P9-DMV-860

Going to College

Expanding Opportunities for People with Disabilities

edited by

Elizabeth Evans Getzel, M.A.

and

Paul Wehman, Ph.D.

Virginia Commonwealth University
Richmond

·P·A·U·L·H·
BROOKES
PUBLISHING Cº ®

Baltimore • London • Sydney

Paul H. Brookes Publishing Co.
Post Office Box 10624
Baltimore, Maryland 21285-0624

www.brookespublishing.com

Copyright © 2005 Paul H. Brookes Publishing Co., Inc.
All rights reserved.

"Paul H. Brookes Publishing Co." is a registered
trademark of Paul H. Brookes Publishing Co., Inc.

Typeset by International Graphic Services, Inc., Newtown, Pennsylvania.
Manufactured in the United States of America by
Victor Graphics, Baltimore, Maryland.

Most of the vignettes in this book are composite accounts that do not represent the lives or
experiences of specific individuals, and no implications should be inferred. Vignettes based
on actual people and events are used by permission, and identifying details have been
changed to protect confidentiality.

Library of Congress Cataloging-in-Publication Data

Going to college : expanding opportunities for people with disabilities / edited
by Elizabeth Evans Getzel and Paul Wehman.
      p.   cm.
   Includes bibliographical references and index.
   ISBN 1-55766-742-X (pbk.)
   1. People with disabilities—Education (Higher)—United States.   2. College
students with disabilities—Services for—United States.   I. Getzel, Elizabeth
Evans.   II. Wehman, Paul.

LC4813.G65 2005
371.9'0474—dc22   2005014680

British Library Cataloguing in Publication data are available from the British Library.

Going to College

Contents

About the Editors

Elizabeth Evans Getzel, M.A., is Director of Postsecondary Education Initiatives with the Rehabilitation Research and Training Center on Workplace Supports at Virginia Commonwealth University. She has extensive experience conducting research, evaluation, and training in the areas of transition planning for secondary students with disabilities, postsecondary education for student with disabilities, and career planning/employment for individuals with disabilities. She currently directs approximately $3 million of grant-funded projects focusing on supported education in postsecondary education, career development for college students with disabilities, faculty professional development focusing on universal design principles, and secondary education transition services. Her research interests include secondary education transition planning, self-determination skills of college students with disabilities, and effective services and supports for college students with disabilities.

Ms. Getzel serves as Associate Editor for the *Journal of Postsecondary Education and Disability* and is on the editorial boards for the *Journal of Vocational Rehabilitation* and *The Journal for Vocational Special Needs Education*. She has authored or co-authored journal articles and book chapters on transition, career development, postsecondary education, and employment. In addition, Ms. Getzel has presented extensively at state, national, and international conferences and at meetings on her projects and research areas.

Paul Wehman, Ph.D., is Professor of Physical Medicine and Rehabilitation, with joint appointments in the Department of Special Education and Disability Policy and the Department of Rehabilitation Counseling. He pioneered the development of supported employment at Virginia Commonwealth University (VCU) in the early 1980s and has been heavily involved in the use of supported employment with people who have severe disabilities, such as those with severe mental retardation, brain injury, spinal cord injury, or autism. At VCU, Dr. Wehman also serves as Director of the Rehabilitation Research and Training Center on Workplace Supports and Chairman of the Division of Rehabilitation Research.

Dr. Wehman has written extensively on the transition from school to adulthood and special education as it relates to young adulthood. He has written more than 150 articles and 24 book chapters and has authored or edited 33 books. He is a recipient of the Joseph P. Kennedy, Jr. Foundation International Awards in Mental Retardation, was a Mary Switzer Fellow for the National Rehabilitation Association in 1985, and received the Distinguished Service Award from the President's Committee on Employment for Persons with Disabilities in October 1992. Dr. Wehman was recognized as one of the 50 most influential special educators of the millennium by a national survey coordinated by the journal *Remedial and Special Education* (December 2000), and he received the VCU Distinguished Service Award in 2001. On April 30, 2002, he testified on behalf of the President's Committee on Excellence in Special Education. He is also Editor-in-Chief of the *Journal of Vocational Rehabilitation*.

About the Contributors

Linda S. Albrecht, M.Ed., M.S., has been at Virginia Commonwealth University (VCU) since 2001. She works as Research Associate with VCU's Rehabilitation Research and Training Center, addressing issues of individuals with disabilities. Her special interests include working with college students with disabilities in both vocational and academic development. In addition, she works on a variety of projects and activities helping to make the campus more aware of the issues of all people with disabilities.

Lori W. Briel, M.Ed., is Research Associate with the Rehabilitation Research and Training Center on Workplace Supports at Virginia Commonwealth University. In addition to her master's degree in education, she has extensive experience providing career development services, resource coordination, and employment supports for individuals with significant disabilities. Ms. Briel currently coordinates a comprehensive career-planning program for postsecondary students with disabilities. Her disability-related research interests include the transition from high school to college, career development for postsecondary students, and employer education.

Sheryl Burgstahler, Ph.D., is Affiliate Associate Professor of Education at the University of Washington in Seattle. Her academic interests are in the areas of universal design, assistive technology, accessible information technology, e-mentoring, and self-determination for people with disabilities. At the University of Washington, she also directs DO-IT (Disabilities, Opportunities, Internetworking, and Technology), which promotes the participation, productivity, and acceptance of people with disabilities in postsecondary education and careers.

Trent Davis, Ed.S., became involved with students with disabilities in higher education through his work on a state-funded research grant. He is employed as an outpatient clinician at New River Valley Community Services in Blacksburg, Virginia. He is also completing his doctoral degree in counselor education at Virginia Polytechnic Institute and State University in Blacksburg.

J. Trey Duffy, M.Ed., is Assistant Dean of Students and Director of the McBurney Disability Resource Center at the University of Wisconsin–Madison. Past president of the Association on Higher Education and Disability (AHEAD) and past president of Access to Independence, an independent living center in Madison, Wisconsin, Mr. Duffy consults in the areas of disability program evaluation, not-for-profit organization board development, and implementing total quality management in higher education. He has undergraduate degrees in interpreting and in sign language studies and a graduate degree in education administration.

Donald E. Finn, Jr., M.S., Ph.D., is Higher Education Disability Training Coordinator at the Rehabilitation Research and Training Center at Virginia Commonwealth University. He specializes in creating and designing disability-related staff development and informational publications for the faculty on VCU's academic and medical campuses. Dr. Finn is also leading an effort to replicate these efforts at other colleges in Virginia, including an outreach to Virginia's 23 community colleges. Dr. Finn obtained a bachelor of science degree in secondary education and a master of science degree in curriculum and instruction in adult education from Radford University in Virginia, as well as a doctoral degree in education from Virginia Commonwealth University.

John Gugerty, M.S., is Researcher and Rehabilitation Faculties Administrator in the Department of Rehabilitation, Psychology and Special Education, School of Education, at the University of Wisconsin–Madison. Since 1975, through both professional and volunteer efforts, Mr. Gugerty has worked to improve career aspirations, preparation, and employment opportunities for youth and adults with disabilities and other risk factors that impede learning. To accomplish these goals, he undertakes research, professional development, technical assistance, program development, program evaluation, organizational capacity building, product development, and dissemination of these results and products nationally. In 2003, he was one of two individuals selected from the 26-campus University of Wisconsin (UW) System to receive the UW Regents Academic Staff Award for Excellence.

Debra Hart, M.S., is Education Coordinator at the Institute for Community Inclusion, located at the University of Massachusetts in Boston. She has more than 25 years of experience working with children and adults with intellectual disabilities. Ms. Hart has directed more than 20 federal and state projects that focus on assisting families, youth, and professionals to create access to and success in high school and postsecondary education for youth with intellectual disabilities and on creating better postschool outcomes for these youth. She has conducted national research on postsecondary education services for youth with intellectual disabilities; served as Director of a U.S. Department of Labor, Office of Disability and Employment Policy State Alignment, grant to assist state and local communities in the conduct of resource mapping to better align transition resources for youth with disabilities prior to exiting school; and served as Director of a U.S. Department of Education, Office of Special Education Programs, model development project to assist several Massachusetts communities in developing an array of individualized supports for youth with intellectual disabilities who are interested in pursuing an inclusive postsecondary education.

Michael F. Hock, Ph.D. is Associate Director and Researcher for The University of Kansas Center for Research on Learning in Lawrence. Dr. Hock is a graduate of The University of Kansas, where he earned his doctoral degree in special education (with an emphasis in learning disabilities) and in teaching and leadership. Dr. Hock's most recent efforts have been directed at increasing student commitment to learning and academic motivation. He was the 1988 recipient of the national Outstanding Teacher Award by the Council for Learning Disabilities.

Joan M. McGuire, Ph.D., is Professor of Special Education in the Department of Educational Psychology at the University of Connecticut in Storrs, Co-director of the university's Center on Postsecondary Education and Disability, and former director of its University Program for College Students with Learning Disabilities. Her research interests include postsecondary disability program development, administration, and evaluation; Universal Design for Instruction (UDI); professional development and training for postsecondary personnel; and assessment and documentation of learning disabilities in adults. She was previously co-editor for the *Journal of Postsecondary Education and Disability*.

Shannon McManus, M.Ed., is Research Associate at Virginia Commonwealth University's Rehabilitation Research and Training Center (VCU-RRTC). While on faculty at VCU-RTTC, she has been involved in many activities that promote self-determination, academic success in postsecondary education, and effective transition services for students with disabilities.

David R. Parker, Ph.D., is Research Associate at the Institute for Community Inclusion, located at the University of Massachusetts in Boston. Dr. Parker enjoyed a 16-year career in human services as a community-based program developer and supervisor in West Michigan and received his doctoral degree in psychology from the University of Notre Dame in 2003. His primary research interests include positive psychology, attitude formation, and the social and psychological impact of institutional policy implementation in response to civil rights legislation, especially in educational environments.

Virginia J. Reilly, Ph.D., is Americans with Disabilities Act (ADA) Coordinator at Virginia Polytechnic Institute and State University in Blacksburg. As a member of the Association on Higher Education and Disability (AHEAD), she conducts annual training for new ADA Coordinators and is past president of AHEAD in Virginia. Dr. Reilly has conducted research on standards of accessibility for higher education and is co-author of the book *The ADA Coordinator's Guide to Campus Compliance* (LRP Publications, 2002). She was awarded a research grant from the Virginia Board for People with Disabilities and is Project Coordinator for the Southwest Virginia Assistive Technology Services site. Dr. Reilly is a member of the Virginia Higher Education Leadership Partners (VA-HELP), which developed statewide guidelines for documentation of disabilities and is developing best practices for transition.

Sally S. Scott, Ph.D., is Associate Professor in the Department of Educational Psychology at the University of Connecticut and Co-director of the Universal Design for Instruction (UDI) Project, a federally funded, 3-year grant from the U.S. Department of Education, Office of Postsecondary Education. Dr. Scott's professional expertise and research interests include postsecondary disability services, UDI, and adults with learning disabilities.

Lisa Donegan Shoaf, P.T., Ph.D., is Director of Clinical Education at Virginia Commonwealth University's Department of Physical Therapy. In this role, she oversees all clinical internships for the entry-level doctorate of physical therapy program, including training of clinical instructors, placements of students, and monitoring performance in the clinical setting. Dr. Shoaf has worked in this role to assist students with disabilities and clinical instructors to establish a plan that addresses needs effectively and gives the students an opportunity for success.

Colleen A. Thoma, Ph.D., is Associate Professor at Virginia Commonwealth University's Department of Special Education and Disability Policy. Dr. Thoma has co-authored (with Dr. Caren Sax) *Transition Assessment: Wise Practices for Quality Lives* (Paul H. Brookes Publishing Co., 2002), as well as articles, guides, and grants related to facilitating student self-determination in the transition planning process.

Michael L. Wehmeyer, Ph.D., is Associate Professor of Special Education at The University of Kansas in Lawrence, Director of the Kansas University Center on Developmental Disabilities, and Associate Director of the Beach Center on Disability. Dr. Wehmeyer's research focus is on self-determination, access to the general curriculum for students with severe disabilities, and technology use by people with intellectual disabilities.

Satoko Yasuda, Ph.D., is Research Associate at the Rehabilitation Research and Training Center at Virginia Commonwealth University. She has been involved in examining return to work for individuals with traumatic brain injury and spinal cord injury and has published numerous journal articles as well as book chapters on these issues. Her other interests include students with disabilities in higher education. Dr. Yasuda has also examined cultural differences in the perception of mothers with children with disabilities.

Karen Zimbrich, M.Ed., is Education Specialist at the Institute for Community Inclusion, located at the University of Massachusetts in Boston. Ms. Zimbrich has worked as a special educator, a school-to-adulthood transition specialist, and an educational consultant to promote inclusive schools, colleges, and communities. She provides training and technical assistance to State Improvement Project and State Alignment Project sites.

Foreword

I am very pleased and honored to write the foreword for *Going to College: Expanding Opportunities for People with Disabilities.* I have always had great respect for the book's editors and their contributions to the field of special education. So, even though I need to say "NO" to more requests, I was not able to turn down the opportunity to discuss this newest resource on such an important topic. This topic is a poignant one for me personally because I have been interested in transition and postschool issues for more than 25 years, and, perhaps more important, I have officially and unofficially worked with many students with disabilities during my career in higher education. I only wish that I had this resource in my possession when I worked directly with students and when I consulted with various programs in institutions of higher education in Hawaii.

What happens when students with disabilities exit high school has been the center of attention of many professionals for decades. Focused efforts on determining what happens after high school and trying to do more about preparing young adults for postschool settings became more formalized in the early 1980s when the federal government funded projects related to transition. It is safe to say that this was the beginning of the "transition initiative" that ultimately resulted in transition requirements being part of the reauthorization of the Individuals with Disabilities Education Act of 1990 (PL 101-476). As we know, the transition mandate of IDEA remains to this day in its newest form, the Individuals with Disabilities Education Improvement Act of 2004 (PL 108-446).

Anyone who enjoys history (there are a few people—I am sure) and those who like to study the history of various aspects of special education/human services (there are one or two of us—I am certain) recognize that early efforts related to preparing students for what I like to call "the life thereafter" (i.e., life after high school) focused almost entirely on the world of work. Will's (1984) seminal piece on transition—*OSERS Programming for the Transition of Youth with Disabilities: Bridges from School to Working Life,* often referred to as the "Bridges" document—clearly had work as the primary outcome on which transition practices were to be focused. Halpern (1985) was the first of a number of other professionals who suggested that postschool outcomes needed to be more expansive in scope.

Consideration of postsecondary education for students with disabilities, especially certain groups, and systematic attention to the issues related to this postschool option are relatively new areas of professional interest. I recognize that some individuals were working with college students with disabilities as early as the late 1970s and early 1980s. To you, I apologize for using the term "relatively new." I am also aware that some school-based personnel predate me and my generational colleagues in their efforts to assist students in going to postsecondary education. To you, I apologize for not providing more acknowledgment of your efforts.

For many years, most of what did exist in the way of "services for students with disabilities" was provided to students with physical or sensory disabilities. Beginning in the 1980s, new types of students with disabilities (e.g., students with learning disabilities, students with psychiatric challenges) were beginning to enter the postsecondary education arena at higher rates.

However, many of us struggled in providing services to students with disabilities for a number of reasons. Key among these reasons was the absence of a comprehensive literature base and access to few useful resources. Contributing to these issues was the fact that almost no professional who was working with students at the postsecondary level had been trained to do so. Professionals came from a wide variety of backgrounds, such as teaching high school special education or working in some aspect of counseling. These types of backgrounds were not bad by any means. However, folks in these emerging roles in higher education were seldom prepared to work with students with disabilities at this level of education and were often given a host of additional duties and responsibilities (e.g., working with veterans attending postsecondary education). These professionals needed resources and assistance to address a system that differed in many significant ways from the nature of services provided to students with disabilities under IDEA.

Even though much has changed in terms of preparing students for postsecondary education, helping them and their families make the transition to these settings, and providing appropriate services to students when they get there, many issues still remain that require professional attention and action. *Going to College: Expanding Opportunities for People with Disabilities* addresses these issues.

Some terrific books have been published on the topic of postsecondary education for students with disabilities: *Postsecondary Education and Transition for Students with Learning Disabilities, Second Edition* (Brinckerhoff, McGuire, & Shaw, 2001), *Transition to Postsecondary Education* (Webb, 2000), *Success for College Students with Learning Disabilities* (Vogel & Adelman, 1993), *Accommodations in Higher Education Under the Americans with Disabilities Act (ADA)* (Gordon & Keiser, 1998), and *College and the Learning Disabled Student: Program Development, Implementation and Selection, Second Edition* (Mangrum & Strichart, 1988). The first edition of *College and the Learning Disabled Student* is notable because it represented, at least for me, the first key resource to which I could refer when I was working with college students with disabilities.

This new book, assembled under the editorship of Elizabeth Evans Getzel and Paul Wehman, adds to that list of notable resources. I refer to those other resources not to distract from Elizabeth and Paul's wonderful new addition to the list of available resources but to emphasize the need for postsecondary personnel who work with students with disabilities to be aware of and have in their possession a variety of valuable tools for serving their clientele. Maybe I am the only one who thinks this way, but I firmly believe that those of us in the field of special education/human services need to acquire all relevant materials that contribute to our expertise in what we do as professionals.

This newest contribution to the field provides an indispensable source of current information on a range of very important and timely topics. It differs from some of the other books in that is covers a wider span of disabilities, with separate chapters on students with psychiatric disabilities and students with intellectual disabilities, for example.

Going to College: Expanding Opportunities for People with Disabilities is also attractive because it highlights certain key elements of the postsecondary education process for students with disabilities. Many of the topics that NEED to be in a book such as this (e.g., legal background for providing services, discussion of disability support services, use of technology, faculty/staff development) are covered very well. Other topics are more unique to this particular book:

- Focus on the preparation of students for postsecondary education—two chapters are specifically dedicated to this issue, one of which is dedicated entirely on the essential topic of "self-determination"

- A complete chapter on Universal Design for Instruction, a theme that has emerging as a preferred way to structure course design and instruction

- Consideration of students with disabilities who attend professional schools, a situation that has received too little attention in the past

- Discussion of the needs of three specific groups of students: those with learning disabilities, those with psychiatric disabilities, and those with intellectual disabilities; the last two groups are seldom given the attention they need, so having chapters dedicated to these groups is very much welcomed

- Consideration of what I call "the forgotten transition"—that is, the transition from postsecondary education to career or post-postsecondary education

I feel fortunate, because in a sense I already have been able to read this book and learn from it. I believe that professionals at the high school level who work with the transition of students to the "life thereafter" and especially professionals who work with students with disabilities at the postsecondary level will find *Going to College: Expanding Opportunities for People with Disabilities* to be an indispensable resource. This book is a tremendous addition to the existing set of resources on this topic. I wholeheartedly recommend it and commend the editors for putting together a valuable resource for those of us who have a passion for assisting students with disabilities who have endeavored to pursue postsecondary education.

James R. Patton, Ed.D.
Independent Consultant
Adjunct Associate Professor
Department of Special Education
The University of Texas at Austin

REFERENCES

Brinckerhoff, L.C., McGuire, J.M., & Shaw, S.F. (2001). *Postsecondary education and transition for students with learning disabilities* (2nd ed.). Austin, TX: PRO-ED.

Gordon, M., & Keiser, S. (1998). *Accommodations in higher education under the Americans with Disabilities Act (ADA)*. New York: The Guilford Press.

Halpern. A.S. (1985). Transition: A look at the foundations. *Exceptional Children, 51,* 479–486.

Individuals with Disabilities Education Act (IDEA) of 1990, PL 101-476, 20 U.S.C. §§ 1400 *et seq.*

Individuals with Disabilities Education Improvement Act of 2004, PL 108-446, 20 U.S.C. §§ 1400 *et seq.*

Mangrum, C.T., & Strichart, S.S. (1988). *College and the learning disabled student: Program development, implementation and selection* (2nd ed.). Philadelphia: Grune & Stratton.

Vogel, S.A., & Adelman, P.B. (1993). *Success for college students with learning disabilities.* New York: Springer-Verlag.

Webb, K. (2000). *Transition to postsecondary education.* Austin, TX: PRO-ED.

Will, M. (1984). *OSERS programming for the transition of youth with disabilities: Bridges from school to working life.* Washington, DC: Office of Special Education and Rehabilitative Services.

Preface

Pursuing a college education remains an American dream. For students with disabilities, this dream is becoming an increasing reality. Whether these students obtain a degree through a community college, 4-year college or university, vocational-technical school or professional school, they are entering postsecondary programs in greater numbers. Research on employment rates of people with disabilities shows that obtaining a college degree significantly improves the likelihood that these individuals will secure meaningful employment and increase their earning potential. As technological capabilities grow and new employment opportunities emerge, the importance of obtaining some level of postsecondary education will continue to increase. Yet, the number of individuals with disabilities is not keeping pace with the number of individuals in the general population who are entering postsecondary education programs. In the long run, this gap in participation rate will have a negative impact on the career and employment opportunities for people with disabilities.

During the 1990s, students with disabilities and their families raised their expectations of continuing educational opportunities beyond high school. Research demonstrates that pursuing postsecondary education, especially at a 2-year college, is more frequently identified as a student's transition goal. Nonetheless, transition to postsecondary education for individuals with disabilities and, more important, retention in these programs continue to present a number of challenges. Students with disabilities must have the academic foundation to meet the entrance requirements of postsecondary education and build on this knowledge to remain in school. Along with these academic skills, students must have the personal skills to manage their educational careers. Some of the demands of college include greater amounts of reading, more independent work outside of the classroom, less contact with instructors, and larger numbers of students seeking specific services and supports. These demands of postsecondary education make it necessary for students with disabilities to understand how to seek services and advocate for the accommodations they need. They must be fully aware of the differences between high school and college when requesting accommodations and of the process for documenting their disabilities to receive these services. This increased responsibility can be especially challenging for students who elect not to self-disclose in college to avoid being identified as someone needing special assistance. In addition, postsecondary institutions can contribute to these feelings in the form of negative attitudes held by some faculty members, staff, or administrators. What emerges from these challenges or issues is the need for systematic planning and preparation of these students to meet academic requirements, develop the skills needed to advocate for services and problem-solve potential barriers, and gain knowledge about and access to services and supports (including technology) to enhance their learning opportunities.

The content of *Going to College: Expanding Opportunities for People with Disabilities* is on the forefront of information and resources regarding the transition and retention of students with disabilities in postsecondary education. The chapters follow a progression of information and materials needed by students, families, secondary and postsecondary education professionals, and community agencies and organizations. Section I provides a discussion of the importance of postsecondary education in today's economy, which is followed by the rights and responsibilities of individuals with disabilities seeking services and supports in higher education settings. Information is offered on self-determination skills and strategies, services and supports provided by disability support services on college campuses, and important considerations when preparing for and applying to college. Section II provides information on Universal Design for Instruction principles that can enhance the learning for all students, including students with disabilities; postsecondary programming using a supported education model; and accommodations in clinical field placements. The critical role of technology in college is also discussed, along with ideas and strategies for providing professional development opportunities for faculty, staff, and administration in postsecondary education settings. Section III discusses specific educational approaches for students with psychiatric disabilities, students with learning disabilities and attention-deficit/ hyperactivity disorder, and students with significant disabilities. Section IV discusses the next stage: exiting school and entering employment, or the "second big transition" for students with disabilities. The section focuses on obtaining experience in work environments through clinicals, practicums, or internships and on employment of college graduates with disabilities. The book is intended to complete a full circle regarding individuals with disabilities in postsecondary schools, beginning with the importance of career opportunities and employment; followed by the process of preparing and entering postsecondary programs, remaining in these programs, and determining a career path; and closing with employment opportunities beyond college.

The design of *Going to College* addresses a number of areas pertinent to stakeholders involved in the preparation of individuals with disabilities for postsecondary education. The range of topics was chosen because of the critical importance that collaboration plays in the successful transition of students with disabilities. It is hoped that this book will assist all members in a student's network to better understand postsecondary education environments and the roles and responsibilities that each member plays in helping students achieve their goals. Students with disabilities are at the heart of the planning process. It is our responsibility as family members and professionals to engage students in this process to the fullest extent possible and to utilize information, resources, and best practices to enable them to obtain the skills and knowledge needed for managing their long-term careers.

Acknowledgments

We express our deepest appreciation to a number of individuals who have helped to contribute so much to the development of this book. Our colleagues at the Rehabilitation Research and Training Center (RRTC) at Virginia Commonwealth University (VCU) have assisted us in obtaining funding to develop and implement new ideas and strategies to assist students with disabilities in meeting the challenges of college, and they have offered their input to strengthen these strategies and approaches. We would especially like to thank Mike West, Jan Hensel-Smith, Darlene Unger, Beth Bader, and John Kregel, who have contributed their expertise and generously shared their knowledge to assist us in our work. We are also grateful for the authors who willingly shared their knowledge and experience. These authors are leaders in their respective fields and we are grateful that Sheryl Burgstahler, Trent Davis, J. Trey Duffy, John Gugerty, Debra Hart, Michael F. Hock, Joan M. McGuire, David R. Parker, Virginia J. Reilly, Sally S. Scott, Michael L. Wehmeyer, and Karen Zimbrich contributed to this book. Our colleagues from VCU's RRTC, Department of Special Education and Disability Policy, and Department of Physical Therapy have assisted us in creating the foundation for a number of the chapters through their work with students and for this we are indebted to Linda S. Albrecht, Lori W. Briel, Donald E. Finn, Jr., Shannon McManus, Lisa Donegan Shoaf, Colleen A. Thoma, and Satoko Yasuda for the nationally recognized work they are performing at VCU.

We are extremely fortunate to have strong administrative support for our work at VCU. Chapters 4, 7, 8, 10, and 14 represent several years of experience working with college students with disabilities. We would like to extend our appreciation to the former Dean of the School of Education, Dr. John Oehler, and to our current Dean, Dr. William C. Bosher, Jr., for their outstanding leadership. We are also very fortunate to have Dr. Henry Rhone, Vice Provost for Student Affairs and Enrollment Services, as an active and involved participant in our work. Dr. Rhone serves as Principal Investigator for our Professional Development Academy project; as a result of his vision to create a welcoming campus for all students, especially students with disabilities, it has been possible to try new ideas and strategies to increase the range of supports and how they are delivered to these students. His leadership, ideas, and vision have had a tremendous impact on our work. We are also grateful for the ongoing support and guidance provided by Dr. Martha Lou Green, Assistant Vice Provost for Student Affairs and Enrollment Services. Her input and ideas have been invaluable to the work that we are doing. In addition, we are grateful to Joyce Knight, VCU Disability Support Services Coordinator, and to Don Roebuck, former Disability Support Services Coordinator, for their support in assisting us to initiate a number of our project activities with students. Finally, we would like to express our gratitude to the VCU Center for Teaching Excellence Director, Dr. Joseph Marolla, and to the Associate Director, Dr. Zachary Goodell, for working closely with us in our efforts to reach faculty, staff, and administrators on successfully educating students with disabilities in higher education.

There are a number of individuals who have influenced our work over the years. These colleagues have helped to shape our ideas about transition, and the specific needs of students with disabilities who are making the transition to postsecondary education programs. Sharon deFur, Susan Asselin, Jeananne Dixon, Kathe Wittig, Erica Lovelace, Ann Deschamps, Kristi Wilson, Bob Stodden, David Johnson, and Bill Kiernan are a few who readily come to mind. We are also privileged to work with the Virginia Higher Education Leadership Partners (VA-HELP), a unique consortium of individuals that has met for approximately 6 years to address the issues of transition and retention of students with disabilities in higher education. This high-energy group has helped to create system wide changes in Virginia. We recognize the following individuals as sources of information, input, and inspiration: Mary Nunnally, Virginia Department of Rehabilitative Services; Marianne Moore, Virginia Department of Education; Shirley Musik, J. Sargeant Reynolds Community College; Gary Krapf, State Council of Higher Education for Virginia; Jim Taylor and Susan Davis Payne, Virginia Department for the Blind and Vision Impaired; Judy Howlett, Richmond Public Schools; Jane Warner, Virginia Tech University; Barbara Ettner, Virginia Board for People with Disabilities; Debby Wilkerson, J. Sargeant Reynolds Community College; Betsy Harrison, John Tyler Community College; Lenna Ojure, Virginia Military Institute; Nancy Bailey, Thomas Nelson Community College; Jack Trammell, Randolph-Macon College; Howard Kallem, Betsy Trice, Judy Risch, and Joe Bardari, U.S. Department of Education; Beverly Harris, Norfolk State University; Christine Young, VCU; Jennifer Bruce, Randolph-Macon College; and Fayne Pearson, Virginia Wesleyan College.

We especially thank and recognize all of the students with disabilities, faculty, staff, and administrators who gave their time and worked side by side with us to create a learning environment that is welcoming for all students.

Finally, we thank our families for their love and support during the development of this book. We appreciate their patience, understanding, and ongoing support of the work that enriches our lives.

To Jerry, Bryant, and Alyssa,
who are life's greatest gifts to me

To my mom and dad,
who taught me about the equality of all people

To my sister,
who is my constant source
of strength and encouragement

And in memory of my beloved brother
—EEG

To Lele—my soul mate, friend, and wonderful wife
—PW

College Planning
and Admissions

CHAPTER 1

The Need and the Challenges Associated with Going to College

Paul Wehman and Satoko Yasuda

There is little doubt that institutions of higher education have become a major part of the fabric of American society. It is a rare community where one cannot find at least a 2-year community college or technical school. It is more likely that within 50–100 miles of most communities, there is a private college, a small state-supported facility, an extension program or center from a large university, and, in many cases, a branch of a large state university. For many people, participation in the college experience represents the American dream. Higher education is viewed by most as the ultimate educational experience and the way to attain greater income, improve the options in one's life, achieve status, make more friends, and promote lifelong networks that allow for individual empowerment and personal capacity. Increasingly, international students are recruited for their expertise in technology, medicine, athletics, and other specialty areas. The diversity seen at some U.S. universities is amazing and clearly serves as a melting pot for different learning opportunities.

Higher education in America is truly a big business. An economic impact statement for Richmond, Virginia, for example, showed the dramatic impact of one state university, Virginia Commonwealth University (VCU), on the hiring and spending trends that occurred in the Central Virginia region. Regarding this economic impact, Trani noted,

> Annual expenditures by VCU and the VCU Health System have grown from three-quarters of a billion dollars in 1990 to more than $1 billion in 2000–01. In 1990, VCU supported 13,000 faculty and staff. In 1999–2000, employment stood at more than 14,500. Throughout the decade, VCU and the VCU Health System have ranked as the city's largest employer. Annually, students and employees have averaged more than $322 million worth of expenditures in the local economy. In 1990, VCU had 75,977 alumni; the total in 2000 exceeds 110,000, 60 percent of whom live and work in Virginia. (2000, p. 15)

3

Another example of college growth as big business is the incredible amount of capital investment that goes into the construction of new buildings for classrooms, of new apartment-style housing options, and especially of athletic facilities and wellness centers. Construction costs rose from $3 billion in 1996 to $6.3 billion in 2001 (Bergsman, 2002). Furthermore, most colleges and universities now have an increased capacity to deliver food service and other hospitality industry features that also require significant capital investment. Bergsman (2002) noted,

> Pick a college. Any college. No matter where you go in the U.S., you'd be hard-pressed to find one without a construction project. Suburban Chicago's Northwestern University? It's in the throes of its biggest building boom in 20 years. Virginia's George Mason University? In excess of $300 million in construction to be finished in 2006. Central Michigan University? Robert Matouka, the Mount Pleasant, Mich., schools' senior officer for facilities management, says it just completed a $50 million library, broke ground on a $50 million health-professions academic building, finished $8 million of work on a baseball stadium, earmarked $33 million for student housing towers and is awaiting funding from the state legislature for a $50 million education building. . . .

In part, the increase in building can be blamed on need. "Two decades ago, the baby boomers went back and had some more kids and we are just seeing the front end of a resurgence in 18- to 24-year-old demographics," says Travis Reindl, director of State Policy Analysis for American Association of State Colleges & Universities in Washington. "Nationwide, we are looking at an additional 1.2 million students that will be on our campuses between 2000 and 2011" (Bergsman, 2003).

The investment in 2- and 4-year colleges is not taken lightly by those in state legislatures and the U.S. Congress. Most of these elected officials have graduated from colleges and universities, and as influential alumni, they often do everything they can to continue to support the mission of their respective universities. Subsequently, large bond funds are floated to maintain this interest, tuitions are raised, and fees are increased, with television revenues fueling the expansion of the top 100–200 universities in this country's sports programs. Fund-raisers to increase endowments are in continual demand as the higher education industry grows and grows.

Colleges have therefore taken on their own lives as separate communities. Faculty, staff, students, adjunct faculty, part-time personnel, and volunteers all play roles in the college community, which is a dominant feature of many smaller communities and takes on a significant complementary role in larger, urban settings. The dramatic growth in college enrollment and the number of degrees granted is presented in Tables 1.1 and 1.2, which indicate that in 2000, there were more than 4,000 colleges with 15 million enrollees, and more than 2 million degrees were awarded.

Table 1.1. College student enrollment

Place of enrollment	Number of students
At public 4-year institutions	6,055,398
At public 2-year institutions	5,697,388
At private 4-year institutions	3,308,460
At private 2-year institutions	251,043
Undergraduate	13,155,393
Graduate	1,850,271
Professional	306,625
American Indian	151,150
Asian	978,224
Black	1,730,318
Hispanic	1,461,806
White	10,462,099
Foreign	528,692
Total	15,312,289

From *The Chronicle of Higher Education*. (2003). The nation: A chart depicting enrollment trends. *The 2003–4 Almanac, 50*(1), A2. Retrieved October 15, 2004, from http://chronicle.com/free/almanac/2003/nation/nation.htm; reprinted by permission.

Table 1.2. Degrees awarded

Associate	578,865
Bachelor's	1,244,171
Master's	468,476
Doctorate	44,904
Professional	79,707

From *The Chronicle of Higher Education*. (2003). The nation: A chart depicting enrollment trends. *The 2003–4 Almanac, 50*(1), A2. Retrieved October 15, 2004, from http://chronicle.com/free/almanac/2003/nation/nation.htm; reprinted by permission.

Up to this point, this chapter's discussions have been limited to traditional on-campus types of programs, but in fact, off-campus/on-line instruction college experiences have been dramatically expanding. For example, companies such as Career Education Corporation; Corinthian Colleges, Inc.; Strayer University; and ITT Technical Institute offer certification programs and professional training (e.g., for teaching, business, and health technology) that allow students to bypass the traditional on-campus environment. This has increased competition for the student tuition dollars by universities, many of which are not particularly well versed in or equipped for the art of rugged market competition. For example, Blumenstyk noted,

While cuts in state aid and philanthropy have put the squeeze on community colleges, state universities, and traditional private institutions, many for-profit education companies are flourishing. The fast-growing Apollo Group, parent company of the University of Phoenix, continues to set the pace. This year it reported enrollments topping 200,000, an increase of 27 percent over 2002. (2003b, p. 37)

According to analysts at *The Chronicle of Higher Education* (Blumenstyk, 2003a), enrollment growth at the seven biggest for-profit companies has rapidly outpaced overall enrollment growth in higher education. Projections indicate that this trend will continue.

As the environment of higher education continues to grow and expand, colleges are forced to generate different types of program and learning arrangements, such as the opportunity for learning from home or the workplace. Because for-profit colleges rely wholly on tuition to cover their costs, they are not dependent on state and private subsidies. This means that each new student they attract contributes to their profits, not their costs, as such enrollment booms sometimes do in the nonprofit sector. In addition, the institutions are attracting students by catering to growing numbers of people who seek job-oriented curricula in fields such as health care and culinary arts, as well as more traditional programs in business and teacher education.

What does all of this mean for students and colleges today, particularly students with disabilities? In a word, opportunity. Meaningful postsecondary education experiences in institutions of higher education correlate highly with the likelihood that people with disabilities will be successful in the workplace and in the community. Without the opportunity to receive additional training and exposure to higher education learning, young people with disabilities may be squeezed into a very limited array of job possibilities, none of which pay well or carry opportunities for significant career advancement. Furthermore, many young people who have entrepreneurial interests may want to start their own businesses, become independent consultants, or work as contractors from home. Hence, some of the more intangible skills that come out of the college experience would be very helpful.

For example, a significant level of self-direction is necessary for college success. There is a need to self-advocate and a need to manage time well. Most college environments carry the expectation that students will come to class, participate, and manage assignments appropriately. Furthermore, if students do not complete these activities, they will likely fail and lose the money that they initially put into the college experience. High school does not carry all of these consequences. This type of personal responsibility is an important aspect of creating the independence that is necessary in the workplace. It is also critical for entrepreneurial ventures, which increasing numbers of Americans are considering as the job market becomes tighter and outsourcing sends more jobs out of the country.

WHY DO PEOPLE GO TO COLLEGE?

The question becomes, "Why do so many students of all ages flock to 2- and 4-year colleges, small and large universities, technical schools, and other types of higher education learning?" Colleges provide settings for major community resources that can apply a pivotal role in many local and state economies. There are, however, a number of very specific tangibles, as well as intangibles, that indicate why college is an attractive part of the life planning and experiences of so many people.

Earnings

The most obvious issue is the perception that those who earn a college degree will accrue much better lifelong earnings. Ample studies have shown that people who receive associate's degrees earn significantly more money than high school graduates and that those with 4-year college degrees earn even more over their lifetimes. With graduate, doctoral, or advanced degrees, the dollar total goes up even higher. Goldstein, Murray, and Edgar (1998) examined the earnings and hours worked of high school graduates with learning disabilities and their peers without disabilities 1–10 years after graduation. The graduates with learning disabilities had higher annualized earnings in the early postgraduate years and lower earnings later, a result largely explained by the greater attendance at postsecondary educational institutions of students without disabilities. This pattern was also reinforced by Hecker's (1998) analysis of employment patterns and earnings of workers with some college credits but no degree. The study showed that these workers were likely to have college-level jobs and to earn substantially more than high school graduates; however, they earned less than workers with associate's or bachelor's degrees. In addition, Crosby (2000) used Current Population Survey data to compare earnings by educational level, from the categories of high school diploma to doctoral degree, in selected occupations. The study found that college graduates earned at least $15,000 more than high school graduates in 1998. Consider the following information cited by InTime (2004):

> [College graduates] will increase [their] overall earning potential by 47%. During . . . [one's] lifetime, a college career will have been worth about $627,480 . . . [and] more than half a million dollars more than somebody with only a high school diploma. . . .
>
> InTime (2004) reports lifetime earnings based on education level:

- High school dropout—.5 million dollars
- High school graduate—.8 million dollars
- Associate's degree—1 million dollars
- Bachelor's degree—1.5 million dollars

A person with a bachelor's degree can earn three times what a high school graduate can hope to earn.

In addition, according to InTime (2004), the earning power of Hispanic individuals with high school diplomas compares as follows to their counterparts with degrees:

- Latinos with bachelor's degrees will earn $500,000 more.
- Latinas with bachelor's degrees will earn $400,000 more.

- Latinos with a master's or a doctoral degree will earn $1.7 million more.

- Latinos with professional degrees—for example, those who work as doctors or lawyers—have a premium of $1.7 million, which is approximately a 200% increase across a lifetime.

It is often true that salaries for teachers, social workers, nurses, and police officers are not exceptional. However, when considering the figures over a person's total work life—say, 25 years—the total numbers are very different.

College often—but not always—makes a difference in a person's ability to earn a comfortable living. So many other factors are involved in earnings and job opportunities, including the economy and one's self-direction and self-drive. In addition, earnings potential has not been as well documented for young people with disabilities, who may struggle to get into the work force or on a meaningful career path. Nevertheless, all indicators suggest that college experiences and degrees lead to more options and better-paying situations for graduates with disabilities.

Benefits

A second reason for going to college is to increase the likelihood of receiving good and stable benefits. In this day and age, benefits are extraordinarily important—almost more important than a specific wage level. Health care, for example, is a major issue for many people. Although older workers have the potential for various health issues, many young people also have preexisting conditions such as congenital heart problems, diabetes, asthma, spina bifida, or mental health issues—all of which would potentially create barriers to employment opportunities that carry health care benefits. Therefore, advanced training and a college degree in hand may provide a greater opportunity to expand the range of jobs that offer health care benefits. Another benefits category is the available amount of vacation, personal, and sick time, which can increase one's quality of life. Furthermore, having a college degree opens the door to working for a company or organization that may pay for some or all of one's retirement—a major, long-term advantage.

Benefits also extend beyond the traditional areas previously listed. Companies sometimes pay for additional course work, provide access to local clubs and organizations, or offer varying discounts on products that they sell.

Career Advancement

Good pay and benefits often are top reasons to make the significant investment of time and money that college requires. However, a third reason—career advancement—may be one of the most compelling reasons to go to college. Many people who are quite capable of supervisory or managerial positions are held back because they do not have a college degree. Although this has changed somewhat over the years, it continues to be an issue in the public sector, such as for state and federal government jobs, and in the private sector, as many corporations require advanced degrees—or at least bachelor's degrees—in a given field to be considered for positions at certain levels. The growth of weekend programs, on-line programs, and other highly flexible college course offerings is directly tied to the fact that many people in the private and public sectors have learned that they cannot get ahead without having an advanced degree. Thus, career advancement and upward mobility is a critical reason why people go to college and need to carefully plan the types of course work and degree programs that work the best for them. Many people have determined that a complementary set of degrees makes the most sense. For example, an individual with a bachelor's degree in business and a master's degree in engineering might be a stronger candidate for a certain position than a person with two degrees in engineering. In similar fashion, an individual with a bachelor's degree in psychology who wants to attend medical school might have a better likelihood of being accepted through appearing more well rounded than one whose major at previous degree levels was life sciences.

Status

A fourth reason why many people go to college is because of the status or perceived status that is associated with being a college graduate. Although the specific advantage or impact of this kind of status is hard to measure and assess, there is a certain level of respect accorded to individuals with college degrees that is not always associated with people who have not graduated from college. Although this judgment is not particularly fair, it may explain why many parents who have not gone to college want their children to be college graduates.

Marketability

Marketability is a fifth factor. Described as the ability to move from job to job or career to career, marketability is substantially enhanced with a college diploma. Again, one might reasonably argue that interpersonal skills and excellent networking, along with a variety of different life experiences, could influence marketability just as well as a college degree. In effect, however, if one uses college experiences appropriately, marketability is highly possible. The capacity to move from job to job or into different industries is clearly tied to complementing the types of training experiences that one receives in college. Therefore, doing field work and obtaining a double major, a major and two minors, or complementary bachelor's and master's degrees demonstrates to employers one's versatility as a potential employee.

Productivity and growth are highly valued in business and industry. Productivity is enhanced not only by increased quality of technology but also by obtaining as much work as possible from a given employee, thereby keeping the number of employees to the minimum required to achieve profit and growth. As a result, individuals who have multiple skills, are able to multitask easily, and have different competencies—both professional and technical—are more valuable in a job market. The interplay of pay, greater benefits, prospects of career advancement, real or perceived status, and substantial marketability combine to create a very powerful reason why people invest so much time and energy in the college experience.

Individuals with disabilities, as well as other "at-risk" and traditionally underserved populations, have not participated in college to the extent that individuals without disabilities have; therefore, it is not surprising that they have not been participating in the American dream as fully either. Achievement in the competitive environment of American industry or attractive employment in the public sector requires appropriate education and training. The marketplace can be brutal, and one needs every advantage possible, starting with an associate's or a bachelor's degree.

Additional Benefits of College Participation

The previously listed five points provide an important base for why people go to college. However, at least three additional types of benefits have to be considered as well. For example, the knowledge accumulated in a good college experience is invaluable. Informed individuals are separated from those who are less knowledgeable about various academic and cultural events in the world. Skills in writing, speaking, reading, technology, planning and organizing, and time management are but a few of the tools needed to be successful in college and in the workplace. Arguably, many on-the-job experiences also encourage competence in writing, planning, thinking, organizing, and so forth. Yet, to avoid getting caught in an entry-level position with fewer chances for promotion, it is often easier to learn these skills in the progressive and independent environment that college offers.

Another benefit is the opportunity to significantly expand one's socialization skills. Making the most of college requires learning how to interact with fellow students, professors, residence hall counselors, traffic and security officers, and the many other people who make up the college community. College helps shape and improve social skills because the inability to learn appropriate social skills can lead to penalties. This can include being left out of activities, not being invited to study sessions with other students, or not knowing how to develop a good relationship with one's professors. These examples show how limited socialization skills can negatively affect an individual who may otherwise be quite intelligent.

A third benefit is the establishment of personal networks, which is the logical progression of good social skills. Among the additional benefits discussed in this section, networking may be the most potent. Some students with good college experiences make lifelong friends who ultimately foster long-term relationships that can be helpful in different walks of life. The personal networks that are established at many universities carry through into general assemblies, large law firms, corporations, churches, and other institutions within American society. Consider a report about a student who graduated May 16, 2004, from the University of Richmond:

> Dan Cellucci, an international-studies major, graduated last Sunday from the University of Richmond. The 22-year-old has since moved back to his Philadel-phia-area hometown, where he hopes to take a job with a communications consulting firm.
>
> He didn't get the connection to the firm through the university's career center or over the Internet, but though networking.
>
> Cellucci, who is Roman Catholic, became involved in helping a nun set up a nonprofit organization near his hometown of Broomall, Pa. Her cousin was president of the consulting firm and offered Cellucci an interview. (Kelley, 2004)

Consider all of the times that connections are made as soon as people learn that they attended the same college or university. There is a type of tie that can bind because of the empathy that accompanies the similar college experience. All levels of networks occur. Clearly, athletic teams, fraternities, sororities, roommates, and clubs all offer opportunities to stay connected. This is truer than ever with e-mail, wireless telephones, and other ways of rapidly communicating and keeping up with others.

In sum, there are some formidable and practical reasons why people go to college. Yet, it is important to remember that college is also about fun and about growing into an independent person.

STUDENTS WITH DISABILITIES AND COLLEGE PARTICIPATION

The chapter now turns specifically to students with disabilities. Who among them is going to college? How do their numbers compare with other groups? What obstacles do they face? This portion of the chapter seeks to answer these key questions.

Like all other students, students with disabilities benefit considerably by continuing their education after high school. In addition to making the psychological adjustment associated with learning to live away from home, establishing new friendships, and experiencing the transition into adulthood (Gilson & Gilson, 1998), students with disabilities who participate in postsec-ondary education are more likely to engage in competitive employment than students with disabilities who do not (Benz, Doren, & Yovanoff, 1998; Black-orby & Wagner, 1996; Getzel, Stodden, & Briel, 1999; Gilmore, Schuster, Zafft, & Hart, 2001; Gilson, 1996; Reis, Neu, & McGuire, 1997; Stodden, 1998; Wehman & Kregel, 1998). In fact, participation in any type of postsec-ondary education—whether vocational education classes, a college certificate program, or even one college course—significantly enhances the ability of individuals with disabilities to secure meaningful employment (Gilson, 1996).

Students with disabilities who earn Bachelor of Arts degrees are also reported to be able to obtain subsequent employment at almost the same rate as those without disabilities (HEATH Resource Center, 1998; Office of Special Education and Rehabilitative Services, 2000).

Factors that Promote Access to College for Students with Disabilities

Since the 1970s, an array of federal legislation has been enacted in an attempt to enhance access and supports to students with disabilities in American education: the Individuals with Disabilities Education Act (IDEA) of 1990 (PL 101-476), the Individuals with Disabilities Education Act (IDEA) Amendments of 1997 (PL 105-17), the Individuals with Disabilities Education Improvment Act of 2004 (PL 108-446), Section 504 of the Rehabilitation Act of 1973 (PL 93-112), the Americans with Disabilities Act (ADA) of 1990 (PL 101-336), and the Carl D. Perkins Vocational and Applied Technology Education Act Amendments of 1998 (PL 105-332). As students with disabilities are increasingly included in prekindergarten through high school general education programs, more students are becoming interested in postsecondary education (Hall, Kleinert, & Kearns, 2000; Halpern, Yovanoff, Doren, & Benz, 1995; Mull, Sitlington, & Alper, 2001; Page & Chadsey-Rusch, 1995; Smith, 1998). Nearly all public postsecondary institutions now enroll students with disabilities and provide some level of services to assist access to education (National Center for Education Statistics [NCES], 2000). Since 1990, there has been a 90% increase in the number of postsecondary institutions offering opportunities for individuals with disabilities to continue their education (Brinckerhoff, Shaw, & McGuire, 1992, 1993; Bursuck & Rose, 1992; Pierangelo & Crane, 1997). The noted legislation, along with social changes, has resulted in more students with disabilities seeking access to colleges, universities, and vocational-technical programs (Adelmen & Vogel, 1992; Benz et al., 1998; Blackorby & Wagner, 1996; Bursuck & Rose, 1992; Fairweather & Shaver, 1991; Henderson, 1995; Stodden, 1998).

Progress and Achievements

Studies in the 1990s showed that the percentage of freshmen with disabilities in 2-year and 4-year colleges more than tripled, from 2.6% in 1978, to 9.2% in 1994, to almost 19% in 1996 (Blackorby & Wagner, 1996; Gajar, 1992, 1998; Wagner & Blackorby, 1996), thus making this the fastest growing group in postsecondary institutions during that time (Norlander, Shaw, & McGuire, 1990). In 1986, 29% of people with disabilities who were older than age 16 enrolled in postsecondary education, compared with 45% in 1994 (Thomas, 2000; U.S. Department of Education, 1996). In 1996, approximately 6% of all undergraduates reported having a disability (HEATH Resource Center, 1998; NCES, 1996a).

The most common category of disability reported by the students since the mid-1990s is learning disabilities, followed by orthopedic, health related, and hearing impairments (Henderson, 2001; NCES, 1996a; Turnbull, Turnbull, Shank, & Leal, 1999). According to the survey *College Freshmen with Disabilities* (Henderson, 2001), the most prevalent disability in 1988 was "partially sighted or blind," but this was the third most prevalent disability in 2000. The actual number of students with visual impairments declined from 1988 to 2000, decreasing from 30% to 16%. The number of college freshmen with learning disabilities also is the fastest growing group of college students (Henderson, 2001; Norlander et al., 1990). The number has more than doubled in 12 years, increasing from 16.1% in 1988 to 40.4% in 2000. Students with more significant disabilities—such as mental retardation, autism, and multiple developmental disabilities—are not typically recruited and generally do not enroll in postsecondary education (Henderson, 1995; Wagner & Blackorby, 1996).

More freshmen males with disabilities are attending 4-year institutions than female freshman with disabilities (52% and 48%, respectively), the opposite of students without disabilities (45% and 55%, respectively) (HEATH Resource Center, 2001). Freshman students—both those with and without disabilities—are predominantly Caucasians, followed by African Americans and Hispanics.

The survey *College Freshmen with Disabilities* (Henderson, 2001) collected data from only 4-year institutions because many students in 2-year institutions are either not first-time students or are not enrolled full time. The percentage of students with disabilities enrolled in 4-year institutions hit its peak in 1994 and is gradually declining, from 8.2% to 6.0%. Yet, more students with disabilities are going to 2-year colleges or vocational colleges (NCES, 1999a, 1999b). These institutions tend to provide more individualized services and more services to students with disabilities compared with 4-year postsecondary institutions (National Center for the Study of Postsecondary Educational Supports [NCSPES], 2000). In particular, 2-year institutions provide greater assistance in the areas of academic accommodations, assistive technology, counseling, tutoring, and assessment (Cocci, 1999). More 2-year college students with disabilities express greater satisfaction and fewer barriers when compared with those attending 4-year institutions (West et al., 1993). In addition, most 2-year colleges have open enrollment policies. From these findings, a prospective college student may be inclined to attend a 2-year college because of all the support services, or a transition coordinator may suggest that the student enroll in a 2-year institution because these tend to better accommodate students with disabilities.

The 1990s showed dramatic increases in the number of students with disabilities completing college. Between 1987–1988 and 1997–1998, the number of students awarded bachelor's and associate's degrees rose by 19% and 28%, respectively; the number of students awarded advanced degrees rose even more sharply: master's degrees by 44% and doctoral degrees by 32% (NCES, 2000b). Although students with disabilities are increasingly enrolling in postsecondary institutions, they are still significantly less likely to go on to

postsecondary education when compared with their peers without disabilities
(Blackorby & Wagner, 1996; Greenbaum, Graham, & Scales, 1995; Murray,
Goldstein, Nourse, & Edgar, 2000). Only 37% of students with disabilities
pursue some type of postsecondary education, as opposed to 78% of all high
school students (Blackorby & Wagner, 1996), and only 15% of students in
special education programs go on to some type of postsecondary education
(Lichtenstein, 1998). The percentage of students with disabilities advancing
in graduate schools is even smaller. As for those enrolling in medical and law
schools, the numbers are impossible to determine because such information
is difficult to locate. For example, web site sources typically only list for
race; however, some do provide information on accommodations provided
for students with disabilities.

Comparisons with Other Minority Groups

Students in colleges and universities have changed drastically in a relatively
short period of time (NCES, 1995, 1996b, 2002). During the 1970s and early
1980s, legislation and social changes that attempted to enhance college access
to minorities, such as the continued Civil Rights movement and affirmative
action, led to dramatic increases in college enrollment. The percentage of
students from ethnic minority groups has almost doubled: In 2000, 31.7% of
all college students were of ethnic minorities, compared with 17.4% in the
mid-1970s. However, college students are still predominantly Caucasian, and
students from ethnic minority groups, especially Hispanic students, are disproportionately represented in 2-year colleges.

Despite the fact that legislation has been implemented and social changes
have occurred for both groups, the rate of enrollment is not the same. Although
similar trends can be seen in the college enrollment between students from
racial minority groups and students with disabilities, the increase in enrollment
is far greater for students from racial minority groups than for students
with disabilities.

Students with disabilities are not participating in college at the level that
they should be. Given the importance of postsecondary education in the
current economy, the underrepresentation of students with disabilities in postsecondary education, and the limited opportunities for students with significant
disabilities to acquire vocational skills, the need for improved access to postsecondary education and support in completing degrees is apparent. In order to
determine what is necessary to achieve these goals, first the barriers that inhibit
the participation of students with disabilities in postsecondary education must
be examined.

CHALLENGES THAT STUDENTS WITH DISABILITIES FACE IN GAINING ACCESS TO POSTSECONDARY EDUCATION

The challenges that students with disabilities face in gaining access to postsecondary education can be broadly divided into two categories: 1) preparation

for postsecondary education and 2) the transition process to postsecondary education.

Preparation for Postsecondary Education

> Karen is a 17-year-old student with mild mental retardation. She takes math and English classes separately from her peers because the content is taught at a speed that she cannot follow and her assignments need to be modified. She has expressed the desire to go to college. However, during one of her individualized education program (IEP) meetings, Karen's parents and teachers pointed out that she does not have the required test scores to enroll in a 4-year college and suggested going to a vocational school.

In order to pursue postsecondary education, students must learn and complete standards-based academic curricula in secondary education. However, students with disabilities are reported to be nationally achieving at lower levels than their peers without disabilities in math and science (American Youth Policy Forum [AYPF] & Center on Education Policy [CEP], 2002), as well as in reading (NCES, 2002). If students with disabilities do not meet the academic criteria that are required to enter college, they are unable to pursue a college education. There are a number of reasons why students with disabilities are unable to achieve sufficient academic criteria.

Substandard Content There is a tendency for secondary schools to place students with disabilities in special education classrooms, separating them from students without disabilities for all or part of the day (Malloy, 1997). Here, they may receive substandard secondary curricular content (Stodden, Conway, & Chang, 2003; Stodden, Galloway, & Stodden, 2003). In these settings, more emphasis is placed on providing students with specialized services and supports that are focused specifically on remedial learning or behavior problems.

Lack of Expectation Teachers, career counselors, administrators, family members, and students themselves often possess low expectations and a limited sense of opportunity (Stodden, Jones, & Chang, 2002). Lack of consensus regarding the definition of "successful outcomes" for students with disabilities can also impede a student's potential. For example, if obtaining a GED or high school diploma is viewed as a successful outcome, then education could be perceived as stopping with the completion of high school and not extending to postsecondary education. These perceptions leave students with a sense of failure before they have even begun to explore their interests and aspirations.

Lack of Qualified Teachers Many students with disabilities spend approximately two thirds of the day in general education classrooms and are taught by general education teachers (U.S. Department of Education, 1999; McLeskey, Henry, & Hodges, 1998), but most of these teachers have little or no training in addressing the individual needs of students with disabilities in learning the standards-based curricula (AYPF & CEP, 2002). Even many special education teachers are reported to lack the basic preparation (Smith, McLesky, Tyler, & Saunders, 2002). State and local education agencies across the United States are experiencing a shortage of qualified personnel to serve children and youth with disabilities (AYPF & CEP, 2002). According to the Consortium for Citizens with Disabilities, approximately 3,000 additional special education teachers are needed in secondary education (Consortium for Citizens with Disabilities, 2003).

Standards-Based Curricula and Standardized Testing   The No Child Left Behind Act of 2001 (PL 107-110) mandates that each state must implement a statewide accountability system for all public schools and their students. Every state requires some type of standardized testing from kindergarten through graduation (Johnson, Kimball, Brown, & Anderson, 2001). Although the No Child Left Behind Act is intended to provide more choices for schools, parents, and students, as well as accountability, it may pose further challenges for students with disabilities in gaining access to postsecondary education.

Students with disabilities may obtain all of the necessary credits for graduation with reasonable accommodations, such as being able to complete worksheets with an open book, having someone read test questions aloud, or taking tests in an alternative format. When taking standardized tests, however, students with disabilities often may not have access to the accommodations that are allowed in a classroom situation. This becomes a huge obstacle for many students with disabilities because standardized tests often are time limited and in a multiple-choice style that requires extensive reading. According to Hishinuma (2001), students with learning disabilities may be at a disadvantage when taking standardized tests because they benefit from accommodations, such as extended time, that students without disabilities do not require. In such a case, a student with disabilities might not be able to pass the test, would not be able to acquire a standard diploma, and hence would not be eligible for college admission.

There are inconsistencies among the state and local agencies regarding policies, procedures, and practices on the use of accommodations. Accommodations are often viewed as unacceptable in meeting test conditions, overused in the hope of enhancing student performance, and too expensive and difficult to implement (Thurlow, House, Boys, Scott, & Ysseldyke, 2000; Thurlow & Johnson, 2000). These perceptions result in students not receiving needed accommodations.

Lack of Self-Advocacy Skills   Students with disabilities often are not active in the decision-making process regarding their own supports (Abery & Stancliffe, 1996). A majority of students with disabilities do participate in their IEP meetings, but professionals, teachers, and parents often make the decisions, which subsequently hinder opportunities for students with disabilities to develop and practice self-determination and self-advocacy (Izzo &

Lamb, 2002). This in part results in students not having the necessary attitudes and advocacy skills when they finish secondary school, as well as not understanding how their disability affects their learning and the potential assistance that they could receive (NCSPES, 2002; Stodden, Conway, & Chang, 2003).

The Transition Process

> Sarah's 16-year-old son David has learning disabilities. He requires accommodations such as extended time for taking tests. David has told his mother and his teachers that he would like to go to college after graduation. Sarah decided to ask the high school guidance counselor about the transition process and her role in it. During this meeting, Sarah was told that David's current services will not be available in college environments and that Sarah should start researching which services and assistance will be available. When Sarah asked the guidance counselor which colleges would be suitable for David in terms of accommodations for his disability, the guidance counselor said that she would look into the matter and contact Sarah later.

Students with disabilities do not only need to be prepared academically and socially to make successful transitions to postsecondary institutions. Students and their parents also need to know what to expect for a smooth transition to occur. Equally critical, teachers must know what to do and how to do it in a timely fashion.

Insufficient Information About the Transition Process   Many students with disabilities and their parents realize the difference between high school and college only when the level of service provision drops off and/or is not automatically extended (Stodden, Conway, & Chang, 2003). This is due to a lack of knowledge about differences in their rights, services, and funding among secondary and postsecondary education—which can discourage or possibly even inhibit students with disabilities from pursuing higher education. Many parents report that they do not have the necessary information to participate in the transition process, such as information on places to go for assistance, available service providers, the student's rights, and community resources (U.S. General Accounting Office, 2003).

There is also a lack of awareness among parents and even teachers regarding the difference in policy between IDEA at the secondary level and the ADA and Section 504 at the postsecondary level. Many secondary schools lack a formal structure to assist students in planning to adjust to the laws governing postsecondary education (Stodden, Galloway, & Stodden, 2003).

Absence of Links Between School Systems and Service Providers   For qualified students who disclose their disabilities and present necessary documentation, postsecondary institutions must provide reasonable accommodations to ensure that the students have full access to programs and services

(Frank & Wade, 1993; McCusker, 1995; West et al., 1993). However, postsecondary institutions are not legally required to assist students with disabilities in making the transition from secondary institutions. Due to lack of time and knowledge about available service providers, many secondary and postsecondary schools do not have designated intermediaries to establish the relationship and communication that would enhance the transition process.

As a result, secondary schools, parents, and students carry the burden of collecting information about postsecondary institutions and the transition process. As parents and students begin to search for information about gaining access to postsecondary education, they may find that circumstances differ significantly from college to college and from state to state. The parents and students may have difficulties first in obtaining the information and then in sorting out the information, as each college provides differing levels of and types of support.

Lack of Knowledge on the Part of Teachers and/or Counselors   Often, students are given inadequate direction and counseling due to the lack of coordination among teachers and counseling staff. In addition, many academic and career counselors lack the necessary skills to provide guidance to students with disabilities. When supports and services are available, they often focus more on the students achieving a single academic outcome than on a continuum of outcomes that will lead to a successful transition (Izzo & Lamb, 2002; Stodden, Conway, & Chang, 2003).

Lack of Transportation   Many students with disabilities may not have access to transportation for getting to campus. For example, rural areas may have limited or no public transportation. In addition, students may have difficulty using public transportation due to their disability (e.g., seizures). They may have difficulties arranging carpooling with others because they may not know that option exists or may not be able to self-advocate for transportation.

CONCLUSION

During the 2000–2001 school year, more than 300,000 students eligible for services under IDEA left high school. (This number includes students who graduated with a diploma or alternative credentials, dropped out, died, or aged out.) Most of these students were identified as having learning disabilities, such as dyslexia, and a smaller number was identified as having some type of mental health or physical impairment.

In an effort to raise expectations for such students and to make school systems more accountable than they have been in the past, the IDEA amendments of 2004 (PL 108-446) required inclusion of these students in state and district assessments to the extent possible. The No Child Left Behind Act of 2001 also required school systems to establish annual assessments in order to demonstrate that all students, including those with disabilities, have made academic progress. Federal law does not mandate that school systems tie assessment results to graduation with a standard diploma; however, it does provide states with the flexibility to implement exit examination policies that require students to pass an examination in order to graduate with a standard diploma.

The challenge of locating and advocating for services, information, and accommodations can be frustrating and time consuming. These processes are difficult to manage, even for the most capable and self-determined students (Whelley, Hart, & Zafft, 2002). Without an effective transition program from secondary to postsecondary education, students with disabilities will continue to face challenges that students without disabilities will not have to confront and will experience difficulties in pursuing postsecondary education.

REFERENCES

Abery, B., & Stancliffe, R. (1996). The ecology of self-determination. In D.J. Sands & M.L. Wehmeyer (Eds.), *Self-determination across the life span: Independence and choice for people with disabilities* (pp. 111–145). Baltimore: Paul H. Brookes Publishing Co.

Adelmen, P., & Vogel, S. (1992). The success of college students with learning disabilities: Factors related to education attainment. *Journal of Learning Disabilities, 25,* 430–441.

American Youth Policy Forum (AYPF) & Center on Education Policy (CEP). (2002). *Twenty-five years of educating children with disabilities: The good news and the work ahead.* Washington, DC: Authors.

Americans with Disabilities Act (ADA) of 1990, PL 101-336, 42 U.S.C. §§ 12101 *et seq.*

Bergsman, S. (2002, June 17). *College building spree boots tuition burden.* Retrieved January 17, 2005 from http://www.realestatejournal.com/propertyreport/newsandtrends/20020617-bergsman.html

Benz, M., Doren, B., & Yovanoff, P. (1998). Crossing the great divide: Predicting productive engagement for young women with disabilities. *Career Development for Exceptional Individuals, 21*(1), 3–16.

Blackorby, J., & Wagner, M. (1996). Longitudinal postschool outcomes of youths with disabilities: Findings from the National Longitudinal Transition Study. *Exceptional Children, 62,* 399–413.

Blumenstyk, G. (2003a). Auxiliary services: Colleges look for more revenue. *The Chronicle of Higher Education, 50*(17), A12.

Blumenstyk, G. (2003b). For-profit colleges: Growth and home and abroad. *The Chronicle of Higher Education, 50*(17), 37.

Brinckerhoff, L., Shaw, S., & McGuire, J. (1992). Promoting access, accommodations, and independence for college students with learning disabilities. *Journal of Learning Disabilities, 25,* 417–429.

Brinckerhoff, L., Shaw, S., & McGuire, J. (1993). *Promoting postsecondary education for students with learning disabilities: A handbook for practitioners.* Austin, TX: PRO-ED.

Bursuck, W., & Rose, E. (1992). Community college options for students with mild disabilities. In F.R. Rusch, L. DeStefano, J. Chadsey-Rusch, A. Phelps, & E. Symanski (Eds.), *Transition from school to adult life: Models, linkages, and policy* (pp. 71–92). Sycamore, IL: Sycamore Publishing.

Carl D. Perkins Vocational and Applied Technology Education Act Amendments of 1998, PL 105-332, 20 U.S.C. 2301 *et seq.*

The Chronicle of Higher Education. (2003). The nation: A chart depicting enrollment trends. *The 2003–4 Almanac, 50*(1), A2. Retrieved October 15, 2004, from http://chronicle.com/free/almanac/2003/nation/nation.htm

Cocci, W. (1997, April–June). The community college choice. *The postsecondary LD report.* Retrieved April 6, 2005, from http://www.ldonline.org/ld_indepth/postsecondary/block_comcol.html

Consortium for Citizens with Disabilities. (2003, May 28). *CCD recommendations regarding Higher Education Act reauthorization.* Retrieved January 14, 2005, from http://www.c-c-d.org/heareautho.htm

Crosby, O. (2000). Degrees to dollars: Earnings of college graduates in 1998. *Occupational Outlook Quarterly, 44*(4), 30–38.

Fairweather, J., & Shaver, D. (1991). Making the transition to postsecondary education and training. *Exceptional Children, 57*, 264–270.

Frank, K., & Wade, P. (1993). Disabled student services in postsecondary education: Who's responsible for what? *Journal of College Student Development, 34*(1), 26–30.

Gajar, A. (1992). University-based models for students with learning disabilities: The Pennsylvania State University in mode. In F.R. Rusch, L. DeStephano, J. Chadsey-Rusch, L. Phelps, & E. Szymanski (Eds.), *Transition from school to adult life: Models, linkages, and policy* (pp. 51–70). Sycamore, IL: Sycamore Publishing.

Gajar, A. (1998). Postsecondary education. In F.R. Rusch & J.G. Chadsey (Eds.), *Beyond high school: Transition from school to work* (pp. 383–405). Belmont, CA: Wadsworth Group.

Getzel, E., Stodden, R., & Briel, L. (1999). *Pursuing postsecondary education opportunities for individuals with disabilities.* Honolulu: University of Hawaii.

Gilmore, D., Schuster, J., Zafft, C., & Hart, D. (2001). Postsecondary education services and employment outcomes within the vocational rehabilitation system. *Disabilities Studies Quarterly, 21*(1). Retrieved January 17, 2005, from http://www.dsq-sds.org/_articles_pdf/2001/Winter/dsq_2001_Winter_08.pdf

Gilson, S. (1996). Students with disabilities: An increasing voice and presence on college campuses. *Journal of Vocational Rehabilitation, 6*, 263–272.

Gilson, B.B., & Gilson, S.F. (1998). Making friends and building relationships. In P. Wehman & J. Kregel (Eds.), *More than a job: Securing satisfying careers for people with disabilities* (pp. 301–318). Baltimore: Paul H. Brookes Publishing Co.

Goldstein, D.E., Murray, C., & Edgar, E. (1998). Employment earnings and hours of high-school graduates with learning disabilities through the first decade after graduation. *Learning Disabilities Research and Practice, 13*(1), 53–64.

Greenbaum, B., Graham, S., & Scales, W. (1995). Adults with learning disabilities: Educational and social experiences. *Exceptional Children, 61*, 460–471.

Hall, M., Kleinert, H., & Kearns, F. (2000). Going to college! Postsecondary programs for students with moderate and severe disabilities. *Teaching Exceptional Children, 32*(3), 58–65.

Halpern, A., Yovanoff, P., Doren, B., & Benz, M. (1995). Predicting participation in postsecondary education for school leavers with disabilities. *Exceptional Children, 62*, 151–164.

HEATH Resource Center (1998). *Profile of 1996 college freshmen with disabilities.* Washington, DC: HEATH Resource Center and American Council on Education.

Hecker, D. (1998). Occupations and earnings of workers with some college but no degree. *Occupational Outlook Quarterly, 42*(2), 28–39.

Henderson, C. (1995). *College freshman with disabilities: A statistical profile.* Washington, DC: American Council on Education.

Henderson, C. (2001). *College freshman with disabilities: A biennial statistical profile.* Retrieved June 16, 2004, from http://www.heath.gwu.edu/PDFs/collegefreshmen.pdf

Hishinuma, E.S. (2001). Summary of test accommodation for SAT and ACT for students who are learning disabled 1999–2000 school year. *LD Online.* Retrieved October 15, 2004, from http://www.ldonline.org/ld_indepth/transition/hishinuma_actsat.html

Individuals with Disabilities Education Act (IDEA) Amendments of 1997, PL 105-17, 20 U.S.C. §§ 1400 *et seq.*

Individuals with Disabilities Education Act (IDEA) of 1990, PL 101-476, 20 U.S.C. §§ 1400 *et seq.*

Individuals with Disabilities Education Improvement Act of 2004, PL 108-446, 20 U.S.C. §§ 1400 *et seq.*

InTime. (2004). *Metro Phoenix ENLACE, College increases your earning power!* http://mphx enlace.asu.edu/earnings.asp

Izzo, M., & Lamb, P. (2002). *Self-determination and career development: Skills for successful transition to postsecondary education and employment.* Retrieved January 17, 2005, from http://www. ncset.hawaii.edu/pdf/self-determination.pdf

Johnson, E., Kimball, K., Brown, S., & Anderson, D. (2001). A statewide review of the use of accommodations in large scale, high stakes assessment. *Exceptional Children, 67*(2), 251–264.

Kelley, J.G. (2004, May 16). A measured approach. *Richmond Times-Dispatch*, pp. F1, F7.

Lichtenstein, S. (1998). Characteristics of youths and young adults. In F. Rusch & J. Chadsey (Eds.), *Beyond high school: Transition from school to work* (pp. 1–31). Belmont, CA: Wadsworth Group.

Malloy, W. (1997). Responsible inclusion: Celebrating diversity and academic excellence. *NASSP Bulletin, 64*, 80–85.

McCusker, C. (1995). The Americans with Disabilities Act: Its potential for expanding the scope of reasonable academic accommodation. *Journal of College and University Law, 21*(4), 619–641.

McLeskey, J., Henry, D., & Hodges, D. (1998). Where is it happening? *Teaching Exceptional Children, 31*(1), 4–10.

Mull, C., Sitlington, P., & Alper, S. (2001). Postsecondary education for students with learning disabilities: A synthesis of the literature. *Exceptional Children, 68*(1), 97–118.

Murray, C., Goldstein, D., Nourse, S., & Edgar, E. (2000). The postsecondary school attendance and completion rates of high school graduates with learning disabilities. *Learning Disabilities Research, 15*, 119–127.

National Center for Education Statistics. (1995). *Condition of education.* Washington, DC: U.S. Department of Education.

National Center for Education Statistics. (1996a). *National Postsecondary Student Aid Study: 1995–96 (NPSAS:96), Undergraduate Data Analysis System.* Washington, DC: U.S. Department of Education.

National Center for Education Statistics. (1996b). *Projections of education statistics to 2006.* Washington, DC: U.S. Department of Education.

National Center for Educational Statistics. (1999a). *An institutional perspective on students with disabilities in postsecondary education* (Prepared by L. Lewis & E. Farris). Washington, DC: U.S. Department of Education.

National Center for Educational Statistics. (1999b). *Students with disabilities in postsecondary education.* Washington, DC: U.S. Department of Education.

National Center for Educational Statistics. (2000). *Digest of educational statistics, 2000 edition.* Washington, DC: U.S. Department of Education.

National Center for Education Statistics. (2002). *Digest of education statistics, 2002 edition.* Washington, DC: U.S. Department of Education.

National Center for the Study of Postsecondary Educational Supports. (2000). *National survey of educational support provision to students with disabilities in postsecondary education settings.* Honolulu: University of Hawaii at Manoa.

National Center for the Study of Postsecondary Educational Supports. (2002, July 8). *Preparation for and support of youth with disabilities in postsecondary education and employment: Implications for policy, priorities and practice.* Proceeding and briefing book for the National Summit on Postsecondary Education for People with Disabilities, Washington, DC, July 8, 2002. (Available online: http://www.ncset.Hawaii.edu/summits/july2002/default.htm)

No Child Left Behind Act of 2001, PL 107-110, 20 U.S.C. 6301 *et seq.*

Norlander, K., Shaw, S., & McGuire, J. (1990). Competencies of postsecondary education personnel serving students with learning disabilities. *Journal of Learning Disabilities, 23,* 426–431.

Office of Special Education and Rehabilitative Services. (2000). *IDEA lessons for all!* Retrieved December 18, 2003, from http://www.ed.gov/offices/OSERS/IDEA25th

Page, B., & Chadsey-Rusch, J. (1995). The community college experience for students with and without disabilities: A viable transition outcome? *Career Development for Exceptional Individuals, 18*(2), 85–96.

Pierangelo, R., & Crane, R. (1997). *Complete guide to special education transition services.* West Nyack, NY: The Center for Applied Research in Education.

Rehabilitation Act of 1973, PL 93-112, 29 U.S.C. §§ 701 *et seq.*

Reis, S., Neu, T., & McGuire, J. (1997). Case studies of high-ability students with learning disabilities who have achieved. *Exceptional Children, 63,* 463–479.

Smith, D., McLesky, J., Tyler, N., & Saunders, S. (2002). *The supply and demand of special education teachers: The nature of the chronic shortage of special education teachers.* Unpublished manuscript, University of Florida, Gainesville.

Smith, J. (1998). *Inclusion: School for all students.* Belmont, CA: Wadsworth Group.

Stodden, R. (1998). School-to-work transition: Overview of disability legislation. In F.R. Rusch & J.G. Chadsey (Eds.), *Beyond high school: Transition from school to work* (pp. 60–76). Belmont, CA: Wadsworth Group.

Stodden, R.A., Conway, M.A., & Chang, K.B.T. (2003). *Professional employment for individuals with disabilities.* Retrieved October 15, 2004, from http://www.ncset.hawaii.edu/institutes/feb2003/papers/txt/PROFESSIONAL%20EMPLOYMENT%20.txt

Stodden, R.A., Galloway, L.M., & Stodden, N.J. (2003). Secondary school curricula issues: Impact on postsecondary students with disabilities. *Exceptional Children, 70*(1), 9–25.

Stodden, R.A., Jones, M.A., & Chang, K. (2002). *Services, supports and accommodations for individuals with disabilities: An analysis across secondary education, postsecondary education, and employment.* Honolulu, HI: Capacity Building Institute.

Thomas, S. (2000). College students and disability law. *Journal of Special Education, 33,* 248–257.

Thurlow, M., House, A., Boys, C., Scott, D., & Ysseldyke, J. (2000). *1999 state assessment policies for students with disabilities: Participation and accommodations.* Minneapolis: University of Minnesota, National Center on Educational Outcomes.

Thurlow, M., & Johnson, D. (2000). High stakes testing for students with disabilities. *Journal of Teacher Education, 51,* 289–298.

Trani, E.P. (2000). *Virginia Commonwealth University 1990–2000: Foundation for our future.* Richmond: Virginia Commonwealth University, Office of the President.

Turnbull, A., Turnbull, R., Shank, M., & Leal, D. (1999). *Exceptional lives: Special education in today's schools* (2nd ed.). Upper Saddle River, NJ: Merrill/Prentice Hall.

U.S. Department of Education. (1996). *Eighteenth annual report to Congress on the implementation of the Individuals with Disabilities Education Act.* Washington DC: Author.

U.S. Department of Education. (2002). *Twenty-second annual report to Congress on the implementation of the Individuals with Disabilities Education Act.* Washington, DC: Author.

U.S. General Accounting Office. (2003). *Special education: Federal actions can assist states in improving postsecondary outcomes for youth.* Washington, DC: Author.

Wagner, M., & Blackorby, J. (1996). Transition from high school work or college: How special education children are. *The Future of Children: Special Education for Students with Disabilities, 6*(1), 103–120.

Wehman, P., & Kregel, J. (Eds.). (1998). *More than a job: Securing satisfying careers for young adults with disabilities* (3rd ed.). Baltimore: Paul H. Brookes Publishing Co.

West, M., Kregel, J., Getzel, E., Zhu, M., Ipsen, S., & Martin, E. (1993). Beyond Section 504: Satisfaction and empowerment of students with disabilities in higher education. *Exceptional Children, 59*(5), 456–467.

Whelley, T., Hart, D., & Zafft, C. (2002). *Coordination and management of services for individuals with disabilities in the transition from secondary to participation in postsecondary education and employment.* Paper presented at the Capacity Building Institute, Honolulu, HI.

CHAPTER 2

Understanding the Regulatory Environment

Virginia J. Reilly and Trent Davis

An understanding of the Americans with Disabilities Act (ADA) of 1990 (PL 101-336) and related statutes, although essential, does not by itself fully convey the realities of college life for students with disabilities. The following fictional story is used to bring alive some of the key issues that students with disabilities face in college as they attempt to succeed in a new environment.

JULIE'S STORY

Julie is a bright and attractive 18-year-old college freshman at a large state university. Witnessing her father's experiences as a part-time cattle farmer influenced her decision to major in biology and become a veterinarian. Julie graduated from a public high school in a rural area outside of Washington, D.C., where she was a popular student who had a leadership role with the school yearbook committee. Julie took her schoolwork seriously, and with much support from her parents and the school, she made honor roll for all but one semester in high school. In order to succeed, Julie learned that she had to become a strong self-advocate. Her teachers in high school came to appreciate Julie's tenacity and assertiveness, although she seemed to make their jobs more complicated at times.

These facts are all the more impressive when one considers that Julie was born with a mild form of multiple sclerosis (MS), which makes it hard for her to stand or sit for long periods of time and requires her to use a wheelchair. Her doctors predicted that her symptoms would intensify as she enters young adulthood. In addition, Julie struggles with spelling and was diagnosed as having a learning disability. Computers have been a tremendous help for her in working with this disability.

Despite Julie's successful high school experience, college requires her to start over in a whole new environment. She purposely chose to attend a school several hours from home and to live in a residence hall in order to establish her independence. However, Julie worries that without her friends and family nearby, she will be overwhelmed. She finds it scary when she imagines approaching professors for accommodations. Although most teachers seem to easily grasp her physical limitations, her "invisible disability" is harder for some to understand. She knows that in college, she has to ask for accommodations—no one will bring them to her, as done in high school. Julie will need all of her self-advocacy skills and knowledge of her rights as a student with a disability to succeed in college. Yet, with the appropriate skills and knowledge, Julie is up for the challenge!

Many students with disabilities and their families do not realize that the transition from high school to college or the workplace involves leaving behind the protection under the Individuals with Disabilities Education Act (IDEA) of 1990 (PL 101-476), its 1997 amendments (PL 105-17), and its 2004 reauthorization (PL 108-446). The transition to higher education involves learning one's rights and responsibilities under the ADA. This is a broad mandate that encompasses public and private colleges, businesses, and testing agencies—such as those administering the Scholastic Aptitude Test (SAT), Graduate Record Examination (GRE), and law school or medical school admission tests—as well as everyday objects such as telephones and televisions. Part of the broad coverage of the ADA includes the requirement that all colleges have an ADA coordinator. Some larger institutions have an ADA coordinator who may oversee physical and program access compliance and a separate office of disability support services (DSS) that works directly with students. The ADA coordinator may be the contact for employees needing accommodations, and the DSS office may only work with students on academic modifications. Smaller campuses may have only a single person responsible for the broad duties of the ADA.

In addition, some faculty do not realize the broad scope of the ADA and worry that students who use academic accommodations may not have that same option at their place of work. Many DSS professionals must educate their co-workers among the college faculty who express reluctance to provide extra time on a test. Such faculty members may say things such as "Well, he won't be able to have extra time when he is an engineer!" not realizing that the ADA will continue to cover a student as he or she makes the transition into the business world.

This chapter introduces the broad scope of the ADA in order to understand how everyone benefits not only from academic and workplace accommodations but also from accommodations such as physical access, text telephones, and captioned television. Often, when the chapter authors conduct disability training sessions, they first ask, "What do you think of when you hear the term *ADA*?" The group invariably replies, "Blue handicapped parking signs" or "Ramps into buildings." Physical access is the first thing that comes to mind for most people, and that is certainly a large part of the ADA. However, the 101st Congress had much more in mind when it crafted this legislation in 1990. To understand the motivation behind adding the ADA to existing disability laws and the manner in which the ADA expanded the coverage of those laws, it is important to examine a short history of how the ADA came about.

HISTORY OF THE AMERICANS WITH DISABILITIES ACT

In U.S. society, the prevailing philosophy governing people with disabilities stemmed from a Judeo-Christian tradition of charity, welfare, and pity (Nagler, 1993; Rioux, 1993). Federal laws to assist people with disabilities grew out of efforts created for veterans who acquired disabilities through war service. These early efforts often ended in a permanent status of dependency and segregation for individuals with mental health disabilities, visual impairments, and physical disabilities and for their families (Percy, 1989; Rothstein, 1995).

The trend of paternalistic services and income support changed with the wave of the Civil Rights movement. The *Brown v. Board of Education of Topeka* (1954) decision articulated the right to equal educational opportunity. This case served as a catalyst not only for the Civil Rights movement but also for children with disabilities who had been placed in separate schools and special classes (Brinckerhoff, Shaw, & McGuire, 1993). Likewise, the Elementary and Secondary Education Act (ESEA) of 1965 (PL 80-10), described by Worthen and Sanders as "the most comprehensive and ambitious education bill ever envisioned" (1987, p. 17), improved schooling for those with disabilities and began the trend toward education and independence.

This trend was strengthened by two landmark cases, *Pennsylvania Association for Retarded Children (PARC) v. Commonwealth of Pennsylvania* (1971) and *Mills v. Board of Education of the District of Columbia* (1972), which resulted in the Education for All Handicapped Children Act of 1975 (PL 94-142). This statute, which was reauthorized as IDEA, serves to outline procedural rights for all children with disabilities in public schools. It guarantees all children, regardless of disability, a free and appropriate public education in the least restrictive environment (Brinckerhoff et al., 1993; Percy, 1989).

The resulting massive changes in K–12 education resulted in many more students who were better prepared to continue their education and expected the same rights as others in their postsecondary education experiences. The Rehabilitation Act of 1973 (PL 93-112) met this need but only by institutions receiving federal funds (Jarrow, 1992). Unlike the explicit guidance in the Education for All Handicapped Children Act of 1975, Section 504 of the Rehabilitation Act was stronger on symbolic statement than on guidelines for implementation, and some colleges took a narrow interpretation of the Section 504 mandate.

The Civil Rights Restoration Act of 1987 (PL 100-259) eliminated many of these limitations for postsecondary students and served as an impetus of vast change (Hill, 1992). Congress found that certain Supreme Court decisions had unduly narrowed the broad application of several civil rights laws, including the Rehabilitation Act of 1973, to those parts of a recipient's operation that directly benefited from federal assistance. The Civil Rights Restoration Act clarified the intent of Congress to include *all* programs and activities of federal aid recipients and restored the broad, institutionwide application of those laws as previously administered. In 1990, President George H.W. Bush signed the ADA into law, extending the provisions of the Rehabilitation Act to the private sector and to all state and local government activities. The ADA has focused attention on disability-related issues as no law before it, protecting the rights of people with disabilities.

The ADA does not replace the Rehabilitation Act but draws a substantive framework from the earlier mandate. Structured much like the sections of the Rehabilitation Act, the ADA is organized around five titles, each addressing a different area of protection for individuals with disabilities. Just as the Rehabilitation Act accomplished some college access for individuals with disabilities in 1973, the ADA has opened the doors a little wider. Students with disabilities can now enter colleges with expectations of access to the campus transportation, accommodation in academics and housing, and provision of their preferred means of communication.

> Julie understands that as a student in the United States, she has the right to equal access and accommodation for her disability at college. Although it remains important that Julie advocate for herself, she is entitled to the same educational opportunities as other qualified students. Julie also knows that she will be covered by the ADA even after she graduates and enters the work force.

THE AMERICANS WITH DISABILITIES ACT: A SMALL SNAPSHOT OF A LARGE FEDERAL MANDATE

Knowing the history of the ADA helps one understand how important this civil rights law is in the history of education in America. In 1990, when there were more than 54 million Americans with disabilities, it was critical to provide protection in public and private entities. As noted previously, most people think of the Rehabilitation Act and the ADA in terms of physical access. It is important to realize that the ADA is a civil rights law that mandates *program* access as well. In fact, the majority of college students with disabilities have learning disabilities, attention-deficit/hyperactivity disorder (ADHD), or psychological disabilities, not physical or sensory disabilities. Thus, it is important to understand the ADA as a civil rights law pertaining to each group. In addition, although the ADA exists to ensure equality of opportunity, it is not an affirmative action statute; it does not specify that quotas or preferences be given in admissions.

The Five Titles of the Americans with Disabilities Act

To comprehend how the ADA guarantees equal opportunity, or equal access, it is helpful to understand how it is organized under five sections, or titles, and to know which federal agencies enforce each title. For example, if a student is unhappy with services at his or her state university, he or she can file an external complaint with the Office of Civil Rights (OCR). The appendix at the end of this chapter provides web sites for each of these federal agencies, which can be consulted for a more in-depth interpretation of the applicable section of the law.

Title I Title I prohibits discrimination in employment; it is enforced by the Equal Employment Opportunity Commission (EEOC). The ADA prohibits discrimination against qualified people with disabilities who can perform the essential functions of the job with or without accommodations. Title I, which applies to businesses that employs 15 or more people, states,

> No covered entity shall discriminate against a qualified individual with a disability because of the disability of such individual in regard to job application procedures, the hiring, advancement, or discharge of employees, employee compensation, job training, and other terms, conditions, and privileges of employment.

In postsecondary education settings, students may also be college or university employees. If they need accommodations in their employment settings, they may arrange those accommodations with staff at the DSS office. A DSS counselor can advise student employees regarding where to apply for workplace accommodations. However, in some institutions, student employees may be required to work with a different office for workplace arrangements. This may be the human resources or personnel office. It is usually best to plan all accommodations through the appropriate office designated by the institution. Accommodations arranged informally with managers or supervisors can have disastrous consequences, and student employees should not share their documentation of disability with anyone other than the offices that are charged with that responsibility through institutional policy. First, a student employee's supervisor is not trained to read the documentation provided by the doctor, therapist, or other professional who verified the disability. This is very private medical information, and most people do not want to share their medical information with people with whom they work daily. Second, the institution has most likely set policies about who is to receive the disability documentation. That person is usually trained to interpret the documentation and to provide the interactive process to determine the most appropriate accommodations for the student employee. A well-meaning supervisor who is very "accommodating" may provide workplace changes that are not appropriate and can later lead to performance issues. In addition, if a new supervisor enters the scene, the student worker who arranged informal accommodations is then seen as not following institutional policies, which is not the best impression to give a new boss.

Title II   Title II prohibits discrimination in connection with state and local governments and is enforced by OCR. It states,

> Subject to the provisions of this title, no qualified individual with a disability shall, by reason of such disability, be excluded from participation in or be denied the benefits of the services, programs, or activities of a public entity, or be subjected to discrimination by any such entity.

Title II covers not only state-operated facilities but also local government services such as courts and jails. Because Title II covers state-operated institutions, this section is the most important to students who attend state colleges and universities, including community colleges and vocational schools.

Title III   Title III prohibits discrimination in businesses that serve the public and are privately owned, such as hotels, restaurants, theaters, and private colleges; it is enforced by the Department of Justice (DOJ). This section states,

> No individual shall be discriminated against on the basis of disability in the full and equal enjoyment of the goods, services, facilities, privileges, advantages, or accommodations of any place of public accommodation by any person who owns, leases (or leases to), or operates a place of public accommodation.

Title III includes private colleges and universities. It also covers testing companies such as Educational Testing Service (ETS), which administers the SAT, and others that administer tests for institutions of higher education (e.g., for law and medical school admissions). As a result, accommodations must be supplied in their testing environments. Although the language of Title II and Title III differs, it indicates that services for students with disabilities and equal access must be provided at state and private institutions. This extension of services to the private sector was one of the major changes brought about by the ADA.

Title IV   Title IV prohibits discrimination in telecommunications; it is enforced by the Federal Communications Commission (FCC). This section provides text telephones for people with hearing impairments and mandates closed-captioning on televisions. Title IV is very important in providing services for college students who have hearing impairments. All telecommunications at state and private institutions must be accessible, and requests for accommodations must be met in a timely manner. This electronic communication includes on-line courses and other types of distance learning.

Title V   Title V, enforced by the EEOC, covers miscellaneous areas; it contains general rules and ensures that other state and federal laws that may provide greater protection for people with disabilities are not preempted by the ADA. The ADA also protects family members of people with disabilities. For example, a college student whose sibling is HIV positive cannot be denied admission or residence hall access on the basis of unfounded fears about spreading the virus.

> Julie has done her homework and is aware of her rights under the ADA. She knows that as an adult, she is now operating under a different set of guidelines and no longer has the protection of IDEA.

DEFINITION OF *DISABILITY*

Who is covered by the ADA? It is important to realize that the ADA and IDEA have different definitions of *disability*. Therefore, a student who received special education services in high school under IDEA may not qualify for accommodations in college. Yet, a student who received services in high school under a 504 plan or who did not meet the qualifications for special education may be covered and receive services under the ADA. The ADA protects those who meet one part of the following three-prong definition:

1. A physical or mental impairment that *substantially limits* one or more *major life activities*

2. A record of such an impairment

3. Being regarded as having such an impairment

It is important to know that accommodations are only provided under the first prong of this definition. Thus, a freshman with a disability who needs accommodations must present the college DSS office with documentation that establishes substantial limitation in a major life activity. These terms and guidelines regarding documentation are discussed in more detail in the following sections. The other two prongs of the definition protect one from discrimination, but they do not establish provision of accommodations. That is, if a student has a record of an impairment (e.g., he or she received special education in fourth grade but has not had any recent evaluations), the college cannot discriminate in the admissions process; however, the college is not responsible for providing accommodations unless the student presents current evaluation information. Likewise, a person who is morbidly obese or who has a severe facial disfigurement may be regarded as having a disability; he or she would be protected from discrimination (i.e., the person would have equal access to education or employment if qualified), but the individual would not be afforded any accommodations. If a student or employee has an obvious disability—for example, a person who needs to use a wheelchair—the college may not necessarily ask for complete documentation of the disability; however, it has the right to ask as a part of informing its safety procedures (e.g., in residence halls, for evacuation plans).

Definition of *Substantially Limits*

To understand the previously described definition of *disability*, one must know the meaning behind some of the related terms. In the first prong of the definition, the term *substantially limits* refers to the inability to perform a major life activity or significant restrictions on the conditions, manner, or duration under which an individual can perform a particular major life activity. Thus, if a student has a learning disability, he or she may be significantly restricted in the manner in which he or she reads. It may take the student an extremely long time to complete written work. If the documentation provides this information about the disability and accommodations, the student may qualify for extended time when taking tests.

Examples of Major Life Activities

The major life activities listed in the ADA do not form an all-inclusive list. They do provide a guide for service providers who must evaluate the documentation presented and assist in establishing the existence of a disability. Table 2.1 provides a partial listing of major life activities. Naturally, a college service provider is most likely to note the areas of learning, concentrating, seeing, and hearing when reviewing documentation of disability.

Qualified Individual and Title II Court Decisions

Whether protected by the ADA's Title I in employment or Titles II or III for students entering state or private colleges, the applicant must be qualified

Table 2.1. Partial listing of major life activities

Breathing
Caring for oneself
Concentrating
Hearing
Interacting with others
Learning
Lifting
Reaching
Reproducing
Seeing
Sitting
Sleeping
Speaking
Standing while performing manual tasks
Thinking
Walking
Working

for the position sought. The language in Title II best applies to potential college students; it explains that a qualified individual is

> An individual with a disability who, with or without reasonable modifications to rules, policies, or practices, the removal of architectural, communication, or transportation barriers, or the provision of auxiliary aids and services, meets the essential eligibility requirements for the receipt of services or the participation in programs or activities provided by a public entity.

An important transition issue for high school students is learning about the admission requirements of the colleges or programs to which they plan to apply. Unlike elementary and secondary school systems and IDEA services providers, colleges (or employers) cannot ask about a disability in the application process. The responsibility of the college is that once the student is accepted and requests accommodations, those modifications and changes needed in physical or program access are provided in a timely manner. The seminal case on the term *qualified individual* is *Southeastern Community College v. Davis* (1979). In this case, brought to court under Section 504 of the Rehabilitation Act, the Supreme Court upheld a nursing program's rejection of a student with a hearing impairment. The court ruled that *otherwise qualified* means, in effect, "in spite of the individual's disability, along with accommodations that do not impose undue financial or administrative burdens."

Later, the important decision in *Bartlett v. New York State Board of Bar Examiners* (2000) provided new guidance on who the ADA considers a qualified individual. Marilyn Bartlett self-accommodated her disability during law school but was denied accommodations for the bar exam. Her learning disability was well documented, but at issue was whether to compare her to average learners and readers or to other law students or lawyers with similar training. Judge Sotomayor's decision confirmed that it is possible to be very smart and still be substantially limited by a learning disability. In this decision, the Supreme Court did not tamper with the EEOC guideline suggesting that in determining whether a disability is substantially limiting, one must consider the "condition, manner, and duration" of the individual's performance of the major life activity under consideration (J.E. Jarrow, personal communication, January 6, 2003, & March 24, 2005). Ms. Bartlett's win, allowing her the extra time on the bar exam, demonstrates the complexity that sometimes emerges in establishing status as a qualified individual with a disability.

Court Decisions on Definitions of *Disability* and *Qualified Individual* Under Title I

In 1999, Supreme Court rulings on three separate cases involving the ADA and disability under Title I changed the way of determining eligibility for accommodations. These cases were called the "Sutton trilogy" because the first case involved the two Sutton sisters, pilots who were found not to qualify as people with disabilities when the court decided their vision was corrected with glasses. (Nonetheless, one airline company refused to hire them because of their vision impairments, even though they had flown for other companies.)

This decision came as a surprise to many college disability professionals, based on previous technical assistance from the enforcing agencies. When the ADA was initially crafted, the federal agencies overseeing the first four titles were charged with composing technical assistance manuals to assist in the interpretation of each title. As noted previously, everyone has access to those technical assistance manuals through each agency's web site. The EEOC interpretation in its technical assistance manual suggested that whether a person's condition meets the definition of *disability* should be determined on the basis of the condition alone, with no mitigating measures (e.g., glasses to correct vision).

Thus, prior to the Sutton decision, if a person asked for accommodations due to a visual impairment, one did not consider the person's vision after corrected with glasses; instead, one determined if the person was substantially limited in the major life activity of seeing *without* his or her glasses. Now colleges can consider the impact of mitigating measures such as glasses or medication. Some colleges use the Sutton decision more strictly than others. For example, if a student has been diagnosed with ADHD and his or her medication is controlling the condition, the college DSS office could determine that the student is not substantially limited in a major life activity such as learning or concentrating. Other colleges have decided to take a more lenient approach, basing eligibility for services on the condition before consideration of the mitigating measure (e.g., medication).

Later guidance from the EEOC instructed its field officers to consider any impact the mitigating measure may have on the person claiming a disability. For example, the mitigation may itself *cause* limitations to a major life activity. A student might have a psychological disability that is controlled by medication, but the treatment causes extreme difficulty with sleeping. Now the service provider in such a situation may determine that the student qualifies for services based on the substantial limitation of the major life activity of sleeping. In turn, the student may be eligible to receive accommodations, such as priority scheduling. This example highlights the importance of students having current, in-depth information on their disabilities, including the effects of their medications.

Difficult decisions must be made by the DSS office and the student who is asking for accommodations. As explained by Friend, Judy, and Reilly (2002),

> Although the Supreme Court decisions indicate the individual is to be viewed with the mitigating measures in place, thereby negating coverage of many persons who have an impairment, there are many others who remain substantially limited in major life activities despite the use of mitigating measures. That fact would then seem to emphasize more clearly the need to address each instance on a case-by-case basis and to more thoroughly investigate the effect of the impairment on a wide variety of major life activities before declaring an individual not eligible for coverage or accommodation. (p. 23)

The preceding extract highlights the importance of students being very familiar with their medical or psychoeducational records and being able to strongly advocate for accommodations, if warranted. Defining disability under the ADA is no simple process, and colleges have great leeway in their decision-making process. Students can be more active participants in this process when they have been actively involved in their own treatment plans and thoroughly understand their disability.

> Julie makes a point of talking with her professors at the beginning of the semester in order to give them a chance to prepare adequate accommodations. She also makes sure that she does her part by contacting the DSS offices as soon as she arrives on campus. Self-advocacy will be a critical factor for her success in college.

GUIDELINES FOR DOCUMENTATION OF DISABILITY

As seen from the discussion in the previous section, clear, current, and complete documentation of disability is vital when beginning the process of receiving accommodations in a college setting. The following guidelines are based on several years of research examining the best standards for disability documentation. The research was conducted by Virginia Higher Education Leadership Partners, the National Association on Higher Education and Disability, and ETS to give colleges a more standardized approach to the evaluations that they would accept. As a result, the guidelines not only help ease transition from high school to college but also provide a smooth transfer from community colleges to 4-year institutions.

This section defines best practices for developing and maintaining consistent, comprehensive, and appropriate guidelines for documenting disabilities and requests for accommodations. It is recommended that the guidelines be used by institutions of higher education, qualified professionals, and secondary education professionals involved in transition planning. In addition, parents and students who are considering different colleges should be well aware of the documentation requirements. This information provides a framework for institutions to establish policies and procedures that are adapted to their specific context while embracing both the spirit and letter of the law. As students and parents consider colleges, they may find that some institutions are using the following framework for their evaluation requirements and others are not. All institutions are encouraged to consult with their legal counsel when establishing this important part of their procedures.

Need for Documentation

Under federal law (i.e., the ADA and Section 504 of the Rehabilitation Act), individuals with disabilities are defined as having "a physical or mental impairment that substantially limits one or more of the major life activities of such individual, a record of such impairment, or being regarded as having such an impairment." Individuals with disabilities are protected from discrimination in admissions to higher education and in employment. With adequate documentation of the current impact of their disabilities, individuals are entitled to appropriate accommodations. Therefore, documentation serves two primary purposes in postsecondary education. First, documentation must establish that an individual has a disability and therefore is protected from discrimination. Second, the documentation must describe the current functional impact of the disability so that potential accommodations can be identified. As learned from *Guckenberger v. Trustees of Boston University* (1997),

> Documentation does not have to be from an M.D. but must be from an appropriate professional. It does not have to be within three years. ADHD documentation may call for a specialized evaluator and more current testing. The process of evaluating documentation must be done by objective review of a knowledgeable individual and accommodations must be based on demonstrated need in the documentation. (Friend et al., 2002, p. 30)

General Documentation Guidelines

Documentation of disability should consist of an evaluation by an appropriate professional and must include a clear statement of the diagnosis, the basis for the diagnosis, and the *current* impact of the disability as it relates to the accommodation request. See Table 2.2 for more information.

Recommendations for accommodations, adaptive devices, assistive services, compensatory strategies, and/or collateral support services should be considered within the context of the individual's current program. Accommodation decisions are to be made on a case-by-case basis, considering the impact

Table 2.2.   Elements to include in documentation of a disability

A diagnostic statement identifying the disability, date of the most current diagnostic evaluation, and the date of the original diagnosis

A description of the diagnostic tests, methods, and/or criteria used including specific test results (including standardized testing scores) and the examiner's narrative interpretation

A description of the current functional impact of the disability—this may be in the form of an examiner's narrative and/or an interview, but it must have a rational relationship to diagnostic assessments; for learning disabilities, *current documentation* is defined using adult norms

A statement indicating treatments, medications, or assistive devices/services currently prescribed or in use, with a description of the mediating effects and potential side effects from such treatments

A description of the expected progression or stability of the impact of the disability over time, particularly the next 5 years

A history of previous accommodations and their impact

The credentials of the diagnosing professional(s), if not clear from the letterhead or other forms; diagnosing professionals should not be family members or others with a close personal relationship with the individual being evaluated

Documentation prepared for specific noneducational venues (e.g., Social Security Administration, Department of Veteran's Affairs) may not meet these criteria

Individualized education program (IEP) or Section 504 plans are not considered sufficient documentation unless accompanied by a current and complete evaluation

From Professional Development Academy, U Success, Resources for University Success. (2001). *Virginia higher education guidelines for documentation of disability.* Retrieved January 11, 2005, from http://www.students.vcu.edu/pda/vahelpguidelines.html; adapted by permission.

of a particular student's disability within the specific context in which that student must function—based on the student's disability, individual needs, and the requirements of the class/program.

Beyond the more objective determination of a disability and its impact that external documentation provides, institutions should recognize that input from the individual with a disability is also a rich and important source of information on the impact of the disability and on the effectiveness of accommodations. Institutions of higher education should give due consideration to records from public school divisions (concerning exiting students who received special education services under IDEA) in determining the presence of a qualifying disability and making decisions regarding accommodations. Nationally, most institutions of higher education utilize guidelines developed by the Association on Higher Education and Disability (AHEAD) and ETS. AHEAD has removed the guidelines for Learning Disabilities from its web site. It is currently in the process of updating those guidelines to meet current practice in the field of higher education and services for students with disabilities. Until the AHEAD guidelines are completed, most colleges and universities are using documentation guidelines such as the following:

- http://www.students.vcu.edu/pda/vahelpguidelines.html (general documentation guidelines)
- http://www.ldonline.org/ld_indepth/postsecondary/ ahead_guidelines.html (learning disabilities guidelines)
- http://www.ets.org/disability/adhdplcy.html (ADHD guidelines)
- http://www.ets.org/disability/psyplcy.html (psychiatric disability guidelines)

Students who begin collecting qualified documentation information during their sophomore or junior year of high school will be ahead of the game when they visit colleges during their senior year. Once a student is accepted at his or her chosen college, having a complete evaluation will speed up the process of deciding on appropriate accommodations, will ensure program or physical access, and will certainly be appreciated by the college DSS office! See Chapter 5 for additional information about documentation.

> Julie was aware that documentation of her disabilities needed to be up to date when she entered college. Thus, she wisely arranged a reevaluation of her learning disability during her last year of high school. She also obtained certification from her family physician, who documented her physical limitations.

PROGRAM ACCESS

The ADA says that businesses and places of higher education must examine their policies, practices, and procedures. Modifications must be made, when necessary, to ensure that *all* services are accessible. This means not just getting in the building but having access to all of the activities and services that *any* student or employee would be able to enjoy.

Approaching the Issue of Program Access

When researching colleges, a student or parent may want to consider the many facets of college participation that will need to be addressed for the student to have equal access at the institution of his or her choice. The goal of program access is not only providing accessibility to all programs, services, and benefits but also establishing independence for the person with a disability. Table 2.3 provides information that may be helpful in evaluating accessibility, depending on the student's type of disability.

> Julie made a point of visiting each college she was considering attending. While on campus, she discussed her needs with staff at the DSS office and visited facilities that she expected to use. Julie then evaluated each college in terms of its accessibility.

Program Access for Family and Guests

Program or physical access does not simply apply to the students at the college or university. Parents and guests with disabilities who are visiting the campus must be afforded access to all activities that are open to other guests. For example, a parent who is deaf must be provided a qualified interpreter while attending his daughter's graduation from college, if this request is made in advance (*Letter to National Holistic University*, 2003).

REASONABLE ACCOMMODATION

Basic Principles

Once a student has found a college that provides his or her planned area of academic study and the best program access for his or her needs, a conversation with a professional at the college DSS office about accommodations should take place. Armed with his or her current documentation, the student is ready to enter the interactive process of establishing appropriate accommodations. Colleges generally follow the rules about accommodations described in Table 2.4.

Workplace Accommodations

As mentioned previously, students are often employed at the university or college they attend. Numerous accommodations may be provided at the work site depending on disability type and the requirements interpreted from the student's documentation. Accommodations in employment might include the following:

1. Restructuring the job

2. Offering part-time or modified work schedules

Table 2.3. College accessibility checklist

Transportation	Transit services offered for people without disabilities must be offered on equal status for people with disabilities. If the college provides bus services, buses must be accessible or the college must provide a paratransit service with comparable schedules.
Parking	Accessible parking should be as close as possible to campus buildings.
Physical access	Physical access includes looking at all features that the student will encounter, such as sidewalks, curb cuts, obstacles along the route (e.g., tree branches, service vehicles, construction sites), railings for stairways, doorways (automatic doors are not required, but doors should open easily), work spaces, aisles, restrooms, and so forth. Residence halls, classrooms, and all public spaces should be accessible. However, this does not mean every building on a campus must be made completely accessible if programs or classes can be moved to an accessible location, which is a common practice, especially for classes originally scheduled to be held in old buildings.
Welcome areas	Welcome desks and reception areas should be at a lower level for wheelchair users.
Signs	Directional assistance should be available for people with low vision, and signs also should be provided in braille.
Safety	Evacuation and emergency routes are clearly marked in all buildings, including residence halls (i.e., evacuation route maps in each room and visible signage in halls). There should be clear, written plans for emergency evacuation of people with disabilities that include buddy systems and plans for people with sensory loss.
Closed-captioning	Classes and campus theaters should provide descriptive and captioned versions of videotapes and films whenever possible.
Computers	Accessibility should be provided through hardware or software, including the following: screen enlargement, voice input/output, and appropriate assistive technology. Prospective students and their families should ask if there is an assistive technology lab. If so, the assistive technology staff should provide training to students requiring technology for means of access to instruction that they may not have learned in high school. It is also critical for the college to provide regular maintenance of assistive technology devices to ensure that access is provided as consistently as possible.
Web pages	Distance education and web-based classes must be accessible and compatible with assistive technology.
Alternate formats	Upon request, the college should be able to provide printed materials in the following formats so that all students can have access to the information at the same time: enlarged, braille, audio, or electronic.
Advertising	Programs, employment, and services should be announced in multiple places and formats.
Events	Presentations, programs, training sessions, and other extracurricular activities should be accessible through the provision of interpreters, auxiliary aids (e.g., notetakers), assistive listening devices, or assistive technology.
Visibility of services	Notice of accommodations and services from the DSS office must be well advertised and easily found on the college's web site.
Americans with Disabilities Act (ADA) coordinator	Students and families should determine if the college has an ADA coordinator who will ensure the provision of the previously listed services.

Table 2.4. Rules that colleges generally follow about accommodations

Accommodations are provided under the auspices of the disability support services (DSS) or other applicable campus office.

Accommodations must be effective.

Accommodations must reduce barriers related to an individual's disability.

Accommodations need not be the best possible, as long as they are effective.

Specifically requested accommodations do not have to be provided if other suitable accommodations are offered.

Accommodations for personal use are not required. (Personal use items include wheelchairs, hearing aids, or provision of private tutoring.)

An institution may provide accommodations beyond those required by the Americans with Disabilities Act (ADA) of 1990 (PL 101-336).

Accommodations are required only for known limitations.

Communication requests for students who are deaf (or who have other communication disorders) may be more stringent in order to provide the preferred means of communication. For example, a student who is deaf and has an interpreter in a class that is highly technical may also request a notetaker because watching the interpreter often precludes being able to take notes.

3. Making facilities accessible

4. Acquiring or modifying equipment and/or devices

5. Modifying exams, training materials, and policies

6. Providing qualified readers, interpreters, and notetakers for work-related activities

Employers are not required to hire two people for one job, so if a student is deaf, a college would not be required to provide a full-time interpreter at the work site (although the college would have to supply a full-time interpreter for the classroom). However, interpreters or notetakers may be provided on occasion when no other method of communication is available, such as during a required training session provided to all employees.

> Julie has realistic expectations about the accommodations she can expect. She knows that they must be effective in providing her with the same opportunities as other students. However, she is willing to accept that these accommodations may not always be what she asked for or the best possible solution. For her introductory psychology course, Julie hoped to have a paid notetaker in class. However, her DSS counselor provided a tape recorder because the professor posts most class materials on his web site.

STUDY ABROAD AND EXCHANGE PROGRAMS

Students should work with the college DSS office regarding accommodations for any required (or desired) global studies. Study abroad is a new issue for many colleges, which are expanding their global studies programs. In its role as enforcer of the ADA's Title II, OCR has addressed what is legally required of a college or university in terms of making accommodations in a study abroad program. OCR stated in *Letter to Arizona State University* (2001),

> Upon reviewing the information provided by the complainant and the University, as well as current OCR policy information, and available case law, it is OCR's determination that Section 504 and Title II programs do not extend extraterritorially. In other words, it is OCR's position that neither 504 nor Title II requires the University to provide auxiliary aids and services in overseas programs. Nor does either statute otherwise prohibit discrimination on the basis of disability in overseas programs.

Because Title II of the ADA does not extend beyond the bounds of the United States, study abroad is not required to be accessible. Although Title II applies to public colleges and universities, the analysis would be the same under Title III, which is the section of the ADA applicable to private colleges and universities. Title I does require accommodations for employees of the institution who are working abroad (the EEOC enforces Title I accommodations for employment).

To what extent a particular college or university wishes to make study abroad programs accessible is a policy decision. Although study abroad and exchange programs are not required to be accessible, best practices would provide a formal mechanism for requesting and assisting students with finding accommodations. Although physical accessibility cannot always be provided, the institution may want to make every effort for program access. The student should meet with the staff from the DSS office and the international studies department to explore resources and strategies for accommodations before the need arises. One idea is for the student to work with these offices to identify disability coordinators at the foreign school. Overall the college should bear in mind the following:

1. Consider offering substitutions for nonaccessible study abroad programs (e.g., substitute an archeological dig in New Mexico for one offered in Egypt).

2. Provide accessibility information on application and marketing materials for study abroad programs.

3. Avoid barring a student from foreign study due to disability.

4. Explore ways to assist in hiring an interpreter to travel with the student (outside funding may be available from other agencies or donors).

5. Remember that accommodations must be provided to international students with disabilities who are studying in the United States. Section 504 of the Rehabilitation Act and the ADA apply to everyone who qualifies, not just U.S. citizens. The college must be ready for creative solutions. For example, students from other countries may have electric wheelchairs that use different voltage; the college might accommodate this need by

obtaining a lower voltage transformer. Information about disability services should be available in offices serving international students.

PHYSICAL ACCESS

No discussion of access is complete without consideration of the physical access to the facilities of the college or university. Although on most campuses few students use wheelchairs, scooters, or other mobility aids, it is critical that colleges provide full access not only to academic areas but also to social, recreational, residential, and other public areas. A finding against Duke University illustrates this point.

On February 23, 2000, Duke University reached an out-of-court settlement with the U.S. Department of Justice to enhance navigability of the campus in general and to improve the accessibility of dormitory rooms and classrooms (see *Settlement Agreement between the United States of America and Duke University*, 2001). The original suit was filed in 1996 by a student who argued that Duke had not made the campus accessible to people in wheelchairs as required by Title III of the ADA, which applies to private institutions. The settlement was significant because it was the first that dealt with campus access on a broad basis. Duke agreed to pay $25,000 in civil penalties and $7,500 to the student and to make wide-ranging improvements on the campus—some taking as few as 10 days to complete and others taking up to 5 years.

In planning for physical accessibility, a student must consider his or her safety in emergency situations. Discussions about safety should occur as early as possible with the DSS office. Mainly, it is the responsibility of the person with a disability to plan ahead for emergency situations. In many emergency situations, elevators will not work, lights may go out, or telephones may not be operable. Always carrying a wireless telephone is helpful, but these do not work inside of all buildings (in a nonemergency situation, the student should take time to check this). Often, stairwells offer a safe area to wait until emergency personnel arrive. However, in some older campus buildings, stairwells may act as chimneys, conducting smoke and flames. The OCR has ruled that pathways must be kept hazard free for evacuation (*Letter to Cosumnes River College*, 2000). In addition, campus facilities must have a plan to evacuate students with disabilities in emergencies (*Letter to University of California, Berkeley*, 2002). Nonetheless, the student should arrange evacuation planning with residence hall advisors, roommates, or classroom faculty; this can save critical time in an emergency situation, especially when elevators are not working. If evacuation information is not posted in buildings as required, the campus physical plant or facilities office should be contacted immediately.

One of Julie's major challenges at college has been getting around campus and obtaining access to her residence hall. She has a great relationship with staff at the DSS office and with her resident hall advisor. With their support, Julie has been able to get the university to provide her with necessary physical accommodations, such as electric doors.

Julie even goes to the university architect directly when she is not satis-fied with the progress being made!

CONFIDENTIALITY

Many students forego seeking accommodations because they do not want to be identified as a person with a disability. However, by disclosing their disability and requesting the necessary accommodations, they can achieve success and still have their disability status protected. Confidentiality is an extremely important issue for records pertaining to students or employees with disabili-ties. The college setting is often more stringent in protecting privacy than the K–12 arena. Elementary and secondary schools fall under IDEA regula-tions, such as the "child find" obligation. The fact that there is no duty to identify students who have a disability under the ADA guarantees that the disability status will remain unknown unless students seek accommodations and disclose their status to the appropriate office.

The right to confidentiality was included in ADA to avoid the stigma that individuals with disabilities often experienced when applying to higher education institutions or for employment. Because colleges are not allowed to ask about disability on any application forms, student disability status should not be known until after acceptance. However, students can choose to reveal their disabilities in the narrative portion that is provided with some college applications. Some applicants believe that this is an opportunity to explain an anomaly such as a low SAT score with a very high grade point average (i.e., due to a disability, standardized testing does not reflect a student's strengths).

Testing companies once commonly flagged scores when students took standardized examinations with accommodations. Because of confidentiality concerns, students took this issue to the courts (*Breimhorst v. ETS Litigation*, 2001). Court rulings eliminated the practice of identifying nonstandard admin-istration of such tests, so colleges could no longer assume that a test score would be flagged due to disability.

A college has an obligation to protect confidentiality throughout a stu-dent's college career. This begins with the application process and continues through notifying faculty of disability status only with the student's consent to protecting accommodation information in records and recommendations. For example, a faculty member cannot provide a reference letter for a graduat-ing senior that states, "This student performed well in my class as long as extra time was used on tests." This statement would reveal disability status to prospective employers. Efforts also must be taken to ensure that disability status is not revealed via e-mail, which is not secure. Students should be aware of this when they choose to discuss their disability with their service provider (DSS) by e-mail.

Another area of confidentiality that often surprises parents is the rules under the Family Educational Rights and Privacy Act (FERPA) of 1974 (PL 93-380). Sometimes referred to as the Buckley Amendment after its principal sponsor, Senator James Buckley, FERPA provides for certain personnel of a given institution to have access to the educational records of enrolled students. This law, which is enforced by the U.S. Department of Education, gives privacy protection to all student education records. FERPA gives parents the right to view their child's educational records, but these rights transfer to the student when he or she attends school beyond the secondary level. *Education records* are defined as materials that are directly related to a student and are maintained by an educational institution or by a party acting for the institution. Such records include grade reports, transcripts, and most disciplinary files. Education records cannot be released to third parties, including parents, without signed and dated written consent from the student, unless that record falls under one of the following specific exceptions (Friend et al., 2002):

1. FERPA permits but does not require disclosure of such records to parents of a dependent student as defined by Internal Revenue Code of 1986. The university should have a policy as to whether it will disclose records to parents.

2. FERPA permits notice to appropriate parties in connection with an emergency in which knowledge of the information is necessary to protect the health or safety of the student or others.

3. FERPA permits but does not require release of campus disciplinary proceedings regarding specified crimes of violence or nonforcible sex offenses.

4. FERPA permits but does not require disclosure to parents regarding the student's violation of federal, state or local law or of any rule or policy of the institution or regarding the student's possession of alcohol or a controlled substance if a) the institution determines that the student has committed a disciplinary violation with respect to that use or possession and b) the student is younger than 21 years of age at the time of the disclosure.

Note that FERPA does not protect attendance records or records of academic major and degrees received.

Medical records are not considered educational information and are specifically exempted from this policy. Because some disability-related information is clearly medical in nature and because the ADA protects individuals equally, regardless of disability type, it is an appropriate extension to consider all disability-related information as medical information and to hold it with the same degree of confidentiality. It should be noted that in addition to the ADA and FERPA, some state regulations regarding privacy of information or doctor–patient relationships may provide overlapping protection (Friend et al., 2002).

It is important to remember that information related to one's disability

1. Is confidential

2. May be shared only on a "need-to-know" basis

3. Must be kept in separate files (not regular student/personnel files)

4. Must be given voluntarily by the person with a disability

5. Cannot be shared via e-mail or in letters of reference or reference checks

> Julie makes it clear that information concerning her disability is confi-
> dential. She expects the DSS office, her professors, and other college
> staff to honor her right to privacy. Julie gets to choose with whom
> and when she discusses her disability.

CONCLUSION

Students need to understand that postsecondary education schools may offer
different accommodations than those provided in elementary and secondary
school under IDEA. The college DSS office must work with students to ensure
equal access; however, this in and of itself does not necessarily guarantee
academic success. Likewise, a student may not get his or her requested accommodations, but those received must be effective. Determining accommodations
is an interactive process that is based on documentation.

It is hoped that this chapter helps prospective students of higher education
to be better consumers and stronger self-advocates. The resources listed in
the chapter appendix may offer further assistance; however, there may still be
times when additional resources and support are needed. All students with
disabilities are strongly advised to work closely with their respective DSS
office. Students with disabilities may also need to stay in close contact with
their ADA coordinator.

REFERENCES

Americans with Disabilities Act (ADA) of 1990, PL 101-336, 42 U.S.C., §§ 12101 *et seq.*

Association on Higher Education and Disability. (1997). *Guidelines for documentation of a learning
disability in adolescents and adults.* Retrieved January 12, 2005, from http://www.ldonline.org/
ld_indepth/postsecondary/ahead_guidelines.html

Bartlett v. New York State Bd. of Law Examiners, 226 F.3d 69, 10 A.D. Cases 1687 (2nd Cir.
N.Y., August 30, 2000).

Breimhorst v. ETS Litigation (N.D. Cal, March 27, 2001).

Brinckerhoff, L.C., Shaw, S.F., & McGuire, J.M. (1993). *Promoting postsecondary education for
students with learning disabilities: A handbook for practitioners.* Austin, TX: PRO-ED.

Brown v. the Board of Education of Topeka, 347 U.S. 483 (1954).

Civil Rights Restoration Act of 1987, PL 100-259, 42 U.S.C.

Education for All Handicapped Children Act of 1975, PL 94-142, 20 U.S.C. §§ 1400 *et seq.*

Educational Testing Service. (1999). *Policy statement for documentation of attention-deficit/hyperac-
tivity disorder in adolescents and adults.* Retrieved November 11, 2004, from http://www.ets.org/
disability/adhdplcy.html

Educational Testing Service. (2001). *Guidelines for documentation of psychiatric disabilities in adolescents and adults.* Retrieved November 11, 2004, from http://www.ets.org/disability/
psyplcy.html

Elementary and Secondary Education Act (ESEA) of 1965, PL 80-10.

Family Educational Rights and Privacy Act (FERPA) of 1974, PL 93-380.

Friend, J.G., Judy, B., & Reilly, V.J. (2002). *The ADA coordinator's guide to campus compliance.*
Horsham, PA: LRP Publications.

Guckenberger v. Trustees of Boston University, 974 F. Supp. 106 (D. Mass. 1997), 13 NDLR 59.

Hill, W.A. (1992). Americans with Disabilities Act of 1990: Significant overlap with Section 504 for colleges and universities. *Journal of College and University Law 18*(3), 389–417.

Individuals with Disabilities Education Act (IDEA) Amendments of 1997, PL 105-17, 20 U.S.C. §§ 1400 *et seq.*

Individuals with Disabilities Education Act (IDEA) of 1990, PL 101-476, 20 U.S.C. §§ 1400 *et seq.*

Individuals with Disabilities Education Improvement Act of 2004, PL 108-446. 20 U.S.C. §§ 1400 *et seq.*

Internal Revenue Code of 1986, 26 U.S.C. § 24.

Jarrow, J.E. (1992). *Title by title: The ADA's impact on postsecondary education.* Waltham, MA: Association on Higher Education and Disability.

Letter to Arizona State University, No. 08012047 (OCR Region VIII 6/7/01); retrieved November 11, 2004, from http://www.nacua.org/documents/OCRComplaint_SignLanguage Interpreter.pdf

Letter to Cosumnes River College, No. 09-00-2054 (OCR Region IX 6/16/00).

Letter to National Holistic University, No. 09-03-2042 (103 LRP 47165) (OCR Region IX, 6/11/03).

Letter to University of California, Berkeley, No. 09-00-2097 (OCR Region IX, 4/23/02).

Mills v. the Board of Education of the District of Columbia, 348 F. Supp. 866 (D. DC 1972).

Nagler, M. (1993). A positive perspective: Introduction to the second edition. In M. Nagler (Ed.), *Perspectives on disability* (pp. x–xi). Palo Alto, CA: Health Markets Research.

Pennsylvania Association for Retarded Children (PARC) v. Commonwealth of Pennsylvania, 334 F. Supp. 1257 (E.D. PA 1971).

Percy, S.L. (1989). *Disability, civil rights and public policy: The politics of implementation.* Tuscaloosa, AL: The University of Alabama Press.

Professional Development Academy, U Success, Resources for University Success. (2001). *Virginia higher education guidelines for documentation of disability.* Retrieved January 11, 2005, from http://www.students.vcu.edu/pda/vahelpguidelines.html

Rehabilitation Act of 1973, PL 93-112, 29 U.S.C. § 794.

Rioux, M. (1993). Rights, justice, power: An agenda for change. In M. Nagler (Ed.), *Perspectives on disability* (pp. 515–523). Palo Alto, CA: Health Markets Research.

Rothstein, L. (1995). *Disability law: Cases, materials, problems.* Charlottesville, VA: Michie Butterworth.

Settlement Agreement between the United States of America and Duke University, Department of Justice Complaint Number 202-54-20 (Re: barrier removal, alterations and new construction, and modification of policies and practices to make classes and programs accessible) (2001).

Southeastern Community College v. Davis, 442 U.S. 397 (1979).

Worthen, B.R., & Sanders, J.R. (1987). *Educational evaluation: Alternative approaches and practical guidelines.* New York: Longman Publishers.

APPENDIX

Additional Resources

Access Abroad, at the University of Minnesota, offers resources on study abroad and exchange programs for students with disabilities. For more information, go to http://www.umabroad.umn.edu/access or call 612-624-6884.

The **Access Board** offers technical assistance on the ADA accessibility guidelines. For publications and questions, go to http://www.access-board.gov or call 800-872-2253 (voice) or 800-993-2822 (TTY).

The Disabilities Rights and Education and Defense Fund (DREDF) offers an **ADA Hotline** that is funded by the Department of Justice to provide technical assistance on the ADA. For more information, go to http://www.dredf.org or call 800-466-4232 (voice/TTY).

The **Americans with Disabilities Act Accessibilities Guidelines (ADAAG)** provide information on whether a building is in compliance with all federal, state, and local codes. Of particular note on ADAAG's web site, Section 4.3.11 addresses areas of rescue assistance and Section 4.28 addresses alarms. For more information, go to http://www.access-board.gov/adaag/html/adaag.htm.

The **Federal Communications Commission (FCC)** offers technical assistance on the ADA telephone relay service (TRS) requirements and FCC regulations. For TRS publications and questions, go to http://www.fcc.gov/cgb/dro/trs.html or call 888-225-5322 (voice) or 888-835-5322 (TTY).

Job Accommodation Network (JAN) is funded by the U.S. Department of Labor's Office of Disability Employment to provide suggestions on accommodating employees with disabilities. For more information, go to http://www.jan.wvu.edu; also, ADA publications can be obtained by calling 800-526-7234 (voice/TTY).

Mobility International offers resources on study abroad and exchange programs for students with disabilities. For more information, go to http://www.miusa.org or call 541-343-1284 (voice/TDD).

Office of Civil Rights (OCR) enforces Title II of the ADA. The OCR publication *Students with Disabilities Preparing for Postsecondary Education: Know*

Your Rights and Responsibilities can be viewed at http://www.ed.gov/about/
offices/list/ocr/transition.html?exp=0; for other information, go to http://
www.ed.gov/policy/rights/guid/ocr/disability.html or call 800-421-3481
(voice) or 877-521-2172 (TDD).

The **Postsecondary Education Programs Network (PEPNet)** offers technical assistance, information, and training to higher education institutions and
to students needing assistance with deaf or hard-of-hearing issues. For more
information, go to http://www.pepnet.org.

The **U.S. Department of Justice (DOJ)** offers technical assistance on the
ADA Standards for Accessible Design and other ADA provisions applying to
businesses, nonprofit service agencies, and state and local government programs; it also provides information on how to file ADA complaints. For more
information, go to http://www.usdoj.gov/crt/ada/adahom1.htm; also, the ADA
information line for publications, questions, and referrals can be reached at
800-514-0301 (voice) or 800-514-0383 (TDD).

The **U.S. Department of Transportation's Federal Transit Administration** offers an ADA assistance line for information and complaints: 888-446-
4511 (voice). For more information, go to http://www.fta.dot.gov/
transit_data_info/ada/ada_info/14524_ENG_HTML.htm.

The **U.S. Equal Employment Opportunity Commission (EEOC)** offers
technical assistance on the ADA provisions applying to employment. It also
provides information on how to file ADA complaints. For more information,
go to http://www.eeoc.gov or call 800-669-4000 (voice) or 800-669-6820
(TTY) for employment questions and 800-669-3362 (voice) or 800-669-3302
(TTY) for information on employment publications.

The **Web Accessibility Initiative (WAI)** provides guidelines for web content
accessibility. For more information, go to http://www.w3.org/WAI/Over
view.html.

CHAPTER 3

Self-Determination
and the Transition to
Postsecondary Education

Colleen A. Thoma and Michael L. Wehmeyer

As a high school senior, Greg, like most seniors, was busy preparing to attend college away from home. Greg's preparations were more extensive, however, because he uses computer-based technology to help him meet his academic and daily living needs. Greg has many technology-support needs due to his physical and learning disabilities; therefore, his preparations were not typical. In fact, it turned out that these needs presented major challenges to his professors and the university's support staff. Computer software programs did not perform as promised, dorm rooms were not wheelchair accessible (except for one room in an all-female dorm), and delays in providing accommodations caused much worry. While many on his high school transition planning team wondered if they would ever be able to facilitate a smooth transition to college, Greg learned a valuable lesson: "You have to be knowledgeable, and you have to be pushy, because you have to be able to articulate what your goals are and what you need to get there."

There is a large body of literature available related to best practices in facilitating the transition from secondary school to adult life for students with disabilities (e.g., Benz & Halpern, 1987; Halpern, 1994; Wehman, 2001; Will, 1984). Much of this literature emphasizes the importance of supporting students to be active participants in the process—that is, to be self-determined (e.g., VanReusen & Bos, 1994; Wehmeyer & Ward, 1995). However, the existing literature does not specifically address the need for students to be self-determined in the process of making the transition to postsecondary education, although there is a literature base addressing the need for students to be self-determined in the general transition planning process (e.g., Wehmeyer & Sands, 1998). As shown in the introductory case study, Greg learned quickly that he needed to be his own advocate and that the support provided to him by teachers and his parents would no longer be so readily available to him. In college, he was expected to know what he needed, to have appropriate documentation to demonstrate his need, and then to advocate for those supports with professionals.

Greg's elementary and secondary schools had the obligation to provide all support necessary for his education; after graduation, however, this was no longer guaranteed to him. The Individuals with Disabilities Education Improvement Act of 2004 (PL 108-446), as well as previous versions of IDEA, mandate that students with disabilities be provided a free and appropriate public education. This education must be based on an individual's strengths and needs as determined by an educational planning team. Central to this premise is a zero reject principle, which means that a public elementary or secondary school cannot decide that a student's support needs are too severe to provide him or her with an appropriate education. In addition, the educational planning team must consider whether an individual student needs assistive technology, and if so, the school must provide that technology.

That is not the expectation at the postsecondary education level, at which the Americans with Disabilities Act (ADA) of 1990 (PL 101-336) and/or Section 504 of the Rehabilitation Act of 1973 (PL 93-112) and Section 508 of its amendments (per the Workforce Investment Act of 1998 [PL 105-220]) apply. These laws do not guarantee that all of an individual's postsecondary educational needs will be met. These laws ensure equal access, and obtaining services becomes an eligibility issue. (See Chapter 2 for more details about the legal implications of providing supports at the postsecondary level for students with disabilities.) For this reason, more preparation needs to go into the transition planning process to ensure that necessary supports are in place—that the student understands his or her disability and what technology or other supports are necessary to help him or her succeed. In short, the student needs to become his or her means of primary support to the greatest extent possible.

Thus, the need to be self-determined becomes very important. This chapter examines the role of promoting self-determination to support the transition of youth with disabilities from secondary to postsecondary education. The chapter begins with an overview of self-determination and of research documenting the impact of self-determination in the lives of students with disabilities. This is followed by an overview of the literature pertaining to success in postsecondary education placements. The chapter then describes methods, materials, and strategies to promote self-determination and closes with an examination of the importance of pursuing such an agenda for successful postsecondary education outcomes.

WHAT IS SELF-DETERMINATION?

Self-determination became an important instructional focus in transition services because of efforts to improve transition-related outcomes for youth with disabilities and as part of IDEA transition mandates requiring student involvement in transition planning. In addition to requiring the delivery of transition-services for youth 16 and older, IDEA 1990 required that goals and objectives related to transition services be based on student needs, taking into account student interests and preferences (Wehmeyer, Agran, & Hughes, 1998). The U.S. Department of Education subsequently funded numerous projects to develop methods, materials, and strategies to promote self-determination (Sands & Wehmeyer, 1996; Ward & Kohler, 1996) and active student involvement in transition planning (Wehmeyer & Sands, 1998).

The historical roots of self-determination for people with disabilities can be found in the normalization, independent living, disability rights, and self-advocacy movements and in legislative protections ensuring equal opportunities for people with disabilities (Ward & Kohler, 1996). Wehmeyer and colleagues (Wehmeyer, 1998; 2001; Wehmeyer, Abery, Mithaug, & Stancliffe, 2003) have presented a functional model of self-determination in which *self-determined behavior* is defined as "acting as the primary causal agent in one's life and making choices and decisions regarding one's quality of life free from undue external influence or interference" (Wehmeyer, 1996, p. 24). Self-determined behavior refers to actions that are identified by four essential characteristics: 1) the person acts autonomously, 2) the behavior(s) are self-regulated, 3) the person initiates and responds to the event(s) in a psychologically empowered manner, and 4) the person acts in a self-realizing manner. These four essential characteristics describe the function of the behavior that establishes whether it is self-determined.

People who consistently engage in "self-determined behaviors" can be described as self-determined, whereas *self-determined* refers to a dispositional characteristic. Dispositional characteristics involve the organization of cognitive, psychological, and physiological elements in such a manner that an individual's behavior in different situations will be similar (although not identical). Eder (1990) described *dispositional states* as frequent, enduring tendencies that are used to characterize people and to describe important differences between people. As such, people can be described as self-determined based on the functional characteristics of their actions or behaviors.

The concept of causal agency is central to this theoretical perspective. Broadly defined, *causal agency* implies that it is the individual who makes or causes things to happen in his or her life. Wehmeyer framed causal agency, and self-determination, within the concept of quality of life. *Quality of life* is a complex construct that has gained increasing importance as a principle in human services. Schalock (1996) suggested that quality of life is best viewed as an organizing concept to guide policy and practice to improve the life conditions of all people and proposed that quality of life is composed of a number of core principles and dimensions. The core dimensions of quality of life include 1) emotional well-being, 2) interpersonal relations, 3) material well-being, 4) personal development, 5) physical well-being, 6) self-determination, 7) social inclusion, and 8) rights.

As discussed in greater detail subsequently, self-determination emerges across the life span as children and adolescents learn skills and develop attitudes that enable them to become causal agents in their own lives. These attitudes and abilities are the component elements of self-determination, and it is this level of the theoretical framework that drives instructional activities. The essential characteristics that define self-determined behavior emerge through the development and acquisition of these multiple, interrelated component elements. Table 3.1 lists these elements. Although not intended as an exhaustive taxonomy, these component elements are particularly important to the emergence of self-determined behavior. A functional model of self-determination is depicted graphically in Figure 3.1 (Wehmeyer, 1999b).

What Do College Students Say About the Importance of Self-Determination?

College students with disabilities were asked to identify which self-determination skills they believed were necessary to be successful in postsecondary education (Virginia Commonwealth University, Rehabilitation Research and Training Center [VCU-RRTC], 2004). Six areas, or skills, were identified by the students, who represented various disabilities, ethnic groups, and college institutions—both 2 and 4 year (VCU-RRTC, 2004). First, students believed that understanding one's disability was critical. Gaining information from doctors, family members, support groups, or others was essential. They also believed that acceptance of one's disability was a large part of understanding their disability.

A second area identified by the students involved understanding their strengths and limitations. The students believed that in most cases this understanding came from trial and error. It was important to try different supports or strategies in different situations to see what worked and what did not work. They believed that gaining information was important in this area as well. Part of learning about their own strengths and weaknesses involved gathering information from their college disability support services (DSS) offices, their

Table 3.1. Component elements of self-determined behavior

Choice-making skills

Decision-making skills

Problem-solving skills

Goal-setting and attainment skills

Self-observation, self-evaluation, and self-reinforcement skills

Self-instruction skills

Self-advocacy and leadership skills

Internal locus of control

Positive attributions of efficacy and outcome expectancy

Self-awareness

Self-knowledge

From Wehmeyer, M.L. (2001). Self-determination and transition. In P. Wehman *Life beyond the classroom: Transition strategies for young people with disabilities* (3rd ed., p. 40). Baltimore: Paul H. Brookes Publishing Co.; reprinted by permission.

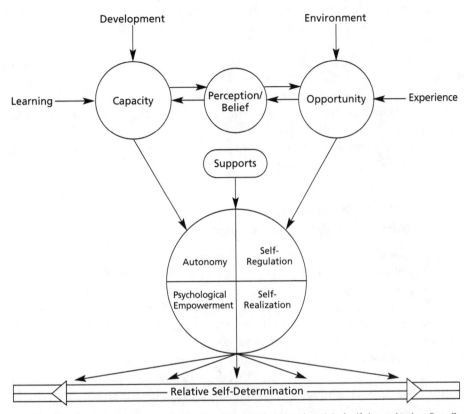

Figure 3.1. Functional model of self-determination. (From "A functional model of self-determination: Describing development and implementing instruction" by M.L. Wehmeyer, 1999b, *Focus on Autism and Other Developmental Disabilities, 14,* p. 40. Copyright © 1999 by PRO-ED, Inc. Reprinted with permission.)

parents, and other resources about strategies to compensate for their disabilities in educational settings.

A third area that the college students identified was learning to succeed despite the impact of their disabilities. Again, gathering information was an important element about which strategies or supports might be helpful. In tandem with this, students believed that understanding their learning styles and how to use accommodations effectively were critical components.

A fourth area involved setting goals and determining how others could contribute to helping set and achieve the students' goals. Students believed that family support and expectations, a desire to be independent, seeing others with disabilities succeed (i.e., having role models), and being involved in activities (e.g., classes, sports) were all essential in teaching them how to set and reach their goals.

The two final areas identified by these students were acquiring problem-solving skills and self-management skills. Students believed that acquiring problem-solving skills was in part learned through trial and error in daily living. They also included talking to others to learn how to develop and implement problem-solving skills and obtaining an understanding of their rights and responsibilities. Learning self-management skills to be aware of limitations, conducting self-evaluation of their performance in any activity, and scheduling and writing to-do lists were other ideas that students believed were important.

In addition, the college students were asked to identify self-determination skills that were essential for high school students to possess for college success. The college students believed that forming relationships with instructors, DSS staff members, friends, and mentors was important. They also identified knowledge of and willingness to use campus resources to assist them and possession of personal skills in addition to self-advocacy, including self-evaluation, perseverance, and coping skills.

Is Self-Determination Important to More Positive Adult Outcomes?

The proposition that self-determination is an important outcome if youth with disabilities are to achieve more positive adult outcomes, including access to postsecondary education, presumes that self-determination and positive adult outcomes are causally linked. The hypothesis that self-determination is important for more positive adult outcomes has support from the literature in two ways: first, by examining the contributions of component elements of self-determined behavior (e.g., choice making, problem solving, decision making, goal setting, self-regulation, self-advocacy) to more favorable school and adult outcomes, and second, by examining studies that tested this hypothesis directly.

A comprehensive review of how component elements of self-determined behavior affect adult outcomes is beyond the scope of this chapter. However, a brief overview still points to the abundant evidence that promoting the component elements listed in Table 3.1 can result in more positive adult outcomes. For example, studies show that improving performance in component elements in turn improves employment, community living, and community integration outcomes for individuals with cognitive disabilities. For example, increased opportunities and capacities to express preferences and make choices have been linked to increased participation of children, youth, and adults with and without disabilities in appropriate or adaptive tasks (Koestner, Ryan, Bernieri, & Holt, 1984; Realon, Favell, & Lowerre, 1990; Swann & Pittman, 1977) and more positive educational or achievement outcomes (Koenigs, Field, & deCharms, 1977). Teaching effective decision-making and problem-solving skills has been shown to improve the adaptability skills (Mithaug, Martin, & Agran, 1987), employment outcomes (Park & Gaylord-Ross, 1989), parenting skills (Tymchuk, Andron, & Rahbar, 1988), and community living outcomes (Foxx & Bittle, 1989) of people with disabilities.

Similarly, research links enhanced self-management and self-regulation skills to positive adult outcomes. Self-monitoring strategies are frequently

used to improve work-related activities, such as attention to task, task completion, and accuracy (Hughes, Korinek, & Gorman, 1991; McCarl, Svobodny, &
Beare, 1991). Lovett and Haring (1989) showed that self-recording activities
enabled adults with disabilities to improve task completion of daily living
activities. Self-instruction techniques have been used to successfully solve
work-related problems (Agran, Fodor-Davis, & Moore, 1986; Hughes & Petersen, 1989; Rusch, McKee, Chadsey-Rusch, & Renzaglia, 1988; Salend,
Ellis, & Reynolds, 1989), improve employment outcomes (Agran, Salzberg, &
Stowitschek, 1987; Lagomarcino & Rusch, 1989; Moore, Agran, & Fodor-
Davis, 1989), and teach social skills critical to independence (Agran et al.,
1987; Hughes & Agran, 1993).

Research on these component elements of self-determined behavior provides strong, though not direct, evidence that youth who are more self-determined achieve more positive adult outcomes. A few studies provide evidence
of the relationship between self-determination and more positive outcomes
for youths' transitions to adulthood. Wehmeyer and Schwartz (1997) measured
the self-determination of 80 students with learning disabilities or mental retardation and then examined adult outcomes 1 year after they left high school.
Students in the high self-determination group were more than twice as likely
(80% of sample) as youth in the low self-determination group to be employed
(40% of sample) and earned, on average, $2.00 per hour more than students
in the low self-determination group who were employed. There were no
significant differences between groups regarding level of intelligence or number of vocational courses.

Wehmeyer and Palmer (2003) conducted a second follow-up study, examining the adult status of 94 students with cognitive disabilities at 1 and 3
years after graduation. One year after high school, students in the high self-
determination group were disproportionately likely to have moved from where
they were living during high school; by the third year, they were still disproportionately likely to live somewhere other than their high school home and were
significantly more likely to live independently. For employed students, those
scoring higher in self-determination (as measured by The Arc's Self-Determination Scale: Adolescent Version [Wehmeyer & Kelchner, 1995]) made statistically significant advances in obtaining job benefits, including vacation, sick
leave, and health insurance—an outcome not shared by their peers in the low
self-determination group. Overall, there was not a single item on which the
low self-determination group fared more positively than the high self-determination group.

SELF-DETERMINATION AND EDUCATIONAL SUCCESS

Self-determination is a key component in promoting the movement from
secondary to postsecondary education, and there are specific component skills
of self-determined behavior that can and should support this transition

throughout its many stages. Although these stages can and do overlap, the chapter presents these stages as distinct steps to ease in the planning process. These stages include transition planning in middle school, transition planning in high school, considering assistive technology, working with the college DSS office, working with professors, organizing the college workload, and problem solving.

Of course, preparation for a transition to postsecondary education needs to begin long before any of these specific stages. Doll, Sands, Wehmeyer, and Palmer (1996) pointed out that students need to be taught skills leading to self-determination long before they begin the transition planning process as adolescents. Most important, they need opportunities to make choices and voice those choices, as well as to have varied experiences in their lives to help with the choice-making and decision-making processes. By the time they begin planning for their lives, they will have the skills and experiences necessary to begin making good decisions.

Transition Planning in Middle School

Transition planning generally begins in middle school (by age 14 or earlier if necessary). At the middle-school level, the focus is on choosing courses based on the student's long-term goals. When college or postsecondary education is the goal, selected courses should be those necessary for graduation and those that are directly related to a career goal. To make these decisions, students need to be able to voice their preferences and interests as well as understand the barriers that their disability may bring. When the barriers are identified, then necessary supports, accommodations, and/or technologies can be found.

The focus on core component skills must be addressed in middle school. Skills such as understanding one's disability and how it affects one's education, understanding how to set goals and measure one's progress on goal attainment, and having an internal locus of control are essential for college success and should begin developing early.

At this stage, Greg was encouraged by his parents to seek assistance from the local assistive technology project to find academic technologies that would help him do his work, as well as technologies that he could use at home to help him with some of his personal care needs. It was important that he tested them because it is impossible to know how a particular technology will work before it is used in appropriate real-life settings.

In addition, Greg knew that he did not perform well on standardized tests, so he began assembling a portfolio of his work to demonstrate his abilities to college admissions committees. His transition planning team suggested this approach, and Greg began the process of collecting this information in middle school. At that stage, it was important to collect various examples; at the time of the college application process, materials that best represent his work over time would be chosen.

Greg's family and educational planning team began focusing on core component skills during his middle school years. During individualized education program (IEP) meetings, Greg described his educational and transition goals. He learned about his disability through collaborative work developed by his teachers—through computer/Internet search skill development, through reading and writing skill development, and in public speaking opportunities. His teachers also helped Greg see that when he worked hard and planned his time through the use of personal planners, he was more successful academically.

Transition Planning in High School

During high school, most students who are planning to continue their education at postsecondary settings visit a variety of colleges and universities to help with making a decision about which one to attend. For students with disabilities, this is even more important. In addition to learning about academic programs and financial aid options, students with disabilities who are planning to attend college also must learn about the supports offered to the students with disabilities, including the college's ability to accommodate students who may have atypical support needs. Unlike elementary and secondary schools, postsecondary schools do not have to provide all options; rather, they assess which accommodations are effective based on the documentation provided. It is imperative that students understand this distinction and talk with staff from the DSS office to determine a good match between support needs and academic programs.

At this stage, it is also important to plan for other aspects of college life. Will the student live in a dorm or an apartment or commute from his or her family's home? If the student plans to live in a dorm or an apartment, it is important to understand his or her ability to care for daily living. Does he or she know how to do laundry? Can he or she cook simple meals? Can he or she wash dishes and/or clean the living area? Most important, can he or she accomplish personal care needs? If help is needed in any of these important areas, then this assistance must become part of the planning process. It is important to know which supports are available, to find funding for those necessary supports, and to identify backup plans. Table 3.2 outlines suggestions for students with disabilities who are preparing for their transition from high school to adult life, particularly to postsecondary education (Held, Thoma, Thomas, Beard, & Pipher, 2003).

Greg's physical disabilities required that he have access to a wheelchair-accessible dorm room and bathroom. Medical issues also required that he be near the accessible bathroom. Only the all-female dormitory had a dorm room and a bathroom that met these requirements. That was fine with Greg, but the college administration did not agree! In the end, the university changed the dorms so that what was previously the all-female dormitory became the all-male dormitory and vice versa,

Table 3.2.   Tips for students with disabilities who are planning for their future after high school

Learn	Increase your self-determination skills such as goal setting, problem solving, and decision making.
	Communicate your preferences and interests with others.
	Set goals, measure progress on goals, and determine when goals have been met.
	Assert your rights within the transition planning process, as well as regarding laws that affect employment, community living, and participation. Examples include the No Child Left Behind Act (PL 107-110), the Americans with Disabilities Act (ADA) of 1990 (PL 101-336), the Rehabilitation Act (PL 93-112), and the Individuals with Disabilities Education Act (IDEA) of 1990 (PL 101-476) and its 1997 amendments (PL 105-17).
	Use technology to meet your goals, as well as to communicate your progress on goals, your preferences and interests, and other important information.
	Discover and communicate your strengths, limitations, and preferred methods of assistance.
	Articulate which supports you need, and learn how to apply for or obtain them.
	Learn what to do when someone disagrees with you (e.g., regarding your goals for an adult life).
	Appreciate that you are the creator of your future.
Create a vision/plan	Communicate the life you want, including opportunities for employment, postsecondary education, recreation and leisure, and connections with others.
	Know what is important to you, and use that to make big decisions.
	Ask for the supports that you need to make your vision a reality.
	Talk with friends who have disabilities to get their opinions about the supports and services they receive.
	Use technology to demonstrate your abilities, preferred supports, and vision for the future.
Take risks	Do not settle for less than what you want, but understand that sometimes good things take longer and/or may be harder to obtain.
	Learn whom to trust, but look beyond paid support services to provide the supports you need.
	Communicate what you want, even if someone does not agree with or like your decisions.
	Meet new people and try new things to help with developing your vision for the future.
	Know that others have accomplished goals that some thought to be impossible or unrealistic. Not trying almost guarantees that your goals will not be met. Trying to achieve the goals might be the only way to tell whether they are possible.

From Held, M.F., Thoma, C.A., Thomas, K., Beard, C., & Pipher, L. (2003, May). *Self-determined transition planning: What happens after the meeting?* TASH teleconference presentation; adapted by permission.

thereby allowing Greg to live in the accessible room near the bathroom. A great deal of planning had to be done to find the right dorm situation for Greg, much more than the typical roommate-matching system that most colleges and universities use.

The College Application Process   An important skill to acquire in high school is learning to fill out college applications and understanding the questions contained in them, including requirements to write an essay and/or personal statement. This is something with which a guidance counselor, as a member of the transition planning team, can help, or it can be incorporated into a high school English class lesson on writing and grammar. Such an assignment would help not only students with disabilities but also students without disabilities who are planning to continue their education past high school.

> Greg's guidance counselor worked with him in the computer lab so that Greg could learn how to research on-line university admissions procedures and practice filling out applications. As a result, Greg also was able to narrow down his search and apply only to those colleges in which he was most interested.

Considering Assistive Technology

Significant advances in both assistive and instructional technology have promise to level the playing field in promoting access to information and learning for students with disabilities (Michaels, Pollack Prezant, Morabito, & Jackson, 2002). Yet, despite the mandate that assistive technology be considered for each student who receives special education under the 2004 reauthorization of IDEA, many students with disabilities are not provided the assistive or instructional technologies they need (Wehmeyer, 1998).

What does it mean to consider assistive technology? The educational planning team must be aware of available assistive technology options and determine, based on a student's needs and disabilities, whether available technology would be of benefit. It is only a first step in the entire assistive technology assessment and decision-making process, but it is critical. If team members are not aware of existing assistive technologies, then they often miss opportunities to find appropriate technologies that can make a student's transition planning goals a reality. This is particularly true when students with disabilities choose to pursue postsecondary education. A variety of computer-based technologies can provide access to education and can help students with completing assignments as required. Alternative keyboards, voice output devices, picture symbols, and word recognition software all can provide supports to students who struggle with writing, reading, and/or fine motor control.

In addition to assistive technology for academic work, assistive technology that provides support in other life areas should also be considered. Some students with disabilities may need assistive technology that helps them with activities of daily living such as eating, getting dressed, getting up in the morning, and/or communicating. These types of assistive technologies should also be considered in the context of transition planning.

It is important that students are actively involved in this process, being as self-determined as possible. Craddock and Scherer (2002) pointed out that special educators often feel alone in the process of matching students with disabilities and assistive technologies and recommended that special educators view themselves as partners with the student in this process. In fact, when students are not actively involved in the assessment and decision-making process, the device often is not used. Scherer (1998) proposed a model for choosing assistive technology that matches an individual's preferences, capabilities, and temperament. The Matching Person and Technology (MPT) model addresses the following components (Craddock & Scherer, 2002, p. 90):

1. Characteristics of the environment and psychosocial setting in which the [assistive technology] is used (milieu)

2. Pertinent features of the individual's personality and temperament (person)

3. Characteristics of the [assistive technology] itself (technology)

Greg was a key partner in choosing appropriate assistive technology that provided access to his educational opportunities in high school. He tried out new technologies that provided access to his computer, including screen readers and word recognition software. He learned to use infrared remote control devices to control his environment, both at home and in the classroom. He also let his team members know when something did not work as described. As a result of his membership on the team, the best assistive technology choices were made for him; these options were communicated with the college DSS staff and with Greg's vocational rehabilitation (VR) counselor. The VR counselor was a key part of this process because funds from the VR office could be used to purchase devices necessary for work/career purposes.

Working with the College Disability Support Services Office

One of the most important resources for students with disabilities is the college or university office that provides and coordinates access to services. Making a successful, smooth transition to postsecondary education is difficult for many students with disabilities because the services and supports offered by this office can vary dramatically from campus to campus. Students and their transition team members need to research the typical services available through this office for each postsecondary setting being considered to be sure that the supports that an individual student needs will actually be available. Unlike a student's elementary and secondary school experiences, not every accommodation and/or support requested will be met. Students with more significant disabilities who use specialized assistive technology will need to be even more conscientious in their review of the supports offered by DSS offices on various campuses.

Many offices for students with disabilities provide on-line descriptions of the services available, making this transition planning process easier. However, it is best to directly contact the offices in person as well because not all postsecondary educational institutions update their web sites on a regular basis.

It is important to discuss documentation of one's disability, as this is a growing concern in the transition from high school to postsecondary educational settings. In public schools, students have an initial evaluation to determine whether they qualify as having a disability and need supports to benefit from their education. Under IDEA, students then are reevaluated every 3 years, unless the team determines that this reevaluation is not necessary. Increasing numbers of high schools are waiving that reevaluation when a student is in high school, believing that if students have qualified for services for many years, a reevaluation at that point would not provide any additional, relevant information. However, if a student is going on to a postsecondary educational setting, this reevaluation is crucial to qualify for services there. Universities and colleges do not accept an IEP document as sufficient documentation of proof that a student has a disability. In addition, they will not accept a reevaluation or initial evaluation report that is more than 3–5 years old. Many students therefore have to arrange and pay for their own evaluations to prove that they qualify to receive supports through a university's DSS office, even if they received special education services for their entire K–12 public school experience.

For Greg, the process of securing services necessitated a great deal of group problem solving. Greg narrowed his choice of universities down to three that were less than a 2-hour drive from home—close enough to go home when needed, but far enough away to feel that he was going away to college. Only two of those universities offered his desired course of study (business management combined with technology). One of those universities had a large student body, and Greg was concerned that he would not receive the individual attention and supports he needed. The other university offered more supports but did not have many of the software programs he needed to use his computer. The transition planning team devised a plan to obtain the needed software, including having VR pay for some of the extra software he needed for a laptop computer that he would use to take notes in class as well as to complete his assignments. In addition, the team worked with his medical insurance to pay for some of the equipment that he would need in his dorm room to take care of his personal care needs (i.e., medically necessary equipment). A local assistive technology community program arranged for a long-term loan of another software program that would allow Greg to use his voice to input information for the computer. His team creatively filled his needs for supports by investigating all options available.

Working with Professors

Students with disabilities often feel uncomfortable disclosing their disabilities especially when they first arrive at college. They are happy to break free of the label from their public school experience, but many more students with disabilities find that it is crucial to self-disclose rather than keep that information private. This is particularly the case in working with professors. It is better to report this information in the beginning than to wait until mid-semester or later, when it is apparent to all that the student is slipping behind.

Disclosing this information to professors must be accomplished in an organized way. Students must determine the proper sequence from the DSS at their college or university. Typically, students must first register with that office, provide the proper documentation about the disability, and then contact their professors. This can take a few weeks to a month to finalize, especially if the necessary documentation is not available (see the preceding discussion for detailed information).

Once students have registered with the proper office on campus and have received a letter of accommodation from this office, it is best for students to contact their professors as soon as possible. This is a time when many of those component skills of self-determination are going to be important. Students should be ready to discuss what supports are being provided by the university and how these supports can be implemented. Students can decide whether to disclose to professors their specific disability. More professors are offering instruction using the principles of universal design for learning, which provides access to instruction for students with diverse learning needs, so students should ask which methods the professor already uses that support their instruction. For instance, many professors use web-based programs such as WebCT and/or Blackboard, which provide a resource for discussions and a place for posting lecture notes, assignments, and calendars to help keep students organized as they go through the semester. Students should become familiar with these programs and how they meet their own learning support needs.

Greg made sure that he registered with the college DSS office. He had the appropriate documentation, and a letter of accommodation was developed. He scheduled his meetings with his professors by talking with them after class to discuss his accommodation needs. Greg had never been exposed to Blackboard, the computer instructional program used at his university. When he spoke with the one professor that used it, Greg and the professor agreed that Greg would try it out for a week and then reschedule a meeting to discuss whether it met his needs or whether he needed additional supports. He found that his voice output computer programs did not interface with the Blackboard system, so he worked with the staff of the DSS office to find a compatible program. They could not find one, so they made arrangements for a staff person in their office to print the information from the Blackboard site (in large print) and for Greg to use his word processing program to type his replies to discussion board questions. The staff person then uploaded the replies for Greg. Greg then rescheduled his meeting with the professor and explained the problem. He asked to be e-mailed if a change was made on the Blackboard site less than a week before class; that way, he could gain access to the information before class. The professor agreed.

Organizing the College Workload

Most college and university students find it difficult to organize their workload; it is a big difference from high school, compounded by the fact that it is often the first time students are living away from home. Unlike high school, where there is nightly homework, college students are more likely to have semester-long projects or research papers and often have only one or two tests to be sure they are mastering the content knowledge.

The self-determination skills that help the most with organizing oneself and the college workload are those of goal setting and attainment, self-management, internal locus of control, and positive attributions of efficacy and outcome expectancy. Students need to have skills in setting their own goals and in working to attain them, managing their time and rewarding themselves for their efforts. Students also need to understand that what they do affects their world. If they do well on a test, it is because of their hard work and/or prior knowledge (internal locus of control), not because of fate or chance. In addition, students need to increase some academic skills so they will believe that they have the ability to learn the material presented in college courses (positive attributions of efficacy) and that if they use those skills, they will do well (positive attributions of outcome expectancy).

Students who are included in high school academic classes are more likely to have the academic skills necessary to attain positive attributions of efficacy and outcome expectancy when they make the transition to postsecondary educational settings. Research has demonstrated that students with disabilities who have been included in general education academic classes while in high school and those who have self-determination skills are more likely to be successful in college (Durlak, Rose, & Bursuck, 1994). Although researchers have made neither a connection between postsecondary success and specific self-determination component skills nor a specific connection between the high school educational setting and acquiring specific core component skills, the chapter authors believe that a focus on acquiring specific self-determination skills leads to postsecondary success.

Colleges and universities frequently offer time management and work organization skills workshops to students in general (see also Chapter 4). Students with disabilities should make every effort to attend such workshops and to incorporate such strategies into their daily routines. Goal-setting skills can be learned in high school and at home prior to the transition to postsecondary education, and active participation in transition IEP meetings can help refine a student's goal-setting and attainment skills. Even with adequate preparation in high school, students with disabilities may need additional support to apply those skills in the new setting of postsecondary education.

Greg led his high school transition IEP meetings and prepared for them by participating in reviews of his progress on current goals, determining what worked and what did not work, and then modifying his goals for the coming year. He presented this information to his team and asked for their input as well as the information they collected since the last meeting. Once Greg got to college, however, it was a different story. Without the structure of the formal yearly meetings, with their long- and short-term goals, it was easy for time to slip by without Greg's completing all of his work. When two of his professors spoke with him about missing assignments, Greg realized that it was time to do something about this situation. He spoke with the DSS staff but found that their office did not offer time management work-shops. Greg then learned that the university counseling center was holding a time management training class that was open to all students, so he registered for it. The Office for Academic Technology was offering training on the use of personal digital assistants (PDAs) for time management, so Greg enrolled in that workshop as well. He found that the PDA with a magnifier was exactly what he needed to organize his time and assignments, and he worked with his VR counselor to purchase one. Greg's comfort with using technology made this a successful method for managing his time and recording his progress on attaining his goals.

Problem Solving

Life at college or a university is like life in general: There is no assurance that things will run smoothly, no matter how thorough one's plans might be. That is why it is important to be able to handle problems and learn from them to make better plans or set new goals. Problem solving is a way to approach those unforeseen bumps in the road, and it is another core component skill of self-determination. A *problem* can be defined as "a specific situation or set of situations to which a person must respond in order to function effectively in his environment" (D'Zurilla & Goldfried, 1971, p. 108).

Problem solving is usually divided into two different types: impersonal problem solving and interpersonal problem solving. Postsecondary students must be ready to handle both types of problems well. Most research on problem solving focuses on impersonal problem solving or dealing with solving puzzles, math problems, or anagrams. Interpersonal problem solving focuses on the interactions among people, which is typically more complex and requires multiple processing demands (Wehmeyer & Kelchner, 1994).

The lack of emphasis on interpersonal problem solving is perplexing, because what college or university student does not run into these complex interpersonal problems? In addition to learning academic skills, college and university life also teaches students about life. They need to learn to work together in groups; live together in dorms; and socialize in student commons, campus events, and organizations. The problem-solving process can help them adjust to new situations and/or new issues as they occur.

Greg noticed one day that his roommate was not happy. He was slamming drawers and banging into his desk, and he finally stormed out of the room without saying anything to Greg. Later, when the roommate returned, Greg asked him what was wrong. "Nothing," was his response, but he still did not talk with Greg and spent most of his time in another friend's room down the hall. When Greg told his counselor about this situation, he confided that he did not know what to do when someone does not talk to him about a problem. They discussed various possibilities: let it go, confront him again, talk with others who might know what is going on, and keep asking questions until he talks. Greg left the office determined to solve the problem. When Greg returned to the room, his roommate was there. Greg asked him if they could talk, and then quickly began to explain how the roommate's behavior made him feel, especially because he was sure that he had offended the roommate without realizing it and could not find a way to change what was so offensive. The roommate seemed surprised at that revelation and some of the anger seemed to disappear. The roommate confided that a problem at home had him upset and he did not know how to deal with it, so he was miserable with everyone. He apologized for taking it out on Greg and resolved that he would deal with his problem at home in a manner similar to how Greg handled this situation.

CONCLUSION

There are obviously many issues to examine when a student with a disability decides to make the transition from high school to a postsecondary educational setting. The benefits of organizing this transition are well documented: Students who attend colleges, even if they do not earn a degree, are more likely to find work they enjoy and earn better wages and benefits than those who have no postsecondary educational experience (Gajar, Goodman, & McAfee, 1995). In addition, students with disabilities who score higher on measures of self-determination have also been shown to be more successful in employment, community living, finances, and postsecondary education. This important component of planning a successful transition to postsecondary education cannot be ignored.

REFERENCES

Agran, M., Fodor-Davis, J., & Moore, S. (1986). The effects of self-instructional training on job-task sequencing: Suggesting a problem-solving strategy. *Education and Training of the Mentally Retarded, 21,* 273–281.

Agran, M., Salzberg, C.L., & Stowitschek, J.J. (1987). An analysis of the effects of a social skills training program using self-instructions on the acquisition and generalization of two social behaviors in a work setting. *Journal of the Association for Persons with Severe Handicaps, 12,* 131–139.

Americans with Disabilities Act (ADA) of 1990, PL 101-336, 42 U.S.C. §§ 12101 *et seq.*

Benz, M.R., & Halpern, A.S. (1987). Transition services for secondary students with mild disabilities: A statewide perspective. *Exceptional Children, 53,* 507–514.

Craddock, G., & Scherer, M.J. (2002). Assessing individual needs for assistive technology. In C.L. Sax & C.A. Thoma, *Transition assessment: Wise practices for quality lives* (pp. 87–101). Baltimore: Paul H. Brookes Publishing Co.

Doll, B., Sands, D.J., Wehmeyer, M.L., & Palmer, S. (1996). Prompting the development and acquisition of self-determined behavior. In D.J. Sands & M.L. Wehmeyer (Eds.), *Self-determination across the life span: Independence and choice for people with disabilites* (pp. 65–90). Baltimore: Paul H. Brookes Publishing Co.

Durlack, C.M., Rose, E., & Bursuck, W.D. (1994). Preparing high school students with learning disabilities for the transition to postsecondary education: Teaching the skills of self-determination. *Journal of Learning Disabilities, 27*(1), 51–59.

D'Zurilla, T.J., & Goldfried, M.R. (1971). Problem-solving and behavior modification. *Journal of Abnormal Psychology, 78,* 107–126.

Eder, R. (1990). Uncovering young children's psychological selves: Individual and developmental differences. *Child Development, 61,* 849–863.

Foxx, R.M., & Bittle, R.G. (1989). *Thinking it through: Teaching a problem-solving strategy for community living.* Champaign, IL: Research Press.

Gajar, A., Goodman, L., & McAfee, J. (1995). *Secondary schools and beyond: Transition of individuals with mild disabilities.* New York: Macmillan/McGraw-Hill.

Halpern, A.S. (1994). Transition: A look at the foundations. *Exceptional Children, 51,* 479–486.

Held, M.F., Thoma, C.A., Thomas, K., Beard, C., & Pipher, L. (2003, May). *Self-determined transition planning: What happens after the meeting?* TASH teleconference presentation.

Hughes, C., & Agran, M. (1993). Teaching persons with severe disabilities to use self instruction in community settings: An analysis of applications. *Journal of the Association for Persons with Severe Handicaps, 18,* 261–274.

Hughes, C.A., Korinek, L., & Gorman, J. (1991). Self-management for students with mental retardation in public school settings: A research review. *Education and Training in Mental Retardation, 26,* 271–291.

Hughes, C.A., & Petersen, D.L. (1989). Utilizing a self-instructional training package to increase on-task behavior and work performance. *Education and Training in Mental Retardation, 24,* 114–120.

Individuals with Disabilities Education Act (IDEA) Amendments of 1997, PL 105-17, 20 U.S.C. §§ 1400 *et seq.*

Individuals with Disabilities Education Act (IDEA) of 1990, PL 101-476, 20 U.S.C. §§ 1400 *et seq.*

Individuals with Disabilities Educaiton Improvement Act of 2004, PL 108-446, 20 U.S.C. §§ 1400 *et seq.*

Kaye, H. (1998). *The status of people with disabilities in the U.S.* Volcano, CA: Volcano Press.

Koenigs, S., Field, M., & deCharms, R. (1977). Teacher beliefs, classroom interaction and personal control. *The Journal of Applied Social Psychology, 7,* 95–114.

Koestner, R., Ryan, R.M., Bernieri, F., & Holt, K. (1984). The effects of controlling versus informational limit-setting styles on children's intrinsic motivation and creativity. *Journal of Personality, 52,* 233–248.

Lagomarcino, T.R., & Rusch, F.R. (1989). Utilizing self-management procedures to teach independent performance. *Education and Training in Mental Retardation, 24,* 297–305.

Lovett, D.L., & Haring, K.A. (1989). The effects of self-management training on the daily living of adults with mental retardation. *Education and Training in Mental Retardation, 24,* 306–307.

McCarl, J.J., Svobodny, L., & Beare, P.L. (1991). Self-recording in a classroom for students with mild to moderate mental handicaps: Effects on productivity and on-task behavior. *Education and Training in Mental Retardation, 26,* 79–88.

Michaels, C.A., Pollack Prezant, F., Morabito, S.M., & Jackson, K. (2002). Assistive and instructional technology for college students with disabilities: A national snapshot of postsecondary service providers. *Journal of Special Education Technology, 17*(1), 5–14.

Mithaug, D.E., Martin, J.E., & Agran, M. (1987). Adaptability instruction: The goal of transitional programs. *Exceptional Children, 57,* 6–14.

Moore, S.C., Agran, M., & Fodor-Davis, J. (1989). Using self-management strategies to increase the production rates of workers with severe handicaps. *Education and Training in Mental Retardation, 24,* 324–332.

No Child Left Behind Act of 2001, PL 107-110, 20 U.S.C. 6301 *et seq.*

Park, H.S., & Gaylord-Ross, R. (1989). A problem-solving approach to social skills training in employment settings with mentally retarded youth. *Journal of Applied Behavior Analysis, 22,* 373–380.

Realon, R.E., Favell, J.E., & Lowerre, A. (1990). The effects of making choices on engagement levels with persons who are profoundly mentally handicapped. *Education and Training in Mental Retardation, 25,* 248–254.

Rehabilitation Act of 1973, PL 93-112, 29 U.S.C. §§ 723(a), 721(a)(9), 793, 794, 795(a), 795(g) *et seq.*

Rusch, F.R., McKee, M., Chadsey-Rusch, J., & Renzaglia, A. (1988). Teaching a student with severe handicaps to self-instruct: A brief report. *Education and Training in Mental Retardation, 23,* 51–58.

Salend, S.J., Ellis, L.L., & Reynolds, C.J. (1989). Using self-instruction to teach vocational skills to individuals who are severely retarded. *Education and Training in Mental Retardation, 24,* 248–254.

Sands, D.J., & Wehmeyer, M.L. (Eds.). (1996). *Self-determination across the life span: Independence and choice for people with disabilities.* Baltimore: Paul H. Brookes Publishing Co.

Schalock, R.L. (1996). Reconsidering the conceptualization and measurement of quality of life. In R. Schalock (Ed.), *Quality of life: Conceptualization and measurement: Vol. 1* (pp. 123–139). Washington, DC: American Association on Mental Retardation.

Scherer, M.J. (1998). *Matching Person and Technology (MPT) model manual* (3rd ed.). Webster, NY: Institute for Matching Person and Technology.

Swann, W.B., & Pittman, T.S. (1977). Initiating play activity of children: The moderating influence of verbal cues on intrinsic motivation. *Child Development, 48,* 1128–1132.

Tymchuk, A.J., Andron, L., & Rahbar, B. (1988). Effective decision-making/problem-solving training with mothers who have mental retardation. *American Journal on Mental Retardation, 92,* 510–516.

VanReusen, A.K., & Bos, C.S. (1994). Facilitating student participation in individualized education programs through motivation strategy instruction. *Exceptional Children, 60,* 466–475.

Virginia Commonwealth University, Rehabilitation Research and Training Center. (2004). *Summary of focus group trends concerning self-determination skills of college students with disabilities.* Richmond, VA: Author.

Ward, M.J., & Kohler, P.D. (1996). Teaching self-determination: Content and process. In L.E. Powers, G.H.S. Singer, & J. Sowers (Eds.), *On the road to autonomy: Promoting self-competence in children and youth with disabilities* (pp. 275–290). Baltimore: Paul H. Brookes Publishing Co.

Wehman, P. (2001). *Life beyond the classroom: Transition strategies for young people with disabilities* (3rd ed.). Baltimore: Paul H. Brookes Publishing Co.

Wehmeyer, M.L. (1996). Self-determination as an educational outcome: Why is it important to children, youth, and adults with disabilities? In D.J. Sands & M.L. Wehmeyer (Eds.), *Self-determination across the life span: Independence and choice for people with disabilities* (pp. 17–36). Baltimore: Paul H. Brookes Publishing Co.

Wehmeyer, M.L. (1998). Self-determination and individuals with significant disabilities: Examining meanings and misinterpretations. *Journal of the Association for Persons with Severe Handicaps, 23,* 5–16.

Wehmeyer, M.L. (1999a). Assistive technology and students with mental retardation: Utilization and barriers. *Journal of Special Education Technology, 14,* 50–60.

Wehmeyer, M.L. (1999b). A functional model of self-determination: Describing development and implementing instruction. *Focus on Autism and Other Developmental Disabilities, 14,* 53–61.

Wehmeyer, M.L. (2001). Self-determination and mental retardation: Assembling the puzzle pieces. In H. Switzky (Ed.), *Personality and motivational differences in persons with mental retardation* (pp. 147–198). Mahwah, NJ: Lawrence Erlbaum Associates.

Wehmeyer, M.L., Abery, B., Mithaug, D.E., & Stancliffe, R.J. (2003). *Theory in self-determination: Foundations for educational practice.* Springfield, IL: Charles C Thomas Publisher.

Wehmeyer, M.L., Agran, M., & Hughes, C. (1998). *Teaching self-determination to students with disabilities: Basic skills for successful transition.* Baltimore: Paul H. Brookes Publishing Co.

Wehmeyer, M.L., & Kelchner, K. (1994). Interpersonal cognitive problem-solving skills of individuals with mental retardation. *Education and Training in Mental Retardation, 29,* 265–278.

Wehmeyer, M.L., & Kelchner, K. (1995). *The Arc's Self-Determination Scale: Adolescent Version.* Arlington, TX: The Arc.

Wehmeyer, M.L., & Lawrence, M. (1995). Whose future is it anyway? Promoting student involvement in transition planning. *Career Development for Exceptional Individuals, 18,* 69–84.

Wehmeyer, M.L., & Palmer, S.B. (2003). Adult outcomes for students with cognitive disabilities three years after high school: The impact of self-determination. *Education and Training in Developmental Disabilities, 38,* 131–144.

Wehmeyer, M.L., & Sands, D.J. (Eds.). (1998). *Making it happen: Student involvement in education planning, decision making, and instruction.* Baltimore: Paul H. Brookes Publishing Co.

Wehmeyer, M.L., & Schwartz, M. (1997). Self-determination and positive adult outcomes: A follow-up study of youth with mental retardation or learning disabilities. *Exceptional Children, 63,* 245–255.

Wehmeyer, M.L., & Ward, M.J. (1995). The spirit of the IDEA mandate: Student involvement in transition planning. *Journal of the Association for Vocational Special Needs Education, 17,* 108–111.

Will, M. (1984). *OSERS programming for the transition of youth with disabilities: Bridges from school to working life.* Washington, DC: Office of Special Education and Rehabilitation Services.

Workforce Investment Act of 1998, PL 105-220.

CHAPTER 4

Preparing for College

Elizabeth Evans Getzel

Obtaining an advanced degree or training beyond high school is essential for individuals to be competitive in today's labor market. Whether it is college, adult and continuing education, or technical preparation, postsecondary education plays a major role in preparing people for employment and career opportunities (Gajar, Goodman, & McAfee, 1995; Getzel, Briel, & Kregel, 2000; Getzel, Stodden, & Briel, 2001). Students who continue their education after high school are more prepared to meet the challenges of a changing marketplace. Increasing numbers of students with disabilities are entering postsecondary education to obtain further skills and knowledge because of a combination of legislative, academic, and social changes (Gilson, 1996). Higher education programs, in particular 2-year colleges, increased as potential transition goals from 1987 to 2001 (Wagner, Cameto, & Newman, 2003). This goal was identified for students across disability categories regardless of gender, race, or income level (Wagner et al., 2003).

Research demonstrates that people with disabilities believe that postsecondary education is a means to enhance their chances of 1) obtaining and maintaining employment, 2) earning a higher annual income, and 3) creating a pathway to lifelong independence and a greater quality of life (Fairweather & Shaver, 1991; Wilson, Getzel, & Brown, 2000). Stodden (1998) found that employment rates for individuals with disabilities show a stronger positive correlation between level of education and rate of employment than is seen in statistical trends for the general population. Therefore, access to postsecondary programs is critical for students with disabilities.

Sarah has been working a long time for this moment! She is in her junior year of high school and moving closer to her goal of graduating and entering college. She has been working closely with her individualized education program (IEP) team on her goals, and has met several times with her guidance counselor. Sarah knows that she must now be thinking more specifically about a career and which college she wants to attend. Her parents want her to go to a school close by, but she does not want to limit her options.

PREPARING FOR COLLEGE

I must learn how to be on my own and make my own decisions. (Old Dominion University [ODU], 2000)

Students with disabilities share many of the same decisions and preparations for college as all students who are considering higher education. Every student needs to consider the size and location of the college, the programs and majors available, extracurricular offerings, the diversity of students, and the availability of scholarships or financial aid. However, students with disabilities must consider other specific areas when determining an appropriate college or university program. Some of these include the availability of support services, campus accessibility, and documentation requirements to obtain services.

The information included in this chapter is based on the available litera-ture on preparing students with disabilities for college and on experiences working with students with disabilities at a 4-year university (Getzel, McMa-nus, & Briel, 2004). Most of the information presented is directed toward students with disabilities who are entering college from secondary education. However, some areas concerning availability of services and supports, docu-mentation requirements, or academic requirements are issues that students with disabilities must understand when matriculating from a 2-year college to a 4-year university or when transferring from one 4-year college to another.

A number of students with disabilities entering college are unprepared for the demands of postsecondary education. From the chapter author's experi-ence at Virginia Commonwealth University and from supporting documenta-tion in the literature (Brinckerhoff, McGuire, & Shaw, 2002; deFur, Getzel, & Trossi, 1996; Getzel et al., 2001; Lock & Layton, 2001), it is apparent that many students do not fully understand their roles and responsibilities concerning accommodations. They do not realize the impact of their disability on learning and have difficulty describing their needs with instructional faculty and staff. They are unaware of the variety of supports and services offered to all students and lack the skills to advocate for services and to manage other aspects of their academic careers—including study skills, time management, and technol-ogy—that can assist in learning.

Preparation for postsecondary education includes learning the skills nec-essary to deal with both the academic and social challenges presented by college. Educators, families, and students may assume that if a student with a disability is academically capable of participating in postsecondary education, then further preparation for college is not needed (deFur et al., 1996; Getzel et al., 2000; Getzel et al., 2004). Unfortunately, without effective planning and preparation, students with disabilities can feel overwhelmed and unable to adapt to a postsecondary environment. Therefore, the transition to college must begin early in their education experience. Activities in middle school could include taking demanding courses in English, math, science, history, or foreign language; learning about high school programs that will help a student pursue academic and career interests; and working on developing strong study skills and learning strategies (Virginia Department of Education, 2003). Several resources describe in detail ideas and strategies that students can implement while in high school to prepare for college. Table 4.1 provides a sample of these strategies; the appendix at the end of the chapter provides more in-depth information.

UNDERSTANDING THE DEMANDS OF COLLEGE

> There is no mother, father, sister, or brother to get mad at when things go wrong. (ODU, 2000)

As previously indicated, secondary students with disabilities seeking a college education (whether in a 2- or 4-year setting) become fully responsible for managing their college career once they are accepted into a program. In postsecondary environments there are 1) fewer contacts with instructors, 2) expectations of higher levels of academic capability, 3) fewer tests covering a larger amount of material, 4) changes in the support systems that students previously had in high school, 5) higher expectations to achieve independently, and 6) changes in social and independent living demands (Brinckerhoff et al., 2002; deFur et al., 1996; Getzel et al., 2000). The reality of this level of responsibility is often not fully realized until the student is in college. However, the more informed a student is about the demands of college, the smoother the transition will be from secondary to postsecondary education.

Academic Preparation

Students with disabilities must be able to demonstrate that they have met the academic requirements to enter a college or university. It is important that students are enrolled in college preparatory classes during high school to build a foundation of knowledge not only to enter college but also to have the academic preparedness to remain in college (Brinckerhoff et al., 2002; Eaton & Coull, 1999; Harris & Robertson, 2001). IEP team members, especially teachers and guidance counselors, should ensure that students are taking the coursework necessary to compete in the college application process. Students with disabilities must be familiar with the math, science, and language requirements for colleges, especially for the higher education programs that they are interested in attending.

One academic area that might need to be thoroughly explored by students and family members is the foreign language requirement for entry into and graduation from a higher education institution. Colleges vary widely on foreign language requirements. The requirements depend on the school's "mission

Table 4.1. Suggested activities to help high school students with disabilities prepare for college

Year	Activities
Freshman year	Understand your disability and how to explain your learning needs to other individuals.
	Actively participate in the development of your individualized education program (IEP).
	Meet with your guidance counselor to review your schedule and ensure that you are taking the correct college prep courses.
	Understand which accommodations you need to enhance your learning.
	Be involved in school and community activities.
Sophomore year	Continue to be an active member of your IEP team meetings.
	Determine if there are community agencies (e.g., rehabilitative services) that need to be contacted about attending an IEP meeting.
	Visit your school's career center or guidance counselor to discuss college requirements.
	Identify your career interests, and begin looking into possible occupational areas.
	Work on any basic skills that need remediation.
	Be involved in school and community activities.
	Take the Preliminary Scholastic Aptitude Test (PSAT) and consider what accommodations you might need for this test.
Junior year	Identify a possible career goal, and begin looking at colleges that meet your interests and abilities.
	Continue focusing on time management, stress management, and study skills.
	Keep working with your IEP team as you move closer to your transition goal of attending college.
	Identify the academic adjustments that you have found most helpful.
	Make sure to consider your technology needs.
	Take the Scholastic Aptitude Test (SAT) or ACT admissions exams. Think about taking them more than one time.
	Visit college campuses and discuss which services and supports are available through the disability support services office.
	Determine the documentation requirements for the colleges to which you are interested in applying. Make sure your documentation is current.
	Learn about financial aid opportunities and available scholarships.
	Continue contact with community agencies for possible support.
Senior year	Determine the application deadlines for the colleges in which you are interested.
	Work on obtaining letters of recommendation.
	Develop your personal essay. Have a number of individuals review the essay—for example, your English teacher and guidance counselor.
	Complete the college applications, making sure that all directions have been carefully followed. Ask someone to proof your application to make sure you have not missed anything.
	Work with your IEP team and community agencies (if appropriate) to determine your support needs.
	Once accepted, consider attending a preadmission summer program (if the college offers one) to help with your transition into college.

From Virginia Department of Education. (2003). *Virginia's college guide for students with disabilities: You know you can do it! Here's how!* (pp. 14–19). Richmond: Virginia Department of Education, Division of Special Education and Student Services; adapted by permission.

and academic competitiveness" (Madaus, 2003, p. 63). Some students with disabilities chose to waive a foreign language requirement during high school to help maintain a higher grade point average. This may limit the number of colleges that they are eligible to attend (Madaus, 2003). Decisions on secondary foreign language coursework must be carefully weighed with the student's potential career goals and what type of postsecondary education program would best meet these goals. Specific questions should be asked of college admission offices about their foreign language requirements (Madaus, 2003, p. 63):

1. Is high school foreign language required for admissions? How many years or units are required?

2. If a certain number of secondary units are required, does the university have a policy on waiving these requirements for students with disabilities, in particular students with learning disabilities?

3. If a foreign language is not a requirement for admissions, does the college "prefer" that a language be taken in high school?

Students with disabilities may be accepted to a specific college without taking many foreign language courses but face difficulties meeting the college's language requirement for graduation. Prior to selecting a college, students need to be aware of policies that the college or university has concerning course substitutions. It cannot be assumed that because course substitutions for a foreign language were provided at the secondary level or even at another postsecondary program that all colleges or universities follow this same policy (Madaus, 2003). Foreign language requirements for college or university graduation differ among the programs of studies offered. Careful consideration must be made as to the policies and procedures for course substitutions at a particular college and the requirements for specific degree programs within the college.

Exploring College Environments

There are several methods for gathering information about specific colleges. The Internet provides a wealth of information through specific college web sites and general web sites providing information about colleges that offer specialized programs for students with disabilities. Also available are resource books that compile information on a number of colleges and universities. These books are available for purchase in bookstores or are developed for students by state departments of education or other non-for-profit groups. It is critical that several sources are used to collect as much information about colleges as possible; this helps ensure that the programs are able to best meet the student's learning needs and career goals. Trying to find a campus that meets the unique needs of students with disabilities can take time and effort. If possible, individuals with disabilities should visit potential schools to learn more about available support services and physical accessibility. Students who are considering a particular school should talk with students with disabilities who attend that school about their experiences. When visiting a specific school or reviewing information about it, the following questions should be used as guidelines for gathering pertinent information (Wilson et al., 2000, p. 38):

1. *Campus climate:* Is the campus atmosphere generally accepting of students with learning differences? Are students encouraged to participate fully in a variety of campus-life activities?

2. *Program philosophy:* Does the college offer a specialized area of emphasis associated with services? Or are supports offered as part of the college's overall program?

3. *Academic adjustment:* How are academic adjustments coordinated? Are there specialized accommodations such as notetakers, real-time captioning, and readers/scribes for examinations? What types of services are typically provided to students with disabilities on campus?

4. *Waivers and substitutions:* Are there written policies and procedures for waivers and substitutions? What kind of documentation is required? Who assists in the process of requesting a waiver or substitution? What is the probability that waivers or substitutions will be granted?

5. *Course load and graduation time:* Is it possible to maintain a reduced course load? Do students with disabilities generally take longer to complete the requirements for graduation? Is priority registration available for students with disabilities?

6. *Student support activities or groups:* Are there ongoing groups that meet to talk about issues or concerns related to the experiences of students with disabilities on campus? Are there specific activities that are designed to assist students with disabilities to network with other students on campus? Are there student leadership/mentoring programs to help students feel connected with other students with disabilities on campus?

7. *Orientation:* Are orientation sessions held designed to address disability-specific needs of students prior to the entering the college? Are these sessions primarily held during the summer or at the beginning of each semester for new incoming students?

Two-Year versus Four-Year Colleges

There are a number of reasons to explore different postsecondary programs to determine the right postsecondary match for a student. There are program considerations that meet the student's career goals; level and type of support services provided; level of academic preparedness required; and general atmosphere, size, diversity of student body, and campus accessibility. Two-year colleges or community colleges provide both vocational programs and academic curricula. These colleges offer associate's degrees and certificates in various occupational fields. They also offer courses that prepare individuals to continue their studies at a 4-year institution (Rioux-Bailey, 2004). It is estimated that 60% of students with disabilities in postsecondary education programs attend community colleges or programs that are less than 2 years (U.S. Department of Education, 2002, as cited in Savukinas, 2002).

Admission to community college significantly differs from admission to a 4-year university or college. Community colleges typically enroll individuals who have a high school diploma or the equivalent (GED certificate) or individuals who are able to benefit from instruction at the college. Some community colleges conduct placement tests to determine if remedial courses are needed. In both 2- and 4-year-colleges, documentation is required for students with disabilities to determine eligibility for services. It is important to note that the admission requirements for community colleges vary, depending on the standards set by each state (Savukinas, 2002).

Students with disabilities need to fully consider the best option in terms of where they would like to begin their postsecondary studies. Savukinas (2002) described the benefits of attending a community college as gaining college experience by taking a few courses at a time, establishing a track record of success, learning a trade, and gaining access to higher education at a cost usually lower than that of a 4-year program. The DO-IT project at the University of Washington developed a briefing paper that discusses some of the issues faced by students with disabilities who transfer from a community college to a 4-year institution. Some of the concerns expressed by students who were interviewed as part of the project included "differences in support services between the two institutions, the transfer process, housing and transportation issues, personal and family issues, and differences in academic requirements" (DO-IT, 2001, p. 2). The project also sought the views of disability support services (DSS) personnel at 4-year colleges on issues that students with disabilities face when transferring from a community college. Some of their concerns focused on similar areas as those noted by students with disabilities: "differences in academic requirements, financial support, and differences in support services provided at the 4-year college. Additional concerns expressed by these professionals included poor study skills, inadequate self-advocacy skills, inadequate academic preparation, and lack of mentors with disabilities" (DO-IT, 2001, p. 2).

When assessing a college or university, it is important to look comprehensively at the programs, college environment, and general feel of the campus and then specifically consider the disability-related supports and services needed. In addition, it is helpful to write down the advantages and disadvantages of each college, whether a 2- or 4-year institution, to help in the decision-making process.

Gaining Access to Supports and Services on Campus

Colleges and universities vary in the types of supports and services provided to students with disabilities. Supports most commonly requested by students include textbooks on tape, notetakers, extended time on tests, distraction-free environment for test taking, use of calculators, and permission to audiotape lectures (Deschamps, 2004; Getzel & Kregel, 1996; Thomas, 2000). Students also need to explore services that are available on campus for all students—for example, counseling services, writing or math labs, and study skills or time-management classes offered either through a counseling center or other entities on campus. There is a full range of services on campus to assist all students in successfully meeting their academic goals, and students with disabilities should take advantage of these services along with any specialized services that they are receiving.

Part of the process for determining the right match for a student and a college is learning about the services and supports available on campus and the process for obtaining these supports. Students with disabilities are not automatically entitled to disability-related services and supports but must meet eligibility requirements through the documentation of a disability. Chapter 2 provides a thorough discussion of the legal responsibilities of colleges and universities to provide services. Students with disabilities must know their rights and responsibilities as these pertain to their college education. Under-standing the process to obtain services and supports on campus is a critical step for determining whether a particular higher education program can meet a student's unique needs.

Most college campuses have a specific office to handle the request for accommodations. Typically, these are DSS offices, but some campuses might locate these services in other offices (see Chapter 2); thus, it is important to obtain information on where students with disabilities must go to self-identify for services. If a student is eligible, there are no costs associated with accommodations authorized by the college DSS office. Some colleges offer programs that provide additional services beyond what the DSS office can provide. Sometimes there is a fee for these services (see Chapter 5). Potential students should find out which services are provided at no cost to eligible students, what additional services are available, and whether there are costs to receive the supplementary services.

How are students with disabilities determined to be eligible for services? Generally, universities and colleges have a documentation policy or procedure in place for determining eligibility. Chapter 2 provides a detailed explanation about documentation requirements for college. It is important for students with disabilities to inquire about the documentation process on campus. Table 4.2 provides a series of questions that students and their families can use as they visit campuses or review information about specific colleges and universities.

Table 4.2. Questions to ask concerning services and supports

What specific documentation does your campus require to be eligible for services?

What types of support services are typically provided to students (i.e., learning disability, attention-deficit/hyperactivity disorder, low vision)?

Is new documentation required every year to remain eligible for services?

Are there orientation classes available that address issues specific to students with disabilities?

What is the process for accessing these support services?

How are instructors notified of a student's disability?

Source: Deschamps (2003).

Unfortunately, too many college students with disabilities are not aware of the supports and services available on campus. Sometimes these students believe that they will gain access to services when they really need them. This may happen after failing their first test or experiencing academic problems after mid-terms (Eaton & Coull, 1999; Getzel et al., 2004). This puts students under more stress to successfully complete a semester. It is important to realize that faculty will only institute accommodations upon receipt of a letter or notification from the college DSS office that a student with a disability presents regarding his or her eligibility to receive specific accommodations. These services are not retroactive, so the sooner students self-identify to the DSS office and become eligible for services, the greater the chance of successfully using these supports in their coursework. Knowing about the services and supports prior to applying for college can assist students in gaining access to services before academic problems occur.

Standardized College Admission Exams

Prior to applying for college, students need to undergo standardized admission testing: the Scholastic Aptitude Test (SAT) and/or the ACT. If a student is going to request accommodations for a standardized exam, ample time is required prior to the date of the test to request these accommodations. The organizations that conduct the SAT and ACT have very specific rules regarding qualification for accommodations (Fuller & Wehman, 2003). The student and his or her family must work closely with the IEP team to provide the necessary information for requesting such accommodations. They should not assume that the process for requesting testing accommodations is the same for each exam. The SAT and the ACT no longer indicate whether an exam was taken using accommodations. The scores are reported in a similar manner whether the test is taken with or without accommodations.

Students with disabilities need a good understanding of what is involved in taking college admission exams. In particular, these students must be fully aware of how their disabilities affect taking these exams. Students need assistance from teachers or other education professionals to help them determine their own personal test-taking strategies (Fuller & Wehman, 2003). Strategies that have helped all students and may help those with disabilities include practice sessions using questions from the test (to learn the design or format of the test questions); relaxation strategies also have been found to be an effective tool when taking these exams (Foster, Paulk, & Dastoor, 1999).

Financial Aid

A majority of students wanting to attend college seek financial resources beyond what their families can provide. Students with disabilities and their families need to explore which types of financial assistance are available, whether they are for disability-related expenses or general college expenses. Financial assistance may be needed to help cover the cost of tuition, room and board, transportation, or other college-related expenses. For students with disabilities, financial aid assistance may be available from programs through the state's vocational rehabilitation agency or from the Social Security Administration. Changes in legislation, eligibility requirements, or policies mean that researching financial aid resources from public and private entities is often a complicated process (HEATH Resource Center, 2005). However, with the rising cost of attending college, identifying financial aid resources is an important part of preparing for college. Four types of financial aid that students with disabilities need to consider are 1) grants (funds that usually do not need to be repaid), 2) loans (funds that are borrowed to cover education costs and repaid over time), 3) work study (employment that helps students earn money to cover costs), and 4) scholarships (awards based on specific criteria such as academic achievement, career goal, and so forth) (HEATH Resource Center, 2005). Information on locating financial aid resources is provided at the end of the chapter. Students can also visit the HEATH Resource Center (http://www.heath.gwu.edu) web site for a thorough review of financial aid options and information on applying for these resources.

Sarah has begun working with the high school's career center staff, looking at college catalogs and information. She has reviewed several college web sites to see which services and supports the colleges offer for students with learning disabilities, but some of the web sites are not very specific about their documentation requirements. Sarah makes a note to herself that when she visits some of the campuses, she should schedule an appointment with the DSS staff to discuss services and to see if she can connect with some of the students with disabilities attending the college to talk with them about their experiences.

She has talked with her parents about wanting to go into business, especially marketing. Sarah spent the summer working for her uncle in an advertising firm, and she loved the experience. Sarah realizes she will need to continue working on strategies to improve her writing and sequencing skills and especially to improve her time-management skills because marketing is a fast-paced field.

APPLYING FOR COLLEGE

College isn't all fun . . . it's hard work and takes self-discipline. (ODU, 2000)

After exploring the college or university programs that seem to best meet a student's needs, it is time to formally apply to the selected postsecondary institutions. It is important that all of the steps in the application process are carefully followed. Students need to be aware of early or regular admission deadlines or whether a specific college has a comprehensive support program for students with learning disabilities that requires documentation during the admissions process (Madaus, 2005). Having more than one person proofread the applications is important to make sure that all sections are completed.

Disclosing During the Application Process

Colleges and university applications cannot include questions about disabilities. However, students and their families often wonder if the student should self-disclose in the written essay or through letters of recommendation included in the application. This is a very personal decision on the part of the student. As noted in Chapter 2, some students self-disclose as part of their essay to demonstrate what they have accomplished; others use the essay as a means to explain discrepancies in grades and standardized test scores. Harris and Robertson (2001) cautioned that an essay or letter should focus on such areas as students' academic strengths, college preparatory program, coping skills, motivation, and maturity. Disclosing a disability at the postsecondary level is only required once a student is accepted and seeking accommodations from the university. In general, college essays or letters are used to provide college admission officers a more personal side or picture of the applicant. Decisions about what information a student with a disability shares should be thoroughly considered.

Writing the Essay

The essay should be carefully written and closely checked for spelling and grammatical errors. Often, high school senior English classes work on developing college essays. It is important for a student to obtain input about his or her essay from a variety of individuals. An English teacher or guidance counselor is an excellent resource. If the same essay is being sent to more than one school, the student must make sure that the correct college name is used in the essay. Not doing this is a very common mistake made by all students applying for college.

Sarah has decided to apply to three colleges, two within her state and one in a bordering state. After much discussion about her grades, financial resources, and ability to manage on her own, Sarah's parents agreed to her college choices. The three colleges that Sarah has selected are medium in size. She believes that they are large enough to offer a number of courses and activities but small enough for her to receive the attention she needs from her professors. Sarah has taken both the SAT and ACT, and her scores put her in the middle range of students typically accepted at these three colleges.

SKILLS NEEDED FOR
MEETING THE DEMANDS OF COLLEGE

Understand what accommodations are needed and how they help. (ODU, 2000)

Students with disabilities need a set of skills to help them make the transition to, adjust to, and remain in college. In essence, the student credo must be "know thyself," including strengths and weaknesses. These sets of personal or interpersonal skills include acceptance of a disability and how it affects learning; understanding which support services are needed; knowing how to describe one's disability and the need for certain supports to service providers, instructional faculty, and staff; being able to self-advocate for needed services; and having the determination to overcome whatever obstacles may be presented (deFur et al., 1996; Eaton & Coull, 1999; Getzel et al., 2000; Getzel et al., 2004). Also included are time management, study, decision-making, and independent-living skills (e.g., maintaining finances, clothing, and other personal needs). Opportunities to develop self-advocacy, self-determination, and independent-living skills prior to entering postsecondary education give students with disabilities the information and resources that they need to address academic and social demands in college. Students who understand themselves and their disability and have confidence to act in their own best interests can then make choices with the full knowledge and understanding of those choices (deFur et al., 1996). Students with disabilities need to consider the personal match to a college or university that will support their developing self-determination skills. Part of the preparation process for college is to investigate the social and academic expectations of postsecondary environments and evaluate one's ability to respond. See Chapter 3 for greater detail on the self-advocacy and self-determination skills needed in postsecondary education settings and how to put these skills into action.

TECHNOLOGY

Chapter 9 discusses the advances in assistive technology for students with disabilities who are preparing for college. Students with disabilities are entering postsecondary education unaware of existing technology (Getzel et al., 2004); they need to be exposed to the growing number of technology devices available to assist. This is a critical need that can make a tremendous difference in students' ability to perform in college. For example, after using a text-to-speech software program, one student was able to significantly raise her grade in a course (Getzel et al., 2004). As a result of this technology, she was able to respond to exam questions and demonstrate the knowledge that she had gained through the course.

> Sarah realized that she needed additional technology skills after meeting students with disabilities while on her campus tour. It was so helpful listening to their experiences about meeting with professors and using technology. They also helped her to see that sometimes things can get tough in college, but you just have to figure out how to overcome these obstacles. Sarah is planning on talking with her IEP team about how she can obtain more information about available technology that could help her in college.

CHANGING ROLE OF FAMILY MEMBERS

When a student enters a postsecondary program, perhaps one that is away from home, it is a major change and adjustment for any family. Yet, this is especially true for families of students with disabilities, as family members have served as advocates throughout their children's educational experience. It can be a difficult transition for some families because of their concern for the student's success and well-being. Often family members become frustrated because they believe that the postsecondary program is unresponsive to their requests or needs. Colleges and universities must operate under very specific policies and laws concerning all students, including students with disabilities. Thus, there are many legal differences between secondary and postsecondary education regarding what information is shared with parents and the delivery of services and supports. It is important that students with disabilities and their families work together to better understand these differences and to begin shifting to the student more responsibility in managing his or her education. Chapters 2 and 3 provide a wealth of information to help students and their families understand the legal responsibilities and process of obtaining services in higher education, along with developing student skills to self-advocate for these services.

Another consideration in the process of planning for college is the cultural aspects of the student and his or her family. Students with disabilities represent a wide variety of ethnic and minority groups, and the values and expectations of their families can play a major role in the decisions made about a particular college. Black, Mrasek, and Ballinger (2003) discussed the individualist and collectivist values of culturally diverse students with disabilities. When exploring postsecondary education as a transition outcome, these authors cautioned that families may have certain expectations about the kind of postsecondary setting that they believe is appropriate for their children. They may want their children to attend a specific type of program—for example, to go to a technical college instead of a university. Careful attention by all IEP team members (including the student and the family) to career goals and the family's beliefs and expectations of postsecondary education are needed to ensure that appropriate planning is done.

CONCLUSION

This chapter has highlighted some of the critical areas that need to be addressed during the transition of students with disabilities to postsecondary settings. Preparing to enter college is only one part of the planning process. Students need the academic preparation and the skills to manage their education to remain in college. There are many aspects to this planning process that need to be done over time. Many of these suggestions begin several years prior to a student's junior or senior year in high school. Assisting students to make the academic and personal match to postsecondary settings can help them to meet the demands of their program and move toward securing a meaningful career.

REFERENCES

Black, R.S., Mrasek, K.D., & Ballinger, R. (2003). Individualist and collectivist values in transition planning for culturally diverse students with special needs. *The Journal for Vocational Special Needs Education, 25*(2, 3), 20–29.

Brinckerhoff, L.C., McGuire, J.M., & Shaw, S.F. (2002). *Postsecondary education and transition for students with learning disabilities* (2nd ed.). Austin, TX: PRO-ED.

deFur, S.H., Getzel, E.E., & Trossi, K. (1996). Making the postsecondary education match: A role for transition planning. *Journal of Vocational Rehabilitation, 6,* 231–241.

Deschamps, A. (2003). Traveling the road from high school to college: Tips for the journey. *Transition Times, 9*(1), 1–2.

Disabilities, Opportunities, Internetworking, and Technology (DO-IT). (2001). *Moving on: The two-four step. How students with disabilities can transition from 2 to 4 year colleges.* Retrieved November 8, 2004, from http://www.washington.edu/doit/Brochures/Academics/24.html

Eaton, H., & Coull, L. (1999). *Transitions to postsecondary learning: Self-advocacy handbook for students with learning disabilities and/or attention deficit disorder.* Vancouver, BC, Canada: Eaton Coull Learning Group.

Fairweather, J.S., & Shaver, D.M. (1991). Making the transition to post-secondary education and training. *Exceptional Children, 57*(2), 264–268.

Foster, S.K., Paulk, A., & Dastoor, B.R. (1999). Can we really teach test-taking skills? *New Horizons in Adult Education, 13*(1), 14.

Fuller, W.E., & Wehman, P. (2003). College entrance exams for students with disabilities: Accommodations and testing guidelines. *Journal of Vocational Rehabilitation, 18*(3), 191–197.

Gajar, A., Goodman, L., & McAfee, J. (1995). *Secondary schools and beyond: Transition of individuals with mild disabilities.* New York: Macmillan.

Getzel, E.E., Briel, L.W., & Kregel, J. (2000). Comprehensive career planning: The VCU career connections program. *Journal of Work, 14,* 41–49.

Getzel, E.E., & Kregel, J. (1996). Transitioning from the academic to the employment setting: The employment connection program. *Journal of Vocational Rehabilitation, 6,* 273–287.

Getzel, E.E., McManus, S., & Briel, L.W. (2004). An effective model for college students with learning disabilities and attention deficit hyperactivity disorders. *Research to Practice, 3*(1). Retrieved January 20, 2004, from www.ncset.org/publications/researchtopractice/NCSETResearchBrief_3.1.pdf

Getzel, E.E., Stodden, R.A., & Briel, L.W. (2001). Pursuing postsecondary education opportunities for individuals with disabilities. In P. Wehman, *Life beyond the classroom: Transition strategies for young people with disabilities* (3rd ed., pp. 247–259). Baltimore: Paul H. Brookes Publishing Co.

Gilson, S.F. (1996). Students with disabilities: An increasing voice and presence on college campuses. *Journal of Vocational Rehabilitation, 6,* 263–272.

Harris, R., & Robertson, J. (2001). Successful strategies for college-bound students with learning disabilities. *Preventing School Failure, 45*(3), 125–131.

HEATH Resource Center. (2005). *Creating options: 2005 financial aid for individuals with disabilities.* Retrieved February 1, 2005, from http://www.heath.gwu.edu/Heath%20Website/PDFs/FinancialAid05.pdf

Kravets, M., & Wax, I. (2003). *The K & W guide to college for students with learning disabilities or attention deficit disorder* (7th ed.). New York: Random House.

Lock, R.H., & Layton, C.A. (2001). Succeeding in postsecondary education through self-advocacy. *Teaching Exceptional Children, 34*(2), 66–71.

Madaus, J.W. (2003). What high school students with learning disabilities need to know about college foreign language requirements. *Teaching Exceptional Children, 36*(2), 62–66.

Madaus, J.W. (2005). Navigating the college transition maze: A guide for students with learning disabilities. *Teaching Exceptional Children, 37*(3), 32–37.

Old Dominion University. (2000). *Taking charge of your college life* [Brochure]. Norfolk, VA: Author.

Peterson's/Thomson. (2003). *Colleges for students with learning disabilities or ADD* (7th ed.). Lawrenceville, NJ: Author.

Rioux-Bailey, C. (2004, March). *Students with disabilities and access to community college: Continuing issues and new directions.* Retrieved February 10, 2005, from http://www.heath.gwu.edu/Templates/Newsletter/Issue9(2004March)/Access.htm

Savukinas, R. (2002, July). *Community colleges and students with disabilities.* Retrieved February 10, 2005, from http://www.heath.gwu.edu/Templates/Newsletter/issue3/commcoll.htm

Stodden, R.A. (1998). School-to-work transition: Overview of disability legislation. In F.R. Rusch & J.G. Chadsey (Eds.), *Beyond high school: Transition from school to work* (pp. 60–76). Belmont, CA: Wadsworth Publishing.

Thomas, S.B. (2000). College students and disability law. *The Journal of Special Education, 33*(4), 248–257.

U.S. Department of Education. (2002). *National postsecondary student aid survey: Data analysis system.* Retrieved February 10, 2005, from http://nces.ed.gov/surveys/npsas/das.asp

Virginia Department of Education. (2003). *Virginia's college guide for students with disabilities: You know you can do it! Here's how!* Richmond: Virginia Department of Education, Division of Special Education and Student Services.

Wagner, M., Cameto, R., & Newman, L. (2003). *Youth with disabilities: A changing population: A report of findings from the National Longitudinal Transition Study (NLTS) and the National Longitudinal Transition Study-2 (NLTS2).* Menlo Park, CA: SRI International.

Wilson, K., Getzel, E., & Brown, T. (2000). Enhancing the post-secondary campus climate for students with disabilities. *Journal of Vocational Rehabilitation, 14*(1), 37–50.

Additional Resources

PREPARING FOR POSTSECONDARY EDUCATION

Colleges for Students with Learning Disabilities or ADD (7th ed.)

Published by Peterson's/Thomson, this is a comprehensive guide to 2- and 4-year colleges and universities offering special services for students with learning disabilities.

DO-IT (Disabilities, Opportunities, Internetworking & Technology)

A comprehensive web site offering information for students with disabilities including using technology, obtaining financial aid, making the transition to college, transferring colleges, obtaining accommodations in college, and learning college survival skills.
http://www.washington.edu/doit

The K & W Guide to Colleges for Students with Learning Disabilities or Attention Deficit Disorder (7th ed.)

Published by Random House, this is a comprehensive college guidebook for students with learning disabilities containing information on programs' admission requirements and graduation policies.

LD OnLine

LD OnLine is a national educational service, which offers on-line services and produces video programs dedicated to improving the lives of children and adults with learning disabilities and attention-deficit/hyperactivity disorder (ADHD). Among the resources offered is a guide on postsecondary education (http://www.ldonline.org/ld_indepth/postsecondary).
http://www.ldonline.org

National Center on Secondary Education and Transition

This resource has information about transition for families, students with disabilities, school personnel, and community organizations and agencies.
http://www.ncset.org

Students with Disabilities Preparing for Postsecondary Education: Know Your Rights and Responsibilities

The Office for Civil Rights (OCR) of the U.S. Department of Education developed this pamphlet to explain the rights and responsibilities of students

with disabilities who are preparing to attend postsecondary schools. This pamphlet also explains the obligations of postsecondary schools to provide academic adjustments, including auxiliary aids and services, to ensure against discrimination on the basis of disability.
http://www.ed.gov/print/about/offices/list/ocr/transition.html

Virginia College Quest

This web site is an excellent resource for students with disabilities who are considering college. The web site assists students in becoming familiar with terminology specific to college and with differences between high school and college, and it provides other helpful background information about making the transition to college.
http://www.vacollegequest.org

COLLEGE ENTRANCE EXAMS

ACT Assessment: Services for Students with Disabilities

This site provides information about the policies established regarding documentation of an applicant's disability and the process for requesting accommodations.
http://www.act.org/aap/disab

College Board: Services for Students with Disabilities

This site provides information about the policies established regarding documentation of an applicant's disability and the process for requesting accommodations.
http://www.collegeboard.com/ssd/student

FINANCIAL AID

Free Application for Federal Student Aid (FAFSA)

FAFSA is used to apply for federal student financial aid, including grants, loans, and work-study programs. In addition, it is used by most states and schools to award nonfederal student financial aid.
http://www.fafsa.ed.gov

HEATH Resource Center

The HEATH Resource Center of The George Washington University, Graduate School of Education and Human Development, is the national clearinghouse on postsecondary education for individuals with disabilities. Support from the U.S. Department of Education enables the clearinghouse to serve as an information exchange about educational support services, policies, procedures, adaptations, and opportunities at American campuses, vocational-technical schools, and other postsecondary training entities.
http://www.heath.gwu.edu

The HEATH Resource Center also published *Financial Aid for Students with Disabilities* (2005 Edition). This resource provides information to help individuals with disabilities seek and obtain financial assistance for postsecondary

education. The guide describes federal financial aid programs, state vocational rehabilitation services, and regional and local sources. It is completed by a listing of nationally awarded grants and a precollege checklist to organize the search for funds.
http://www.heath.gwu.edu/Heath%20Website/PDFs/FinancialAid05.pdf

CHAPTER 5

The Role
of Disability Support Services

J. Trey Duffy and John Gugerty

In discussing the role of disability support services (DSS) in higher education, this chapter reviews alternative philosophical frameworks. It sketches
program policies, designs, and operational procedures. The chapter then
discusses personnel configuration and qualification issues, reviews budgetary
considerations, and outlines program evaluation considerations. Finally, it
previews possible future trends and challenges.

PHILOSOPHY

Why Is There a Need for a
Disability Support Services Program?

In a perfect, universally designed world, perhaps there would be no need for
a specialized program facilitating support services that provide equal access
to university programs for students with disabilities. However, until that day
arrives, all U.S. colleges need to take affirmative steps to ensure that students
with disabilities have access to their educational programs and services on an
equal basis with other students.

There are two primary reasons for having a disability services program.
First, U.S. civil rights laws require the provision of equal access to people
with disabilities, and the likelihood of achieving equal access is amplified by
the presence of personnel, policies, and programs dedicated to executing these
rights. Second, and more important, it is proper pedagogy. Educators are
concerned with student learning; disability services help ensure that all students
have an equal opportunity to learn. Throughout this chapter, one objective
should remain clear: It is the role of disability services personnel to seek,
nurture, and preserve institutional commitment and support for ensuring

that students with disabilities have equal access to educational opportunities available to all other students.

Access versus Success: Is Equal Opportunity Enough?

The Americans with Disabilities Act (ADA) of 1990 (PL 101-336) requires colleges to provide accommodations to ensure that students with disabilities have equal access to all educational opportunities. The ADA promotes access, equal opportunity, and nondiscrimination; it does not concern itself with an individual's ultimate success. Students are concerned with both access and success, and they do not necessarily draw a distinction between the two. DSS programs are continually faced with the dilemma of determining when an accommodation request crosses the line from ensuring access to attempting to facilitate success. Should DSS programs design accommodations so students have the maximum opportunity for success? Is there a conflict of interest if a DSS program is charged with the responsibility of determining appropriate accommodations based on existing laws (ADA, Section 504 of the Rehabilitation Act of 1973 [PL 93-112]) and with helping students succeed? For example, appropriate accommodations needed for equal access for a student who is deaf might be interpreting, notetaking, and preferential seating. However, if the ultimate concern is the student's success, the argument could also be made for providing priority registration, alternative testing, Communication Access Realtime Translation (CART), tutoring, proofreading, different test formats, pass/fail grading options, and late withdrawals if needed.

The line between access and success can be easily blurred when colleges implement fee-for-service programs such as The University of Arizona's SALT Center (http://www.salt.arizona.edu) and Harper College's Program for Achieving Student Success (PASS) (http://www.harpercollege.edu/services/ads/ldadd/programs.shtml). These programs typically offer services beyond mandated auxiliary aids developed by postsecondary education in response to Section 504 and the ADA. They are intended to help students succeed. Balancing services designed for equal access with those designed for student success can be challenging.

It is critical for campus administrators to clarify, both to DSS staff and to students, the expectations charged to the DSS program and whether these expectations surpass the goal of equal access and enter into a realm of promoting success. Administrators can accomplish this by bringing together campus stakeholders (e.g., faculty leaders, academic and student affairs administrators, legal counsel) to thoughtfully discuss and, if possible, develop consensus on campus values, directions, resources, limitations, and, ultimately, expected outcomes. Without this stakeholder-derived conceptual framework, the decisions that determine where the line between ensuring access ends and promoting success begins fall to DSS staff. For detailed expositions of student stakeholder voices, see Lehmann, Davies, and Laurin (2000); Mooney and Cole (2000); National Center for the Study of Postsecondary Educational Supports (n.d.); Rodis, Garrod, and Boscardin (2001); Roessler and Kirk (1998); Skinner (2004); and Whelley and Yeganeh (n.d.).

CENTRALIZED VERSUS DECENTRALIZED PROGRAM MODELS

Centralized Disability Support Services

A centralized DSS program provides comprehensive services covering a vast array of curricular and cocurricular areas for all students with disabilities—and frequently also for employees, guests, and visitors. The key characteristic of a centralized program is that it serves essentially as a one-stop center for any and all disability services and accommodations. For example, Disability Services (DS) at the University of Minnesota offers employee services (http://ds.umn.edu/employees). In this capacity, DS serves as an objective resource in balancing the rights and responsibilities of employees and those of the institution. DS does this by documenting disabilities, adhering to employment policies and procedures established by the university, and determining reasonable accommodations. The Disability Resource Center at The University of Arizona (http://drc.arizona.edu) has developed a state-of-the-art assistive technology computer facility that provides specialized tools for students and staff with disabilities. The Virginia Commonwealth University's supported education model emphasizes a one-stop approach designed for students with disabilities who are at high risk for failure (Getzel, McManus, & Briel, 2004).

The advantages of a centralized program are consistency and influence. Faculty, staff, students, guests, and visitors with disabilities all know exactly where to go regardless of their access issue. Also, centralized programs tend to be larger than decentralized programs and, as such, can leverage their human resources broadly. A centralized system tends to work well in large, complex institutions. A disadvantage of centralized programs is that there can be a tendency for segregation and duplication of services. For example, if a center is designed to be a one-stop focal point, then many students may expect their needs that are not related to disability to be met as well. This gives rise to adaptive technology labs, academic advising, specialized tutoring, and the like. Another drawback is that institutions may expect their disability centers to solve all access matters, regardless of the issue. For example, the chemistry department is remodeling its laboratory and seeks confirmation that its plans comply with accessibility codes. In a centralized model, the first call may be to the DSS program. Because this is primarily a facilities construction issues, consultation from an architect would be more suitable.

Decentralized Disability Support Services

A decentralized DSS program provides only those services not available elsewhere on campus and expects existing campus departments and service units to develop expertise in meeting the needs of its students and customers who have disabilities. One primary function of a decentralized disability services program is providing consultation and training. The decentralized program delivers direct, disability-related access services such as interpreting/captioning, notetaking, adaptive materials, electronic text, alternative testing, and disability management advising. Although applicable to institutions of varying sizes, a decentralized system tends to work particularly well in medium to small institutions.

A drawback of a decentralized system is the threat of inconsistencies if individual departments are charged with meeting the access needs of all their students. For example, computer labs, facilities management, or career advising may develop disparate levels of responsiveness. In most cases, however, the concept of responding to the needs of individuals in the most inclusive fashion possible overrides the fear that individual departments cannot respond effectively. The University of Wisconsin–Madison is an example of a decentralized program (http://www.wisc.edu/wiscinfo/policy/disability.html).

Programs reflect the specific campus communities from which they evolve. There is no perfect program for every campus (Brown, 1994).

Academic Division versus Student Affairs

An often-asked question is whether disability services are more aptly located in an academic department or a student affairs unit. The following sections explore the advantages and disadvantages of each.

Pros and Cons of Placement within an Academic Division An academic unit offers closer ties to curricular issues and to the people making decisions affecting learning. Learning is the major life activity affected by the vast majority of students now served by DSS programs (e.g., Asperger syndrome, attention-deficit/hyperactivity disorder [ADHD], learning and psychiatric disabilities). Affiliation with an academic unit may enhance understanding of disability-related learning issues more effectively. Disability policies initiated and endorsed by an academic administrator may better serve students than policies originating from nonacademic sources. However, because teaching and learning are the priorities of an academic unit, affiliated academic support units often suffer in times of financial difficulty. Even during the best of times it is hard to compete with academic priorities.

Pros and Cons of Placement within a Student Affairs Unit Most disability programs tend to be housed in student affairs units; however, placement ranges, as shown from the following examples: the Division of Student Affairs (University of Michigan), University Counseling Services (Oklahoma State University), and the Office for Campus Relations (Stanford University). Students may ultimately benefit from services housed in student affairs because the primary focus, training, and expertise of staff are specifically in the delivery of services. Students with disabilities require specific actions, services, modifications, and adaptations that student services personnel are accustomed to administering. Kroeger and Schuck noted,

> Whether or not the disability services office is housed in the student services unit, student affairs administrators can play a key support role by becoming well informed about the ADA, establishing access as a priority goal in the mission of the institution, infusing access within all other student services divisions, providing ample staff development and training opportunities, and advocating funding for disability services. (1993, p. 67)

The best answer is that a disability services program should be located in a unit that wants it. Campus culture and politics will dictate more clearly than a philosophical underpinning the administrative or pedagogical advantages of one area over another.

PROGRAM AND OPERATIONAL PROCEDURES

Mission Statements

In reviewing various DSS office mission statements, several themes emerge. The following extracts are illustrative of common elements:

- Create "an accessible community where individuals with disabilities have an equal opportunity to participate in or benefit from all college programs, activities, and services" (Adams State College, Alamosa, CO)

- "Facilitate support services that provide equal access to university programs for students with disabilities" (California State University–Chico)

- Provide "the opportunity to take part in [the university's] educational programs and services on an equal basis with other students" (University of Mary Washington, Fredericksburg, VA)

- Ensure that "all programs and facilities of the University are accessible to all persons in the University community [and] . . . develop programs and services that permit students to, independently as possible, meet the demands of University life" (The University of North Carolina at Chapel Hill)

- "Function as a resource to University faculty in offering students equity and excellence in education, maximizing each student's educational potential while helping him or her develop and maintain independence" (University of Massachusetts–Boston)

- Encourage "self-awareness, self-determination, self-advocacy and independence in a comprehensively accessible environment" (University of Massachusetts–Boston)

See the Mission and Goals of the University of Wisconsin–Madison's McBurney Disability Resource Center (http://www.mcburney.wisc.edu/information/mission.php) for a complete mission statement example.

Program Standards

Association on Higher Education and Disability   In 1997, the first (and, to date, only) study was conducted to examine the essential components of DSS programs (Dukes, 2001). Sampling more than 800 disability service practitioners in North America, 80% of whom were Association on Higher Education and Disability (AHEAD) members, resulted in the identification of 27 program standards across 9 categories (see a complete listing of AHEAD's Program Standards at http://www.ahead.org/about/AHEAD_Program_Stan dards.doc). Considered a living document with room for development and expansion, the program standards are under consideration for revision by AHEAD. In essence, the standards emphasize the importance of DSS programs serving as advocates and consultants for students and disability issues, as well as being the primary coordinator of direct services and accommodations. In addition, the standards include the role of participating in policy and program development, disability training, program evaluation, and information dissemination.

Perhaps Standard 4.3 is the most controversial item among AHEAD's standards: "Have final responsibility for determining academic accommodations which do not fundamentally alter the program of study." Many argue that there are other more appropriate sources (e.g., individual faculty members, department chairs, faculty committees) for determining whether an accommodation fundamentally alters a program of study and that the process should be collaborative, not authorized by DSS personnel. It should be noted that this standard stems from responses from the more than 800 practitioners in the original survey. The survey did not include college administrators or faculty, who may have a different opinion on who has final responsibility. Although not exhaustive, the standards resulting from this study serve as a strong foundation for measuring a DSS program's design and effectiveness.

Council for the Advancement of Academic Standards in Higher Education   The Council for the Advancement of Academic Standards in Higher Education (CAS) has developed the *Disability Services Standard and Guidelines Self-Assessment Guide*, which translates into a format enabling self-assessment. Educators can use this guide to gain informed perspectives on the strengths and deficiencies of their services and programs and plan for improvements. Grounded in the self-regulation approach to quality assurance in higher education endorsed by CAS, this self-assessment guide provides institutions with a tool to assess their programs and services using national standards of practice. (To obtain a copy, go to http://www.cas.edu/catalog.)

SERVICES

Determining Eligibility for Services

Once a student decides to self-disclose his or her disability, the first and perhaps most perplexing task is determining whether the individual satisfies the definition of the term *student with a disability.* Once thought to be a fairly straightforward undertaking, U.S. Supreme Court decisions over the years have narrowly interpreted the definition such that it is increasingly more difficult for students to demonstrate that they are substantially limited in a major life activity. Chapter 2 outlines the regulatory environment. In any case, it is incumbent upon the student to provide sufficient documentation demonstrating a substantial limitation to one or more major life activities. The role of a college's DSS office is to develop and distribute clear, concise criteria for what the college accepts as appropriate documentation. Documentation from an appropriate treating clinician is the primary resource for determining disability. Figure 5.1 is an example of a form that can be sent to a student's clinician in order to obtain information regarding the student's impairments and disabilities.

Assessing Service Needs

Once a student is determined to be eligible for disability-related services and accommodations, a professional staff member should evaluate the impact and functional limitations imposed by the individual's disability. It is important to make tangible connections between the impairment, the major life activities affected, and the resulting substantial limitations. Assessing a student's accommodation needs involves 1) reviewing relevant written documentation, 2) understanding the student's expressed needs, 3) noting prior services and accommodations that the student used in an educational setting, and 4) using professional judgment.

Documenting Decisions

A DSS staff member should be prepared to adequately respond to the question, "On what basis did you determine that this student should have XYZ accommodations and services?" The answer occurs by drawing a direct line between an impairment (e.g., low vision), a major life activity (e.g., seeing), and the accommodation (e.g., document conversion). The rationale for accommodation decisions should be documented. For a sample of such documentation, see the McBurney Disability Resource Center's Disability and Accommodations Assessment for Eligibility Form (Figure 5.2).

Clinician Disability Assessment

To Whom It May Concern:

A patient/client of yours has requested disability-related services from the McBurney Disability Resource Center, University of Wisconsin-Madison. Legal protection and eligibility for such services is based on an individual providing sufficient information to conclude that he or she has an impairment that substantially limits one or more major life activities. As this student's treating specialist, you are asked to provide the following information to allow the university to consider this student's service request(s).

PLEASE COMPLETE THE FOLLOWING:

1. Patient/Client Name:

---

2. The Condition of Patient/Client:

A. What is the diagnosis/impairment?

B. When was the diagnosis originally made?

C. Is the patient/student currently under your care?

D. When did you last see the patient/student?

E. Is the impairment temporary (< 3 months) or persistent?

F. Please identify any factors that may affect the severity of the impairment (e.g., to what degree might the impairment be *minimized* by medications, hearing aids, etc.?) Alternatively, could there be an adverse affect (e.g., medication side effects)?

---

3. Please complete the following: FUNCTIONAL IMPACT ASSESSMENT

LIMITATION IS: 1 = Unable to Determine   2 = Mild   3 = Moderate   4 = Substantial

1	2	3	4	Major Life Activity		1	2	3	4	Major Life Activity
				Caring for oneself						Learning
				Talking						• Reading
				Hearing						• Writing
				Breathing						• Spelling
				Seeing						• Calculating
				Walking/Standing						• Concentrating
				Lifting/Carrying						• Memorizing
				Sitting						• Listening
				Performing Manual Tasks						Other:
				Eating						
				Working						
				Interacting with Others						
				Sleeping						

Figure 5.1.   McBurney Disability Resource Center's Clinician Disability Assessment Form. (Reprinted by permission.)

4. What method(s) were utilized to assess functional limitation? Please list or attach under separate cover.

5. Please list your recommendations for accommodations within the academic environment. Please provide a rationale for any recommendation made utilizing data from objective measures, the educational record, or other data sources. Please list or attach under separate cover.

6. Certifier Information:

Clinician Name

Medical Specialty

License

Address

Phone

Email

Date

Please send this completed form and any additional information to the McBurney Disability Resource Center.
If you have questions, please feel free to contact our office. Thank you.

Disability and Accommodations Assessment for Eligibility Form

Student:

Accommodation Specialist: **Date:**

I. DISABILITY/MAJOR LIFE ACTIVITY LIMITATION ASSESSMENT

Limitation is: 1 = Unable to Determine   2 = Mild   3 = Moderate   4 = Substantial

Major Life Activity	1	2	3	4
Caring for oneself				
Talking				
Hearing				
Breathing				
Seeing				
Walking/Standing				
Lifting/Carrying				
Sitting				
Performing Manual Tasks				
Eating				
Working				
Interacting with Others				
Sleeping				

Major Life Activity	1	2	3	4
Learning				
• Reading				
• Writing				
• Spelling				
• Calculating				
• Concentrating				
• Memorizing				
• Listening				
Other:				

Rating Scale: 1 = Unable to Determine   2 = Mild   3 = Moderate   4 = Substantial   NA = Not Applicable

Documentation is Complete	Yes	No				
Impact is:	Current	Potential				
Impact of Mitigating Measures is:	Positive	Negative	1	2	3	4	NA
Impact is seen in Condition, Manner or Duration	Yes	No	1	2	3	4	NA
Impact seen in Academic Record	Yes	No	1	2	3	4	NA
Qualifies as a Disability:	Yes	No	Unable To Determine			
Permanent:	Yes	No	If NO, duration of temporary disability _____			

Disability (Common Description)

Regent Code	Primary: _____	Secondary: _____	Tertiary: _____
McBurney Code	Primary: _____	Secondary: _____	Tertiary: _____

Duration:

Code: R for *accommodations* determined to be reasonable under the ADA (i.e., they accommodate a substantial limitation to a major life activity).
D for *discretionary* accommodations that would not be required under the ADA (i.e., these accommodations are determined to be helpful for mild to moderate limitations but would not be required under the ADA).

Accommodations / Functional Limitation	Alternative Testing										Document Conversion			Other							Deaf/HH	
	Accessible Room	Computer	Small Group	Test Alone	Scribe	Doc. Conversion	1.5 Time	Seating	2.0 Time	Other	Braille	Electronic	Audio Tape/CD	Priority Reg.	Lab Assistance	Lib.Assistance	Notetaker	NT Paper only	Red.Course Load	CART	CART	Sign Language Interpreter
Caring for Oneself																						
Talking																						
Hearing																						
Breathing																						
Seeing																						
Walking/Standing																						
Lifting/Carrying																						
Sitting																						
Performing Manual Tasks																						
Eating																						
Working																						
Interacting with Others																						
Sleeping																						
Learning																						
• Reading																						
• Writing/Spelling																						
• Calculating																						
• Memorizing																						
• Concentrating																						
• Listening																						
Other:																						

Figure 5.2. McBurney Disability Resource Center's Disability and Accommodations Assessment for Eligibility Form. (Reprinted by permission.)

Types of Services

Common accommodations provided to college students with disabilities include the following:

- Alternative testing: Provides accommodations such as extra time, audio versions, and small-group testing sites for course exams

- Interpreting: Provides sign language or oral interpreters for students who are deaf or have hearing impairments

- Real-time captioning (or CART): Provides text alternatives to classroom lectures

- Notetaking: Provides copies of classroom notes from a fellow student

- Document conversion: Provides reading materials in three formats—audio, enlarged text, and braille (audio formats include four-track audiocassettes, digital audio, and electronic media—i.e., print materials in electronic format)

See Table 5.1 for additional possible accommodations; for examples from a specific university, see the McBurney Disability Resource Center's listing of services to students with disabilities. The McBurney Disabilities Resource Center also provides an individualized services plan called VISA, or Verified Individualized Services and Accommodations (see Figure 5.3).

Training for Students Who Receive Services It is imperative that students receive orientation and training on how to request and gain access to support services. Accommodations can be intricate because numerous courses,

Table 5.1. Additional services and accommodations

Adaptive technology access
Advocacy/liaison
Assistive listening devices
Braille
Class relocation
Commencement ceremony accommodations
Counseling/advising
Course substitution
Early registration
Elevator keys
Laboratory assistance
Library assistance
Notetaking assistance
Preferential seating
Priority registration
Reduced credit load

Source: http://www.mcburney.wisc.edu/services

McBurney Center VISA

(Verified Individualized Services and Accommodations)

Original VISA Date:

Expiration:

Revised On:

Recommended services are effective through the above expiration date unless otherwise indicated by a duration date.

Student _____

Email _____

Accommodations Specialist _____

The following accommodations are recommended for this student by the McBurney Disability Resource Center. Recommendations are based upon documentation of disability and an evaluation of the student's needs. Revisions may occur pending additional information, changes in disability status, or periodic review. You may contact the student's accommodations specialist with questions or concerns regarding the provision of accommodations and services or visit McBurney's website at www.mcburney.wisc.edu. *This information should remain confidential.*

LEVEL I INSTRUCTIONAL SERVICES AND ACCOMMODATIONS

Duration	Service	Duration	Service
_____	Alternative Testing:*	_____	Course Substitution Evaluation
_____	accessible room	_____	Document Conversion:*
_____	computer/standard or adaptive	_____	audio
_____	tests alone	_____	Braille
_____	tests in a small group	_____	enlarged text
_____	scribe/voice recognition	_____	Laboratory Assistance
_____	audio exam/Brailed exam	_____	Notetaker *
_____	enlarged text	_____	Notetaker Paper Only
_____	time and a half	_____	Preferential Seating
_____	double time	_____	Priority Registration/Linked/Modified
_____	_____ time	_____	Reduced Credit Load
_____	other: _____	_____	Computer Assisted Transcription*/CART*[1]
_____	other: _____	_____	Registration Assistance
_____	other: _____	_____	Sign Language/Oral Interpreter*
_____	Assistive Listening Device*	_____	Other: _____
_____	Class Relocation		

LEVEL II GENERAL ACCOMMODATIONS AND SERVICES

_____	Adaptive Technology Access	_____	Library Assistance:
_____	Advocacy/Liaison	_____	MLRR access
_____	Accommodation Advising	_____	paging service
_____	Elevator Keys	_____	Other

* Training required prior to receiving this service.   [1]Computer Assisted Real-time Transcription

---

I understand that provision of these services may involve McBurney staff disclosing disability record information provided by me with appropriate university personnel participating in the accommodation process.

Student Signature: _____ Date: _____

(continued)

White Copy: AT Coordinator / Student   Yellow Copy: Student File

Figure 5.3. McBurney Disability Resource Center's Verified Individualized Services and Accommodations (VISA) form. (Reprinted by permission.)

(continued)

The McBurney Disability Resource Center, a division of the Dean of Students Office, is the disabled student services office at the University of Wisconsin-Madison. The McBurney Center's mission is to create an accessible university community for students with disabilities. Creating this community is a collaborative effort involving the student, the faculty and the McBurney Center staff. The University of Wisconsin-Madison faculty, in collaboration with McBurney Center staff, has established policies regarding instructional access and accommodation via Faculty Documents 1143 (http://www.wisc.edu/adac/students/assess.html) and 1071 (http://www.wisc.edu/adac/1071.html).

The **VISA** (Verified Individualized Services and Accommodation) is a written record of the accommodations recommended by the McBurney staff for the student whose name appears on the document. Accommodations are designed to provide the student with an equal opportunity to participate in all educational activities. The roles of the student, faculty and McBurney Center in the development and implementation of the **VISA** are described below.

Student's Role:

Students request support services/accommodations; provide the McBurney Center with sufficient disability-related documentation from an appropriate licensed professional; and describe the impact of their disability in an academic setting. Students are expected to request accommodation in a timely manner with the appropriate university personnel.

McBurney Center's Role: (http://www.mcburney.wisc.edu/)

The McBurney Center reviews disability documentation, verifies that the documentation satisfies disability verification guidelines and implements an intake process with the student to assess the impact of the disability or disorder. McBurney Center staff may also communicate with departments or individual faculty members to better understand the nature of the course or program as part of the intake process. At the conclusion of the intake process, students receive a **VISA** and training on the *recommended* services.

Faculty's Role:

As needed, the faculty member meets with the student to discuss accommodation recommendations and make suitable arrangements for those accommodations as appropriate. If faculty have questions regarding the provision or appropriateness of the recommended accommodations, they are encouraged to contact the McBurney accommodations specialist noted on the **VISA,** or the departmental Access and Accommodation Resource Coordinator (AARC).

Access and Accommodation Resource Coordinator's (AARC) Role:
(http://www.wisc.edu/adac/facstaff/coord.html)

The AARC is a departmentally designated representative responsible for providing information and referral to address accommodation concerns for faculty and students, and for providing information to students who wish to initiate a formal appeal.

Current federal and state legislation (Americans with Disabilities Act, 1990, Section 504 of the Rehabilitation Act, 1973, Wisconsin State Statute 36.12) states that academically qualified students with disabilities be reasonably accommodated in instruction and academic assessment. In order to be eligible for services, students must have a documented disability. A disability is legally defined as a physical or mental impairment substantially limiting one or more major life activities (e.g., walking speaking, seeing, hearing, sitting, breathing, learning, or caring for oneself). Recommended accommodations are intended to provide equal access as required by law; they are not intended to fundamentally alter the course/program or to create an undue financial or administrative burden to the faculty or university.

Additional information, faculty documents, and disability service handouts can be obtained by calling the McBurney Center or by visiting the McBurney website.

faculty, and service providers are usually involved. Training can be provided individually or in small groups, although the latter is more time efficient. Orientations and trainings may also be provided on line via multimedia presentations. Individuals providing services (e.g., notetakers, proctors) also need orientation and training. See http://www.mcburney.wisc.edu/services/ servicetraining.php for an example of student training services provided by the McBurney Disability Resource Center.

POLICIES

All colleges and universities need a complete, concise, fair, and comprehensive set of disability policies and procedures. Policies fall into two main categories: DSS policies for services and accommodations and college policies for nondiscrimination and access. The lynchpin, regardless of a policy's origin, is a viable and expedient appeals process. Students have a right to due process if they are denied a request for a reasonable accommodation or if they believe they have been discriminated against on the basis of disability.

Documentation Policy

To qualify for disability services, students are required to provide diagnostic documentation from a licensed clinical professional familiar with the history and functional implications of the impairments. As noted in Chapter 2, disability documentation should adequately verify the nature and extent of the disability in accordance with current professional standards and techniques, and it should clearly substantiate the need for all of the student's specific accommodation requests. All documentation should be submitted on the official letterhead of the professional describing the disability. The report should be dated and signed and include the name, title, and professional credentials of the evaluator, including information about his or her license or certification. If the original documentation is incomplete or inadequate for determining the extent of the disability or reasonable accommodation, the college has the discretion to require additional documentation. Any cost incurred in obtaining additional documentation when the original records are inadequate is borne by the student. If the documentation is complete but the college desires a second professional opinion, the college bears the cost. In general, it is not acceptable for such documentation to include a diagnosis or testing performed by a member of the student's family.

Services Policy

Each core service should have its own set of policies and procedures. Services policies include time lines, roles and responsibilities, and processes. Although not all accommodations and services require explicit policies and procedures, it is wise to develop them for services such as interpreting/captioning, alternative testing, notetaking, and document conversion (e.g., electronic media).

Campus Policies

Campus policies about service animals, emergency evacuation, parking, tele-typewriters (TTYs), assistive listening systems, commencement ceremonies, visitors and guests with disabilities, confidentiality, employee accommodation requests, and appeals/complaints need to be established through a formal process. In turn, this process must be approved by appropriate governing bodies, formally available, and well publicized.

Appeal Process Many campuses falter in their appeal processes. Colleges are required to have adequate, impartial, and timely grievance procedures to respond to complaints of discrimination. Students must be made aware of these procedures, and colleges are required to comply with their own procedures. The following guidelines are recommended:

- Grievance procedures should be published and posted in a clear and conspicuous place.

- Published grievance procedures should be followed carefully.

- Expulsion hearings may be held in any manner deemed reasonably necessary for safety.

- Office of Civil Rights (OCR) complaints generally must be filed within 180 days of discrimination.

- An internal disability grievance must be brought through the appropriate process.

- Internal grievance procedures should be exhausted before filing a complaint with OCR.

- When a college makes an effort to resolve a student's complaint and the student withdraws the OCR complaint, OCR will not investigate.

- Universities must ensure that they comply with Section 504 of the Rehabilitation Act by adopting and publishing grievance procedures and providing a notice of nondiscrimination.

- Once a timely discrimination claim is made to the appropriate agency, the claimant must prove discrimination and overcome any legitimate reasons his or her employer gives for the adverse employment action (LRP Publications, 2003).

PERSONNEL

Professional Standards

Shaw, McGuire, and Madaus (1997) developed standards of professional practice, and Shaw and Dukes (2001) developed program standards that were adopted by AHEAD. Professional practice standards are the skills, abilities, and knowledge that should be required of professionals working in disability services. Program standards are the essential expectations for all postsecondary institutions in terms of minimum supports that must be available to provide equal access for students with disabilities.

Using these program and professional standards as a guide, DSS personnel should engage in 51 activities enabling them to accomplish no less than 27 specific responsibilities. For example, in order to "serve as an advocate for students with disabilities to ensure equal access" (Program Standard 1.1), the DSS program collaborates with the physical plant to ensure modifications to campus facilities (Professional Standard 3.2) and communicates program activities to the campus community (Program Standard 3.6). (For a complete listing, see http://www.ahead.org/about/AHEAD_Professional_Standards.doc for AHEAD's Professional Standards.) Consider some of the tasks and skills a DSS administrator ought to demonstrate: develop program policies and procedures, evaluate program effectiveness, maintain and compile statistical data on students and services, and interpret court and government agency laws and rules. Furthermore, an administrator needs to determine students' program eligibility, determine appropriate services and accommodations, instruct students and campus personnel on roles and responsibilities, consult with faculty to ensure that appropriate accommodations are delivered, and process appeals and complaints that are relevant to the program's services. In addition, this person should also conduct outreach activities for prospective students, train staff on disability issues, and hold memberships in relevant professional organizations to develop and sustain professional peer networks and keep abreast of the latest research.

Staffing

A common ratio professional staff to students is 1:100, although many colleges have survived (but not thrived) with much higher ratios. According to Henderson (2001), approximately 6% of first-time, full-time freshmen attending 4-year institutions in fall 2000 self-reported a disability. However, discussion on the often-used Disabled Student Services in Higher Education e-mail discussion group (DSSHE-L@LISTSERV.buffalo.edu) demonstrates that it is more common for DSS offices to register and serve approximately 2%–3% of enrolled students with disabilities. Thus, on a campus of 10,000 students, the DSS office might serve 200–300 students and should have at least two professional staff members. This does not include administrative support personnel or service providers such as interpreters, notetakers, or proctors.

Positions in DSS offices tend to be defined by disability type or by job function. Examples of a disability-defined position are learning disabilities counselor or blind/low vision specialist. Functional positions are accommodation or disability specialist, support services coordinator, and adaptive technology specialist.

The most mystifying and vexing personnel issue in disability services is the recruitment, hiring, and supervising of interpreters and captioners. Finding a balance between hiring interpreters/captioners who work on an hourly basis and employing them as salaried staff is confounding and challenging. These services are expensive, and practitioners vary from those determined to be contractual, those who are freelance entrepreneurs, and those who want an employer–employee relationship. Work standards, hourly rates, confidentiality, and parking are some of common issues in the hiring process. For example, some freelance interpreters may view their relationship being as between the students (consumers) and themselves and not with the college. Agreeing on payment for travel, preparation time, no-shows, and dropped courses can be contentious. Determining when two interpreters need to be assigned for a class or an event has both human and financial resource ramifications. Seasoned DSS directors with more than 20 years experience continue to face the challenges of delivering quality services to students who are deaf or hard of hearing while maintaining their budgets and level of services to students with other types of disabilities.

A good resource is the Postsecondary Education Programs Network (PEPNet) (http://www.pepnet.org). PEPNet is a national collaboration of the four Regional Postsecondary Education Centers for Individuals who are Deaf and Hard of Hearing. The Centers are supported by contracts with the U.S. Department of Education's Office of Special Education and Rehabilitative Services. PEPNet's goals are twofold: assisting postsecondary institutions across the nation to attract students with hearing impairments and effectively serving students who are deaf and hard of hearing.

ADA only requires that accommodations be effective; it does not prescribe how this can be accomplished. Accommodations are often mandated, but there is nothing preventing the use of volunteers or other unpaid staff to carry out accommodations. Many colleges use volunteers and interns to augment their meager ranks. On some small campuses (fewer than 3,500 students), committees often serve in an assistive capacity to what is generally a staff of one or two people. Examples of descriptions for such jobs are found on various online bulletin boards.

Americans with Disabilities Act Coordinators

Every college should have an ADA coordinator. This person tends to serve one of two roles: compliance officer or consultant. In far too many cases, these roles are combined, creating the uncomfortable situation of having one person both give advice (consultant) and then evaluate the appropriateness of the advice (compliance officer) when a complaint is filed. It is far better to separate these two functions. ADA coordinators are often the key to enhancing—or thwarting—the overall campus climate for people with disabilities. It is an important role and requires administrative recognition at a senior administrative level.

BUDGET

Providing services and accommodations to students with disabilities is sometimes referred to as an "unfunded mandate." This means that an institution is required to provide certain services for which it receives no direct funding. Another way of looking at it is that accommodating students is simply sound pedagogy. Why would postsecondary schools not want to provide students who are blind or who have low vision with print in alternative formats, or to ensure that students who are deaf understand lectures, or to give students with learning disabilities ample time to explain their understanding of course material? What makes accommodating students complicated is often not expense but, rather, students who do things differently and educational institutions that do not always deal well with such differences.

The previous discussion about personnel mentioned that 2%–3% of a student body could be expected to seek services. The University of Wisconsin System's annual DSS report, *Big Ten Universities Informal Annual Surveys*, and a survey of large colleges (enrollments greater than 15,000) conducted by Bonnie Martin (2001) of Clemson University consistently show that in large colleges, after removing expenses for students who are deaf, the average cost per student with a disability is less than $1,000 per year. Interpreter/captioning services for students who are deaf, however, can cost well over $20,000 per year.

Types of Funding

Funding sources for disability services include university general funds, federal grants, student fees, and private contributions. General university funds are the most common source of funding. For state institutions, this typically means general-purpose revenues received through the legislative budget process supporting state higher education.

In 1965, Congress began creating a series of programs to help Americans overcome class and social barriers to higher education. These services, geared toward low-income and first-generation students, were called Special Programs for Students from Disadvantaged Backgrounds. Today, they are known as the Federal TRIO Programs. Congress initially authorized most of the programs in the Higher Education Act of 1965 (PL 89-329) and its subsequent amendments. After their authorization, Congress appropriated money for the programs. One of the TRIO programs is Student Support Services, which helps low-income and first-generation college students and individuals with disabilities graduate from college. Services include assistance with securing financial aid; personal, academic, and career counseling; academic instruction; assistance with making the transition from 2-year to 4-year institutions; assistance with applying to graduate and professional programs; and activities specially designed for students with limited English proficiency (see http://www.trioprograms.org/clearinghouse/shared/DoYouKnowTRIOSheet1.doc for more information).

The Carl D. Perkins Vocational and Applied Technology Education Act (PL 98-524) is federal legislation that provides more than a billion dollars nationally in funds for vocational-technical education programs at the secondary and postsecondary levels. Funds are directed to programs that provide academic and occupational skills to participants, including "special populations" (see http://www.state.co.us/gov_dir/wdc/pubs/TEsection_iv_perkins.htm for more information).

On occasion, a college may partially support disability services by means of student fees, similar to fees that support health services, recreation, and/ or technology services. Finally, ambitious administrators may tap into philanthropic campus efforts to include disability service needs in capital campaigns and other fund-raising initiatives.

Fixed and Variable Expenses

Accommodations are usually not expensive: 71% of job accommodations cost less than $500 (Job Accommodation Network, 2004), and 69% of people with disabilities do not need special equipment to do their jobs effectively (Stoddard, Jans, Ripple, & Kraus, 1998). College students' needs and accommodations are comparable to the needs that they will experience in the workplace.

Tracking accommodation costs can most easily be accomplished by dividing a disability services budget into two separate budgets: one for fixed costs, the other for variable costs. Fixed costs are known and predictable expenses that can accurately be budgeted. Salaries, supplies and expenses, capital equipment, and student help are fixed costs. Variable costs are expenses associated with direct services that are dependent on the number of students and the frequency of requests. Interpreting/captioning, notetaking, document conversion, adaptive materials, and proctors for alternative testing are examples of direct services with variable costs.

Separating fixed from variable expenses allows a clear understanding of actual costs for direct services and actual costs for staffing and infrastructure. For example, if all funds are commingled and the expenses for notetaking services exceed the budgeted amount, funds from another line, such as student help or office supplies, would be tapped to cover these unanticipated and unpredicted overruns. At year's end, it may appear that a deficit occurred in one line (student help) when in actuality it was in direct services (notetaking). Separating fixed from variable expenses allows for better tracking of actual costs in specific areas.

During the 2002–2003 fiscal year the University of Wisconsin System— composed of 13 4-year colleges and one college system of 13 small, locally owned campuses—provided services to 4,054 students with disabilities. This equaled 2.5% of the entire system's enrollment of 160,635 students. Total expenses were $4,077,236—of which $1,132,931 (28%) was for costs for variable expenses assistance (interpreting/captioning, notetaking, document conversion, laboratory/library, adaptive materials, and alternative testing); $844,511 (75%) was for interpreting/captioning for 58 students who were deaf (1.4% of all students with disabilities). The average cost for each full-time student who was deaf (in which one student who was deaf = 24 credits a year of interpreting or captioning services) was $19,193. The average cost for all other students was just over $800 per year. Average annual costs for other services included notetaking ($183 per student); document conversion—that is, taping or providing adaptive materials ($288); and alternative testing ($86).

Clearly, other than interpreting and/or captioning services, services to students with disabilities incur modest costs.

Predicting Direct Services Expenses

Using the previously described 2%–3% figure, it is possible to predict fixed costs for providing staffing and infrastructure in a disability services program. Using the figures from the University of Wisconsin System gives a rough idea of per-student and per-service costs. Accurately predicting services expenses for individuals who are deaf is key to budget planning, due to the enormous per-student cost for this disability. One method of calculating costs for services for people who are deaf is to obtain a per-credit cost for interpreting and captioning services. A baseline year is needed for even approximate accuracy. The University of Wisconsin System data for 2002–2003 indicated the costs for providing interpreting services to be $835 per credit. Therefore, a full-time Deaf student (i.e., one carrying 24 credits per year) using interpreting services averaged $20,047, with the median being $23,648.

To obtain a per-credit cost, one divides the number of credits in which students who are deaf are enrolled by the total expenses for services in a given year. For example, in 2002–2003, 45 students who were deaf took 859 credits (also called units). Interpreting expenses for this period were $717,314, or $835 per credit. This calculation is replicated to obtain a per-credit cost for captioning services. When a new student who is deaf arrives on campus and accommodation decisions are made regarding interpreting and/or captioning—and an assessment is made as to the likely number of credits in which the student will enroll—an estimate of costs can be obtained.

Because some students take one class per term and others take five or six, it is far more accurate to develop a calculation based on credits than on actual numbers of students. One warning, though: Students in programs requiring internships or practicum distort predictions. A traditional credit is approximately 3 hours of class per week, whereas an internship could be 20 hours per week and 3 credits. One solution is to convert internship or practicum hours into credits to get a more accurate prediction of anticipated costs.

PROGRAM EVALUATION

Too often, practitioners view program evaluation as an onerous add-on couched in a foreign language—the language of the professional program evaluator. Contrary to this misperception, ongoing evaluations of specific services and the overall program are, or at least should be, critical to success. DSS programs and DSS staff are not an institutional expense, although many decision makers might consider them to be. Rather, DSS programs and staff are a value-added service, in that effective DSS programs and services promote student retention, academic success, and program completion. These outcomes add to the institutional variables often measured (and valued) by administrators and policy makers. These variables include credits attempted versus credits attained, cumulative grade point average, year-to-year reenrollment, and program completion/graduation. For many institutions, state support (funding) is tied directly to these outcomes. Thus, retention of students with disabilities brings in revenue—that is, support from state and/or local tax revenue, not to mention continued tuition revenue from students who continue their courses of study until they complete a program.

As part of the program evaluation process, students should be surveyed annually for their satisfaction levels and comments. DSS programs themselves should undergo a comprehensive review at least once every decade. To help focus program evaluation efforts more succinctly on key student process and outcome variables, DSS programs should consider systematically addressing GOALS that are SMART (Gugerty & Foley, 2004). Each of the GOALS— knowledge, behavior, attitudes, skills, and aspirations—should be SMART— that is, specific, measurable, attainable, results oriented, and time specific. Including evaluation as an integral component of program/service delivery, and framing it in terms of SMART GOALS, will result in an increased focus on measurable, attainable goals and objectives throughout the program.

Data Collection and Annual Reports

Data are crucial for policy and program planning, as well as for advocacy efforts. Systematic data collection can

- Document the successes and needs of students with disabilities
- Provide information on existing resources and identify gaps in services
- Inform policy and program planning
- Allow for comparisons across colleges and states or with a national average
- Help plan for improvements and set benchmarks for the future
- Offer justification for and accountability around the use of public funds or leverage other resources
- Advocate for policy and program changes when necessary

The basic information needed for a disability services program involves the numbers and types of students with disabilities served and the associated costs. Although disability classifications vary considerably, most colleges use the following categories: visual (e.g., blind, low vision), hearing (e.g., deaf, hard of hearing), mobility/physical (e.g., spinal cord injuries, neuromuscular disorders, other conditions in which mobility is the primary limitation), learning, psychiatric/psychological, health (e.g., cardiovascular/pulmonary diseases, blood diseases, multiple organ system disorders, bone and joint diseases), and temporary (e.g., broken bones, severe muscular sprains, recovery periods after illness or surgery, hospitalization due to illness or surgery). Due to an increase in prevalence, two other conditions have emerged as distinct categories for tracking: attention deficit disorder (ADD)/attention-deficit/hyperactivity disorder (ADHD) and autism spectrum disorder.

Data are also needed on budget, sources of funding, and expenses. In addition to overall program costs, it is helpful to document costs for specific auxiliary aids and services, including (but not limited to) notetaking, document conversion, interpreting/captioning, and alternative testing. Additional programs and services, if offered, should also be tracked. These include tutoring, assistive technology, transportation, physical therapy, diagnostic assessment, adaptive equipment, and mobility orientation and training. It is also useful to include information on staffing, particularly professional full-time equivalent positions, in order to benchmark student–staff ratios.

For a detailed description of program evaluation processes, see Brinckerhoff, McGuire, and Shaw (2002, pp. 462–483). An extensive collection of program evaluation resources has also been compiled by Gibson and Gugerty (2003, 2004) and made available in CD-ROM format. These resources cover all aspects of program evaluation design and implementation and integration of results into program improvement.

FUTURE TRENDS AND CHALLENGES

Technology

Access to web-based information, electronic conversion of print materials, and remote captioning and interpreting are significant issues facing disability providers. See Chapter 9 for details on advances in assistive technology and the accompanying challenges.

Funding

Many colleges once relied on state vocational rehabilitation (VR) agencies to provide funding for auxiliary aids and services such as interpreting, braille, and notetaking. In recent years, there has been a national trend for state VR agencies not to provide funding for accommodations and services to their clients attending institutions of higher education. Although some federal monies are available (most notably TRIO program dollars; see http://www.ed.gov/about/offices/list/ope/trio/index.html), there are precious few opportunities for outside funding to cover basic services. Colleges need to identify internal operating funds to support DSS programs. The cost of providing services to students who are deaf and hard of hearing are expected to rise for the following reasons: 1) students who are hard of hearing and previously got by with inexpensive notetakers will likely desire and request the more effective and expensive CART services and 2) increased incidents of repetitive motion syndrome among interpreters means assigning two interpreters for classes in which one interpreter used to be sufficient.

Testing Accommodations

Chapter 6 examines the role of universal design in instruction and testing students' knowledge of course material. This is a laudable arena for experimenting with universal design. Students with learning disabilities comprise the largest group of students requesting overall accommodations. For these students, the most sought after accommodation is more time on exams. If it were no longer necessary to limit exams to a certain time space, the single largest issues in disabilities services would be resolved.

Defining Who Is Eligible for Services

At one time, the most controversial issue in providing services revolved around whether certain accommodations were reasonable. Because the U.S. Supreme Court has since issued several options on disability cases, the focus has become whether the individual requesting services is in fact a person with a disability. Most Supreme Court decisions have determined that the individual does not have a disability and thus is not eligible for accommodations. Most DSS programs were developed prior to this body of court cases that has narrowed the definition of *disability*. It may be time for administrators to reexamine policies and procedures.

Developing New Students' Academic and Survival Skills

The demand for summer school in the K–12 arena has dramatically increased since the early 1990s (Boss & Railsback, 2002), as has the recognition that there is a significant "summer skills slide" attributed to students who take the summer off (Boss & Railsback, 2002) and the dawning realization that this skills slide can be minimized or prevented (e.g., Borman, 2001; Borman & Boulay, 2004). At the postsecondary level, however, the possibility of a summer skills slide between completion of secondary education and entrance into postsecondary education, and the implications of that skills slide for students with disabilities, has not received comparable attention. For example, Mull, Sitlington, and Alper (2001) made a comprehensive synthesis of 26 research articles published in peer-reviewed journals from 1985–2000 that recommended or reported on postsecondary education services for students with learning disabilities; summer preparation programs/services were not a component. Conway (2003–2004) described approaches designed to improve postsecondary education access and results for youths with disabilities. Her success strategies did not include summer orientation and/or preparation programs designed to prevent summer skills slides and to increase readiness for postsecondary education among youth with disabilities.

Should it be inferred that summer preparation and transition programs are not worth the time and expense needed to establish and operate them? Not necessarily. Rather, data indicate precisely the opposite. The dropout/noncompletion rates among postsecondary students with disabilities are totally unacceptable. As reported by Wolanin and Steele (2004), 73% of students with disabilities enroll in higher education, compared with 84% of their peers without disabilities; only 28% of students with disabilities achieve diplomas in 4-year public institutions, compared with 54% of their peers without disclosed disabilities. In addition, Carey (2004) reported that one in five postsecondary students (not just those with identified disabilities) who start as full-time, first-time freshmen in public, 4-year institutions take at least one remedial reading, writing, or math course. These are courses for which the students pay tuition, but the courses do not count toward a degree or other credential. As Carey (2004) described, the consequences of this weak preparation are severe. Remedial students are much less likely to graduate, particularly if they need help in reading.

Some institutions of higher education have recognized the importance of formal summer transition/preparation programs designed to level the playing field for students with disclosed disabilities. For example, the George Washington University HEATH Resource Center (2004) compiled a list of 15 summer precollege programs for students with disabilities who seek ways to prepare for college and thus enhance their chances of success. Brinckerhoff et al. (2002, pp. 286–292) described procedures to set up and operate summer transition programs. As part of their online professional development course, Gibson and Gugerty (2003, 2004) have vetted and compiled more than 250 resources that practitioners can use to design, operate, and evaluate summer preparation programs for new students with disabilities.

There is much room for improvement in the postsecondary completion rates of students with disabilities. Strong evidence shows that the summer skills slide exists (for K–12 students), and documentation indicates that new postsecondary students who take remedial courses after enrollment are much more likely to attain diplomas than those who do not take such courses. Therefore, colleges and universities might explore formal summer transition/preparation opportunities for their new students with disabilities as a value-added factor.

CONCLUSION

This chapter's "Mission Statements" section outlines the primary roles of DSS programs. DSS programs can most effectively fulfill these roles when they do the following: arise from a strong institutional commitment and pursue a clearly articulated mission; create program and professional standards based on existing publishing criteria; clearly define who is eligible for which services; develop and disseminate clear, concise, and equitable policies; hire competent, well-trained personnel; and receive and judiciously expend adequate funding based on accurate assessment of numbers and types of students on campus.

REFERENCES

Adams State College, Office of Student Affairs' Disability Services Program. (n.d.). *Mission statement.* Retrieved May 18, 2005, from http://www.sa.adams.edu/mission%20and%20 objectives.htm

Americans with Disabilities Act (ADA) of 1990, PL 101-336, 42 U.S.C. §§ 12101 *et seq.*

Borman, G.D. (2001). Summers are for learning. *Principal, 80*(3), 26–29.

Borman, G.D., & Boulay, M. (Eds.). (2004). *Summer learning: Research, policies, and programs.* Mahwah, NJ: Lawrence Erlbaum Associates.

Boss, S., & Railsback, J. (2002). *Summer school programs: A look at the research, implications for practice, and program sampler.* Portland, OR: Northwest Regional Educational Laboratory.

Brinckerhoff, L.C., McGuire, J.M., & Shaw, S.F. (2002). *Postsecondary education and transition for students with learning disabilities* (2nd ed.). Austin, TX: PRO-ED.

Brown, J.T. (1994). Effective disability support services program. In D. Ryan & M. McCarthy (Eds.), *A student affairs guide to the ADA and disability issues* (pp. 98–110). Washington, DC: National Association of Student Personnel Administrators.

California State University–Chico, Disability Support Services. (n.d.). *Role of disability support services.* Retrieved May 18, 2005, from http://www.csuchico.edu/dss/fh_role.htm

Carey, K. (2004). A matter of degrees: Improving graduation rates in four-year colleges and universities. *National Educational Longitudinal Survey, 88,* 1–20.

Carl D. Perkins Vocational and Applied Technology Education Act, PL 98-524, 98 Stat. 2435, 20 U.S.C. §§ 2301 *et seq.*

Conway, M.A. (2003–2004, Fall/Winter). Improving postsecondary education access and results for youth with disabilities. *Impact, 16*(3), 8–9.

Dukes, L. (2001). The process: The development of the AHEAD's program standards. *Journal of Postsecondary Education and Disability, 14*(2), 62–80.

The George Washington University HEATH Resource Center. (2004). *Summer pre-college programs for students with disabilities.* Washington, DC: Author.

Getzel, E.E., McManus, S., & Briel, L.W. (2004). An effective model for college students with learning disabilities and attention deficit hyperactivity disorders. *Research to Practice Brief, 3*(1), 1–6.

Gibson, C.C., & Gugerty, J.J. (2003, May). *From here to there* [CD-ROM for on-line version, developed with permission of original authors from the print document of the same name]. Madison: University of Wisconsin Center on Education and Work.

Gibson, C.C., & Gugerty, J.J. (2004, Spring). *Success from the start: Preparing Students with disabilities for their first semester of colleges—Resources.* Madison: University of Wisconsin Center on Education and Work.

Gugerty, J.J., & Foley, C. (2004, April 15). *Success from the start: Preparing students for their first semester in college.* Paper presented at the 2004 Council for Exceptional Children's Annual Convention and Expo, New Orleans, LA.

Henderson, C. (2001). *College freshman with disabilities: A biennial statistical profile.* Retrieved June 16, 2004, from http://www.heath.gwu.edu/PDFs/collegefreshmen.pdf

Higher Education Act of 1965, PL 89-329, 20 U.S.C. § 1001 *et seq.*

Job Accommodation Network. (2004). *Low cost accommodation solutions.* Retrieved January 14, 2005, from http://www.jan.wvu.edu/media/LowCostSolutions.html

Kroeger, S., & Schuck, J. (1993, Winter). Essential elements in services delivery. In S. Kroeger & J. Schuck (Eds.), *Responding to disability issues in student affairs: New directions for student affairs, 64* (p. 67). San Francisco: Jossey-Bass.

Lehmann, J.P., Davies, T.G., & Laurin, K.M. (2000). Listening to student voices about postsecondary education. *Teaching Exceptional Children, 32*(5), 60–65.

LRP Publications. (2003, August). Make sure grievance procedures are prompt, equitable. *Disability Compliance for Higher Education.* Horsham, PA: Author.

Martin, B.S. (2001). *Survey of disability services of top 20 public universities.* Unpublished manuscript, Clemson University's Student Disability Services Program, Clemson, SC.

Mooney, J., & Cole, D. (2000). *Learning outside the lines.* New York: Simon & Schuster.

Mull, C., Sitlington, P.L., & Alper, S. (2001). Postsecondary education for students with learning disabilities: A synthesis of the literature. *Council for Exceptional Children, 68*(1), 97–118.

National Center for Study of Postsecondary Educational Supports. (n.d.). *Postsecondary education and employment for students with disabilities: Focus group discussion on supports and barriers in lifelong learning.* Honolulu, HI: Author.

Rehabilitation Act of 1973, PL 93-112, 29 U.S.C. § 794.

Rodis, P., Garrod, A., & Boscardin, M.L. (Eds.). (2001). *Learning disabilities and life stories.* Boston: Allyn & Bacon.

Roessler, R.T., & Kirk, H.M. (1998). Improving technology training services in postsecondary education: Perspectives of recent college graduates with disabilities. *Journal of Postsecondary Education and Disability, 13*(3), 48–59.

Shaw, S.F., & Dukes, L. (2001). Program standards for disability services in higher education. *Journal of Postsecondary Education and Disability, 14*(2), 81–89.

Shaw, S.F., McGuire, J.M., & Madaus, J.W. (1997). Standards of professional practice. *Journal of Postsecondary Education and Disability, 12*(3), 26–35.

Skinner, M.E. (2004). College students with learning disabilities speak out: What it takes to be successful in postsecondary education. *Journal of Postsecondary Education and Disability, 17*(3), 91–104.

Stoddard, S., Jans, L., Ripple, J., & Kraus, L. (1998). *Chartbook on work and disability in the United States, 1998* (an InfoUse Report). Retrieved January 14, 2005, from http://www.infouse.com/disabilitydata/workdisability/4_5.php

University of Mary Washington, Disability Services. (2004). *Our mission.* Retrieved May 18, 2005, from http://www.umw.edu/disability/resources/instructor/our_mission.php

University of Massachusetts–Boston, The Ross Center for Disability Services. (2002). *Philosophy and mission statement.* Retrieved May 18, 2005, from http://www.rosscenter.umb.edu/fh1.shtml

The University of North Carolina at Chapel Hill, Disability Services. (2004). *Mission statement.* Retrieved May 18, 2005, from http://disabilityservices.unc.edu/welcome

Whelley, T., & Yeganeh, M. (n.d.). *Students speak: Stories of postsecondary education.* Manoa, HI: National Center for the Study of Postsecondary Educational Supports.

Wolanin, T.R., & Steele, P.E. (2004). *Higher education for students with disabilities: A primer for policymakers.* Washington, DC: The Institute for Higher Education Policy.

Creating a Welcoming Environment Through Design and Implementation

Implementing Universal Design for Instruction to Promote Inclusive College Teaching

Sally S. Scott and Joan M. McGuire

Lynn Bennett, newly hired as an assistant professor of education, felt butterflies in her stomach as she walked to her first class. She had completed her doctoral program in July and arrived at her new home the following month, enthused and ready to start off on her professional career. She had impeccable credentials in research for someone so young, and she had completed a term as a teaching assistant with one of the best-known scholars in the field. As she approached the podium for her Introduction to Educational Psychology course, she was glad that she had prepared thoroughly for the class. She was using a familiar textbook from her graduate training and had created a syllabus delineating time lines and expectations. She looked at the 125 students in the auditorium and managed a smile before launching into her welcoming comments and lecture for the day.

The 50-minute period went rapidly, and Lynn felt a surge of relief as she made her closing comments. A few times during the lecture, she had noticed that some of the students looked bored, and she was irritated that one student kept asking her to repeat information or to spell educational terms. She made a note to herself that she would have to think about how to address these issues before next week's class. She reflected that the lecture must have gone well enough, though, because when she asked if there were any questions, no one raised a hand. She sighed, looked at her watch, and felt satisfied that she had 15 minutes to get across campus for the committee meeting she needed to attend. As she gathered up her notes, she was surprised that several students stayed behind to speak with her. Their comments and questions included the following:

- "I need to miss the first test because of my work schedule. Is that a problem?"

- "I have a learning disability and need you to make an announcement in class to find a notetaker for me."

- "Starting next week, I have to leave early to catch the bus to pick up my child at the child care center before it closes."

- "Can I make an appointment to talk with you about taking tests in a separate room and having additional time to complete them?"

In addition, two students handed Lynn letters on letterhead from the Office for Students with Disabilities—what was this about? She would have to follow up later, as the students left without giving an explanation. Her head was spinning. She thought she was prepared and had made her expectations clear in her syllabus. These requests and exceptions seemed chaotic and unreasonable. Did the students think that they could take advantage of her because she was new, or were these legitimate requests? She was late for her committee meeting now and would have to hurry.

INCREASING DIVERSITY OF COLLEGE STUDENTS

Dr. Bennett has just been introduced to the increasingly diverse college student population. Student demographic data reveal that a variety of factors are changing the complexion of college classrooms. Nearly 40% of the student population is 25 years of age or older; 34% are attending college part time; 31% of college students come from ethnic backgrounds that differ from the majority; and 12% more women than men are enrolled; in addition, the rate of enrollment among international students increased 20% from 1998 to 2000 (*The Chronicle of Higher Education*, 2003).

Students with both visible and "invisible" disabilities are also represented in the growing diversity of college students. In a longitudinal study of full-time, first-time college freshmen, Henderson (1999) noted that student self-report of a disability rose from 2.3% in 1978 to 9.8% in 1998. Numerous conditions are included in the category *disability*, such as speech, orthopedic, hearing, and health-related disabilities; the largest category of disability, however, is learning disabilities, representing 41% of college students with disabilities.

Across categories of disability, this largest group is still far from homogeneous. These students also represent various ages, ethnicities, genders, and levels of income (Henderson, 1999). As professionals in higher education increasingly acknowledge the educational value of diversity on college campuses (American Council on Education, 2000; American Council on Education and American Association of University Professors, 2000), faculty must recognize the implications of student diversity for the design and delivery of instruction.

TRADITIONAL APPROACHES TO INSTRUCTIONAL ACCESS

For many years, the instructional needs of college students with disabilities have been addressed within the context of legal mandates for nondiscrimination.

Legislation, including the Americans with Disabilities Act (ADA) of 1990 (PL 101-336) and Section 504 of the Rehabilitation Act of 1973 (PL 93-112), established that qualified students with disabilities are entitled to equal access to postsecondary education. Typical approaches to nondiscrimination consist of accommodating the regular class procedures for instruction and assessment. For example, a college's accommodation procedures might require a student with a disability to identify his or her disability to the class instructor within the first few weeks of class, provide documentation to authorized campus disability professionals that verifies eligibility for accommodations, request specific accommodations based on the manifestations of the disability, and wait for adjustments to be implemented (e.g., confirming and clarifying coordination with the college disability support services office, obtaining a notetaker, identifying a reader).

This approach has been valuable and important for nondiscriminatory treatment, but retrofitting classroom instruction for only some students has some inherent pitfalls. As illustrated in the opening case example, frequently requested classroom accommodations, such as extra time on tests or the provision of a notetaker in class, are retrofits to a course that minimize the impact of a disability. Although such accommodations emanate from civil rights law and are nondiscriminatory in intent, they are rarely based on pedagogical decisions by faculty concerning the best way to promote student learning. Indeed, faculty have reported concerns that such after-the-fact changes to instruction and assessment of learning may risk lowering standards, compromising academic integrity, and being unfair to classmates without disabilities (Leyser, Vogel, Wyland, & Brulle, 1998; Scott & Gregg, 2000).

Students with disabilities report that there are limitations to the current system of retrofitted accommodations as well. In multiple student focus groups reflecting diverse institutions and geographical areas (Madaus, Scott, & McGuire, 2002b; National Center for the Study of Postsecondary Educational Supports, 2000), students with disabilities reported difficulties in attaining accommodations and negative attitudes of faculty, leading to frustration with the current system of self-identifying and advocating for modified treatment in the classroom based on a disability.

Is there another way to achieve a nondiscriminatory learning environment for college students with disabilities? Might the field be able to broaden the vision of inclusive classrooms through the proactive design of instruction that is inclusive of students with disabilities and an even broader range of diverse learners?

UNIVERSAL DESIGN FOR INSTRUCTION

Universal Design for Instruction (UDI) is a new paradigm for addressing diverse learning needs in college settings. It is an approach to teaching that consists of the proactive design and use of inclusive instructional strategies that benefit a broad range of learners, including those with cognitive disabilities (e.g., learning disabilities, attention-deficit/hyperactivity disorder, traumatic brain injury) (Scott, McGuire, & Embry, 2002). UDI is designed to support faculty in the challenging process of planning and delivering instruction that is responsive to diverse learning needs and offers an alternative to retrofitting changes that accommodate only those students with documented disabilities.

The Development of Universal Design for Instruction

From 1999 to 2003, efforts to support faculty in ensuring equal opportunities for instructional access have received increasing attention, in part because of two cycles of grant funding from the U.S. Office of Postsecondary Education. By virtue of grant awards in each funding cycle, the Center for Postsecondary Education and Disability (CPED) at the University of Connecticut is actively engaged in the development of the construct of UDI. Expanding on the work of Silver, Bourke, and Strehorn (1998), who introduced the concept of universal design (UD) for the instructional milieu of higher education, CPED envisions and is developing an approach to teaching that supports faculty in proactively building in strategies that expand opportunities for learning access.

A multifaceted approach has guided CPED's work on this new paradigm, including consideration of the theory base of UD and literature on effective instruction. The concept of *universal design*, a term coined in the early 1970s by Ronald Mace (founder of the Center for Universal Design at North Carolina State University), emanated from the fields of architecture and product design. UD is defined as the design of products and environments to be usable by all people to the greatest extent possible (The Center for Universal Design, 1997). Designers and architects embracing UD assert that they have a responsibility to proactively consider human diversity in the design of public spaces so that resulting environments and products are usable by the intended audience: the diverse public (Welch, 1995; Wilkoff & Abed, 1994).

When principles of UD are applied to the physical environment, adaptations are built in rather than added on as an afterthought. These modifications benefit a broad range of users. For example, a ramp to a building is viewed as an accommodation for an individual using a wheelchair, but it is also useful for a parent pushing a baby stroller or a delivery person carrying large packages. When the ramp is an integral component of the architectural and landscape designs from the outset, aesthetics of the building are not compromised, and its usability by the public is broadened. Other examples of UD include the use of large-print signage (benefiting older adults, individuals with visual impairments, or people in a hurry); electronic door openers; and adjusted-height elevator call buttons, drinking fountains, and public telephones (increasing usability by individuals in wheelchairs, children, and people of short stature). UD, therefore, entails awareness of human diversity, anticipation of a variety of needs, and an intentional approach to designing an inclusive environment (The Center for Universal Design, 1997; Covington & Hannah, 1997).

Applying the concept of UD to instruction in higher education is powerful. As faculty anticipate the predictable diversity of students in their classrooms, they can approach planning and delivering instruction and assessing student learning in a manner that is more inclusive. This proactive design results in an instructional environment that is more universally designed and usable by a broader range of students while maintaining the aesthetics of the product (i.e., the academic integrity of the course). The principles of UD as adapted and applied to college instruction provide tools for addressing disability access and other legitimate student needs in a proactive way; they preserve the integrity of a course while promoting learning by diverse students. A component of CPED's work has been establishing a foundation based in the literature to explore more universal approaches to instruction that can guide faculty as they reflect on their pedagogy and expand their approaches to inclusive teaching.

In addition to a foundation in UD, development of the construct of UDI has been informed by literature bases regarding effective instruction in higher education and by effective instruction for students with learning disabilities in both secondary and postsecondary educational settings (Scott, McGuire, & Foley, 2003). CPED included the area of students with learning disabilities because these students, by definition, represent a broad range of learning and cognitive differences that often challenge traditional notions of college instruction. Several references emerged as seminal resources for practice in the areas of postsecondary instruction and instructional strategies for students with learning disabilities:

- Chickering and Gamson's (1987) *Seven Principles of Good Practice in Undergraduate Education* (see also Chickering & Ehrmann, 1996; Cross, 1998)

- The work of Kame'enui and Carnine (1998) at the University of Oregon National Center to Improve the Tools of Educators (NCITE)

- The work of the Center for Applied Special Technology (CAST) in the area of Universal Design (Center for Applied Special Technology, 2003; Orkwis & McLane, 1998)

By extrapolating from the Principles of Universal Design (The Center for Universal Design, 1997) and infusing elements from the work of Chickering and Gamson, NCITE, and CAST, the resulting Principles of UDI were articulated. (For a detailed description of the construct development process, see Scott et al., 2003.)

The Principles of Universal Design for Instruction

As faculty reflect on their teaching in increasingly diverse classrooms, particularly on planning and delivering instruction and assessing student learning, they should consider the nine principles that comprise the framework for implementing UDI (McGuire & Scott, 2002; Scott, McGuire, & Shaw, 2001; Shaw, Scott, & McGuire, 2001). These Principles of UDI and examples of their application in the college classroom are presented in Table 6.1.

Table 6.1. The Nine Principles of Universal Design for Instruction (UDI)

Principle	Definition	Example(s)
Principle 1: Equitable Use	Instruction is designed to be useful to and accessible by people with diverse abilities. Provide the same means of use for all students—identical whenever possible, equivalent when not.	Class notes are provided on line. Comprehensive notes are available, to which all students have access in the same manner, regardless of hearing ability, English proficiency, learning or attention disorders, or notetaking skill level. In an electronic format, students can utilize whatever individual assistive technology is needed to read, hear, or study the class notes.
Principle 2: Flexibility in Use	Instruction is designed to accommodate a wide range of individual abilities. Choice is provided in the methods of use.	Varied instructional methods (e.g., a lecture with a visual outline, group activities, use of stories, web-board based discussions) are used to provide different ways of learning and expressing knowledge.
Principle 3: Simple and Intuitive	Instruction is designed in a straightforward and predictable manner, regardless of the student's experience, knowledge, language skills, or current concentration level. Unnecessary complexity is eliminated.	A grading rubric is provided that clearly lays out expectations for exam performance, papers, or projects. A syllabus is provided with comprehensive and accurate information. A handbook is provided to guide students through difficult homework assignments.
Principle 4: Perceptible Information	Instruction is designed so that necessary information is communicated effectively to the student, regardless of ambient conditions or the student's sensory abilities.	Textbooks, reading material, and other instructional supports are in a digital format or on line so students with diverse needs (e.g., vision impairments, learning or attention disorders, English as a second language) can gain access to the materials through the traditional hard copy or with the use of various technological supports (e.g., screen reader, text enlarger, on-line dictionary).
Principle 5: Tolerance for Error	Instruction anticipates variation in individual students' learning pace and prerequisite skills.	A long-term course project is structured so that students have the option of turning in individual project components separately for constructive feedback and for integration into the final product. On-line "practice" exercises are provided to supplement classroom instruction.
Principle 6: Low Physical Effort	Instruction minimizes nonessential physical effort in order to allow maximum attention to learning. (*Note:* This principle does not apply when physical effort is integral to essential requirements of a course [e.g., lifting requirements in a physical therapy program]).	Students are allowed to use a word processor for writing and editing papers or essay exams, thereby facilitating document editing without the additional physical exertion of rewriting portions of text. This is helpful for students with fine motor or handwriting difficulties or extreme organizational weaknesses and for those who are more adept at and comfortable with composing on a computer.
Principle 7: Size and Space for Approach and Use	Instruction is designed with consideration for appropriate size and space for approach, reach, manipulations, and use regardless of a student's body size, posture, mobility, and communication needs.	In small class settings, a circular seating arrangement is used to allow students to see and face speakers during discussion—an important component for students who have attention-deficit/hyperactivity disorder or hearing impairments.

Principle 8: A Community of Learners	The instructional environment promotes interaction and communication among students and between students and faculty.	Communication among students is fostered in and out of class by structuring study groups, discussion groups, e-mail lists, or chat rooms.
		Personal connections with students and motivational strategies are used to encourage student performance through learning students' names or individually acknowledging excellent performance.
Principle 9: Instructional Climate	Instruction is designed to be welcoming and inclusive. High expectations are espoused for all students.	A statement in the class syllabus affirms the need for class members to respect diversity in order to establish the expectation of tolerance as well as to encourage students to discuss any special learning needs with the instructor.
		The instructor highlights diverse thinkers who have made significant contributions to the field or shares innovative approaches developed by students in the class.

From Scott, S.S., McGuire, J.M, & Shaw, S.F. (2001). *Principles of Universal Design for Instruction* (pp. 1–2). Storrs: University of Connecticut, Center on Postsecondary Education and Disability; © 2001 S.S. Scott, J.M. McGuire, & S.F. Shaw; adapted by permission.

Although each example in Table 6.1 demonstrates an application of a principle, the examples are not necessarily universal in reflecting all nine principles; rather, they illustrate the intent of the principle under consideration. The Principles of UDI form a framework to inform faculty planning and practice rather than a rigid procedure or prescription for instruction. To illustrate the application of the principles, elaboration on several examples from Table 6.1 is useful.

Principle 2, Flexibility in Use, posits that instruction is designed to accommodate a wide range of individual abilities. This principle can apply both to the delivery of instruction (e.g., using multiple methods: lectures, small group activities, on-line exercises, cooperative learning exercises) and to the assessment of student learning. Heterogeneity, a hallmark of diverse classrooms, encompasses students' background knowledge and experiences. In designing methods for assessing student learning of content, providing multiple options for demonstrating mastery can tap into areas of student strength. For example, students might be given the choice of completing a take-home final examination, producing a CD-ROM according to specified criteria, or completing several individual projects. Such flexibility acknowledges the range of student interests and strengths and differentiates the method of measuring learning from the demonstration of mastery of essential course concepts.

Principle 3, Simple and Intuitive, states that instruction is designed to be useful to and accessible by people with diverse abilities. Providing explicit guidelines for students to inform them of which criteria will be used in evaluating papers or class projects not only eliminates ambiguity regarding expectations for grades but also helps students as they consider the process of demonstrating their understanding of course content. Providing an on-line model or an exemplar of an *A* paper and then explaining how its attributes reflect the grading rubric or criteria provides all students with a straightforward illustration to guide their work.

The Principles of UDI do not constitute a checklist or prescription for inclusive instructional practice, and the examples in Table 6.1 do not necessarily reflect new teaching strategies. Indeed, in a study of university Teaching Fellows, tenured faculty recognized for their teaching expertise were interviewed about which instructional strategies and techniques they incorporate into their teaching. All 18 Fellows cited examples of instructional methods and strategies that are congruent with the Principles of UDI (Madaus, Scott, & McGuire, 2002a). In the rapidly changing environment of college classrooms, faculty will need support to respond to student diversity. UDI provides a framework that promotes creative thinking about pedagogy and respects faculty members' autonomy as the architects and designers of their courses.

APPLYING THE PRINCIPLES OF UNIVERSAL DESIGN FOR INSTRUCTION

There are some distinct differences between the educational environments of colleges and K–12 classrooms that influence the application of the Principles of UDI (Scott, McGuire, & Shaw, 2003). It is important to be aware of these context differences in order to understand the educational practices of faculty at the college level as they plan and deliver instruction.

Context Differences Between K–12 and Postsecondary

Though all educational environments exist for the purpose of promoting student learning, different mandates for serving students with disabilities, distinct means of selecting and adapting academic curricula, and diverse requirements for personnel preparation create very different contexts for considering inclusive teaching.

Different Legal Mandates for Serving Students with Disabilities   The Individuals with Disabilities Education Act (IDEA) of 1990 (PL 101-476), its 1997 amendments (PL 105-17), and its 2004 reauthorization (PL 108-446) clearly prescribe protections and services for elementary and secondary students with disabilities. Every student with a disability in the K–12 system is entitled to a free and appropriate public education. If related services are required to ensure this education, they too must be provided at no cost to the student and his or her family. In contrast, students with disabilities are not entitled to a postsecondary education; in fact, not every student with a disability can pursue higher education. Colleges are not required to alter academic and technical standards, meaning that students with disabilities must demonstrate that they are academically qualified (Rothstein, 2002). Colleges must provide reasonable accommodations and auxiliary aids on a case-by-case basis, but there is no mandate to create an educational program to meet individual needs.

Distinct Means of Selecting and Adapting Academic Curricula   A second area of difference relates to curricula and curricular materials. Under the 2004 reauthorization of IDEA, students with disabilities must be ensured access to the general education curriculum. Curriculum and instructional materials in the K–12 system are regulated through state education codes, and there is a growing trend for states to require textbook series adopted by school districts to include digital or technology-based materials (Texas Education Agency, n.d.). In postsecondary settings, the role of state governance in delineating elements of the curriculum is generally far less prescriptive. Curricula and courses differ tremendously among liberal arts, research, and vocational and technical colleges and universities (Morelli, 1999). Although certain disciplines (e.g., education, accounting, occupational therapy) are guided in their curricular offerings by professional standards and certification requirements, many more reflect flexibility of curriculum. Faculties often are autonomous in their selection of course textbooks, and they may decide to use a different text or a revised edition every year.

Different Requirements for Personnel Preparation   Another attribute that distinguishes K–12 from postsecondary settings and has an impact on instruction is the preparation of personnel. A comprehensive system of personnel development is an integral component of IDEA. Elementary and secondary classrooms are staffed with teachers and paraprofessionals trained in special education and related services fields. Government funding of personnel preparation projects has targeted both preservice and professional development initiatives, and there are more than 875,000 certified teachers and related services personnel providing services to children with disabilities (U.S. Department of Education, 2002). In contrast, preparation for teaching in higher education settings derives primarily from graduate and professional training programs. Faculty typically have expertise in content, not pedagogy. There are no requirements for training in effective instructional strategies, let alone training requirements for working with students with disabilities. Paradoxically, despite the absence of specialized professional training or preparation, postsecondary instructional environments are by nature fully inclusive. That is, all students with disabilities are educated in the same classrooms and settings as their peers without disabilities (Alper, Ryndak, & Schloss, 2001). With only a few specialized postsecondary settings or programs that are exclusively geared toward the instruction of students with learning disabilities (Brinckerhoff, McGuire, & Shaw, 2002), college students with disabilities are most often fully included in classes and programs with their peers who do not have disabilities. Yet, faculty are often unaware of validated instructional products and practices that can enhance the learning environment for students with disabilities.

In the case presented at the beginning of this chapter, it is clear that Dr. Bennett has been well prepared for one of her major roles as a new faculty member: research. As is typical of many college faculty, her professional preparation for college teaching, however, has been a much more informal process of learning through trial and error. In a study of outstanding college teachers, Madaus et al. (2002a) found a similar pattern of minimal preparation of college faculty for the role of teaching. As one faculty member noted, "When it comes to research, we are professionals. When it comes to being teachers, we're amateurs" (Madaus et al., 2002a, p. 12). Given the often informal nature of faculty preparation to teach, it is important to examine how these highly accomplished professionals can be supported in improving their teaching practices.

Supporting College Faculty in Enhancing Instruction

Effective college teachers are problem solvers concerned about student learning (Baiocco & DeWaters, 1998; Chickering & Gamson, 1987). Teaching revolves around the ability to identify, analyze, and solve all types of instructional challenges. Traditional approaches to college faculty development pertaining to students with disabilities (e.g., workshop presentations, newsletters, faculty handbooks) have not resulted in permanent changes, in part because solutions to complex academic problems do not come as quick fixes (Baiocco & DeWaters, 1998). In fact, early efforts in the field to provide simple tips for addressing the needs of college students with disabilities may have precluded more focused examination and discussion by faculty of the most effective ways to address *instructional* needs of students with disabilities (Scott & Gregg, 2000). UDI reverses this trend by addressing essential elements of pedagogy and providing a framework for faculty reflection about inclusive instruction that can be used in a number of ways. Depending on faculty needs, the Principles of UDI can be applied to the design of a new course or used to reflect on practices in an existing class. They can inform a variety of teaching issues and approaches—ranging from assessing student learning, to broadening learning experiences, to considering how an inclusive classroom climate can be established. All nine principles will not apply to all aspects of instruction. However, each principle will come into play differently when applied to the design and delivery of instruction as well as to the determination of student mastery of course concepts. Although the principles can serve as a useful reference point for experienced faculty from diverse academic disciplines, they have particular relevance for junior faculty and graduate teaching assistants seeking support and direction as emerging teachers.

Applying Universal Design
for Instruction in College Teaching

As an approach that supports faculty reflection and problem solving, the following case studies illustrate applications of the Principles of UDI by diverse faculty in various postsecondary settings. The first example returns to the case of Dr. Lynn Bennett to see how a new faculty member at a competitive research institution might benefit from beginning to implement the Principles of UDI while planning instruction.

Lynn Bennett made it through her first semester of teaching. During that time, she had called the college disability support services (DSS) office and found it to be a campus resource for helping to address the access needs of students with disabilities. When Lynn received an electronic announcement about a workshop on UDI that was being co-sponsored by DSS and the Teaching and Learning Center, she was curious. The message said that UDI was purposely developed to support faculty in providing inclusive instruction for students with disabilities, as well as other diverse learners. That seemed to describe the many learning needs she had encountered in her large lecture class in the fall, so she marked the date on her calendar.

The workshop was very interesting, and the Principles of UDI really challenged her to think about her teaching in new ways. At the advice of the workshop leaders, Lynn decided to focus on a limited number of course revisions as she prepared for the spring term, with a goal of enhancing her instruction by increments each semester. She was most interested in Principle 1 (Equitable Use) and Principle 2 (Flexibility in Use), as these seemed to resonate with the student needs she had encountered.

As Lynn prepared her class web site, she had a new appreciation of some of the inclusive features that were enhanced by this increasingly popular technology resource. She would certainly post her class syllabus, assignments, and due dates to the web site, as she had last semester, making sure all students had access to essential course information. This semester, however, Lynn also planned to provide class notes on the site. When a student with a learning disability in her fall course obtained a notetaker, Lynn had wondered if some of her students who spoke English as a second language would benefit from this service as well. Thus, by posting the notes on the web site, she could ensure that students with learning disabilities received a complete set of notes while providing this resource to all students in the class. Thinking further, she also decided to post her reserve readings for the class. The previous semester, commuting students faced a number of logistical difficulties in getting to the library. Some students with reading difficulties complained that they did not have enough time to complete the reading assignments in the library. By making materials available on the class web site, students could gain access to the reading materials at their own pace and in locations and times that were more convenient for the diverse schedules and real-life demands of students. Lynn was satisfied that these additions to the class web site added some needed flexibility to key elements of her class while making materials more uniformly available to all students. She would monitor her own satisfaction with the enhanced class web site for the spring term and ask students for direct feedback about the usefulness of these strategies. Her mind was already racing ahead,

however. Next semester she wanted to explore how she might integrate Principle 8 (A Community of Learners) into her class activities
and web site. . . .

In this next case, a veteran faculty member at a community college explores
the Principles of UDI in delivery of instruction.

Janet had been teaching food science at the local community college
for more than a decade. During that time, she had encountered many
tips and resources for making learning nondiscriminatory for students
with disabilities. Janet was very committed to students with disabilities, and a number of them were very talented students who completed the program in food science, but she was always bothered by
the focus on special accommodations rather than on supporting student learning in the best way possible. When Janet saw an article on
UDI in one of her preferred publications for getting new teaching
ideas, she read it thoroughly. She was interested in this idea of enhancing inclusive teaching, and true to her hands-on style, she decided to
go straight to the students in her program and ask for their input.
With a kitchen lab as an instructional environment, she was curious
about the feedback of students with disabilities regarding what was
most helpful or detrimental to their learning. Walking through the lab
and talking about some typical class assignments generated a windfall
of ideas; the students offered numerous suggestions for making the
learning environment more usable, among them

- "Why don't you label the drawers so we are sure to put cooking
  utensils back in the right place?" (Principle 3: Simple and Intuitive)

- "If we had a digital clock, it would be easier to monitor cooking
  times." (Principle 4: Perceptible Information)

- "I wish we had a conversion chart for measurements. It gets tricky
  sometimes to make the calculations in a hurry." (Principle 5: Tolerance for Error)

The students did not use the language of UDI in their feedback, but
the suggestions resonated with what Janet had read about UDI in the
newsletter. She decided to modify the kitchen lab. Later, she reflected
that incorporating UDI made a more effective learning environment,
as the other students in the program kept coming over to use her
modified kitchen lab.

In the following example, two associate professors at a 4-year liberal arts
institution reconsider their approach to student assessment.

Ken and Bob are colleagues in the biology department. They meet for
a game of racquetball during lunch hour when their schedules permit.

Occasionally, as they cool down after a game, their conversation turns to the topic of teaching and to some of the frustrations or successes they are experiencing in their classes. After the most recent game, Bob started to tell Ken about a new web site he had found. The site was focused on UDI, and it provided sample instructional products and methods that reflected inclusive approaches to teaching diverse learners that had been developed by faculty across the United States.

When Bob later e-mailed the Internet address, Ken went to the web site to check out the information on UDI. After agreeing that they would both take a look at the training materials available on the web site, Bob and Ken began to dialogue about ways of making their own instruction more inclusive. They both prided themselves on engaging class sessions—Ken through multimedia PowerPoint presentations and Bob by collaborative, group problem solving. Yet, when thinking about the area of student assessment, they both agreed that they could probably improve on the multiple-choice testing that shaped student grades. Every semester, each encountered multiple requests for an alternative format, both from students with disabilities and from others who convincingly spoke about their difficulty with this type of assessment. It had never occurred to Ken and Bob to view such requests as part of an instructional design issue. As creative teachers and competitive colleagues, they decided to reexamine their use of multiple-choice testing and compare solutions. Ken reasoned that the multiple-choice format was not a problem for many of his students and was still the quickest format for him to grade (no small consideration given his demanding teaching and student advising load) but that Principle 2 (Flexibility in Use) might be relevant. His test item coverage was good, he thought, but perhaps he could add more flexibility around question format and time issues. These seemed to be the areas in which students with disabilities requested accommodations. Ken was pleased with the new design options that he described to Bob: "I will still give multiple choice tests," he explained, "but students will have the option of writing in their own answers if they don't think the correct option is in the question response choices. Knowing some students rely on diagrams and other visuals, I'll even give them the option to draw their response if they choose. As for time, I never really thought about it before, but the kind of performance I'm asking for in knowledge of biology concepts is not really dependent on timed outcomes. It's always been determined by class logistics. So I decided to shorten my tests. I'll plan for a 45-minute test and give all students the 75-minute class period to complete it."

Conversely, Bob had seen Principle 8 (A Community of Learners) as being compatible with his teaching style and had focused on combining this principle with Principle 5 (Tolerance for Error). He too had decided to keep the multiple-choice test format, but after taking the test individually and receiving an independent grade, a new feature would be added: Students would have the opportunity during a class period to work in groups and retake the same test together, with the possibility for extra credit if the group work could bring up the score of the highest individual grade in the group. "I'm always impressed with how much students learn from each other," Bob explained, "and this way the test really becomes a learning opportunity as well as an evaluation."

Observations from the Case Studies

The Principles as a Flexible Framework   As reflected in the case studies, teaching in higher education varies widely along a number of factors. Campus size and mission create a different climate and result in diverse resources for the enhancement of teaching. Faculty reflect diversity in academic discipline, instructional experience, and teaching philosophy. Class settings may vary by student numbers, physical layout, or available technology. All of these elements come into play when considering how best to support college faculty in providing more inclusive instruction. As the case studies emphasize, it is essential that faculty are actively engaged in reflection about their own teaching through the use of this flexible framework for enhancing inclusive instructional practices.

The Process of Implementing the Principles   Traditional faculty development materials often structure discussion of teaching around the areas of planning, delivery of instruction, and assessment of student learning. For example, Bob and Ken identified assessment as a focus area that might be made more inclusive.

Other faculty may prefer to approach implementation of UDI from the perspective of exploring an individual principle. On the one hand, Lynn believed that Principles 1 and 2 (Equitable Use and Flexibility in Use) were most in line with the student needs she had observed in her class the previous semester. Bob, on the other hand, believed that Principle 8 (A Community of Learners) was compatible with his teaching style and saw an opportunity to expand this teaching philosophy into his approach to assessment of student learning.

A third perspective that faculty may find helpful in approaching implementation of UDI is to examine frequently requested disability accommodations in the class and consider if a component of instructional design could better address student needs in a proactive way. For example, Ken and Bob realized that the accommodations of alternate test formats and extended time on tests reflected characteristics of multiple-choice testing that might easily be adapted to benefit and provide options for many students in the class.

Resources on Universal Design for Instruction   Faculty approach enhancements to their teaching in a variety of ways. Some intentionally seek workshops and learning opportunities to garner new ideas for teaching. In the case studies, Lynn Bennett attended an on-campus workshop on UDI provided by DSS and the Teaching and Learning Center. An increasing number of college campuses have campus offices or instructional labs to support faculty in enhancing their teaching.

Other faculty prefer to access more informal means of teaching support. College faculty typically have heavy time demands, so it is important to have multiple options available for faculty support. Janet, for example, enjoyed reading a newsletter with ideas for college teaching. Bob and Ken, as regular Internet users, found a web site resource most helpful.

There are growing resources available to college faculty in a variety of media and formats on the topic of UD and instruction. One approach that the chapter authors have found particularly useful for diverse college faculty in a variety of disciplines is providing a platform for faculty to share innovative teaching strategies and methods that they have found to be effective and inclusive of diverse learners. The Facultyware web site (http://www.faculty ware.uconn.edu) contains information on UDI and offers an on-line publication process for faculty who want to share their teaching ideas. As seen in the case with Bob and Ken, institutional reward structures encourage faculty to publish their work, but there are limited opportunities to publish innovative teaching ideas that other faculty may find beneficial. The scholarship of teaching (Boyer, 1990) is promoted by some professional associations in higher education as a way of bringing rigor and academic integrity to the enhancement of college teaching. The Facultyware web site publishes instructional products that undergo a peer review and selection process similar to that of an academic journal—an approach that is in keeping with the spirit of Boyer's scholarship of teaching.

Expectations and Outcomes UDI offers a proactive alternative for ensuring access to higher education for college students with disabilities. By providing faculty with a framework and tools for designing inclusive college instruction, the dialogue surrounding college students with disabilities changes from a focus on compliance, accommodations, and nondiscrimination to an emphasis on teaching and learning. Implementing significant changes in faculty views of disability and inclusive teaching, however, takes time. As noted in Lynn's case, faculty should be encouraged to view changes in their instructional practices as incremental and as an opportunity to evaluate the impact on students. Over time, increasingly inclusive classrooms will be achieved.

Some faculty may be resistant to the idea of UDI or may not see the value of inclusive teaching—an approach without a legal mandate. However, it is anticipated that as UDI is embraced as a tool for meeting diverse learner needs, faculty will hear and learn from other faculty (particularly within their own disciplines) about the value of these inclusive practices for student learning.

In dialoguing with outstanding college teachers, the chapter authors have found that even the best instructors acknowledge that they can always improve their teaching practices (Madaus et al., 2002a). Similarly, in applying UDI, even the most inclusive classrooms can continue to be made more inclusive when instruction is based on the foundation of UD. It is important to acknowledge that UDI does not preempt legal mandates for nondiscriminatory treatment of students with disabilities. Services for these students will continue to occupy a pivotal role in promoting and ensuring equal educational opportunity on college campuses. Some students will need accommodations that are not addressed through instructional design efforts. However, it might be anticipated that with the growing implementation of UDI, some commonly requested accommodations (e.g., notetakers, test accommodations) may become obsolete as more faculty adopt inclusive instructional practices.

IMPLICATIONS FOR SECONDARY SETTINGS

The value of UD as it applies to educational settings and instruction is under exploration in a number of areas (Bowe, 2000; Center for Applied Special Technology, 2003; McGuire & Scott, 2002; McGuire, Scott, & Shaw, 2003). As discussed previously, there are significant differences between secondary and postsecondary settings, including the legal mandates relating to educational access, specification of the curriculum, and the preparation of instructors.

Despite contextual differences between the settings, secondary personnel play an important role in preparing students for the transition to higher education. Self-awareness on the part of college-bound students with disabilities is critical, as they often face additional challenges when they enter a system in which educational access, not educational entitlement, is the mandate. Although colleges are now characterized by more diverse student populations, they differ regarding their missions and their requirements. For students with disabilities, flexibility in curricular requirements at the postsecondary level speaks to the importance of carefully choosing a college or program that constitutes a suitable match with learning strengths, weaknesses, and interests.

Faculty flexibility in choice of curricular materials can, however, create a challenge for students who rely on an audio or electronic version of a text because timely ordering of materials is essential and a decision to change a textbook shortly before the start of a semester can create a barrier. In the process of transition planning, supporting students in understanding their needs for accommodations, as well as their learning strengths and interests, is critical as they consider the array of postsecondary options from which to choose. Four-year colleges and universities, community and junior colleges, private vocational schools, apprenticeship programs, and distance learning programs are among the choices (Sitlington, Clark, & Kolstoe, 2000). Faculty and student diversity is an existing reality, so as the notion of UD becomes more widespread, the possibilities for innovative approaches to inclusive instruction may create learning environments that are more diverse with respect to teaching styles and learner options.

Because of 1997 IDEA requirements, secondary special educators are addressing how to ensure access to the general education curriculum for students with disabilities. King-Sears (2001) proposed an approach for determining the accessibility of the general education curriculum, with suggestions for modifications (e.g., accommodations—audiotaped books, graphic organizers) and strategies (e.g., delineating the explicit standards for evaluation of student learning). Such an approach to inclusive instruction at the secondary level may be a precursor of the skills that students will bring to postsecondary settings. As students become more advanced in their knowledge and use of supports that enhance their access to the educational environment (e.g., assistive technology), they may advocate for these supports from college faculty. As the makeup of college classrooms changes with respect to student and faculty diversity, UDI offers tremendous potential to broaden thinking about teaching so that inclusive strategies for instruction become the norm rather than retrofitted changes to accommodate individual needs.

THE FUTURE OF UNIVERSAL DESIGN FOR INSTRUCTION IN THE POSTSECONDARY ENVIRONMENT

UD is indeed a new paradigm for providing equal educational access for students with disabilities in postsecondary education. In keeping with the fundamental concept of UD—making environments more usable for a broader range of people—UDI supports faculty in anticipating student diversity in the classroom and intentionally incorporating inclusive teaching practices. The UDI model shifts the primary focus for providing equal education access from compliance with legal mandates to consideration of student learning needs. As we saw in the cases of Lynn, Janet, Ken, and Bob, the Principles of UDI support faculty to think in more inclusive ways as they plan and deliver instruction and assess student learning while also acknowledging the broad diversity of faculty, their disciplines, and the postsecondary settings in which they work.

With the "graying" of the American professoriate and a host of incoming college instructors (Bowen & Schuster, 1986), it is an opportune time to provide faculty with the powerful paradigm of UDI. Other trends in higher education are supportive of UDI as well. Colleges and universities, including research universities, are paying greater attention to teaching and teaching-related activities (Gillespie, 2002). The escalating use of technology and its potential for augmenting accessible learning environments is a leading force for instructional change on college campuses (Baiocco & DeWaters, 1998). The impact of student diversity cannot be overstated. As noted by Baiocco and DeWaters, "It has accentuated our inadequacies in the classroom as never before. What we are coming to understand is that this new student population does not simply look different, but it presents an entirely new set of instructional challenges" (1998, p. 3).

CONCLUSION

The UDI paradigm is in sync with the trends and challenges facing higher education in the early 21st century. The beneficiaries of UDI extend beyond those protected by civil rights nondiscrimination laws (i.e., students with disabilities) to the growing number of diverse learners found on college campuses. Perhaps most important, UDI provides a powerful, tacit message—student diversity is now the norm, not the exception, and college instructors can welcome *all* students through the creation of inclusive instructional environments.

REFERENCES

Alper, S., Ryndak, D.L., & Schloss, C.N. (2001). *Alternate assessment of students with disabilities in inclusive settings.* Boston: Allyn & Bacon.

American Council on Education. (2000). *Facts in brief: Enrollment in postsecondary education institutions increases, NCES report shows.* Retrieved October 26, 2004, from http://www.acenet.edu/resources/HigherEdFacts/facts_in_brief/2000/02_28_00_fib.cfm

American Council on Education & American Association of University Professors. (2000). *Does diversity make a difference? Three research studies on diversity in college classrooms.* Washington, DC: Authors.

Americans with Disabilities Act (ADA) of 1990, PL 101-336, 42 U.S.C. §12101 *et seq.*

Baiocco, S., & DeWaters, J. (1998). *Successful college teaching: Problem-solving strategies of distinguished professors.* Boston: Allyn & Bacon.

Bowe, F. (2000). *Universal design in education: Teaching nontraditional students.* Westport, CT: Bergin & Garvey.

Bowen, H., & Schuster, J. (1986). *American professors: A national resource imperiled.* New York: Oxford University Press.

Boyer, E. (1990). *Scholarship reconsidered: Priorities of the professoriate.* Princeton, NJ: The Carnegie Foundation for the Advancement of Teaching.

Brinckerhoff, L.C., McGuire, J.M., & Shaw, S.F. (2002). *Postsecondary education and transition for students with learning disabilities.* Austin, TX: PRO-ED.

Center for Applied Special Technology. (2003). *Universal design for learning.* Retrieved October 27, 2003, from http://www.cast.org/udl

The Center for Universal Design. (1997). *The Center for Universal Design: Environments and products for all people.* Retrieved October 27, 2003, from http://www.ncsu.edu/ncsu/design/cud/index.html.

Chickering, A.W., & Ehrmann, S.C. (1996). *Implementing the seven principles: Technology as lever.* Retrieved May 24, 2000, from http://www.tltgroup.org/programs/seven.html

Chickering, A.W., & Gamson, Z.F. (1987). *Seven principles for good practice in undergraduate education.* American Association for Higher Education, Washington, DC. (ERIC Document Reproduction Service No. ED282491)

The Chronicle of Higher Education. (2003). *The Chronicle of Higher Education Almanac.* Retrieved October 27, 2003, from http://chronicle.com/free/almanac/2003/index.htm.

Covington, G.A., & Hannah, B. (1997). *Access by design.* New York: Van Nostrand Reinhold.

Cross, K.P. (1998). *What do we know about students' learning and how do we know it?* Paper presented at the American Association for Higher Education's 1998 National Conference on Higher Education, Washington, DC. Retrieved October 27, 2003, from: http://www.aahe.org/nche/cross_lecture.htm.

Gillespie, K. (Ed.) (2002). *A guide to faculty development: Practical advice, examples, and resources.* Bolton, MA: Anker Publishing Co.

Henderson, C. (1999). *College freshmen with disabilities: Statistical year 1998.* Washington, DC: HEATH Resource Center and American Council on Education.

Individuals with Disabilities Education Act Amendments of 1997, PL 105-17, 20 U.S.C. §§ 1400 *et seq.*

Individuals with Disabilities Education Act (IDEA) of 1990, PL 101-476, 20 U.S.C. §§ 1400 *et seq.*

Individuals with Disabilities Education Improvement Act of 2004, PL 108-446, 20 U.S.C. §§ 1400 *et seq.*

Kame'enui, E.J., & Carnine, D. (1998). *Effective teaching strategies that accommodate diverse learners.* Upper Saddle River, NJ: Prentice Hall.

King-Sears, M.E. (2001). Three steps for gaining access to the general education curriculum for learners with disabilities. *Intervention in School and Clinic, 37,* 67–76.

Leyser, Y., Vogel, S., Wyland, S., & Brulle, A. (1998). Faculty attitudes and practices regarding students with disabilities: Two decades after implementation of Section 504. *Journal of Postsecondary Education and Disability, 13*(3), 5–19.

Madaus, J.W., Scott, S.S., & McGuire, J.M. (2002a). *Addressing student diversity in the classroom: The approaches of outstanding university professors* (Universal Design for Instruction Project Technical Rep. No. 02). Storrs, CT: University of Connecticut, Center on Postsecondary Education and Disability.

Madaus, J.W., Scott, S.S., & McGuire, J.M. (2002b). *Barriers and bridges to learning as perceived by postsecondary students with learning disabilities* (Universal Design for Instruction Project Technical Rep. No. 01). Storrs, CT: University of Connecticut, Center on Postsecondary Education and Disability.

McGuire, J., & Scott, S. (2002). Universal Design for Instruction: A promising new paradigm for higher education. *Perspectives, 28*(2), 27–29.

McGuire, J.M., Scott, S.S., & Shaw, S.F. (2003). Universal Design for Instruction: The paradigm, its principles, and products for enhancing instructional access. *Journal of Postsecondary Education and Disability, 17*(1), 10–20.

Morelli, R.A. (1999). The World Wide Web and the liberal arts: Threat or opportunity? In M.W. McLaughlin, D.A. Hyland, & J.R. Spencer (Eds.), *Teaching matters: Essays on liberal education at the millennium* (pp. 168–182). Hartford, CT: Trinity College.

National Center for the Study of Postsecondary Educational Supports. (2000). *Postsecondary education and employment for students with disabilities: Focus group discussion on supports and barriers in lifelong learning.* Honolulu, HI: Author.

Orkwis, R., & McLane, K. (1998). *A curriculum every student can use: Design principles for student access* (ERIC/OSEP Topical Brief). Arlington, VA: ERIC Clearinghouse on Disabilities and Gifted Education.

Rehabilitation Act of 1973, PL 93-112, 29 U.S.C. § 794.

Rothstein, L.F. (2002). Judicial intent and legal precedents. In L.C. Brinckerhoff, J.M. McGuire, & S.F. Shaw, *Postsecondary education and transition for students with learning disabilities* (2nd ed., pp. 71–106). Austin, TX: PRO-ED.

Scott, S., & Gregg, N. (2000). Meeting the evolving needs of faculty in providing access for college students with LD. *Journal of Learning Disabilities, 33,* 158–167.

Scott, S., & McGuire, J. (2001, April). *The application of Universal Design for Instruction (UDI) to college instruction: Creating a web site resource.* Paper presented at the annual convention of the Council for Exceptional Children, Kansas City, MO.

Scott, S., McGuire, J., & Embry, P. (2002). *Universal Design for Instruction fact sheet.* Storrs: University of Connecticut, Center on Postsecondary Education and Disability.

Scott, S.S., McGuire, J.M., & Foley, T. (2003). Universal Design for Instruction: A framework for anticipating and responding to disability and other diverse learning needs in the college classroom. *Equity & Excellence in Education, 36,* 40–49.

Scott, S.S., McGuire, J.M, & Shaw, S.F. (2001). *Principles of Universal Design for Instruction.* Storrs: University of Connecticut, Center on Postsecondary Education and Disability.

Scott, S.S., McGuire, J.M., & Shaw, S.F. (2003). Universal Design for Instruction: A new paradigm for adult instruction in postsecondary education. *Remedial and Special Education, 24*(6), 369–379.

Shaw, S.F., Scott, S.S., & McGuire, J.M. (2001). *Teaching college students with learning disabilities* (ERIC Digest E618). Arlington, VA: ERIC Clearinghouse on Disabilities and Gifted Education.

Silver, P., Bourke, A., & Strehorn, K. (1998). Universal instructional design in higher education: An approach for inclusion. *Equity & Excellence in Education, 31*(2), 47–51.

Sitlington, P.L., Clark, G.M., & Kolstoe, O.P. (2000). *Transition education and services for adolescents with disabilities.* Boston: Allyn & Bacon.

Texas Education Agency. (n.d.). *A brief overview of the adoption process.* Retrieved January 12, 2005, from http://www.tea.state.tx.us/textbooks/adoptprocess/overview.html

U.S. Department of Education. (2002). *Twenty-fourth annual report to Congress on the implementation of the Individuals with Disabilities Education Act.* Washington, DC: Author.

Welch, P. (Ed.). (1995). *Strategies for teaching universal design.* Boston: Adaptive Environments.

Wilkoff, W.L., & Abed, L.W. (1994). *Practicing universal design: An interpretation of the ADA.* New York: Van Nostrand Reinhold.

CHAPTER 7

Expanding Support Services on Campus

Elizabeth Evans Getzel and Shannon McManus

S tudents with disabilities attending college face an entirely new set of challenges managing their academic program. These students now become one of potentially hundreds of students seeking services through a disability support services (DSS) office on campus. They are responsible for requesting their supports and services, providing documentation to receive these accommodations, and interacting with faculty to implement their supports. Along with these increased responsibilities, students with disabilities must also adjust to an educational environment much different from that of their secondary school experiences (see Table 7.1 for examples). These changes have in part contributed to students with disabilities feeling overwhelmed and unable to complete their advanced degree program, which results in low retention and completion rates (Getzel, Stodden, & Briel, 2001).

In addition, institutional factors affect students' ability to remain in school and earn a degree. Because of the increased number of students with disabilities entering postsecondary programs, the range of services provided by postsecondary institutions is still relatively new and not yet well known by faculty

Table 7.1. Ways that postsecondary environments differ from secondary environments

Higher instructor–student ratio

Less contact with instructors

Expectations of higher levels of academic competence

Fewer tests covering a broader base of knowledge

Changes in personal support systems

Greater expectations to achieve independently

Changes in social and independent living demands

Sources: Brinckerhoff, McGuire, & Shaw (2002); deFur, Getzel, & Trossi (1996); and Getzel, Stodden, & Briel (2001).

members (Getzel et al., 2001; Mellard, 1994; Minskoff, 1994; Wilson, Getzel, & Brown, 2000). Faculty and other stakeholders may find it difficult to accommodate students simply because they lack understanding of students' needs or familiarity with campus services (deFur & Taymans, 1995; Scott, 1996). Furthermore, the heavy workload of many DSS offices presents significant barriers to students seeking and securing needed services (McGuire & Scott, 2001). There are also obstacles in the form of negative attitudes held by faculty members, administrators, and other students (Greenbaum, Graham, & Scales, 1995; West et al., 1993; Wilson et al., 2000). In too many instances, students with disabilities are made to feel that they do not belong in advanced educational programs because of the need to self-identify for specific services. As a result, students may elect not to disclose their disability to the university in order to avoid being labeled (Gordon & Keiser, 1998; National Center for the Study of Postsecondary Educational Supports [NCSPES], 2000).

To meet the educational support needs of students, DSS offices across the country are faced with providing more varied and specialized services to meet the increased demand. These support services cover a wide spectrum regarding the amount and type of support services offered, and services often vary from campus to campus. Typically, these programs can be categorized by level of services offered as in minimal, moderate, or intensive (Brinckerhoff, Shaw, & McGuire, 1993; Mooney, 1996). Minimal programs are described as offering general academic support services and developmental classes. Moderate programs have coordinated services, and students are fully included in their academic studies. Intensive programs provide a specialized service component and an advocacy component. Medium and large institutions are more likely than smaller institutions to provide specific services or accommodations to students, and they are more likely to provide more than one service or support (Horn & Berktold, 1999).

Some universities and colleges are testing new models of service delivery for all students. For example, Lehigh University in Bethlehem, Pennsylvania, established a peer mentoring program for any student experiencing academic problems (Bartlett, 2004). Bartlett noted that an increasing number of colleges are establishing programs to help students who are struggling with their course work in order to increase the likelihood of staying in school. In addition, Chapter 5 discusses various models of service delivery that are specifically designed to expand the level and type of services offered to students with disabilities beyond those provided through the formal accommodation process. These models are designed to provide more individualized and ongoing services to assist students in managing their educational program. Exploring the effectiveness of services and supports is especially critical as more students with disabilities are identifying postsecondary education as a transition goal (Wagner, Cameto, & Newman, 2003). Yet, there is a limited body of knowledge within the postsecondary education and disability field on which services and specific accommodations are appropriate under various conditions (Eichorn, 1997; NCSPES, 2000).

The expansion of services to assist students with disabilities in partnership with the DSS office is an approach that Virginia Commonwealth University (VCU) has implemented since 2000. The idea for a model resulted from an evaluation of services and supports provided on the VCU campus. The VCU Office of Vice Provost for Student Affairs and Enrollment Services was interested in information that would 1) serve as documentation of unmet needs, 2) clarify and justify the need for increased or diverse funding to support the identified unmet need, 3) offer recommendations regarding administrative and programmatic best practices, and 4) recommend strategies for building a comprehensive approach for providing supports and services on campus. The external review was conducted with the coordinators of the DSS offices; VCU students with disabilities; and administrators, faculty, and staff from a variety of university schools and administrative divisions who served in integral student support roles. A series of recommendations were developed based on the evaluation results. One of the recommendations addressed the expansion of supports for students with disabilities.

The model developed by VCU uses the principles of existing supported education models that were developed for individuals with psychiatric disabilities or attention-deficit/hyperactivity disorder (ADHD). The principles of a supported education model emphasize a consumer-driven, individualized support system utilizing community and university resources. The model structures these resources around the students' career choices to help them meet both their short- and long-term goals (Cooper, 1993; Egnew, 1993; Unger, 1998). Supported education models vary in the types of services provided and the locations in which participants receive services (Cooper, 1993). At VCU, it was decided that the model would be designed to provide supports within the existing DSS structure on campus, using both university and community resources. This would enable students to receive services as part of their typical experience on campus.

COMPONENTS OF SUPPORTED EDUCATION PROGRAMS

Mowbray, Moxley, and Brown (1993) identified five components for building and implementing a supported education program. These are described in the following sections.

Linking with Community Resources

The first component is establishing and using critical community linkages. Creating these linkages helps to blend community and university resources to provide a range of supports for students who may need specialized services beyond those available only on campus. The VCU supported education model has a strong emphasis on linking community resources to students while they are in college. The program creates connections to community-based services and to the business sector. Establishing a link to the community through participation in support groups, rehabilitation services, and independent living organizations prepares students to understand and utilize the adult service system before exiting higher education. Connections to the business community take the form of informational interviewing, job shadowing, and internships. Because the supported education model is designed to provide services around a student's career choice, linking to the community becomes an important part of the supports provided.

Recruiting Students

The second component is student recruitment (Mowbray et al., 1993). It is essential that students with disabilities learn about the range of services and supports available on campus and how to obtain them. Several strategies are used to recruit students in need of a supported education program. Most of the student participants are recruited through the university's DSS office. These students have been identified by the DSS staff as needing more individualized and intensive services. Typically, these students are seeking assistance through the DSS office because they are failing in one or more classes, are on academic probation, or are significantly behind in their coursework. Students are also referred to the program through faculty members, counseling center staff, other staff on campus, or students. Information is disseminated throughout the campus using the university's web site, student organizations, student and university publications, electronic bulletin boards, and residence hall bulletin boards. The program also provides information to community partners in rehabilitation, independent living, and support groups to inform them of the supported education program.

Developing an Academic and Career Plan

The third component is the intake of students (Mowbray et al., 1993). Students entering the VCU supported education program represent all disability categories. Specific services are designed around each student's expressed need and documented using an academic and career plan (see the chapter appendix). The plan serves as a mechanism to help guide students through their academic coursework. A combination of techniques is used to generate a plan that is student centered, focusing on students' preferences and needs. The four major elements of the academic and career plan include the following:

1. Establish a career objective that becomes the focus of the students' academic course work and program of study. The career objective can be modified at any point in time.

2. Identify effective learner skills or strategies that are needed to promote successful progression in students' program of study.

3. Identify other services and supports—such as time management, personal counseling, and financial aid resources—to address issues that could be preventing students from being successful.

4. Identify technology as a compensatory tool when applicable. Staff provide individualized training with the technology and thereby help students customize the technology to meet their own unique needs.

Implementing the Academic and Career Plan

The fourth component of a supported education program is implementing the services and supports to address the needs identified on the academic and career plan. This component implements the core service elements of the program (Mowbray et al., 1993). The VCU program is student centered and self directed, so student participants can determine the amount of assistance and support they receive. Students and program staff decide how often they should meet to discuss any problems that may be occurring or to follow up on the effectiveness of the supports or strategies identified. Program staff members also work with students to connect with community and campus agencies and organizations when needed. If specific strategies are not working for a student, the staff and student meet to develop alternative methods and incorporate these changes in the student's plan.

Evaluating Program Effectiveness

The fifth component is evaluating and monitoring the effectiveness of the program (Mowbray et. al, 1993) in meeting the needs of the student participants. The VCU supported education program uses a variety of evaluation methods to determine needed programmatic changes as well as student satisfaction with services. Tables 7.2 and 7.3 describe the series of evaluation activities conducted by program staff.

Table 7.2. Virginia Commonwealth University supported education program evaluation: Effectiveness of program services and supports

Evaluation components	Method of evaluation
Quality of academic and career plans	Student interviews Review of strategies implemented by students
Student demographic characteristics	Descriptive statistics
Services and support needs of students with disabilities	Review of academic and career plan
Types of services and supports received by students	Review of academic and career plan at beginning and end of semester Descriptive statistics
Frequency and intensity of services and supports	Review of academic and career plan Student interviews Review of staff contact sheets
Identification of barriers to student retention and success	Student interviews Descriptive statistics
Components of program that contribute to academic success and student satisfaction	Student interviews Descriptive statistics

Table 7.3. Virginia Commonwealth University's supported education program evaluation: Impact of program on people served

Evaluation components	Method of evaluation
Academic outcomes	Review of study indicators (e.g., grade point average, retention, persistence in program)
Utilization of services and supports	Review of academic and career plan Student interviews
Student satisfaction	Structured interviews Descriptive statistics

PROGRAM FRAMEWORK

The intent of the VCU supported education program is to assist students to increase their capacity to direct and manage their education and, ultimately, their careers. In order to facilitate these goals, VCU adapted a three-step model framework that moves students toward greater independence (Brinckerhoff, Shaw, & McGuire, 1992). Figure 7.1 describes the framework VCU uses with students—beginning in the direct coaching phase, then moving to students consulting with the program staff, and ending with monitoring. The direct coaching of students is the first and most direct intervention of the program. Student participants and the staff jointly determine how often they will meet

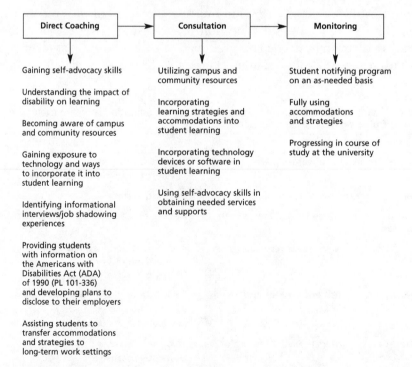

Figure 7.1. Three steps toward increasing independence: framework used by Virginia Commonwealth University for its supported education model. (*Source:* Brinckerhoff, Shaw, & McGuire, 1992.)

face to face or communicate by e-mail or telephone. On average, students who are actively involved in the program contact the staff one to three times per week. The supports provided during the direct coaching phase involve identifying and structuring supports around specific needs. For example, a student with ADHD was struggling with completing assignments on time. He often missed tests and deadlines or would finish assignments at the last minute. The student requested meeting with the staff on a regular, intensive basis—at least two times per week. His academic and career plan began by developing an organizational plan that involved notebooks. The student bought four different colored notebooks in order to quickly identify them by subject matter. He then made tabs for each section: lecture notes, reading notes, assignments, handouts, and tests, with the syllabus placed prominently in the front of each notebook. Prior to organizing his notebooks, he often spent hours in search of his syllabi to find out the requirements for each class. Next, the student and the staff worked on developing a master wall calendar of important due dates. Each class was color coded to match the notebooks. This calendar was placed in a prominent location in the student's dorm room. At the beginning of the week, the student would develop a weekly to-do list from this calendar and prioritize that list. At the end of each week, the student would e-mail the staff to discuss what he was able to accomplish.

The second phase of the model framework is consultation. Students in this phase implement the supports identified in the academic and career plan. Students primarily contact the staff by e-mail or by telephone, and some face-to-face contact occurs during this time period. The staff obtains feedback from students on the effectiveness of the strategies and supports, and the plan is modified if it is jointly determined that changes need to be made. Student contact varies, but typically during this phase student contact averages approximately one to two times per month.

The final phase is monitoring. This represents the highest level of student independence. Students notify the staff on an as-needed basis about issues they would like to discuss, or they stop by to update the staff on how things are going. It is not unusual for students to go as long as a semester before contacting the staff about something they would like to discuss. The program has an open-entry, open-exit design, which enables students to obtain services and supports when needed.

AREAS OF PROGRAM SERVICES AND SUPPORTS

The VCU supported education model provides a variety of supports and services for students with disabilities. The services are highly individualized to meet each student's unique areas of difficulty. The focus is to assist the students in compensating for their weaknesses by focusing on their strengths, using a variety of methods in such areas as promoting the utilization of accommodations, strengthening student academic skills, and exposing students to technology.

Promoting the Utilization of Accommodations

Students with disabilities in higher education sometimes have difficulty obtaining and utilizing their accommodations. Reasons for not using accommodations include not knowing how to receive accommodations, being embarrassed about having a disability, trying to be successful without using accommodations, and being newly diagnosed (Getzel, McManus, & Briel, 2004; Getzel et al., 2001; Smith & Sowers, 2003). Table 7.4 discusses several strategies that are employed to assist students with successfully obtaining and using accommodations. For example, one student met with a staff member of the supported education program to discuss why she was doing poorly in her courses. She had recently acquired a traumatic brain injury and did not know what types of services were available for students with disabilities or how to receive them. Staff gave her a copy of the student handbook for individuals with disabilities and discussed the process of receiving accommodations in higher education. The student was then directed to the DSS office to begin the process of requesting accommodations. Another student, who had a learning disability, felt uncomfortable approaching faculty with an accommodation letter. In addition to not wanting to be labeled as a student with a disability, he believed that his professors would think that he was getting an unfair advantage. This student and the supported education staff first discussed the purpose of accommodations in college and what the laws stated about receiving accommodations. They then discussed the reasons for his feeling uncomfortable, and they brainstormed several ways to approach faculty. The student and staff members role-played on how to talk with his professors about accommodations. This reduced the student's anxiety, and he was able to approach his professors.

Student participants provided the following comments concerning the supported education program's emphasis on helping students understand the importance of using their university accommodations:

- "It's a wonderful program. . . . Now I have an accommodation. In fact, I have become an advocate for it."

Table 7.4. Ways to promote the utilization of accommodations

Provide information on university policies regarding disability-related issues.

Develop steps within students' academic and career plans on how to self-identify to the disability support services office, using the university's student handbook as a guide, and on how to hold discussions with staff members on appropriate strategies for requesting accommodations.

Discuss the importance of using accommodations provided by the university.

Explore effective ways to disclose to professors or clinical staff.

Provide opportunities for students with disabilities to network with one another to share their college experiences and discuss the services, supports, or strategies that have proven helpful.

Sources: deFur, Getzel, & Trossi (1996); Getzel, McManus, & Briel (2004); and Getzel, Stodden, & Briel (2001).

- "[The program] made me aware of the accommodations that are available for me. [It] gave me a good start on realizing my strengths and how to strengthen my weaknesses."

- "It was very helpful to be able to talk to someone about my disability without feeling stupid."

Strengthening Student Academic Skills

Students with disabilities in higher education sometimes find that the strategies they used to compensate for their disabilities often do not transfer from high school to college, from an undergraduate to a graduate curriculum, or from an undergraduate to a professional school. These students may find it difficult to change or adjust compensatory strategies to meet a more demanding curriculum. The VCU supported education program works with students to strengthen their academic skills and thereby utilize their strengths to compensate for the impact of their disability. Examples of the types of academic skills strengthened in the program are in Table 7.5.

A student at a professional school who had a learning disability was able to strengthen his academic skills through the program. This student believed that he had spent sufficient hours studying and had studied proficiently; however, his test grades did not reflect his efforts. The VCU staff and the student began by analyzing a test that he had recently taken in order to identify any patterns of error. After analyzing the test, the student realized that he was recognizing the information but was not committing it to memory. He was having difficulty with the vast amount of information that he had to memorize. As the information had common categories, the student and the staff developed cell charts to organize it. Not only was the student able to better organize the information (hence, making it easier to retrieve), but he also used the cell chart as a way to check his memory.

The following remark, made by a student during the program evaluation, reflects a participant's experience with strengthening academic skills:

Table 7.5. Examples of areas for strengthening academic skills

Writing strategies

Reading skills

Proofreading strategies

Color-coding information

Mnemonics for memorization

Test-taking strategies

Time-management strategies

Organizational strategies

Cell charts and time lines for organizing information

Videotaping for self-evaluation

Role playing practicum exam questions

Study skills

- "[The staff] really showed me that I was competent to do much more than I had previously believed I could. [The staff] introduced me to a number of great organizational strategies as well as software that help me cross academic roadblocks."

Exposing Students to Technology

A key component of the VCU supported education program is the exploration and utilization of technology to assist students with their academic coursework. As a result of implementing the program, staff members have found that a majority of students have had little to no experience with technology prior to entering college. Table 7.6 lists examples of the technology used in VCU's program. These types of technology are used in myriad ways, depending on each student's needs, strengths, weaknesses, and familiarity with technology.

During the development of the academic and career plan, students are assessed to determine the most appropriate and effective method for assisting them in compensating for their disability. If the staff member and student decide that technology is the option that would be most suitable and effective, technology options are explored. Background information on the technology is given, such as the purpose, the people it may benefit most, possible uses, and ways that the technology is applied. The technology is demonstrated and customized to meet the student's unique needs. Following the demonstration, a practice session is held so the student can try the technology with the assistance of the program staff. This enables the student to learn how to correctly use the technology and to determine if it is suitable for his or her needs. It also increases the likelihood that the student will use the technology and not abandon it should he or she encounter difficulties in operating it. When students face problems with the technology, the staff immediately meets with them to determine the issues and seek solutions.

If a student decides that he or she would like to continue to explore a technology independently and in relation to his or her academic coursework, the student receives a demonstration disk (when available), which allows the individual to explore the software prior to purchasing it. In addition, the student receives information about the availability of technology on campus as well as possible sources of financial assistance for funding the technology. For example, if the student finds the technology beneficial but is unable to

Table 7.6.   Types of technology explored in Virginia Commonwealth University's supported education program

Text-to-speech software for reading, writing, and taking exams

Speech-to-text software

Personal digital assistants

Templates for recording information

Graphic organizer software

Word prediction software

Handheld spellers

financially obtain it, the supported education program will purchase it for the student on a loan basis. The student is able to use the technology throughout his or her enrollment at VCU and participation in the program. Technical assistance is provided on an ongoing basis, and once the student leaves the program, the technology is returned for use by other students.

A program participant with ADHD was experiencing difficulties with time management. She used a paper planner but often would not look at it, thereby missing deadlines. In addition, she was not utilizing her accommodation of taking a test in a room with limited distractions because she could not remember to contact the DSS office 1 week prior to the test in order to secure the room. The student and the staff explored the use of a personal digital assistant (PDA). The student was given a PDA on a loan basis, and she input all of her assignments, tests, quizzes, and papers. The student set up reminders for each area in order to receive a visual and auditory reminder of due dates. In particular, she set up reminders for her test date to go off 1 week in advance of the actual date so that she would remember to contact the DSS office about securing a testing room.

Program participant feedback shows that many students have positive experiences with using technology as a result of meeting with staff. This point is reflected in the following remarks made by students during the program evaluation:

- "The staff helped me to get a fresh start in field and I went from a *D* on a test to an *A* because of the software I was introduced to."

- "Using [speech-to-text software] to help my spelling problem, I'm sure you have noticed by now. Because of the staff great attitude about everything, it has rubbed off and given me the confidence to do well."

Summary

Student participants have expressed a high level of satisfaction with the program's focus regarding the three broad areas discussed in the preceding sections. Students stated that the program enabled them to gain a better understanding of their accommodation needs. The increased exposure to technology programs and software was extremely beneficial in assisting them to progress in their program of studies, and the program's person-centered, student-directed philosophy helped students to take responsibility for developing and implementing their educational support needs. Student participants reported the following in a survey concerning overall satisfaction with services:

- "[The staff] was willing to do what was needed to help me. That meant meeting with me every week, sitting in on field liaison meetings, and helping me find way to compensate for things I may not be good at."

- "I needed help, and I needed it before I just gave up on school completely."

- "The help I received with this program is much more than I ever thought possible, and I am very grateful."

ASSESSING THE IMPACT OF SUPPORTED EDUCATION

To assess the impact of VCU's supported education program on student outcomes, program staff analyzed a subset of 26 students with learning disabilities and/or ADHD who participated in the program across a 16-month period. These students entered the program as a result of academic difficulties, including failing one or two courses, being on academic probation, or falling behind in their coursework. Students represented undergraduate and graduate students from both the VCU academic and medical campuses. The evaluation focused on a number of areas, but for the purpose of this chapter, the discussion covers the following:

- Students' self-report of strategies incorporated into their learning routine
- Students' reasons for frequent versus infrequent participation
- Students' academic outcomes

The staff members decided that to determine the effectiveness of the program, an examination of the relationship between 1) intensity and frequency of services and 2) student performance and retention would be conducted. Intensity of services was defined as the number of contacts that students had with staff members, including office visits, telephone contacts, or e-mail correspondence. Frequency of services was measured by the number of times that students used services and supports. Students self-reported their use of services and supports during contacts with the staff and during follow-up structured interviews. After the staff reviewed the information collected, the group of 26 participants was divided into two groups for comparison (i.e., frequent and infrequent). Eleven of the students were identified as part of the frequent group based on their continual contact with staff members and the incorporation of supports into their learning routine. Fifteen of the students were identified as being in the infrequent group, because they either did not return for follow-up meetings or were in contact with the staff only a limited number of times during a semester. After the group was divided, a comparison was made between the groups to determine students' educational outcomes (i.e., overall grade point average [GPA], academic progress, and retention).

For the 11 students who frequently participated in the program, the services and supports reported as being most helpful included writing strategies, proofreading strategies, color-coding information, developing mnemonics, organizational strategies for research articles, and cell charts for organizing information. Students with disabilities whose academic course of study had a clinical component also identified role playing as a useful study skill. Students were able to practice answering potential application questions that they were likely to face during their clinical or practicum experience. In addition, students reported that assistance from the supported education program enabled them to use their university accommodations more fully and to increase their ability to meet the academic challenges of college.

Staff members analyzed contacts made with the 15 students with disabilities who did not fully use the program. Reasons identified for their limited participation included personal life issues (7 students), a belief that the program did not meet their needs (3 students), and the sufficiency of short-term strategies previously offered by the program (2 students). No contact information was available for the 3 other students who left the program.

Student Outcomes

A comparison of academic outcomes between the two groups was obtained for 24 of the 26 students in the evaluation study (see Table 7.7). The information obtained showed that 8 of the 11 students in the frequent group obtained good academic standing during their course of study. Of these 8, 1 student graduated, 2 were on the dean's list, and 5 progressed in their program. None of these students were placed or remained on academic probation or warning. One student was dismissed from his program of study, but not from the university, and 2 students left VCU for personal reasons. In the comparison group (i.e., the 13 students who participated on an infrequent basis), 8 students progressed in their program of study, 1 student was dismissed from her program of study (not from the university), and 4 were placed on academic probation or warning. When staff analyzed grades earned across the 16-month period, the evaluation results indicated that the overall GPA earned by the students who frequently participated in the program was higher than that of their counterparts who received services on an infrequent basis. For some students in the frequent group, this meant earning a GPA that removed them from academic warning or probation status.

Students expressed the following about their experiences with the supported education program:

- "I would have passed my classes without [the program,] but life would be no picnic and I definitely would not be doing as well as I am now."

- "It gave me life long skills to help me succeed. If I do have a problem I can always come back, which is extremely important."

Table 7.7. Comparison of academic outcomes for students who frequently and infrequently used services offered by Virginia Commonwealth University's supported education model

Outcomes	Frequent (N = 11)	Infrequent (N = 13)
Graduated	1	0
Progressing in the academic program to the level of making the dean's list	2	0
Progressing in the program to the level of having good academic standing	5	8
Dismissal from program of study	1	1
Academic warning or academic probation	0	4
Left school for nonacademic reasons (e.g., financial, personal)	2	0

NOTE: From An effective model for college students with learning disabilities and attention deficit hyperactivity disorders, in *Research to Practice, 3*(1), retrieved January 20, 2005, from http://www.ncset.org/publications/researchtopractice/NCSETResearchBrief_3.1.pdf, by E.E. Getzel, S. McManus, & L.W. Briel, 2004, Minneapolis: University of Minnesota, National Center on Secondary Education and Transition. Adapted with permission.

- "Without the help the staff has given over the past few months, I would have given up on applying for graduate school."

- "Through the staff's guidance I was able to post my best grades to date . . . !"

- "Was thinking about leaving the school before coming to [the program]."

The staff also collected information on grades, class attendance, types of supports used, the number of resources obtained on campus and in the community, and overall adjustment to college. It was collected during structured interviews with each participant who was located. The structured interviews also provided insight on students' satisfaction with services, feedback concerning the delivery of services through the program, strategies and supports that proved useful, and university and community resources that were effective.

Evaluation Implications

The evaluation of this subgroup of students served through the VCU supported education program provides initial results of the program's impact on students' educational outcomes. There are limitations of the evaluation, including a need to conduct the evaluation with a larger number of students to further analyze the effectiveness of the program and the services provided. Comparison data are also needed to determine the outcomes of students with disabilities who receive services through a supported education model versus those who do not. The criteria used to divide students with disabilities posed limitations to the evaluation. For example, the eight students who did not fully participate but were progressing in their program in good standing did receive some services and supports; however, staff members were unable to determine the extent that these services were used and the possible benefits students received from their limited interaction with staff. In addition, the model needs to be tested in a variety of postsecondary settings, including 2- and 4-year colleges and universities.

However, the evaluation does indicate that for some students experiencing academic problems, access to supports through this program can be beneficial. Students who frequently participated in the program were able to progress in their program of studies, earning grades that removed them from academic probation or potentially prevented them from failing in one or more classes. Students in the infrequent group did receive some level of services from the program, and in some cases the amount of help they received might have been enough for them to succeed in college. The amount and intensity of services and their impact are evaluation areas that will be continually studied to better understand the effectiveness of the program.

The evaluation also revealed (through student interviews) that issues students experience outside of the classroom—particularly personal issues— still make it difficult for them to manage and direct their academic studies. In the group of students who did not frequently obtain services from the program, personal issues were cited as forming one of the primary reasons for not doing so. Two of the students who frequently received services also indicated personal issues as a reason for leaving VCU. Further efforts are needed to 1) prepare students with disabilities enrolled in higher education programs to manage their personal needs and supports and 2) explore institutional changes that will enhance the availability and delivery of services.

CONCLUSION

Although the number of students with disabilities entering postsecondary education has increased, issues and challenges remain that prevent these students from successfully completing their degree programs. Universities and colleges concerned with the retention rates of all students are beginning to explore strategies that enable students to fully benefit from the educational experiences offered in higher education. Students with disabilities form one of several groups of diverse college learners, and some may need service options beyond the formal accommodation process established on campus. As universities and colleges explore the expansion of these service options, programs such as the one established at VCU need further study to document their effectiveness in meeting the unique learning needs of college students with disabilities.

REFERENCES

Americans with Disabilities Act (ADA) of 1990, PL 101-336, 42 U.S.C. §§ 12101 *et seq.*

Bartlett, T. (2004). Back from the brink: More colleges try to help students who struggle with their courses. *The Chronicle of Higher Education, 50*(36), A39.

Brinckerhoff, L.C., McGuire, J.M., & Shaw, S.F. (2002). *Postsecondary education and transition for students with learning disabilities* (2nd ed.). Austin, TX: PRO-ED.

Brinckerhoff, L.C., Shaw, S.F., & McGuire, J.M. (1992). Promoting access, accommodations, and independence for college students with learning disabilities. *Journal of Learning Disabilities, 25,* 417–429.

Brinckerhoff, L.C., Shaw, S.F., & McGuire, J.M. (1993). *Promoting postsecondary education for students with learning disabilities: A handbook for practitioners.* Austin, TX: PRO-ED.

Cooper, L. (1993). Serving adults with psychiatric disabilities on campus: A mobile support approach. *Psychosocial Rehabilitation Journal, 17*(1), 25–38.

deFur, S.H., Getzel, E.E., & Trossi, K. (1996). Making the postsecondary education match: A role for transition planning. *Journal of Vocational Rehabilitation, 6,* 231–241.

deFur, S.H., & Taymans, J. (1995). Competencies needed for transitions specialists in vocational rehabilitation, vocational education, and special education. *Exceptional Children, 62,* 38–51.

Egnew, R.C. (1993). Supported education and employment: An integrated approach. *Psychosocial Rehabilitation Journal, 17*(1), 121–127.

Eichorn, L. (1997). Reasonable accommodations and the awkward compromises: Issues concerning learning disabled students and professional school in the law school context. *Journal of Law and Education, 26,* 31–63.

Getzel, E.E., McManus, S., & Briel, L.W. (2004). An effective model for college students with learning disabilities and attention deficit hyperactivity disorders. *Research to Practice, 3*(1). Retrieved January 20, 2005, from http://www.ncset.org/publications/researchtopractice/NCSETResearchBrief_3.1.pdf

Getzel, E.E., Stodden, R.A., & Briel, L.W. (2001). Pursuing postsecondary education opportunities for individuals with disabilities. In P. Wehman, *Life beyond the classroom: Transition strategies for young people with disabilities* (3rd ed., pp. 247–259). Baltimore: Paul H. Brookes Publishing Co.

Gordon, M., & Keiser, S. (1998). Underpinnings. In M. Gordon & S. Keiser (Eds.), *Accommodations in higher education under the Americans with Disabilities Act* (pp. 3–19). DeWitt, NY: GSI Publications.

Greenbaum, B., Graham, S., & Scales, W. (1995). Adults with learning disabilities: Educational and social experiences during college. *Exceptional Children, 61*(5), 460–471.

Horn, L., & Berktold, J. (1999). *Students with disabilities in postsecondary education: A profile of preparation, participation, and outcomes.* Washington, DC: U.S. Department of Education, National Center for Education Statistics.

McGuire, J., & Scott, S.S. (2001, July). *Universal design for instruction: Promoting equal access through a new paradigm.* Presented at the annual conference of Association on Higher Education and Disability (AHEAD), Portland, OR.

Mellard, D.F. (1994). Services for students with learning disabilities in community colleges. In P. Gerber & H. Reiff (Eds.), *Learning disabilities in adulthood: Persisting problems and evolving issues* (pp. 130–140). Boston: Andover Medical Publishers.

Minskoff, E. (1994). Postsecondary education and vocational training: Keys for adults with learning disabilities. In P. Gerber & H. Reiff (Eds.), *Learning disabilities in adulthood: Persisting problems and evolving issues* (pp. 111–120). Boston: Andover Medical Publishers.

Mooney, D. (1996, March). *You can go to college.* Paper presented at the meeting of the International Conference of the Learning Disabilities Association of America, Dallas, TX.

Mowbray, C.T., Moxley, D.P., & Brown, K.S. (1993). A framework for initiating supported education programs. *Psychosocial Rehabilitation Journal, 17*(1), 129–149.

National Center for the Study of Postsecondary Educational Supports. (2000, June). *National focus group project: Perspectives of students with disabilities in postsecondary education: A technical report.* Honolulu: University of Hawaii at Manoa.

Scott, S.S. (1996). Understanding colleges: An overview of college support services and programs available from transition planning through graduation. *Journal of Vocational Rehabilitation, 6*, 217–230.

Smith, M.R., & Sowers, J. (2003). *A day in the life of health science students: Faculty in-service training guide.* Portland: Oregon Health & Science University, Center on Self-Determination.

Unger, K.V. (1998). *Handbook on supported education: Providing services for students with psychiatric disabilities.* Baltimore: Paul H. Brookes Publishing Co.

Wagner, M., Cameto, R., & Newman, L. (2003). *Youth with disabilities: A changing population: A report of findings from the National Longitudinal Transition Study (NLTS) and the National Longitudinal Transition Study-2 (NLTS2).* Menlo Park, CA: SRI International.

West, M.D., Kregel, J., Getzel, E.E., Zhu, M., Ipsen, S.M., & Martin, E.D. (1993). Beyond Section 504: Satisfaction and empowerment of students with disabilities in higher education. *Exceptional Children, 59*(5), 456–467.

Wilson, K., Getzel, E.E., & Brown, T. (2000). Enhancing the post-secondary campus climate for students with disabilities. *Journal of Vocational Rehabilitation, 14*(1), 37–50.

Virginia Commonwealth University (VCU) Academic and Career Plan

The VCU supported education program uses the following form to document academic and career plans. These individualized and student-centered plans help guide students through their academic coursework.

Form developed by Elizabeth Evans Getzel, Shannon McManus, and Lori W. Briel at Virginia Commonwealth University's Rehabilitation Research and Training Center on Workplace Supports; reprinted by permission.

Academic and Career Plan

Rehabilitation Research and Training Center on Workplace Supports
Virginia Commonwealth University

Student Information

Name: _____   Social Security number: _____

Address: _____   Telephone number: _____

_____   E-mail address: _____

Date of birth: _____   Date of intake: _____

How you learned of the program: _____

Long-term career goal: _____

Learning style: _____

Strengths: _____

Academic or career challenges: _____

Previous Academic Information

Standardized test for admissions: Type: _____   Scores: _____

Transfer student: ___ yes   ___ no   If yes, name of college: _____

Previous Support Services

What is your disability (if willing to disclose)?

When were you first diagnosed with a disability?

___ Elementary school   ___ Middle school   ___ High School   ___ College   ___ Professional School

Did you receive support services prior to college/professional school? ___ yes   ___ no

If yes, check all that apply:

   LD resource center   Private tutoring

   Speech therapy   Collaborative teaching

   Individualized classes: _____

Community Support Services

Have you received services or supports outside of the university? ___ yes   ___ no

If yes, check all that apply:

___ Department of Rehabilitative Services

   Services received: _____

   Current counselor: _____

Form developed by Elizabeth Evans Getzel, Shannon McManus, and Lori W. Briel at Virginia Commonwealth University's Rehabilitation Research and Training Center on Workplace Supports; reprinted by permission.

___ Social Security Administration
    ___ SSI benefits   ___ SSDI benefits
___ Central Virginia Independent Living Center
    Services received: _____
___ Disability-specific organizations or support groups (e.g., Spinal Cord Injury Association, CHADD)
___ Job Accommodation Network or Virginia Assistive Technology System
___ Other: _____

VCU Information

Academic status: _____ Academic major: _____
Number of months/years at VCU: _____ Current grade point average (GPA): _____
Current Schedule:

Course	Credits	Grade	Date and Time

Supports/Services at VCU

Have you formally disclosed your disability to the University? ___ yes ___ no

What accommodations is the university *currently* providing?
___ Priority registration   ___ Notetakers
___ Tutoring   ___ Taped text
___ Exam modifications   ___ Extended time on assignments
    ___ Extended time   ___ Books on tape
    ___ Proctor   ___ Tape-record lectures
    ___ Reader   ___ Extended program (e.g., leave of absence, deceleration of program)
    ___ Scribe   ___ Other _____
    ___ Alternative testing room

Form developed by Elizabeth Evans Getzel, Shannon McManus, and Lori W. Briel at Virginia Commonwealth University's Rehabilitation Research and Training Center on Workplace Supports; reprinted by permission.

What additional supports/services are you using on campus?

___ Tape-record lectures   ___ University Counseling Center

___ Small-group study sessions   ___ Academic Success Workshops (Counseling Center)

___ Academic counseling   ___ Math Lab

___ Support group for students with disabilities   ___ Writing Center

___ Other: _____   ___ Academic Success Program

What type of assistive technology have you used while at the university?

_____

_____

Career-Related Information

Are you currently employed?   ___ Yes   ___ No

If yes, what type of work do you do?

_____

_____

What types of jobs have you held in the past?

_____

_____

Did you disclose your disability to your employer? _____

What kinds of accommodations, if any did you use in your previous jobs?

_____

_____

Does your course of study have any internship or field placement requirements? _____

        If so, describe: _____

Are you eligible for work study? _____

Have you used the university career center?   _____

        If so, what services are you receiving? _____

Which of the following career- related services interest you?

___ Information on ADA	___ Time management	___ Organizational skills
___ Résumé development	___ Interview skills ___	Internship
___ Disclosure plan ___	Career exploration ___	Effective accommodations
___ Informational interviews	___ Job shadow/mentor	___ Evaluate technology
___ Interpersonal skills	___ Stress management	___ Work experience

Are there any other career-related services that you would like?

_____

Form developed by Elizabeth Evans Getzel, Shannon McManus, and Lori W. Briel at Virginia Commonwealth University's Rehabilitation Research and Training Center on Workplace Supports; reprinted by permission.

Academic and Career Action Plan

Short-term goal(s):

Immediate activities to implement:

Future/ongoing activities:

Next meeting date:

Update information

Date of contact:

Review outcome from previous activities:

Activities initiated/changes to plan:

Next meeting date/time: _____

Form developed by Elizabeth Evans Getzel, Shannon McManus, and Lori W. Briel at Virginia Commonwealth University's Rehabilitation Research and Training Center on Workplace Supports; reprinted by permission.

Academic and Career Plan

Rehabilitation Research and Training Center on Workplace Supports
Virginia Commonwealth University

Plan Update

Name: _____

Date: _____

Review of previous activities:

Short-term goals:

Immediate activities to implement:

Future/ongoing activities:

Next meeting date: _____

Form developed by Elizabeth Evans Getzel, Shannon McManus, and Lori W. Briel at Virginia Commonwealth University's Rehabilitation Research and Training Center on Workplace Supports; reprinted by permission.

CHAPTER 8

Strategies for Students with Hidden Disabilities in Professional School

Shannon McManus and Lisa Donegan Shoaf

Doug is a student in an occupational therapy program and has demonstrated strong academic and social skills. He is extremely motivated
and has a strong desire to succeed. When he enrolled in the program,
Doug disclosed his disability to the university's disability support services (DSS) office to receive classroom accommodations for attention-
deficit/hyperactivity disorder (ADHD). As a result, he was able to use
notetakers, receive extended time on tests, and take tests in a separate room to limit distractions. He also learned to compensate for
attention difficulties during class by audiotaping lectures. Doug is
entering his first clinical placement next semester and looking forward
to the experience. Because he has been doing well academically, he
has decided not to disclose his disability to his clinical instructor. Doug
believes that he can handle the placement without accommodations.

A significant number of students in higher education are pursuing careers
that require professional degrees. Since the late 1970s, enrollment
in graduate programs and first-professional programs has increased
between 26% and 39%. By 2012, it is estimated that enrollment will increase
for first-professional programs to approximately 350,000 (Choy & Geis, 2002;
National Center for Education Statistics [NCES], 2003). Examples of these
programs include veterinary medicine, medicine, dentistry, optometry, pharmacy, theology, and law. As enrollment has continued to increase, the types
of students pursing higher education also has changed by ethnicity, gender,
and enrollment status (Choy & Geis, 2002; NCES, 2003). Students seek
admission to a professional program after completing their undergraduate
work. For example, a student interested in a health career may seek admission
to medical, dental, pharmacy, or physical therapy school, to name a few.

Professional programs range from 2 to 4 years in length and usually include some type of fieldwork as part of the curriculum.

Professional programs are finding that a growing number of students with disabilities are attending (Keys, 1993, and Wu, Tsang, & Wainapel, 1996, as cited in Smith & Sowers, 2003). Furthermore, some students with disabilities are being newly diagnosed as having disabilities while attending school. As many as a third of students with learning disabilities were first identified in postsecondary education, and more than 40% of students with ADHD (National Center for the Study of Postsecondary Educational Supports, 2002). Students who are first identified with a disability in a postsecondary or professional program face the added challenge of learning about their disability, coping with the emotional component of having a disability, and finding new ways to compensate while learning new material in their classes or clinical placements (also called *clinical experiences* and *clinicals*).

Professional programs present new challenges not found in undergraduate education. The degree of rigor is significantly higher than in the undergraduate curricula. Students are typically in classes a majority of the day, taking multiple graduate courses of varying difficulty. Many of these programs are specifically sequenced so that course material builds within the curriculum. Along with the demand of the curricula, there are also increased expectations about adult learning behaviors. Students are expected to assimilate large amounts of material quickly and apply information at higher levels of learning. Students must be able to apply material at the synthesis, analysis, and evaluation levels. They are also expected to demonstrate self-directed learning skills that include an accurate self-assessment of their performance, advocacy on their behalf with professors, the ability to problem solve about their learning needs, and the ability to seek assistance on their own. These skills require a certain level of maturity and readiness, which may create difficulties for some graduate students.

In addition to the academic components of the curricula, most professional programs require that students complete one or more field placements to demonstrate competency of skills, knowledge, and behaviors beyond the academic setting. These clinical placements can present challenges to all students, such as integrating expected professional behaviors, applying higher level problem solving in real-world situations, and performing recently learned skills and knowledge in a fast-paced environment that students cannot control. The clinical environment can present additional unique challenges for students with disabilities. This chapter focuses on strategies both for faculty and for students with hidden disabilities (i.e., learning disabilities, ADHD, psychological disorders, and traumatic brain injury) to enable them to compensate for potential challenges and successfully meet the academic standards of their professional school experiences.

STRATEGIES FOR FACULTY AND STAFF TO CREATE A WELCOMING ENVIRONMENT

Students with disabilities are entering professional degree programs and finding success in the health care field. Many students with hidden disabilities progress through these programs with minimal additional supports. However, some students with disabilities may encounter challenges that require specific supports while attempting to complete their professional degree programs. Obtaining accommodations or supports while in graduate school has helped students with disabilities, particularly those with learning disabilities, to compensate, thus reducing some of the learning challenges and providing them with an opportunity for success (Getzel, McManus, & Briel, 2004).

Not only are accommodations and supports important, but the learning environment also plays an essential role in the successful progression of students with disabilities in professional school. A student with a disability may feel nervous and unsure about beginning a professional program. Academic and clinical faculty who work with the student can apply several strategies to provide a more welcoming environment that helps reduce student anxiety, fear, and concerns about the ability to perform in a challenging academic setting. Some professional programs have developed the following strategies, which have been successful in creating this positive environment for students with disabilities:

- Development of clear identification of affective professional behaviors with reinforcement throughout the program of the expectations of these behaviors and feedback to students about performance in both the classroom and clinical settings

- Establishment of regular meetings among a DSS staff member (e.g., the DSS coordinator), the student, and the faculty to determine needed accommodations, expectations for progress, and strategies to provide the accommodations

- Establishment of regular meetings among the student, his or her faculty advisor, and the clinical coordinator to discuss academic and clinical issues, the student's progress, and any student concerns

- Development of collaborative relationships between academic departments and other campus resources (e.g., on-site coaching, additional tutoring on disability strategies, education to increase faculty awareness) to assist the student with disability-related issues.

- Delivery of educational workshops for clinical instructors on disability-related information and information on effective Universal Design for Instruction strategies for all learners (see Chapter 6)

- Creation of a network of clinical instructors to develop additional knowledge and skills in working with students with disabilities so when the need arises, a clinical coordinator has a core group of individuals to work with students (these individuals should have a commitment to the education of individuals with disabilities, a positive attitude about providing a learning experience that can meet the student's need, and additional knowledge in order to provide an effective learning experience)

- Creation of strong relationships among the clinical coordinator, the DSS coordinator, and the core clinical faculty working with students with disabilities so that communication and understanding are facilitated

- Creation of a mentorship program (involving current students with disabilities and program graduates who have disabilities) to demonstrate accomplishments, provide encouragement, and offer additional strategies to address disability-related issues

Essential Functions and Generic Abilities

Each professional program should have a set of essential functions. These functions outline the physical, mental, and emotional requirements in the student's field or profession. In some instances, they also address the cognitive, psychomotor, and affective behaviors and skills that are required to perform in the profession effectively and safely. Technical standards of a profession address items such as the amount of lifting required or the amount of fine motor activity or vision needed to safely perform a function. Students in professional programs are asked to verify whether they can, with or without accommodation, meet the stated functions. It is important to remember that any student with a disability will be asked to meet these essential functions but may do so with accommodations. It is also important that all academic faculty, all clinical faculty, and the student understand that having a disability and requesting an accommodation does not preclude the student from the requirement of meeting the expected professional competencies. Those competencies may be met in a manner that is nontraditional or requires additional time, but the outcome must be the same in order for the student to matriculate through or graduate from a professional program.

A strategy that is helpful for all students is the development of expected affective professional behaviors for a given profession, with reinforcement of these behaviors throughout the curriculum. Students will gain a better understanding of what will be expected of them in their chosen professional field. The field of physical therapy provides a good example of how this strategy can be utilized. During the 1990s, the field explored which generic, global characteristics an individual should possess to be successful in physical therapy. A research project (May, Morgan, Lemke, Karst, & Stone, 1995) completed at the University of Wisconsin–Madison yielded a set of 10 Generic Abilities (see Table 8.1). These abilities were then broken down further into specific items and divided into beginning, developing, entry-level, and post-entry-level skill levels. The field of physical therapy embraced these Generic Abilities and embedded them into various national documents, including a national clinical performance tool, the Clinical Performance Instrument (CPI) that evaluates students in the clinical setting (American Physical Therapy Association, 1998). Many physical therapy curricula have adopted these abilities and have embedded them into course content, clinical evaluations, and self-assessment tools. Several other health professions have reviewed the Generic Abilities and concluded that the 10 items were the same for their profession. It appears that these abilities may have global applications across health fields, although no specific research to date has tested this assumption.

The Generic Abilities give the student a framework by which to assess his or her readiness to learn and adopt expected skills and behaviors as part

Table 8.1. Generic Abilities

Generic Ability	Definition
1. Commitment to Learning	The ability to self-assess, self-correct, and self-direct; to identify needed resources of learning; and to continually seek new knowledge and understanding.
2. Interpersonal Skills	The ability to interact effectively with patients, families, colleagues, other health care professions, and the community and to deal effectively with cultural and ethnic diversity issues.
3. Communication Skills	The ability to communicate effectively (i.e., speaking, body language, reading, writing, listening) for varied audiences and purposes.
4. Effective Use of Time and Resources	The ability to obtain the maximum benefit from a minimum investment of time and resources.
5. Use of Constructive Feedback	The ability to identify sources of and seek out feedback and to effectively use and provide feedback for improving personal interaction.
6. Problem-Solving	The ability to recognize and define problems, analyze data, develop and implement solutions, and evaluate outcomes.
7. Professionalism	The ability to exhibit appropriate professional conduct and to represent the profession effectively.
8. Responsibility	The ability to fulfill commitment and to be accountable for actions and outcomes.
9. Critical Thinking	The ability to question logically; to identify, generate, and evaluate elements of logical argument; to recognize and differentiate facts, illusions, assumptions, and hidden assumptions; and to distinguish the relevant from the irrelevant.
10. Stress Management	The ability to identify sources of stress and to develop effective coping behaviors.

From May, Morgan, Lemke, et al. "Model for Ability-based Assessment in Physical Therapy Education. Journal of Physical Therapy Association" 1995: 9(1): P4; reprinted by permission.

of a professional program. If the student (with or without a disability) can utilize this tool for accurate and useful self-assessment, it may enhance his or her ability to increase learning, apply information more fully, and demonstrate expected professional behaviors more consistently. The Generic Abilities model has not yet been tested with individuals with disabilities, but the possible application of self-assessment skills, as well as attention to how well these abilities are met, may be useful for those with additional challenges in academic and clinical environments.

STRATEGIES FOR STUDENTS WITH DISABILITIES IN PROFESSIONAL SCHOOL

Although not all students with disabilities require accommodations or additional support, some students with hidden disabilities may need to compensate and enhance success during clinical placements by developing and implementing strategies to meet their needs. The following strategies are intended for students with hidden disabilities, but they may be effective for all students. In addition, due to the heterogeneous nature of students with disabilities, the strategies should be used only as a guideline and should be modified to meet each student's unique set of needs and environments. Several common challenges that students with disabilities encounter in professional school include limited self-assessment skills, disclosure decisions, and inadequate compensatory strategies.

Preparing for Clinical Placements

Clinical experiences are a critical element of professional school. Students must be able to apply the principles and knowledge that they have gained in the academic setting. Clinical placements are frequently in fast-paced and complex settings, which are extremely demanding and often overwhelming. Students with hidden disabilities may require extra time to become acclimated to the environment and to learn the wealth of information presented to them. Some of the strategies used to compensate for learning differences can be acquired prior to the beginning of the clinical experience.

A student can prepare for the clinical experience by visiting the site early. During this time, the student should meet with the clinical instructor to get to know him or her. This may result in the student having a better understanding of how the site operates as well as what will be expected of him or her. In addition, the clinical instructor can identify typical cases found in the setting to give the student an opportunity to review relevant content such as class notes and textbooks.

The student can observe at the site prior to beginning the clinical experience. This may assist the student in adjusting to the pace, staff, and various treatment philosophies in the setting, as each placement has unique features. Also during this time, the student should become familiar with the setting's documentation systems, billing systems, and forms so it will be easier to use these forms once the clinical experience begins.

A student can also become familiar with the most common diagnoses or types of clients or patients seen at that facility. This allows the student to review course material for these areas. In addition to visiting the site prior to the clinical experience, the experience could be extended by 1–2 weeks. This would give the student extra time to process information. It is helpful to determine by the clinical's mid-point if additional weeks will be added. The clinical coordinator, the student, and the clinical instructor should work together to set specific goals and expected outcomes for the additional time in the clinical setting. This strategy should be used judiciously and only when all parties involved have identified clear objectives that can reasonably be met in the additional time provided.

During the first 2 weeks of his clinical, Doug realized that he was having difficulty generalizing information he learned in the classroom to the clinical setting. He also had difficulty with the fast pace of the clinic and with self-assessment of his performance. He struggled with interviewing clients and recording accurate written information from his interview. In addition, he had difficulty completing the written evaluation once he had collected the data. When providing feedback, the clinical instructor stated that Doug was not performing well and needed to try harder.

Disclosure Strategies

Students with hidden disabilities—whether in undergraduate, graduate, or professional school programs—often struggle with deciding whether to disclose their disability to their instructors. There are several reasons for the apprehension of disclosure: embarrassment, fear of the stigma attached to the disability label, feelings of inadequacy, belief that using accommodations gives an unfair advantage, and/or feelings that disclosure will lead to scrutiny and being held to a higher standard (Smith & Sowers, 2003). If a student is uncomfortable with disclosure, he or she may decide not to disclose or to disclose late in the semester or clinical placement. Disclosure is frequently a result of failing or nearly failing a class or a clinical experience (Ashland Regional Technology Center, 1997; Briel & Getzel, 2001; Smith & Sowers, 2003). When this occurs, it may be difficult to provide appropriate accommodations or develop compensatory strategies in time to pass the class or clinical placement.

Students have the choice about whether and how much information to disclose. They must evaluate the advantages and disadvantages of disclosing their disabilities. If students require accommodations in order to perform the requirements of their jobs, then they will need to seriously consider disclosing their disabilities. A student may need the assistance of a DSS coordinator to help facilitate this procedure and to determine techniques for disclosure. Effective communication among the student, the DSS office, and the clinical coordinator can enhance this process and can help the student feel more comfortable with disclosure if a plan for accommodation is discussed prior to telling the clinical instructor.

If students choose to disclose, doing so is recommended before the clinical experience begins, although students can disclose at any point during the clinical. Accommodations generally start at the point of disclosure and are not retroactive. By disclosing prior to the beginning of the clinical experience, students will have an equal opportunity for learning throughout the duration of the placement. While disclosing, students should discuss the characteristics of their disabilities and the types of necessary accommodations. Students need only to divulge pertinent information about their disabilities as it relates to the clinical placement. When negotiating accommodations with the clinical instructor, students must discuss how the accommodations and strategies can be implemented in the setting. Students should be specific and customize the accommodations and strategies to each setting. Ideally, the discussion of accommodations can be a joint meeting of a student, his or her clinical coordinator, his or her clinical instructor, and the DSS coordinator. In this meeting, the student can take the lead in discussing accommodations but also have the support of other individuals if needed. By doing this, all parties involved participate to develop a plan for the clinical experience.

> After receiving feedback from his clinical instructor, Doug decided he needed to disclose his disability and receive accommodations. He contacted the university's DSS office and asked the DSS coordinator if she would act as a liaison when Doug met with the clinical instructor. A week later, Doug, the DSS coordinator, and the clinical instructor met to discuss the situation. Doug talked about his disability and the accommodations or compensatory strategies he thought he needed. The DSS coordinator also offered suggestions, and everyone discussed what would be most appropriate in the clinical setting.

Self-Assessment Skills

An integral factor of a student's success during clinical placements is developing an awareness of the characteristics of his or her disability, his or her strengths and weaknesses, and how the disability affects learning and performance. The ability to regularly and appropriately assess one's performance is critical, particularly in relation to a clinical placement. Clinical instructors routinely ask students to discuss their performance and to propose methods to improve areas of weakness. It is also important for students to respond to feedback and to show improvement at the next learning opportunity. This requires that students be able to take ownership of areas that need improvement, receive constructive feedback, apply specific strategies to improve skills, demonstrate the ability to apply learning across similar and different situations, and accurately assess performance.

Some students with hidden disabilities may have difficulty monitoring their proficiency due to issues with interpreting social cues or subtle cues given by clinical instructors or supervisors regarding behavior or aptitude. If students are unable to self-assess accurately, they may not realize that their performance in the clinical environment is not meeting expectations. As a result, a student with a disability may be unaware that he or she is at risk of failing a clinical placement until well into the experience (Briel & Getzel, 2001; Smith & Sowers, 2003).

Because regular self-assessment is essential during a clinical experience, a student may need to structure this process to effectively reflect on his or her performance. This can be accomplished by keeping a daily journal of activities in the clinical setting, thoughts on areas of strength and weakness, reflections from observing other professionals, and notes about how to learn clinical skills more effectively. In addition, consistent and regular feedback from the clinical instructor is essential. The clinical instructor and student must determine at the beginning of the clinical experience how often and in what format feedback will be provided. The clinical instructor should provide the student with an opportunity to assess his or her performance as soon as reasonably possible following a learning opportunity. For example, if the clinical instructor and the student meet briefly in the hall after treating a patient, the instructor could ask, "What did you do well in treating that patient?" "In what areas did you struggle?" Such questions will give the student an opportunity to respond openly and possibly to assist in identifying strengths and weaknesses. In addition, the clinical instructor might ask the student to reflect on the experience more fully outside of the clinical setting and be prepared the next day to identify two or three specific ways to improve any areas of weakness.

Videotaping role-playing sessions or interactions with patients (with their permission) may help students with disabilities in determining skill level and appropriate social interactions (Briel & Getzel, 2001). Students can then review these privately and be prepared to self-assess their performance with the clinical instructor at a later time. The clinical instructor can provide specific feedback on student–patient interactions and skills as observed in the videotape. If a student was previously unable to self-identify performance areas, viewing the videotape with instructor feedback can assist in more accurately self-assessing performance in the future.

Daily feedback on a student's performance should be provided if at all possible. The clinical instructor should provide oral feedback at various times throughout the day depending on his or her availability. It is helpful for students to receive small amounts of feedback specifically directed toward learning experiences. If feedback is received immediately after a learning experience, students are better able to assess their performance and apply constructive feedback. Summative feedback at the end of the day or at the end of a week can also be helpful in pulling together a series of learning experiences. This process can then be used to generate ideas for further improvement or illustrate the need for other specific learning opportunities to address a particular skill or behavior.

A student may also benefit from regular written feedback. A grid-style form can be used to track each day's learning opportunities. The clinical instructor can then provide brief comments on specific strengths and challenges. This can be used for discussion between the student and the clinical instructor to determine specific strategies or action items for improvement. The student can also use these written methods of feedback as a way to follow or track improvement through the clinical experience. It is important for the clinical instructor to remember that positive feedback should always be provided in addition to feedback on areas of improvement. Even struggling students do well in certain areas and should be acknowledged for those skills or behaviors. By receiving regular feedback and being a part of the assessment process through reflection, students can further develop their self-assessment skills. For additional input on strategies to address disability issues that arise through the feedback and evaluation process, students and clinical instructors should have regular communication with the DSS coordinator.

Students who disclose their disabilities should also determine short-term and long-term goals prior to beginning the clinical experiences. They should share these goals with the clinical instructor and discuss how the goals can be met and which possible barriers exist. At the mid-term summative assessment, a student and his or her clinical instructor should fully evaluate implemented strategies to determine their effectiveness. This is also a good time to communicate with the DSS office, if the student believes that this would be beneficial, to obtain additional information or assistance in developing more effective strategies. Even if only contacted by telephone, the clinical coordinator should be informed of the student's progress and asked to discuss any areas of concern.

At the completion of each clinical experience, the student should assess which learning strategies were effective and consider if additional strategies are needed for subsequent experiences. If possible, the student should generalize the effective strategies from this clinical experience to future clinical settings.

Compensatory Strategies

Some students may have difficulty compensating for their hidden disabilities during their clinical experiences. These students may have learned appropriate ways to compensate at the undergraduate level, but as the demands increase and change with more emphasis on analysis and synthesis, the ability to manage and compensate can also change. In addition, students may find that the strategies they used in academic settings may not transfer to clinical experiences. Students must develop an entirely new set of strategies, which may be a time-consuming process. However, without the appropriate accommodations, strategies, and compensatory skills already in place, a student may be unable to keep up with the rigorous demands of professional school. For example, a student with a disability in an undergraduate program may audiotape lectures, transcribe the lectures, and then review the material afterward. In a graduate program, time constraints make it difficult to create such transcriptions in time for study and application to the next round of lecture material. In the clinical experience, a student may find that the accommodation of having additional time to process information is no longer effective because clinical decisions about patients must be made quickly to address safety issues. These types of situations can present new challenges for students with disabilities as they determine new, more viable strategies for success.

Written Communication Strategies   For students in clinical experiences, writing difficulties may be identified when the student documents patient or client records. Students are required to write concisely and to include pertinent, appropriate information. In addition, accurate spelling is expected, which can be a source of great difficulty for some students with hidden disabilities. Students can use several strategies to address writing and documentation challenges:

- Examine current clinical instructor notes to ascertain what information should be included and how it should be written.

- Study other clinicians' patient charts and use these charts as guides for what information needs to be included and how it should be written.

- Develop a template or form on which to record information that is critical for clinical notes and patient charts.

- Write a simulated set of notes and then give the notes to the clinical instructor for constructive feedback.

- Carry a list of commonly used medical terms, carry a list of commonly misspelled words along with correct spellings, and/or use an electronic handheld medical speller. An electronic handheld medical speller enables students to enter the phonetic spelling of a word. The correct spelling of the word then appears on the device's screen.

- Utilize speech-to-text software. This software enables users to dictate into a microphone and have their dictations transcribed into text that can be edited on the computer.

Communication Strategies   Communication is critical in clinical placements. Students must be able to communicate with patients, families, and other related professionals. They need to demonstrate expected professional behaviors, including appropriate nonverbal responses. Students must be able to communicate with family members in appropriate layman's terms and then discuss specifics of the patient or client with other health professionals. Furthermore, students have to communicate openly with the clinical instructor. Because they are being evaluated, students may have difficulty with articulating their thoughts and needs to others. Specific learning opportunities can be provided to help the student develop stronger communication skills:

- Clinical instructors can assign practice patients for the student to work with and then ask students to provide specific information about the patients.

- Instructors and students can discuss the plan for interacting with particular patients, specify which procedures to use with those patients, consider what may go wrong (and how to address such situations), and determine how information for the patient will be provided. Articulating these concepts prior to performing them can help students sequence activities, organize oral information that will be given to patients, and address word choices.

- Instructors can ask students to paraphrase information in order to check for comprehension of directions, feedback, and information.

- Instructors can ask students to begin with basic types of communication, such as interacting with a patient or consulting with another colleague from the same discipline. More advanced communication skills might include conducting family education or presenting a patient's information at an interdisciplinary meeting to discuss the patient's status and care plan. With these types of communication, the student would interact with others, both "laypeople" and professionals, to provide information and dialogue about patient issues. Allowing success in less formal, more basic communication areas can enhance student confidence for more difficult communication situations.

Memory Strategies   During clinical placements, students are required to remember a wealth of information (e.g., patient information, different types of treatment and medication). Not only do students need to recall this information they also need to communicate it rapidly. Some tips for enhancing memory may include the following:

- Use protocol cards with an outline of the information that needs to be included in each protocol (e.g., diagnosis, treatment, limitations, goals).

- Use medication cards to have a quick reference for the vast amount of prescription products available.

- Practice treatment protocols on fellow students or clinical instructors when appropriate. This will help to reinforce the information learned.

- Utilize personal digital assistants and download essential information for quick reference.

- Use audiotape or digital recorders to quickly record important information for future review.

During the meeting with the DSS coordinator and Doug's instructor, it was determined that Doug could review his clinical instructor's notes and use them as a model for taking good notes. Because Doug had difficulty remembering to ask certain questions during the client intake, it was decided that he would develop a template for taking client notes to help minimize the amount of writing required. He would also use a color-coding system to prompt him at different points during the interview. To compensate for his lack of self-assessment and generalization skills, Doug would receive additional practice by role playing client–therapist interactions with the clinical instructor. These interactions would be videotaped and viewed for self-assessment. Finally, Doug would receive regular and consistent feedback from the clinical instructor.

ADDRESSING FACULTY AND CLINICAL INSTRUCTOR CONCERNS ABOUT EDUCATING STUDENTS WITH DISABILITIES

Faculty and clinical instructor attitudes concerning practitioners with disabilities form another potential challenge that students may face. When students with disabilities enter higher education, specifically professional graduate programs, faculty must be prepared to address their learning needs. Findings from various studies indicate faculty concerns about the time involved in providing accommodations, the laws in regard to their roles and responsibilities, instructional strategies for specific disabilities, and who to contact on campus for information and support (Getzel, Briel, & McManus, 2003; Leyser, Vogel, Wyland, & Brulle, 1998; Salzberg, Peterson, Debrand, Blair, Carsey, & Johnson, 2002; Scott & Gregg, 2000; Szymanski, Hewitt, Watson, & Swett, 1999; Wilson & Getzel, 2001). Along with these issues, clinical faculty also express a primary concern about patient safety (Sowers & Smith, 2003). (For more information about faculty training, see Chapter 10.) Faculty member attitudes generally fall into three categories regarding readiness to address learning issues with students with disabilities. The first category includes faculty who are open to the admission of students with disabilities and, from previous experience, may feel prepared to address any unique learning needs and accommodations. Faculty in the second category are willing to work with these students but feel ill prepared to appropriately address the students' learning needs. The third category includes faculty members who are not particularly open to working with students who have disabilities.

Some faculty members have not encountered accommodating students with disabilities, especially hidden disabilities, in college or professional school settings. A faculty member who has directly encountered a student with a disability may have relied on support from DSS offices to address the necessary accommodations and to determine the student's needs for that academic setting. However, in professional programs, in which students are more closely tracked by the faculty and must be evaluated in clinical or field environments, faculty need to be better informed about implementing instructional strategies and accommodations. Faculty must have a better understanding about educating students with disabilities. In turn, faculty can form strategies for addressing the educational needs in the classroom or the clinic, thereby avoiding a "guessing game" approach to providing a better learning environment for the student.

In addition, students often do not specifically know how to apply strategies more effectively to meet their needs. For example, in the clinical environment a student may initially need additional time to review medical chart information about a patient or client. The clinical instructor may not realize that this is needed (and may even have strategies to allow for this process), so the student then looks unprepared to discuss the patient or client and becomes frustrated and intimidated. It is critical that discussions occur among the clinical instructor, the student, and the academic faculty about how to best address issues that occur in clinical settings.

As noted, academic faculty often do not understand various disabilities or applicable strategies. Clinical faculty may also express concerns that a student with a disability will be accommodated and matriculated forward in the program without accomplishment of the required competencies. It is important to remember that a student with a disability must still meet the required competencies of the clinical placement and the profession but may do so in a nontraditional way. The importance of good, ongoing communication among the academic faculty, the clinical faculty, and the student concerning learning needs in the clinical setting cannot be overstated. It is paramount that these groups work together openly, honestly, and continuously to give the student with a disability a reasonable opportunity for success in the clinical or field environment.

FUTURE DIRECTIONS IN PROFESSIONAL SCHOOLS

Based on future projections provided earlier in the chapter, individuals with disabilities will continue entering professional programs. Many colleges and universities still need to determine a more comprehensive program for addressing student learning needs in all areas of the professional curriculum. Professional program directors should seek available resources by communicating and collaborating with colleges and universities that already have programs in place to address disability issues with their students. Although all higher education programs have DSS offices, the programs vary in the degree to which they have developed support staff and programs to assist students. Colleges and universities can utilize information on the Internet, as well as workshop attendance, to build the skills and knowledge of faculty members. In addition, specific learning activities such as workshops for clinical instructors can help extend learning to clinical environments. Assessment is needed in the following areas: communication lines across departments, resources available to assist students, attitudes about working with students with disabilities, and plans for enhancement of needed programs.

CONCLUSION

This chapter has focused on the involvement of all parties in the professional school setting to enhance the learning needs of students with disabilities and create a welcoming learning environment. When academic and clinical faculty support a student's matriculation through the program, provide guidance and understanding of disability issues, and work with the student to provide a reasonable opportunity for success, they form a partnership that will enable the student to meet the standards and qualifications of the professional program.

REFERENCES

American Physical Therapy Association. (1998). *Clinical Performance Instrument.* Alexandria, VA: Author.

Ashland Regional Technology Center (KY), Case No. 07-96-1285, 10 NDLR 303 (OCR Region VII 1997).

Briel, L.W., & Getzel, E.E. (2001). Internships in higher education: Promoting success for students with disabilities. *Disabilities Studies Quarterly, 21*(1), 38–48.

Choy, S.P., & Geis, S. (2002, July). *Student financing of graduate and first-professional education, 1999–2000: Profiles of students in selected degree programs and their use of assistantships (statistical analysis report).* Retrieved November 2, 2004, from http://nces.ed.gov/pubs2002/2002166.pdf

Getzel, E.E., Briel, L.W., & McManus, S. (2003). Strategies for implementing professional development activities on college campuses: Findings from the OPE funded project sites (1999–2002). *Journal of Postsecondary Education and Disabilities, 17*(1), 59–78.

Getzel, E.E., McManus, S., & Briel, L.W. (2004). An effective model for college students with learning disabilities and attention deficit hyperactivity disorders. *Research to Practice Brief*, *3*(1), 1–6.

Leyser, Y., Vogel, S., Wyland, S., & Brulle, A. (1998). Faculty attitudes and practices regarding students with disabilities: Two decades after implementation of Section 504. *Journal of Postsecondary Education and Disability*, *13*(3), 5–19.

May, W.W., Morgan, B.J., Lemke, J.C., Karst, G.M., & Stone, H.L. (1995). Model for ability-based assessment in physical therapy education. *Journal of Physical Therapy Education*, *9*(1), 3–6.

National Center for Education Statistics. (2003). *Participation in education: Graduate and professional education: Trends in graduate/first-professional enrollments*. Retrieved January 1, 2005, from http://nces.ed.gov/programs/coe/2003/section1/indicator07.asp

National Center for the Study of Postsecondary Educational Supports. (2002, July 8). Preparation for support of youth with disabilities in postsecondary education and employment: Implications for priorities and practice. In *Proceedings and briefing book for the National Summit on Postsecondary Education for People with Disabilities*. Retrieved October 7, 2004, from http://www.ncset.hawaii.edu/summits/july2002/default.htm

Salzberg, C.L., Peterson, L., Debrand, C.C., Blair, J.J., Carsey, A.C., & Johnson, A.S. (2002). Opinions of disability service directors on faculty training: The need, content, issues, formats, media, and activities. *Journal of Postsecondary Education and Disability*, *15*(2), 101–114.

Scott, S., & Gregg, G. (2000). Meeting the evolving educational needs of faculty in providing access for college students with LD. *Journal of Learning Disabilities*, *33*(2), 158–167.

Smith, M.R., & Sowers, J. (2003). *A day in the life of health science students: Faculty in-service training guide*. Portland: Oregon Health & Science University, Center on Self-Determination.

Sowers, J., & Smith, M.R. (2003). A field test of the impact of an inservice training program on health sciences education faculty. *Journal of Postsecondary Education and Disability*, *17*(1), 33–48.

Szymanski, E.M., Hewitt, G.J., Watson, E.A., & Swett, E.A. (1999). Faculty and instructor perception of disability support services and student communication. *Career Development for Exceptional Children*, *22*(2), 117–128.

Wilson, K.E., & Getzel, E.E. (2001). Creating a supportive campus: The VCU Professional Development Academy. *The Journal for Vocational Special Needs Education*, *23*(2), 12–18.

CHAPTER 9

The Role of Technology in Preparing for College and Careers

Sheryl Burgstahler

Technology is used in almost every educational, employment, community, and recreational setting. Access to technology can promote positive postsecondary academic and career outcomes for students with a wide range of abilities and disabilities and, for those who have the interest and aptitude, open doors to high-tech career fields that were once unavailable to people with disabilities. However, the potential of technology to level the playing field in education and employment will not be realized unless students have access to these powerful tools and are adequately prepared to effectively use them.

Taking advantage of the power that technology offers in promoting achievement in academic studies and employment is critically important because people with disabilities experience far less career success than their peers without disabilities (National Council on Disability, 2000; National Organization on Disability, 1998; Phelps & Hanley-Maxwell, 1997; Wagner & Blackorby, 1996). However, these differences in achievement diminish as individuals gain more education (Yelin & Katz, 1994). Clearly, technology access and use that leads to greater success in college has the potential to improve career outcomes for people with disabilities (Kim-Rupnow & Burgstahler, 2004).

The benefits of technology use may be even greater for people with disabilities than for those without disabilities (The Alliance for Technology Access, 2002; Anderson-Inman, Knox-Quinn, & Szymanski, 1999; Blackhurst,

This chapter was funded by the National Science Foundation (Cooperative Agreement No. HRD0227995) and the U.S. Department of Education (Grant Nos. H324M990010 and P116D99013801). The opinions expressed in this chapter are those of the author and do not necessarily reflect those of the funding agencies.

179

Lahm, Harrison, & Chandler, 1999; Goldberg & O'Neill, 2000). However, significantly fewer individuals with disabilities own computers and use the Internet (Kaye, 2000). In addition, some people with disabilities cannot access web pages, instructional and applications software, telecommunications equipment, and other electronic tools because the designs of these products erect barriers to them (Burgstahler, 2002; Opitz, Savenye, & Rowland, 2003; Schmetzke, 2001). For example, individuals who are blind use speech and braille output systems that can only read text on a computer screen; when web designers embed content within graphic images and do not provide text alternatives, users who are blind cannot access the content. Similarly, software with an unnecessarily high reading level may not be accessible to some people with learning disabilities or developmental disabilities. Much of the content of videotapes without captions is inaccessible to viewers who are deaf. In addition, office equipment that cannot be operated from a seated position is not accessible to an intern or employee who uses a wheelchair.

The full potential of using technology to prepare young people with disabilities for postsecondary education is not being realized (National Council on Disability & Social Security Administration, 2000), in part because accessibility is rarely identified as an important factor when purchasing or developing educational technology (National Council on Disability, 2000). Consequently, inaccessible hardware and software are purchased, inaccessible web sites are developed, and inaccessible computing facilities are constructed. Many computer support staff, general education teachers, and special education teachers are not sufficiently aware of how technology can maximize access to education for students with disabilities (National Center for Education Statistics, 2000a, 2000b). Because of differences in laws and funding for technology between K–12 and postsecondary environments, even students who are fortunate enough to gain access to empowering technology in K–12 settings may not be allowed to take it with them when they exit high school. Rarely is there a seamless transition of availability of technology as students move from K–12 to postsecondary to career environments.

This chapter explores the role that technology can play in helping students with disabilities make successful transitions to postsecondary studies and, ultimately, employment. It discusses the broad issues of assistive technology and universal design (UD), relevant legislation, and self-determination; provides examples of how technology can be used to promote academic and career success for students with disabilities; describes the types of technology available for students with a wide variety of disabilities; discusses funding strategies; and outlines technology considerations in choosing a college and in succeeding in college studies and careers.

BROAD ISSUES

Myriad issues need to be addressed in order to maximize the access and effective use of technology for people with disabilities. Considerations include assistive technology and UD, relevant legislation, and self-determination.

Assistive Technology and Universal Design

Throughout this chapter, the term *technology* refers to both mainstream information technology and assistive technology that provides access to mainstream technology. *Information technology* includes computers, telephones, office equipment, educational and applications software, calculators, science equipment, and personal data assistants.

Assistive technology is defined as "any item, piece of equipment, or system, whether acquired commercially, modified, or customized, that is commonly used to increase, maintain, or improve functional capabilities of individuals with disabilities" (Technology-Related Assistance for Individuals with Disabilities Act of 1988 [PL 100-407]). Assistive technology helps people with disabilities accomplish daily living tasks, communicate, succeed in education, secure employment, and participate in recreational and community activities. It can maximize physical or mental functioning and minimize the impact of a disability. Examples of assistive technology include wheelchairs, hand-controls for automobiles, computer-based environmental controls, communication aids, hand splints, hearing aids, and alternative keyboards for computers. This chapter focuses on assistive technology that interfaces with information technology, such as alternative keyboards, speech output systems, spelling and grammar checkers, and braille embossers (Closing the Gap, 2005).

As noted in Chapter 6, UD is the process of creating products and environments that are usable by people with a wide range of abilities, disabilities, and other characteristics. It is defined as "the design of products and environments to be usable by all people, to the greatest extent possible, without the need for adaptation or specialized design" (The National Center for Universal Design, 2002, p. 1). The concept of UD has been applied to many areas that ultimately affect the success of students with disabilities, including the selection of teaching methods and curriculum; the development of student services; the design of computer labs; and the creation of accessible web pages, distance learning courses, and other information technology (Bar & Galluzzo, 1999; Bowe, 2000; Burgstahler, 2002, 2004b; The Center for Applied Special Technology, 2002; Hitchcock & Stahl, 2003; Schmetzke, 2001).

When developers apply UD principles as they create information technology, they minimize the need for assistive technology and, in those situations where assistive technology is needed, they ensure that new products are compatible with commonly used assistive hardware and software. There are many ways that universally designed technology benefits students with disabilities. Universally designed web pages allow students who are blind and using text-to-speech systems to gain access to information, communicate with peers and teachers, and take advantage of distance learning options. Accessible instructional software (on disks, CDs, or other media) allows students with many types of disabilities and students without disabilities to participate side by side in simulations and other computer-based activities.

Applying the UD approach to K–12 and postsecondary technology environments, facilities, information resources, and services is a critical step toward ensuring that students with disabilities are afforded full access to academic and career preparation activities. Educators, administrators, technology specialists, parents, and students with disabilities can all play roles in the promotion of UD. Adopting technology accessibility policies and standards, such as those established by the federal government (Office of the Federal Register, 2000), is one way for educational entities to move closer to this goal. Librarians, educators, and others who purchase technology products for schools should demand that accessibility considerations be included in the procurement process. Similarly, distance learning program providers should employ UD principles so that their courses are accessible to potential students with a wide variety of abilities and disabilities. A UD approach to the selection, development, and use of information technology in schools can facilitate student transition from secondary to postsecondary educational and career settings by reducing the need for assistive technology, promoting compatibility between assistive technology and mainstream technology in educational settings and the workplace, and making it easier for service providers to respond to the changing technology needs of clients.

Relevant Legislation

The Individuals with Disabilities Education Improvement Act of 2004 (PL 108-446), a reauthorization of the Education for all Handicapped Children Act of 1975 (PL 94-142), mandates that each state provide a free and appropriate education for all children, regardless of their disabilities. It requires individualized education programs (IEPs) to be developed for students with disabilities who meet certain criteria and assistive technology and transition issues to be considered in the development of IEPs. Elementary and secondary schools are covered by IDEA; postsecondary education is not.

Section 504 of the Rehabilitation Act of 1973 (PL 93-112) prohibits discrimination against individuals with disabilities in programs and services that receive federal funds. The vast majority of educational entities at all levels receive federal funds and are therefore covered entities under Section 504. The Americans with Disabilities Act (ADA) of 1990 (PL 101-336) reinforces and extends the requirements of Section 504 to public programs and services, regardless of whether they receive federal funds. Therefore, in K–12 programs, all students with disabilities, even those who do not have IEPs, have a right to full access to content and activities that make use of technology whenever such access is provided to students without disabilities. In postsecondary settings, qualified students who disclose their disabilities and present appropriate documentation also have a right to reasonable accommodations that ensure nondiscrimination and access to courses, programs, and information in an inclusive setting whenever possible (Frank & Wade, 1993; McCusker, 1995). Although the ADA does not specifically mention information technology, the U.S. Department of Justice clarified that the ADA applies to technology resources: "Covered entities that use the Internet for communications regarding their programs, goods, or services must be prepared to offer those communications through accessible means as well" (Patrick, 1996, p. 1). Provisions of the Carl D. Perkins Vocational and Applied Technology Education Act Amendments of 1998 (PL 105-232), the Rehabilitation Act Amendments of 1992 and 1993, the School-to-Work Opportunities Act of 1994 (PL 103-239), and the Technology-Related Assistance for Individuals with Disabilities Act of 1988 (PL 100-407) affirm that individuals with disabilities have a right to full access to public programs and resources. Furthermore, the New Freedom Initiative demonstrates a commitment by the federal government to remove barriers to equality faced by people with disabilities (U.S. Department of Health and Human Services, 2001). It promises to expand research and access to assistive and universally designed technologies that promote the inclusion of people with disabilities in the workforce.

Although educational institutions have legal obligations to provide technology access to students with disabilities, barriers to such access persist. Many educators and service providers have difficulty understanding and applying the maze of conflicting definitions, eligibility criteria, and policy implications of legislation that affects the provision of technology access for individuals with disabilities (National Council on Disability, 2000). In addition, students with disabilities and their advocates are often unaware of their rights regarding access to technology. A simple approach in both K–12 and postsecondary environments is to itemize which resources and activities are supported by technology for students without disabilities and then to take steps to ensure that students with disabilities receive equivalent, independent access to the same resources and activities within an inclusive setting.

Self-Determination

As noted in Chapter 3, *self-determination* refers to the skills, knowledge, and beliefs that enable a person to participate in goal-directed, self-regulated, autonomous behavior. It requires an understanding of one's own strengths and limitations and of how technology and accommodations can maximize functionality. Self-determined people consider options and make informed choices as they take control of their lives and gradually assume the roles of successful adults (Field, Martin, Miller, Ward, & Wehmeyer, 1998). *Self-advocacy* is an important skill employed by people who are self-determined and is essential for success in higher education and employment. Students who understand their strengths and needs, set and pursue goals, and seek the information and support they need are prepared for a successful future.

The skills and attitudes necessary for self-determination should be developed throughout a young person's life, but particular attention should be given to this area during high school as part of the transition process. As with all other aspects of the transition process, applications of technology should be addressed in ways that maximize the involvement of students with disabilities, and transition plans should require that students develop and apply self-determination skills in this area. Ideally, by high school graduation, students with disabilities are experts in how their disabilities affect their learning; know how specific mainstream technology and assistive technology can maximize their potential to reach personal, educational, and career goals; know the technical support requirements of their systems and resources available to them; and are prepared to articulate their technology needs to teachers, professors, on- and off-campus service providers, and employers. Students with disabilities should be included at all stages of technology selection, support, and use so that they learn to self-advocate regarding their needs for accessible technology in the classroom, computer lab, and workplace.

Students can practice self-determination skills by inviting a technology specialist to join their IEP team, planning and leading their IEP meetings, and practicing how to ask for accommodations with a teacher or computer lab instructor. Students should "test drive" options and ultimately determine what works best for them.

Young people with disabilities should be given opportunities to practice skills in advocacy for others as well as advocacy for themselves. For example, students with disabilities who find web sites inaccessible to them or other people with disabilities should be encouraged to do something about it. Educators and advocates can help them e-mail web masters, ask for an alternate format of site contents, and encourage web site sponsors to make their pages accessible to everyone. Promoting UD provides opportunities for students with disabilities to develop and practice leadership and self-determination skills and leads to a more accessible world for everyone.

USES OF TECHNOLOGY TO PREPARE FOR COLLEGE

Technology can help people with disabilities fully participate in academic and employment offerings. Unfortunately, sometimes technology is employed in a very narrow range of ways to enhance the education of students with disabilities (if used at all). For example, a computer and assistive technology might occasionally be available to a student in a special education resource room but not in general education classrooms where, if available, the technology could be used to complete in-class assignments. This situation may be a result of the teacher not being aware that the student can use this technology. In addition, educators are often not sensitive to the need for students with disabilities to complete their work independently, particularly as they prepare for postsecondary studies and careers. Because of this lack of understanding, educators may not see that providing a personal aide to perform writing tasks is less empowering than providing technology so that the student can "write" independently. Dependence and passive behaviors are barriers to postsecondary education and careers.

It is also true that assistive technology is not always readily available to students who, with it, might be able to participate in work-based learning experiences, such as summer internships. Educators, service providers, and parents should ensure that appropriate technology is available when and where students with disabilities need it.

Students with disabilities should be taught to use technology in ways that 1) maximize their independence, productivity, and participation in all academic and employment activities; 2) facilitate successful transitions between academic settings and employment; and 3) lead to successful, self-determined adult lives. Technology can be used for supporting mentoring relationships, gaining access to information, participating in science labs, communicating in class discussions, practicing self-advocacy, conducting independent living tasks, engaging in work-based learning opportunities, and partaking in other academic and career preparation activities. Teaching students how to make the most of their technology should build on existing interests. For example, a student with a learning disability that affects reading can be motivated to use a scanner, screen-reading software, and a speech synthesizer by his desire to read for recreation. Another student might be encouraged to master spell-checking software if she is allowed to use it while communicating with her friends via e-mail.

The following examples[1] illustrate some of the many ways that technology can be creatively used by students with disabilities to maximize their independence, productivity, and participation in academic studies and careers.

- *Maximize independence in academic and employment tasks.* A student with a mobility impairment uses a hands-free keyboard and mouse to operate a computer to take class notes, gain access to library resources, and complete papers rather than have an assistant write for him.

- *Participate in classroom discussions.* A student who cannot speak uses a computer-based communication device to deliver speeches and participate in class discussions.

- *Gain access to peers, mentors, and role models.* In a supported Internet community, a student who is deaf uses e-mail to chat with other teenagers, gain support for college, obtain career transition help from mentors, and meet role models (Burgstahler, 1997; Burgstahler & Cronheim, 2001).

- *Self-advocate.* A student who is deaf uses a teletypewriter (TTY) and relay service to arrange appointments regarding internship accommodations with her supervisor.

- *Gain access to the full range of educational options.* A student who is blind and uses speech output technology fully participates in an Internet-based distance learning course that employs UD principles to assure access to people with disabilities.

- *Participate in experiences not otherwise possible.* A young man with no functional use of his arms and legs experiences completion of a chemistry

---

[1]From Burgstahler, S. (2003). The role of technology in preparing youth with disabilities for postsecondary education and employment. *Journal of Special Education Technology, 18*(4), 7–20; adapted by permission.

experiment through a computer simulation and observation of sea life while swimming in the ocean through virtual reality.

- *Succeed in work-based learning experiences.* A student who has no use of her hands independently uses a computer with an on-screen keyboard and a mouse operated with head movement to draft and edit articles in a journalism internship at the local newspaper office.

- *Secure high levels of independent living.* A young person who has a developmental disability uses a cellular telephone to maintain regular contact with caregivers as he participates in community activities. A teenager with a mobility impairment uses a voice-controlled system to operate the television, turn lights on and off, open doors, and perform other tasks of daily life.

- *Prepare for transitions to college and careers.* A student with a learning disability that makes it difficult for her to read uses a computer with a text-to-speech output system to explore internship and career opportunities, take self-paced career readiness and interest tests, and research the academic programs and services for students with disabilities offered at colleges of interest.

- *Work side by side with peers.* A girl who is blind and a boy who has no use of his hands work on the school newsletter with fellow journalism students; she uses speech output technology, he uses a voice recognition system, and other students use standard input and output devices on a local area network in the computer lab.

- *Master academic tasks that they cannot accomplish otherwise.* A student with a learning disability uses a set of software tools to support her management of reading, writing, and study demands in a postsecondary setting (Anderson-Inman et al., 1999).

- *Enter high-tech career fields.* A child who shows interest in engineering at a young age but does not have the fine motor skills to manipulate objects gains technical knowledge using the Internet, operates computer simulations of engineering tasks, and develops a solid foundation for college studies and a career in engineering.

- *Participate in community and recreational activities.* An adult who is blind can privately cast his vote for president of the United States because the voting booth is designed to be accessible to everyone.

These and countless other examples demonstrate the wide variety of roles that technology can play as young people with disabilities prepare for and then succeed in college and careers. Students with disabilities realize the same benefits as individuals without disabilities—they write, develop spreadsheets, use the Internet, and participate in technology-rich internships. In addition to the benefits others secure, however, some people with disabilities can use technology as compensatory tools, allowing them to do things that are otherwise impossible as a result of their disabilities. Computer-based technology can provide a voice for those who cannot speak and a pencil for those without functional use of their hands.

College-bound students with disabilities should begin exploring postsecondary options long before their senior year in high school. They can take tours of college campuses that include school computer labs. They can also begin to prepare for college and to explore academic and career options on line. A sample of the many on-line resources that can help students with disabilities prepare for college and beyond can be found in *Preparing for College: An Online Tutorial* (Burgstahler, 2004a).

SELECTING TECHNOLOGY

With appropriate computing tools and well-defined strategies for their use, students with disabilities can demonstrate and apply their knowledge and fully participate in educational, career, and recreational activities. Long before high school graduation, students with disabilities and their advocates should be thinking about technology that students will use in college and employment. Technology specialists should work closely with students to first determine what they need to accomplish by using a computer. Technology choices for people with disabilities should be driven by both short-term and long-term needs. Once basic tools and strategies are initially selected, students can test, discard, adapt, and/or refine them. The end-user of the technology should ultimately determine what works best. The following sections, organized by disability type, describe some of the many types of assistive technology to consider for students with disabilities.

Mobility Impairments

Some accessibility features are built into operating systems. For instance, the Accessibility Options control panel in Microsoft Windows and the Easy Access control panel or Universal Access system preference in Macintosh contain a variety of settings to make a standard keyboard easier to use. For a person who uses a single finger, mouth-stick, head-stick or other single-selection device, software utilities create "sticky keys" that electronically latch the shift, control, and other keys, thereby allowing sequential keystrokes to input commands that normally require two or more keys to be pressed simultaneously. The repeat function key can also be disabled to eliminate repeated keystrokes for a person who tends to depress a key for too long.

The standard keyboard and mouse present barriers to computer access for many people. Fortunately, there is a wide range of enhancements and alternatives from which to choose. For example, trackballs, rather than mice, are easier for some individuals to use because they can rest their hands on the top and the buttons can be activated without inadvertently changing the position of the cursor on the screen. Touchpads, joysticks, and other devices can also be used to replace the mouse. In addition, speech recognition products provide an alternative to standard keyboard and mouse functions. They convert words spoken into a microphone into a computer-readable format and can be efficiently used by people who have high levels of stamina with respect to speaking and breathing.

Sometimes simply repositioning the system components can enhance accessibility. For example, mounting keyboards perpendicular to tables or wheelchair trays at head height can assist individuals with limited mobility. Placing the keyboard on the floor can allow the use of feet instead of hands for typing. Wireless keyboards can provide a great deal of flexibility in positioning. A keyguard, a plastic or metal shield that fits over a standard keyboard and has holes over each key, helps individuals with limited fine motor skills press desired keys without inadvertently pressing other keys nearby.

Alternative keyboards for people who cannot use a standard keyboard include mini-keyboards for people who have a limited range of motion and keyboards with extra-large keys for those who have reduced fine motor skills. In addition, specialized software can present a virtual keyboard on the computer screen so that a student can use a mouse or alternative input device to select the "keys." For individuals who need to operate the computer with one hand, left- and right-handed keyboard layouts are available. They provide more efficient key arrangements than standard keyboards designed for two-hand users.

Word prediction programs are often used with alternative keyboards to increase accuracy and typing speed. As users begin to type a word, the word prediction software prompts them with a list of likely word choices based on words they have used previously. Standard features within word processing programs can also assist with text entry. For example, large blocks of commonly used text, such as school contact information, can be represented by short character sequences.

Keyboard and mouse emulation can be provided using scanning and Morse code input systems. In each case, special switches make use of at least one muscle over which the individual has control (e.g., in the eyebrow, neck, knee, or mouth). In row-column scanning input systems, lights or cursors scan letters and symbols displayed on computer screens or external devices. To make selections, students use switches activated by movement of the selected muscle. Hundreds of switches tailor input options to individual needs. In a Morse code system, users input Morse code by activating switches (e.g., a sip-and-puff switch registers a dot with a sip and a dash with a puff). Special hardware and software translate Morse code into a form that computers understand so that standard software can be used. Most learners quickly adapt to using Morse code and achieve high entry speeds.

Low Vision

For some people with visual impairments, the standard size of letters on the screen or printed in documents is too small to read. Some people cannot distinguish one color from another. Others have visual field limitations that result in tunnel vision or alternating areas of total blindness and vision. Some are hypersensitive to light.

The most common computer adaptation for people with visual impairments is software to enlarge screen images. Most screen magnification software can also reverse the screen from black on white to white on black for people who are light sensitive. Some software programs also provide speech output to reduce the eye strain associated with reading large blocks of text with screen enlargement alone. For individuals with some visual impairments, software to adjust the color of the monitor or change the foreground and background colors is also of value. In addition, antiglare screens can make screens easier to read.

A standard desktop scanner can be combined with screen enlargement technology to magnify printed text. With this system, each page of text is scanned and the results are displayed in large print on the computer screen. Closed-circuit television (CCTV) magnifiers, available in both stationary and portable models, can also be used to magnify printed materials, pictures, and objects. Wearable cameras and binoculars can be used to magnify whiteboard content or other mid-distance objects or displays.

Blindness

Most individuals who have no functional sight use standard keyboards; however, braille input devices are available and braille key labels can assist with keyboard use. For people who are blind, speech output is the most popular form of assistive technology. Screen reader software and a speech synthesizer read text presented on the screen by word processing, web browsers, e-mail, and other software.

Refreshable braille displays deliver a line-by-line translation of screen text into braille on a display area where vertical pins move into braille configurations as screen text is scanned. Braille displays can be read quickly by those with advanced braille skills and are good for detailed editing, such as in computer programs and articles for publication. They also offfer an alternative to speech output when privacy is an issue. Refreshable braille displays are essential for computer users who are deaf and blind. Braille embossers provide hard copy output for users who are blind.

Scanners with optical character recognition combined with an accessible computer system provide independent access to printed materials for students who are blind. These systems read printed content and store it electronically on computers, where it can be read using speech synthesis or printed using braille translation software and braille embossers. Talking calculators, thermometers, and other specialized devices that provide audio output can enhance the participation and success of students who are blind, particularly those in science and engineering fields.

Speech and Hearing Impairments

Speech and hearing limitations alone do not generally interfere with computer use. However, speech synthesizers can act as substitute voices and thus provide a compensatory tool for students who cannot communicate vocally. Once computers provide them with intelligible speaking voices, students with speech impairments can participate in class discussions and other communications in academic, career, and community settings.

Alternatives to audio output can assist computer users who are hearing impaired. For example, if the sound volume is turned to zero, the computer may flash the menu bar when audio output is normally used. Similarly, software and web sites that provide content in auditory form should include captions or transcriptions for individuals with hearing impairments. Students can use FM systems to increase the volume of a speaker.

Specific Learning Disabilities

Students with learning disabilities are often neglected when it comes to the provision of assistive technology. However, mainstream and specialized hardware and software can further the academic and career goals of many people with learning disabilities.

A specific learning disability is unique to the individual, but it usually affects function in one or more of four broad categories: spoken language, written language, arithmetic, and reasoning skills. Specific types of learning disabilities include the following:

- *Dyslexia:* An individual with dyslexia may mix up letters within words and words within sentences while reading; misspell words, often using letter reversals; and/or have difficulty navigating using right and left and/or compass directions.

- *Dysgraphia:* An individual with dysgraphia has difficulty forming letters and words and producing legible handwriting on paper.

- *Dyscalculia:* A student with dyscalculia has difficulty understanding math symbols and/or applying concepts.

- *Dyspraxia:* The language comprehension of a person with dyspraxia is higher than language production, often resulting in the mix up of words and sentences while talking.

Educational software—especially when a computer provides multisensory experiences, interaction, positive reinforcement, individualized instruction, and repetition—can be useful in skill building for students with learning disabilities. Assistive technology can also help these students demonstrate their intelligence, knowledge, and skills. Students with disabilities such as dyslexia can compensate for high rates of input errors by using the spell-checker, thesaurus, and grammar-checker in a standard processing program. In addition, word prediction programs can help some students with learning disabilities by predicting whole words from fragments. Similarly, macro software, which expands abbreviations, can ease the entry of regularly used text. Many word processing programs also include tools for outlining thoughts and providing alternative visual formats that may compensate for difficulty in organizing words and ideas.

For individuals with learning disabilities who find it difficult to organize and integrate thoughts and ideas while writing, concept mapping software (e.g., Inspiration) allows for visual representation of ideas and concepts. It presents the ideas in graphic images connected with arrows to show their relationship. These images can be linked, rearranged, color coded, and matched with icons that make sense to the user. Concept mapping can help students organize content for writing assignments.

Spelling words correctly while typing can be a challenge for people with some types of learning disabilities. Again, word prediction programs can help by prompting users with a list of most likely word choices based on what they have typed so far. Students can then choose the desired word from the list presented, reducing the impact of poor spelling skills. Some people with specific learning disabilities spell phonetically. For them, software that renders phonetic spelling into correctly spelled words may be a useful tool.

Some individuals with learning disabilities find adaptive devices designed for those with visual impairments useful. In particular, large-print displays and alternative color combinations on the computer screen can overcome some reading challenges. People who have difficulty interpreting visual material may improve comprehension and the ability to identify and correct errors when words are spoken or printed in large fonts or in alternate color combinations. Individuals who receive information much better by listening than by decoding printed words may benefit from using reading systems. A scanner, along with optical character recognition software, can be used to read printed text into the computer. The printed material is placed on the scanner, where it is converted from an image file into a text file, using optical character recognition to make the characters recognizable by the computer. The computer then can read the words back using text-to-speech software and a speech synthesizer and can simultaneously present the words on screen. Reading systems include useful options such as highlighting a word, sentence, or paragraph by using contrasting colors.

Speech recognition software can help some individuals with learning disabilities that affect their ability to express themselves in writing or to use a standard keyboard. With speech recognition software, words spoken into a microphone are displayed on the computer screen while the individual is operating a word processor or other software.

Organizing schedules and information is difficult for some people with learning disabilities. Personal information managers or organizational software can provide these students with a centralized and portable organizer. The cues provided by these tools help them stay on task and provide visual representations of work schedules and assignment deadlines.

Talking calculators and other scientific tools with speech output provide useful assistive technology for people with dyscalculia. The verbal feedback helps them check input accuracy. Hearing a numerical answer can also provide a check for transposition of numbers, which is common for people with dyslexia.

Health Impairments

Students with health impairments can benefit from remote access to assignments, class notes, and instructors. Internet-based learning options should also be considered for those who have difficulty attending on-site activities. When computer and Internet access are available at home or in the hospital, students with health impairments can move forward with their education without meeting on campus.

FUNDING TECHNOLOGY

Funding is reported as the top barrier to providing computer access to people with disabilities by educators, service providers, and policy experts (National Council on Disability, 2000). Consumers identify the two biggest barriers to be lack of knowledge of stakeholders about appropriate assistive technology and lack of funding to purchase assistive technology (Fichten, Barile, & Asuncion, 1999; National Council on Disability, 2000). There is often a lack of available trained professionals to evaluate assistive technology and ensure that information technology is accessible in educational institutions (National Council on Disability, 2000).

To ensure that good choices are made regarding the purchase of technology for students with disabilities, stakeholder groups need to be aware of the types of technology options available to enhance the academic and career outcomes for individuals with disabilities. These stakeholder groups include general and special education teachers, occupational therapists, rehabilitation counselors, policy makers, employers, service providers, students, families, technology professionals, and postsecondary DSS staff. In addition to questions about initial purchase, questions about who is responsible for upgrades and technical support must be answered. Federal, state, regional, and local agencies should collaborate on planning, funding, selecting, and supporting assistive technology to ensure continuous technology access and support as students with disabilities make transitions through academic levels and to employment.

Stakeholders should be creative in identifying funding sources for technology. For example, if assistive technology is needed for a student with a disability to participate in a science or computer lab, perhaps the funding source for the inaccessible equipment and software should purchase the accessible items as well. Similarly, central computing dollars should be used to ensure that central computing resources such as web pages and computer labs are accessible to everyone on K–12 and college campuses, including students who are blind. Too often administrators assume that only special education dollars or specific campus resources earmarked for students with disabilities should be used for these purposes.

SELECTING A COLLEGE

Myriad considerations should be addressed when selecting a college. One of them should be the availability and accessibility of technology used in academic departments, programs, and campus services. The level of importance of this area of consideration depends on specific accessibility issues, academic interests, and the prospective student's perceived need for access to specific services and programs. The needs of a computer science major who is blind and plans to live in a campus dormitory will be quite different from those of a student with a learning disability who plans to major in social work and commute from home.

When investigating a college, students should ask what types of assistive technology are currently available on campus, where they are located, and how they are supported. Students should also inquire about how specific requests for assistive technology are handled. Campus policies and standards regarding web accessibility and the accessibility of science and computer labs should also be explored.

Regarding campus services, prospective students with disabilities should find out about the accessibility of on-line registration systems and library resources. They should inquire whether the availability of tutoring centers, career services, and other student services are fully accessible to them. Those who plan to live in a campus dormitory should ask about the accessibility of computing services that are provided in campus housing and about how requests for assistive technology are handled there.

Prospective students with disabilities should find out to whom they would submit requests or complaints regarding the accessibility of technology and technology services on campus. Although prospective students cannot expect satisfactory responses to all of their questions about technology access, asking enough individuals or organizations a suitable number of questions will give students a good idea about what they can expect regarding technology access on a specific campus. A campus with a commitment to nondiscrimination regarding information and technology access and with clear policies, procedures, and departmental responsibilities is likely to be a better fit for students with disabilities than one without these characteristics.

SUCCEEDING IN COLLEGE
AND PREPARING FOR A CAREER

Choosing a college and getting enrolled are big steps for anyone, particularly for those who have disabilities. Yet, entering college is just the beginning of an important chapter of a person's life. College enrollment provides opportunities to further develop and apply self-determination, study, and technical skills in a new, challenging environment. Throughout their college years, it is important that students with disabilities employ self-advocacy skills with professors and student services staff. They should clearly articulate to computer support staff exactly what they need and where. They should request that assistive technology be provided in an inclusive setting when reasonable. For example, if students in an accounting class are working in the business school computer lab, a student with a disability should be able to work in this lab as well. Computer registration for classes, campus web sites, and other technology-related services should be accessible. In addition, students with disabilities who wish to make the campus a more accessible place for everyone should promote UD of campus technology environments. An effective way to contribute in this way is for the students to volunteer as members of advisory committees that identify and solve accessibility problems on campus.

High-tech careers are particularly accessible to individuals with disabilities because of the combined effect of advancements in assistive technology and the increasing use of information technology in these career fields. Although few students with disabilities pursue high-tech postsecondary programs and careers and the attrition rate is high (National Science Foundation, 2000; Office of Disability Employment Policy, 2001), those who succeed in these fields demonstrate that opportunities do exist (Presidential Task Force, 1999).

Individuals with disabilities who complete postsecondary studies are likely to have fewer work-based learning experiences than those who do not have disabilities. Because lack of job skills and related experiences before graduation create barriers to employment (Blackorby & Wagner, 1996; National Council on Disability, 2000; National Council on Disability & Social Security Administration, 2000; Unger, Wehman, Yasuda, Campbell, & Green, 2001), it is important for students with disabilities to engage in work-based opportunities while still in school. At both the high school and college levels, they should participate in internships and other work-based learning experiences where they can practice using technology in work settings. Internships, job shadows, service learning, and other work-based learning experiences can help students with disabilities gain job skills, explore accommodation options, and learn to use technology in work settings (Burgstahler, 2001; Luecking & Fabian, 2000). Such experiences can improve their chances for a successful school-to-work transition.

Individuals who coordinate work experiences for high school and college students as well as participating employers need to be aware of the potential contributions and accommodation needs (including assistive technology) of students with disabilities. Stakeholders should work together to ensure that students have access to appropriate technology for employment settings and that students are included in the process in order for them to gain the knowledge and self-advocacy skills that they need for success in postsecondary education and careers.

Steps to Success

In summary, as students with disabilities prepare for the transition to college, they should consider the role of technology in all aspects of their plans and preparations. Specifically, with the help of parents, educators, and other advocates, students should

- Take the initiative and responsibility to explore their learning styles, their disability-related challenges, and the role that technology can play in helping them build on their strengths to succeed in college and careers

- Find sources of authoritative and up-to-date information on assistive technology related to their own needs

- Seek assistive technology solutions that maximize self-reliance and self-determination

- Be willing and prepared to educate teachers and others involved with their education regarding assistive technology

- Become acquainted with technology typically used in postsecondary academic and career paths of interest

- Advocate for access to appropriate tools at their schools and/or find alternate access to technology that supports vocational goals

- Develop skills using computers, assistive technology, and the Internet

- Employ technology to take advantage of opportunities to participate in classroom activities, such as discussions and interactive projects, at the same levels as others

- Become acquainted with academic tools, expectations, and services in advance of making the transition to postsecondary studies

- Learn which postsecondary schools are best at supporting mainstream technology in specific disciplines, assistive technology in inclusive settings, and the design and procurement of accessible technology campuswide

- Connect with role models, mentors, and peers who can assist them in acquiring and using assistive technology and in learning to advocate for access to programs and resources in education and employment

- Use technology to participate in work-based learning opportunities, such as job shadows, internships, and community service

- Develop independent daily living skills, using technology as appropriate, for life on and off campus

CONCLUSION

The use of information technology is ubiquitous—in education, employment, community service, and recreation. Computers, the Internet, and other technologies have the potential to promote positive postsecondary and career outcomes for people with disabilities. However, this potential will not be realized unless stakeholders secure funding; are knowledgeable about technology; comply with legal mandates; and develop policies, standards, and procedures that maximize the independence, participation, and productivity of people with disabilities throughout their lives. Educators, service providers, and other stakeholders must work to ensure that all individuals with disabilities have access to technology and learn to use technology in ways that contribute to positive academic and career outcomes and self-determined lives. In addition, they should work toward a seamless transition of availability of technology as individuals with disabilities move from secondary schools to postsecondary institutions to employment work sites. Ensuring that the opportunities technology provides are accessible to everyone contributes to a level playing field in college and employment, results in successful careers for more citizens, and thereby strengthens the economy.

REFERENCES

The Alliance for Technology Access. (2002). *Success stories.* Retrieved January 14, 2005, from http://www.ataccess.org/resources/fpic/successes.html

Americans with Disabilities Act (ADA) of 1990, PL 101-336, 42 U.S.C. §§ 12101 *et seq.*

Anderson-Inman, L., Knox-Quinn, C., & Szymanski, M. (1999). Computer-supported studying: Stories of successful transition to postsecondary education. *Career Development for Exceptional Individuals, 22*(2), 185–212.

Bar, L., & Galluzzo, J. (1999). *The accessible school: Universal design for educational settings.* Berkeley, CA: MIG Communications.

Blackhurst, A.E., Lahm, E.A., Harrison, E.M., & Chandler, W.G. (1999). A framework for aligning technology with transition competencies. *Career Development for Exceptional Individuals, 22*(2), 153–183.

Blackorby, J., & Wagner, M. (1996). Longitudinal postschool outcomes of youth with disabilities: Findings from the National Longitudinal Transition Study. *Exceptional Children, 62,* 399–413.

Bowe, F.G. (2000). *Universal design in education: Teaching nontraditional students.* Westport, CT: Bergin & Garvey.

Burgstahler, S. (1997). Peer support: What role can the Internet play? *Information Technology and Disabilities, 4*(4). Retrieved January 14, 2005, from http://www.rit.edu/~easi/itd/itdv04n4/article2.htm

Burgstahler, S. (2001). A collaborative model promotes career success for students with disabilities: How DO-IT does it. *Journal of Vocational Rehabilitation, 16*(3–4), 209–216.

Burgstahler, S. (2002). Distance learning: Universal design, universal access. *Educational Technology Review, 10*(1). Retrieved January 14, 2005, from http://www.aace.org/pubs/etr/issue2/burgstahler.cfm

Burgstahler, S. (2003). The role of technology in preparing youth with disabilities for postsecondary education and employment. *Journal of Special Education Technology, 18*(4), 7–20.

Burgstahler, S. (2004a). *Preparing for college: An online tutorial.* Retrieved January 17, 2005, from http://www.washington.edu/doit/Brochures/Academics/cprep.html

Burgstahler, S. (2004b). *Universal design.* Seattle: University of Washington. Retrieved January 14, 2005, from http://www.washington.edu/doit/Resources/udesign.html

Burgstahler, S., & Cronheim, D. (2001). Supporting peer–peer and mentor–protégé relationships on the internet. *Journal of Research on Technology in Education, 34*(1), 59–74.

Carl D. Perkins Vocational and Applied Technology Education Act Amendments of 1998, PL 105-232, 20 U.S.C. 2301 *et seq.*

The Center for Applied Special Technology. (2002). *Universal design for learning.* Retrieved January 14, 2005, from http://www.cast.org/udl

Closing the Gap. (2005). 2005 Closing the Gap resource directory. *Closing the Gap, 23*(6), 37–194.

Education for All Handicapped Children Act of 1975, PL 94-142, 20 U.S.C. §§ 1400 *et seq.*

Fichten, C., Barile, M., & Asuncion, J.V. (1999). *Learning technologies: Students with disabilities in postsecondary education.* Montreal, Canada: Dawson College, Office of Learning Technologies Adaptech Project.

Field, T., Martin, J., Miller, R., Ward, M., & Wehmeyer, M. (1998). Self-determination for persons with disabilities: A position statement of the Division on Career Development and Transition. *Career Development for Exceptional Individuals, 21*(2), 113–128.

Frank, K., & Wade, P. (1993). Disabled student services in postsecondary education: Who's responsible for what? *Journal of College Student Development, 34*(1), 26–30.

Goldberg, L.B.G., & O'Neill, L.M. (2000). Computer technology can empower students with learning disabilities. *Exceptional Parent, 30*(7), 72–74.

Hitchcock, C., & Stahl, S. (2003). Assistive technology, universal design, universal design for learning: Improved learning opportunities. *Journal of Special Education Technology, 18*(4), 45–52.

Individuals with Disabilities Education Act (IDEA) Amendments of 1997, PL 105-17, 20 U.S.C. §§ 1400 *et seq.*

Individuals with Disabilities Education Improvement Act of 2004, PL 108-446, 20 U.S.C. §§ 1400 *et seq.*

Kaye, H.S. (2000). Disability and the digital divide (Disability Statistics Abstracts No. 22). Washington, DC: U.S. Department of Education, National Institute on Disability and Rehabilitation Research.

Kim-Rupnow, W.S., & Burgstahler, S. (2004). Perceptions of students with disabilities regarding the value of technology-based support activities on postsecondary education and employment. *Journal of Special Education Technology, 19*(2), 43–56.

Luecking, R., & Fabian, E. (2000). Paid internships and employment success for youth in transition. *Career Development for Exceptional Individuals, 23*, 205–222.

McCusker, C. (1995). The Americans with Disabilities Act: Its potential for expanding the scope of reasonable academic accommodations. *Journal of College and University Law, 21*(4), 619–641.

McNeil, J.M. (1997). *Current population reports: Americans with disabilities 1994–95.* Washington, DC: U.S. Department of Commerce (Document Number 1246).

National Center for Education Statistics. (2000a). *Teachers' tools for the 21st century: A report on teachers' use of technology.* Retrieved January 14, 2005, from http://nces.ed.gov/pubsearch/pubsinfo.asp?pubid=2000102

National Center for Education Statistics. (2000b). *What are the barriers to the use of advanced telecommunications for students with disabilities in public schools?* Retrieved January 14, 2005, from http://nces.ed.gov/pubsearch/pubsinfo.asp?pubid=2000042

The National Center for Universal Design. (2002). *What is universal design?* Retrieved January 14, 2005, from http://www.design.ncsu.edu/cud/univ_design/ud.htm

National Council on Disability. (2000). *Federal policy barriers to assistive technology.* Washington, DC: Author.

National Council on Disability & Social Security Administration. (2000). *Transition and post-school outcomes for youth with disabilities: Closing the gaps to post-secondary education and employment.* Washington, DC: Author.

National Organization on Disability. (1998). *Harris survey of Americans with disabilities.* Washington, DC: Author.

National Science Foundation. (2000). *Women, minorities, and persons with disabilities in science and engineering.* Washington, DC: U.S. Government Printing Office.

Office of Disability Employment Policy. (2001, November). *Improving the availability of community-based services for people with disabilities.* Washington, DC: Author.

Office of the Federal Register, National Archives and Records Service, General Services Administration. (2000, December 21). Electronic and information technology accessibility standards. *The Federal Register, 65*(246), 80499–80528.

Opitz, C., Savenye, W., & Rowland, C. (2003). Accessibility of state department of education home pages and special education pages. *Journal of Special Education Technology, 18*(1), 17–27.

Patrick, D.L. (1996, September 9). *Correspondence to Senator Tom Harkin.* Retrieved January 14, 2005, from http://www.usdoj.gov/crt/foia/cltr204.txt

Phelps, L.A., & Hanley-Maxwell, C. (1997). School-to-work transitions for youth with disabilities: A review of outcomes and practices. *Review of Educational Research, 67*(2), 197–226.

Presidential Task Force on Employment of Adults with Disabilities. (1999). *Recharting the course: If not now, when?* Washington, DC: Author.

Rehabilitation Act Amendments of 1992 and 1993, 34 C.F.R. 361.42 (a) (3) (b); RSM 1513-1523.

Schmetzke, A. (2001) Online distance education: "Anytime, anywhere" but not for everyone. *Information Technology and Disability, 7*(2). Retrieved January 14, 2005, from http://www.rit.edu/~easi/itd/itdv07n2/axel.htm

School-to-Work Opportunities Act of 1994, PL 103-239, 108 Stat 568, 20 U.S.C. §§ 6101–6235.

Section 504 of the Rehabilitation Act of 1973, PL 93-112, 29 U.S.C. § 794(a).

Section 508 of the Rehabilitation Act of 1973 (1998, amended). 29 U.S.C. § 794(d).

Technology-Related Assistance for Individuals with Disabilities Act of 1988, PL 100-407, 29 U.S.C. §§ 2201 *et seq.*

Unger, D., Wehman, P., Yasuda, S., Campbell, L., & Green, H. (2001, March). *Human resource professionals and the employment of persons with disabilities: A business perspective.* Paper presented at the National Capacity Building Institute, University of Hawaii at Manoa.

U.S. Department of Health and Human Services. (2001). *New Freedom Initiative.* Retrieved January 14, 2005, from http://www.hhs.gov/newfreedom

Wagner, M.M., & Blackorby, J. (1996). Transition from high school to work to college: How special education students fare. *The Future of Children, 6*(1), 103–120.

Yelin, E., & Katz, P. (1994). Labor force trends of persons with and without disabilities. *Monthly Labor Review, 117,* 36–42.

CHAPTER 10

Training University Faculty and Staff

Elizabeth Evans Getzel and Donald E. Finn, Jr.

There is an increased need for faculty development in response to the number of diverse learners, including students with disabilities, entering postsecondary education programs. A combination of legislative, academic, and social change has resulted in greater numbers of students with disabilities seeking advanced degrees (Gilson, 1996). The National Longitudinal Transition Study-2 (Wagner, Cameto, & Newman, 2003) findings reflect the increased interest by students (and their families) in attending institutions of higher education. For students with disabilities, postsecondary education, especially in the form of 2-year colleges, was more likely to be a transition option in 2001 than in 1987. This identified outcome was for youth of all disability categories regardless of gender, race, or income level (Wagner et al., 2003).

Professional development activities for faculty and instructional staff are critical for creating a welcoming campus for all students, especially those with disabilities. More than any other campus entity, faculty members and other instructional staff influence the academic success of students with disabilities (Wilson, Getzel, & Brown, 2000). In a review of the literature, Vogel, Leyser, Wyland, and Brulle (1999) reported that two important factors contributed to students with learning disabilities successfully completing their degree programs: 1) a positive faculty attitude and 2) a willingness to provide accommodations. These authors found that faculty members who were more knowledgeable about disability characteristics and their effects on learning or who had experience teaching students with disabilities were more likely to display a positive attitude about teaching these students (Vogel et al., 1999).

Scott and Gregg (2000) raised another important aspect in the professional development of faculty. These authors concluded that institutions require faculty members to perform an increasing number of individual, institutional, and disciplinary responsibilities. For example, faculty members sit on grievance committees or academic standards committees that require an understanding not only of the universities' policies and procedures but also of ways for obtaining equitable decisions when considering students with disabilities (Scott & Gregg, 2000). On an individual level, faculty members are responsible for ensuring that academic standards are maintained and for providing accommodations for students with disabilities in their courses. When designing and implementing faculty development activities, it is critical to assist faculty in better understanding their roles within the university and to offer information, strategies, and techniques to enhance and increase their participation in these roles (Scott & Gregg, 2000).

There is a growing body of literature studying the need for professional development programs for postsecondary education faculty (Getzel, Briel, & McManus, 2003; Salzberg et al., 2002; Scott & Gregg, 2000; Szymanski, Hewitt, Watson, & Swett, 1999; Thompson, Bethea, & Turner, 1997; Wilson et al., 2000; Wilson & Getzel, 2001). Salzberg and colleagues (2002) conducted a national survey of disability support service (DSS) directors on their perceptions of faculty concerns and the professional development activities needed. Most respondents identified the following faculty concerns:

- Maintaining academic standards

- Understanding their rights and responsibilities

- Obtaining information on course modifications

- Understanding the rights and responsibilities of students with disabilities

- Discussing issues surrounding students disclosing disabilities to professors

- Understanding the process students use to become eligible for accommodations

When asked which topics should be included in professional development activities, the DSS directors identified information on the services available to students on campus, contact information for assistance, legal responsibilities of faculty members, ethical considerations (e.g., privacy issues), and information about specific disability characteristics (Salzberg et al., 2002).

Providing effective faculty development activities can be challenging. Yet, as the field of higher education and disability continues to advance, strategies and techniques to assist faculty in educating students with disabilities are being studied for effectiveness (Getzel et al., 2003; Salzberg et al., 2002; Scott & Gregg, 2000; Vogel et al., 1999). This chapter presents suggested strategies and activities to address identified challenges when creating and implementing faculty development programs. The information and resources described are based on current literature in the field and on the experiences of the chapter authors designing professional development programs at Virginia Commonwealth University (VCU) in Richmond. The chapter context is based on a comprehensive program developed by the VCU Rehabilitation Research and Training Center (VCU-RRTC), in collaboration with the Vice Provost's

Office for Student Affairs and Enrollment Services, to assist faculty, staff, and administrators in creating a more welcoming campus for students with disabilities. The Professional Development Academy (PDA) program was established as a result of in-depth needs assessments conducted for the Vice Provost's Office. Since 1999, the PDA staff members have designed multiple approaches and strategies to support four broad objectives:

1. Foster a more welcoming and supportive campus environment for students with disabilities.

2. Equip administrators and support staff with the information and resources to better meet the unique and varied needs of students with disabilities.

3. Provide training and technical assistance to instructional faculty and staff to assist them in teaching, advising, and ultimately facilitating successful academic outcomes for students with disabilities.

4. Establish a campuswide network that supports a more decentralized support and delivery model.

VCU, along with other universities and colleges across the United States, was awarded funds from the U.S. Department of Education's Office of Postsecondary Education (OPE) to develop and implement faculty development activities. Since 1999, VCU has worked to create a series of approaches to address the specific needs of faculty, staff, students with disabilities, and administrators to enhance and expand the educational experiences of students with disabilities. The chapter provides descriptions of products and materials developed by VCU and other national postsecondary programs, along with evaluation and follow-up strategies to use with faculty and staff.

ASSESS NEED FOR PROFESSIONAL DEVELOPMENT ACTIVITIES

Faculty/Staff Input

One of the best methods for planning and implementing professional development activities is to assess the needs of faculty on campus. Getzel and colleagues (2003) found that faculty input was a critical component in the development and implementation of successful professional development programs. Depending on the amount of time and resources that can be devoted to such an activity, several methods can be used. Focus groups constitute one method that colleges and universities use to obtain input on topics to cover and on the format for providing information. This type of inquiry allows for a detailed, more in-depth process to gain insight into faculty and staff experiences with teaching students with disabilities (Krueger, 1994; Wheeler, 1996). Structured interviews form a similar inquiry technique but are more in depth. These interviews can be conducted by telephone or in person and allow faculty and staff to thoroughly discuss their perceptions on needed training or information. To reach an even wider audience, surveys (completed on line or through regular mail) provide a broader range of faculty and staff responses concerning professional development needs. Table 10.1 provides sample questions for obtaining faculty input. Suggested questions for student input are also included in the table. It is important when assessing faculty and staff training needs that a variety of perceptions is obtained to ensure that the training materials and information are comprehensive and inclusive. In previous faculty development activities, VCU has sought the opinions of faculty, staff, administrators, DSS coordinators, and students with disabilities.

When collecting ideas for professional development activities, it is important to obtain information from a holistic approach. In other words, training opportunities should reflect the needs of faculty in the various roles they play at the individual, institutional, and disciplinary levels (Scott & Gregg, 2000). All too often, faculty development activities focus primarily on content areas such as instructional strategies, rights, responsibilities, and so forth. There is a great need for training in these areas; however, questions need to focus on all of their roles and responsibilities concerning students with disabilities on campus. Asking questions about faculty members' responsibilities in addition to their teaching role provides an opportunity to address other pressing issues that could have a tremendous impact on the experiences of college

Table 10.1. Sample questions on professional development needs

Faculty/administrator questions	Student questions
Have you worked in any capacity with students with disabilities? If so, describe your role.	What major barriers have you encountered during your postsecondary education as a result of being a student with a disability?
Are the faculty and administration equipped with the necessary knowledge, information, and resources to adequately provide support services to students with disabilities?	What would you change about our campus's program of services for students with disabilities (e.g., policies, services offered)?
What methods or strategies should be used to disseminate information or materials on educating students with disabilities in higher education settings?	What are your major concerns for you and other students with disabilities on this campus?
What should be the university's highest priorities regarding the provision of services for students with disabilities? What strategies should be employed to most effectively address these priorities?	Are campus organizations that support student activities considerate of and responsive to the needs and interests of students with disabilities?
What are some specific ways in which faculty/administration might be better supported and encouraged to seek information and assistance when working with students with disabilities?	Have you found the faculty and administration to be knowledgeable and sensitive regarding disability-related issues?
In what specific areas has the university been most responsive to and supportive of the needs of students with disabilities?	Do you think the general campus climate—with respect to understanding, sensitivity, and acceptance of students with disabilities—has affected your success as a student? How?
In what areas could the university be more responsive to the needs of students?	

Source: Wilson, Kregel, & Getzel (1999).

students with disabilities. Faculty members often sit on financial aid commit-tees, deciding whether a student is making enough progress in his or her studies to continue receiving aid, or on academic probation committees. Understanding the policies and the range of issues faced by students with disabilities in higher education can assist faculty in making informed decisions concerning students with disabilities who come before these kinds of commit-tees.

Another aspect of gathering information for training purposes is assessing the campus environment. It is important to understand the culture of the campus when designing and implementing professional development activities. The content might cover areas that faculty and staff rate as highly needed, but the mode of delivery can seriously affect the participation of interested individuals. For example, would it be more effective for someone already on campus, rather than someone from outside the university, to deliver faculty development? Sometimes bringing in a speaker from another university is helpful because doing so provides instructional faculty and staff the opportunity to learn what others have found effective for educating students with disabili-ties. Yet, if faculty members perceive the speaker's teaching load, access to graduate students as assistants, or other factors as greatly different from their own experiences, the content, although very helpful, could appear irrelevant.

Determining whether honoraria or other incentives are needed to obtain faculty participation is a question that training developers need to consider. Some universities within the network of U.S. Department of Education's OPE faculty development projects (Getzel et al., 2003) found that the use of incentives was an effective method to obtain participation. In some instances, the incentives were used to compensate faculty for the time involved in sharing information with their colleagues or providing feedback for an evaluation process to document curriculum materials, policies, or teaching strategies (Getzel et al., 2003). Again, the campus climate will determine the effectiveness of using incentives for participation; some campus administrators may believe that professional development activities are faculty responsibilities and that incentives, particularly financial ones, should not be a part of the training package (Wilson, Getzel, & Brown, 2000).

Obtain Input from Other Campus Entities

Obtaining input from service providers on campus—particularly staff members in the DSS office, counseling centers, career centers, and other support services offices—is also critical. At VCU, an in-depth campuswide assessment of ser-vices for students with disabilities was conducted to help facilitate a comprehen-sive strategic planning effort (Wilson, Kregel, & Getzel, 1999). As part of this assessment, interviews were conducted with the coordinators of services for students with disabilities on the university's academic and medical cam-puses. One primary area of focus was the training and program development needs of faculty and staff serving students with disabilities. The perceptions of DSS coordinators, along with those of students with disabilities who were interviewed as part of this process, were then compared with the responses provided by faculty, staff, and administrators. The information obtained from all of these groups helped to form a picture of the gaps in training and information provided for faculty and staff. As a result of the assessment, implementation of a comprehensive training program was recommended to VCU's administration to provide university personnel with adequate information on educating and working with students with disabilities. Some avenues of training were identified, including existing faculty development programs, department in-service training sessions, short Internet courses, and new faculty orientation. Various entities on the VCU campus (e.g., DSS coordinators, counseling center staff) were also identified as being equipped to serve as potential trainers.

CONDUCT OUTREACH EFFORTS

Faculty Networks

University personnel responsible for developing and implementing professional development activities face a lack of understanding or buy-in by faculty and staff members regarding the relevancy of the information or materials provided. This issue, along with time constraints of university personnel, can present tremendous challenges to any outreach effort (Getzel et al., 2003). Often, obtaining administrative support for professional development activities helps to increase the visibility and importance of these activities. A critical initial step in the design and implementation of professional development programs or activities is to build collaborative relationships with all parties involved, including faculty, administrators, and students with disabilities.

One approach to building collaborative relationships is the use of faculty liaisons. Individuals who serve as liaisons are not disability experts; however, they serve as representatives in their respective departments to disseminate disability-related information to their colleagues, and they provide input on topics for training sessions. At VCU, these liaisons are called Professional Development Partners (PDPs). The recruitment of a PDP is individualized. Some PDPs are recruited after attending a training session sponsored by the PDA. During the training, staff members talk about the network of faculty in each of the schools and departments who serve as PDPs. Other faculty members become PDPs as a result of working with the PDA staff on other projects. The PDA staff recruits faculty members across the academic and medical campuses at VCU. Department chairs or associate deans are contacted about the PDA concerning the services and supports that can be provided. During this discussion, members talk about how these partners are administrative and teaching faculty who act as the eyes and ears in their departments regarding disability-related issues and needs. In addition, these individuals maintain information on campus resources and support services that faculty can obtain when a particular need arises. Other universities and colleges have used a similar approach to identify faculty liaisons to support faculty development initiatives (Getzel et al., 2003).

The PDA staff members hold meetings or training sessions with the PDPs at least once during each semester. The content of the training or meeting is structured around the needs that the partners have expressed. For example, the initial meeting of the fall semester covers the roles and responsibilities of the PDPs and provides updated information that might be useful to faculty in their departments. Other meetings may cover the range of resources and supports on campus, assistive technology devices, and community resources available to students with disabilities. These sessions help to establish a group identity and solidify a network of liaisons. Having individuals serve in the capacity of resource providers helps to keep information current within university departments and serves as a mechanism to obtain continuous feedback and input on topics for professional development activities.

Centers for Teaching Excellence

An effective outreach method involves working with university centers for improving instruction, which are commonly called Centers for Teaching Excellence (CTEs). Typically CTEs offer a range of professional development activities focusing on effective instructional practices, classroom management, and new technologies. These centers offer resources and training in a variety of ways, including on-line modules, large- and small-group seminars, or large-group training sessions. Collaborating with an established entity on campus that focuses on improving and enhancing university teaching creates opportunities to present current practices in assisting college students with disabilities. Several universities found that incorporating concepts of universal design (UD) into the information that centers disseminated to faculty and staff was an effective outreach method (Getzel et al., 2003). Providing information within the context of UD enabled teaching professionals to learn how changes in their instruction, curriculum, and use of technology could benefit all students— including students with disabilities—which helped to expand their perception of teaching these students. (See Chapter 6 for a detailed description of UD principles.)

At VCU, a collaborative relationship with the CTE and other entities providing training on disability-related information has provided a wealth of opportunities for training and resource development across campus. At the heart of this partnership is the goal of effectively reaching and teaching all students, including students with disabilities. Although disability awareness and sensitivity training sessions are important, the collaboration has placed emphasis on classroom practices and strategies to effectively reach students with disabilities. The approach showing the greatest potential has been opening a discussion about the increased diversity of learners attending college. Presenting disability along a continuum of diversity or learner differences gives faculty a new framework for viewing these students. This approach sensitizes faculty to students with disabilities and helps to cultivate a receptive atmosphere to UD concepts and practices in face-to-face training sessions/seminars and through print and on-line materials.

Among the most effective outreach methods utilized on the VCU campus to foster awareness surrounding disability-related issues has been the collaborative effort to develop, design, and distribute a print and electronic newsletter for faculty through the CTE. This publication, *VCU Teaching*, is printed and distributed (via campus mail) semiannually to teaching and administrative faculty, including adjunct professors, across the academic and medical campuses. Each issue of *VCU Teaching* includes an article featuring principles and effective practices for working with students with disabilities. This newsletter not only provides exposure for both the CTE and entities on campus providing disability specific information but also provides an effective means for reaching faculty across campuses and exposing them to disability-related topics on a regular basis. Figure 10.1 provides a sample page of *VCU Teaching*.

Use of Different Training Formats

University centers established for teaching faculty are one of many outreach mechanisms. If a university or college does not have an identified entity on campus, such as a CTE, a variety of outreach methods can be used. In the survey conducted by Getzel and colleagues (2003), universities and colleges emphasized the importance of infusing disability-related information into existing programs and activities on campus whenever possible. This is especially important if face-to-face or on-site training sessions are planned. Unless faculty members have requested a special training session, incorporating information into other established events helps to increase the number of faculty members receiving the information and overcomes the time constraint barrier that limits the number of training sessions or programs that faculty can attend. Some universities incorporate disability-related information into annual graduate teaching assistant orientations or departmental meetings. Others infuse learner-centered concepts and instructional strategies into academic departments on their campus (Getzel et al., 2003).

Web-based training and information forms another method that is widely used by many universities and colleges. A web site can become a primary vehicle for sharing information and conducting training. Teaching professionals, administrators, and other university personnel can retrieve the information at their convenience. Web sites enable individuals to explore a particular topic thoroughly and independently or to retrieve information on a need-to-know basis (i.e., when confronted with a particular issue or concern). However, it is important to carefully plan and present any information or training provided on the web site. Although the Internet offers extensive resources, learning does not naturally occur just through "surfing." Some new information may be acquired this way, but chances are that the information is limited in scope

A publication from the Virginia Commonwealth University Center for Teaching Excellence

CTE

Volume 2, Number 1   Spring, 2004

Summer 2004 CTE VITAL Workshops

TLC Series
2-day workshop

◆ Teaching Large Classes
◆ Infusing Technology
◆ Active Learning
◆ Teaching with BlackBoard

Dates:
- June 7th & 8th -- 9:00 - 3:30
  Academic Campus
- July 27th & 28th -- 9:00 - 3:30
  Academic Campus
- Aug. 2nd & 3rd -- 9:00 - 3:30
  Health Sciences Campus

New Faculty Institute
2-day workshop

◆ Teaching Philosophies
◆ Creating a Syllabus
◆ Teaching and Assessment

Dates:
- August 10th & 11th -- TBA
- August 12th & 13th -- TBA

For more information, contact the CTE at:
cte@vcu.edu
(804) 827-0838

Greetings from the Center for Teaching Excellence. Once again this has been an extremely busy year for us and the many faculty who help us with all of our programs. This past spring and fall we will have conducted over 25 workshops with faculty on both campuses. Later this spring we will be doing special workshops for the School of Medicine, School of Dentistry, the College of Humanities and Sciences and possibly a few other schools that we are currently working with on focused programs.

This past fall we instituted a number of programs, some of which are described within the newsletter. One of our major initiatives was the CTE Junior Faculty Mentoring Program. This is an integrated program whereby we link a 1st or 2nd year faculty member with a senior member within their school or college. We also conduct at least one workshop every month on topics that the new faculty have determined are important to them. The highlight of last semester was a workshop in getting started with writing for publication. The program now includes 25 faculty from almost every school in the university. The mentors are paid a stipend for their participation. We are looking for faculty who would like to be mentors next year so if you are interested please contact us at cte@vcu.edu and we will put you on our list. During the summer we will meet with all new faculty and offer this program to them.

This summer we will rerun our very successful series of summer workshops on teaching in the large classroom, integrating active learning in the classroom and integrating technology into large classes. We will also run another series of workshops on Teaching with Blackboard during the summer. Finally, Don Forsyth has agreed to work with us to develop a two-day workshop on teaching for all new faculty. We intend to do this workshop twice during the summer.

On a final note I want you to be aware that the CTE is heavily involved in almost all the major university initiatives involving teaching. We are a major part of the PRISM grant that is working with chemistry, biology and math in Humanities and Sciences. We are also a major part of the Quality Enhancement Program (QEP) that will be instituted over the next ten years as part of our response to the SACS accreditation process. But most importantly I feel the CTE is the voice of the faculty in the classroom. We are here to serve you and your interests. The Classroom Performance System (CPS) described below was initiated by the CTE in an attempt to promote active learning and student engagement in the classroom. We are committed to helping you improve student learning and making your experience as a faculty member at VCU a more positive one. Contact us or join our mailing list at http://www.vcu.edu/cte. Help us make the university the kind of place you want it to be.

Best Regards,

Joseph Marolla, Director, CTE

Figure 10.1. Sample of *VCU Teaching*. (From the Virginia Commonwealth University Center for Teaching Excellence. [2004]. *VCU Teaching, 2*[1], 1; reprinted by permission.)

and application (Garrison & Anderson, 2003). For meaningful learning to occur in an on-line environment, courses of study need to be constructed with the learner, as well as specific learner outcomes, in mind. The design of a web site can serve as an example of how information and materials should be formatted to make the site accessible to everyone. A general rule of thumb is to use a simple, basic layout for all pages. For example, too many buttons, colors, or background designs that obscure text can be distracting, particularly for people with learning disabilities or visual impairments.

One very critical component of professional development activities for teaching faculty and university administrators is creating web pages that are accessible for students with disabilities. The emphasis is on good practice and incorporating UD principles. Training sessions focus on illustrating web pages that are designed to meet the needs of students with diverse disabilities. The content is filled with examples that include web features of large, easy-to-read buttons and "alt" tags. Examples of graphics or pictures are illustrated showing longer descriptive captions that are beneficial for all site visitors. Information is provided on the use of on-line captioned video or video transcripts to help enrich the web experiences of users with hearing impairments. In addition, information on how to organize information on the web for screen readers is discussed. Regardless of the features that are covered during the training, participants are shown how to obtain resources to review their sites for accessibility. Participants are asked to compare their web pages with accessibility guidelines such as those developed by the World Wide Web Consortium (W3C) (http://www.w3.org) or through commercially available software packages such as Watchfire's Bobby™ (see Figure 10.2 for this software's logo, which is often displayed on accessible sites).

The use of campus mail can be an effective alternative for reaching out to faculty and other instructional staff, especially adjunct faculty members. The advantage of this method is that it does not require any action by the recipient. Providing resources in this way does not guarantee that the recipient will review them, but the probability of recipient review may be enhanced by the design of the materials. The PDA program has successfully used the campus mail system at VCU to distribute disability-related information for faculty. These materials have included Internet links to sources of additional

Figure 10.2. Bobby logo. (The Bobby Logo is a Trademark of Watchfire Corporation. Used with permission. All rights reserved.)

information, generally the PDA web site. Some materials have included information about upcoming training opportunities offered in face-to-face and online formats.

Two critical (and often costly) ingredients are having these materials created by an experienced graphic designer and printed by a professional. Even individuals who have an eye for layout and design and own desktop publishing software (allowing the creation of professional-looking publications that can be printed on a color printer) may encounter some problems. First, although color printers produce nice-looking documents, there is no substitute for professionally printed materials. Second, securing the services of someone trained in graphic design and layout can create a professional and appealing publication that includes elements to pique the interest of the recipient. The colors, pictures, graphics, and titles used in the publication are all important elements that should be handled by a professional. Exploring the availability of a graphic designer within the university community could be achieved through an in-house print shop or through relationships with off-campus shops that provide services at predetermined or prenegotiated prices. The important point is to present information in a professional manner that is appealing to the targeted audience.

PROVIDE TRAINING OPPORTUNITIES

Face-to-Face Training

Training events constitute the most common method for delivering information to faculty, and face-to-face interactions form the most common mode of training delivery. Arranging for these training efforts may be done through one office or as a cooperative effort with another office. The VCU PDA has utilized each type of training outreach and has found advantages to both. For training sessions delivered by the PDA alone, topics have been designed and directed toward specific schools or geared toward an area of interest to multiple schools. A training session about providing physical accommodations in a laboratory setting may only be of interest to the biology department; a workshop addressing issues for working effectively with students with disabilities in field placements may appeal to faculty members from the school of education, the school of social work, or various medical departments. Regardless of which school or department is the focus of the training, the assistance of faculty liaisons (e.g., VCU's PDPs) is invaluable for determining specific training needs.

In some instances, training sessions may be conducted in cooperation with another department and may be offered as one segment of a daylong or multiday institute. In its cooperative work with the VCU CTE, the PDA has offered 1 hour or 90-minute workshops on the integration of UD techniques into learning settings as part of a $1^{1}/_{2}$-day institute focusing on myriad topics related to effective teaching practices.

Many universities and colleges are using training teams that are comprised of students with disabilities and faculty members and are used for the creation and implementation of professional development activities (Getzel et al., 2003). Student input and involvement is critical for two important reasons. Having the involvement of students with disabilities maximizes the personal contact between students and faulty, thereby enhancing communication and understanding between these two groups, and it increases faculty awareness of students' on-campus educational experiences (Getzel et al., 2003).

Visibility is an important ingredient for increasing faculty awareness. As previously discussed, this visibility can be achieved through working with faculty liaisons, working cooperatively with individual departments and schools, or partnering with CTEs. Another more indirect way to raise faculty awareness of disability and disability-related issues is through the presence of applicable staff at various types of training sessions and university-sponsored events. VCU's CTE and PDA have discussed the value of having a PDA representative present at various university training sessions, regardless of topic, to help field any questions that arise about disability and diversity issues. The advantage of this approach is twofold. First, the presence of a representative at such a meeting may help to draw the attention of participants to issues of disability. Second, this presence gives faculty and staff a chance to ask disability-specific questions and to receive informed answers.

On-Line Training

An area of growth since the mid-1990s has been the use of the Internet in education. Internet-based instruction has seen tremendous growth in public 2-year and 4-year institutions of higher education. Waits & Lewis (2003) reported that during the 2000–2001 academic year, 90% of public postsecondary institutions offered courses or course components to their students via the Internet. Although specific numbers regarding on-line development opportunities for college faculty are not readily available, trends in business and industry suggest that on-line development programs are growing. The PDA at VCU is in the process of implementing Internet-based faculty development opportunities on a number of topics, such as specific information about learning disabilities, general disability sensitivity, and the successful integration of UD techniques into the instructional environment. The advantages of such training modules include completing the training sessions at the convenience of the participant's schedule, offering links to additional on-line resources, and having the ability to revisit the module repeatedly. Such modules may appeal to administrative faculty because they form a cost-effective training method and may fit into the technology integration goals of many colleges and universities.

ASSESSING THE EFFECTIVENESS OF RESOURCES DEVELOPED

Assessing the impact of professional development programs through evaluation measures or follow-up strategies is a key component of any activity planned and implemented. Without continuous and ongoing feedback from faculty and staff, the opportunity to collect vital information about the immediate and long-term effects will be missed. It is especially critical to conduct follow-up or assessment activities to assess the level of knowledge or understanding gained from the training and, more important, what behavior changes occurred as a result of participating in the training (Sowers & Smith, 2003). For example, evaluation results of a 2-day conference on assistive technology found faculty members expressing high satisfaction with the conference's content, yet a number of the participants were not implementing what was learned several weeks after the training because of a need for ongoing technical assistance (Getzel, 1993). These faculty members expressed the need for a person to contact when questions or problems occurred with the technology. Incorporating follow-up activities as part of the faculty development process is essential to ensure that the knowledge gained through the training translates into action by the faculty and staff.

Ongoing Technical Assistance

As mentioned previously, the VCU PDA has developed a network or faculty liaisons called PDPs, who are faculty and staff within the schools and departments across the university. These individuals can serve as facilitators to gauge whether questions or concerns are being raised after training sessions. PDPs are not experts in disability issues but serve as internal touchstones for the program to ensure that issues or concerns are being addressed on an ongoing basis, including technical assistance needs after training sessions have occurred. This enables the PDA training staff to develop further information to assist with implementing new information or materials. For example, during a UD training session conducted by a member of the PDA staff, a faculty participant raised the issue of technical standards and the legalities of disability disclosure for students in field placements, primarily during student teaching. Later, while discussing potential staff development opportunities with the Associate Dean for Faculty Affairs, this PDA staff member raised the issue of technical standards for field placements. This resulted in the decision to bring a nationally recognized ADA presenter and author to the campus to conduct workshops regarding students in field placements. In attendance were teaching and administrative faculty from the schools of education and social work as well as from departments on the medical campus. Had the issue not been raised and addressed, faculty in these departments might still have questions concerning these issues.

The PDA has also developed a Resource Team consisting of community agency members and faculty or staff members who have expertise in the disability field. This group does not meet regularly, but holds an orientation on the program's goals and objectives and on team members' roles. These individuals respond 24–48 hours after receiving a request for information or assistance. For example, a faculty member had questions concerning the use of particular assistive technology in his course. A Resource Team member from the Virginia Assistive Technology System contacted the faculty member by telephone to discuss the issue. In another instance, the VCU Career Center staff attended a training session on college students with disabilities and had questions about working with these students in particular career fields. A Resource Team representative from the Virginia Department of Rehabilitative Services was notified, and contact was made to answer specific questions.

There are multiple approaches for follow-up activities. Often the decision on the type of activity is driven by staff time and resources. Providing participants discussion boards, question-and-answer features on web sites, and periodic e-mails containing updated information are methods that can be used to keep in touch with faculty and staff. Regardless of method, the objective is to keep a continuing dialogue with faculty and staff after a training session or event. This dialogue can build further training agendas based on the input received through these follow-up activities.

Evaluation Activities

Evaluating the reactions or experiences of individuals who have participated in a training session, an on-line course, or a conference is a common method of obtaining feedback and input for developing future activities. Asking participants about the content, the ease of obtaining the information, the setting of the session or conference, or the time allotted for each session are examples of information typically collected. This type of evaluation activity helps program developers to gauge the immediate impact of the information provided. It is equally important to evaluate the long-term impact of the training on the participants.

Evaluation activities should be an integral part of planning for professional development activities—not an afterthought. Planning an evaluation assists in determining the scope of the feedback needed and the resources or time required to effectively implement the evaluation. For example, an evaluation strategy can be designed to be initiated over time. Faculty and staff members might receive a brief e-mail survey 3–6 months after the training session. This survey could ask which ideas or strategies were implemented as a result of participation in the training session. It also could ask which information was not implemented and why. Follow-up activities can then be planned, or additional training sessions can incorporate ideas on how to overcome similar barriers in the future.

PROFESSIONAL DEVELOPMENT RESOURCES

The continuing demand for faculty development resources and information has led to the creation of specific grant-funded projects across the United States to develop, implement, and evaluate the effectiveness of training formats and materials. The U.S. Department of Education's OPE has funded demonstration projects, through a request for a proposal process, to community colleges and 4-year institutions to provide technical assistance or professional development for faculty and administrators of higher education. The intent of these grant funds is to ensure that students with disabilities receive a quality postsecondary education through the use of faculty development activities (information on the materials and products developed as a result of these projects can be found at http://www.ed.gov/programs/disabilities/awards. html). There is a wide variety of resources that other universities and colleges can adapt for their use, including training materials, web accessibility information, ways of assessing the campus environment, and ideas on creating collaborative relationships.

These resources can be used to supplement materials developed by universities or colleges or can become the basis for creating further professional development activities. Much has been learned about effective strategies and approaches by these participating demonstration sites that can potentially reduce some of the cost and effort of other higher education programs creating professional development activities. In addition, evaluation activities have been a key part of these projects, helping to assess their effectiveness and potential outcomes. For example, one college was able to establish clearer guidelines for obtaining accommodations though the DSS office and to have faculty implement these accommodations (Getzel et al., 2003). This change resulted from increased interaction and collaboration among university services, faculty, and administrators. In addition, some colleges and universities have been able to establish new positions within the DSS networks on campuses, including the hiring of DSS staff, faculty development personnel, and a consultant to assist in creating a stronger process to assess student services. The knowledge gained through the development and implementation of faculty and staff training activities is an excellent source for colleges and universities.

CONCLUSION

Creating professional development activities for faculty, administrators, and staff is an evolving and ongoing process. It is essential that information, materials, and resources reflect current practice in the higher education and disability field, helping to keep university personnel abreast of new trends in practice and policy. Even with the increase of technology to assist in easier access to information and training, establishing collaborative relationships among all of the entities on campus remains critical for creating a welcoming campus for students with disabilities. Multiple approaches must be used to provide faculty, staff, and administrators with information, materials, and products to enhance and expand their knowledge of educating college students with disabilities. The key to the success of these programs is creating the right fit between the training methods and the campus environment. Ultimately, this can lead to innovative practices in higher education that meet the unique needs of diverse learners, including students with disabilities.

REFERENCES

Garrison, D.R., & Anderson, T. (2003). *E-learning in the 21st century: A framework for research and practice.* New York: Routledge.

Getzel, E.E. (1993). *Evaluation findings on faculty use of assistive technology: Follow-up study of usage after attending training.* Richmond: Virginia Commonwealth University, Rehabilitation, Research, and Training Center.

Getzel, E.E., Briel, L.W., & McManus, S. (2003). Strategies for implementing professional development activities on college campuses: Findings from the OPE funded project sites (1999–2002). *Journal of Postsecondary Education and Disability, 17*(1), 59–76.

Gilson, S.F. (1996). Students with disabilities: An increasing voice and presence on college campuses. *Journal of Vocational Rehabilitation, 6,* 263–272.

Krueger, R.A. (1994). *Focus groups: A practical guide for applied research* (2nd ed.). Thousand Oaks, CA: Sage Publications.

Salzberg, C.L., Peterson, L., Debrand, C.C., Blair, R.J., Carsey, A.C., & Johnson, A.S. (2002). Opinions of disability service directors on faculty training: The need, content, issues, formats, media, and activities. *Journal of Postsecondary Education and Disability, 15*(2), 101–114.

Scott, S.S., & Gregg, N. (2000). Meeting the evolving needs of faculty in providing access for college students with LD. *Journal of Learning Disabilities, 33*(2), 158–167.

Sowers, J., & Smith, M.R. (2003). A field test of the impact of an inservice training program on health sciences faculty. *Journal of Postsecondary Education and Disability, 17*(1), 33–48.

Szymanski, E.M., Hewitt, G.J., Watson, E.A., & Swett, E.A. (1999). Faculty and instructor perception of disability support services and student communication. *Career Development for Exceptional Children, 22*(1), 117–128.

Thomspon, A.R., Bethea, L., & Turner, J. (1997). Faculty knowledge of disability laws in higher education: A survey. *Rehabilitation Counseling Bulletin, 40,* 166–180.

Vogel, S.A., Leyser, Y., Wyland, S., & Brulle, A. (1999). Students with learning disabilities in higher education: Faculty attitude and practices. *Learning Disabilities Research and Practice, 14*(3), 173–186.

Wagner, M., Cameto, R., & Newman, L. (2003). *Youth with disabilities: A changing population: A report of findings from the National Longitudinal Transition Study (NLTS) and the National Longitudinal Transition Study-2 (NLTS2).* Menlo Park, CA: SRI International.

Waits, T., & Lewis, L. (2003). *Distance education at degree-granting postsecondary education institutions: 2000–2001* (NCES Publication No. 2003-017). Washington, DC: National Center for Education Statistics.

Wheeler, J.J. (1996). The use of interactive focus groups to aid in the identification of perceived service and support delivery needs of persons with developmental disabilities and their families. *Education and Training in Mental Retardation and Developmental Disabilities, 31,* 294–303.

Wilson, K.E., & Getzel, E.E. (2001). Creating a supportive campus: The VCU Professional Development Academy. *The Journal for Vocational Special Needs Education, 23*(2), 12–18.

Wilson, K.E., Getzel, E.E., & Brown, T. (2000). Enhancing the post-secondary campus climate for students with disabilities. *Journal of Vocational Rehabilitation, 14*(1), 37–50.

Wilson, K.E., Kregel, J.J, & Getzel, E.E. (1999). *VCU External review final report: Services for students with disabilities.* Richmond: Virginia Commonwealth University, Rehabilitation, Research, and Training Center and School of Education.

Applications for Students with Disabilities

CHAPTER 11

Students with Psychiatric Disabilities

Linda S. Albrecht

College students with psychiatric disabilities are men and women who report conditions affecting their thinking, feeling, and ability to cope on a day-to-day basis. In today's world, psychiatric disabilities present myriad labels to describe a wide range of emotions—anger, frustration, despair, helplessness, anxiety, or fear—that may dominate the individual's daily life and functioning. Amid this flood of feelings, it must be remembered, however, that people with psychiatric disabilities desire the same things in life as other people, perhaps more so (Vander Stoep, Davis, & Collins, 2000). The fact that individuals with psychiatric disabilities may have the abilities to pursue higher education, seek and retain employment, and live satisfying lives is sometimes not understood by educators, mental health workers, families, and the individuals themselves (Megivern, Pellerito, & Mowbray, 2003). With the passage of the Americans with Disabilities Act (ADA) of 1990 (PL 101-336), hope in the form of these pursuits was reinvigorated as discrimination of all types, including that related to college and university entrance for people with disabilities, was outlawed. Subsequent judicial rulings have shaped the ADA and its present path. Likewise, as more students with psychiatric disabilities have enrolled in colleges, their issues and challenges have come into clearer focus.

This chapter examines current thinking and practice related to students with psychiatric disabilities in higher education. Areas covered include demographics and matriculation rates of students with psychiatric disabilities, transition from high school to college, current campus challenges and potential solutions, and the research implications for transition services.

STUDENTS WITH PSYCHIATRIC DISABILITIES

College-Related Demographic Information

To gain a better understanding of the numbers of students with psychiatric disabilities attending postsecondary schools, it is helpful to look at information collected from a variety of studies. These studies track the movements and preparation of all students with disabilities as they enter differing phases of life: graduating from school, obtaining jobs, or matriculating into technical or 2- or 4-year colleges. To put students with psychiatric disabilities into perspective, it is necessary to paint a broader statistical picture of students with disabilities in general.

Since 1990, approximately five million children with disabilities were receiving federal support in U.S. schools. By 2000, the figure had increased to six million. This figure reflects approximately 13% of the total number of all school-age children younger than age 21. Of that 13%, students with psychiatric disabilities represented 8% (The Institute for Higher Education Policy, 2004).

As of 2001, increased percentages of students with disabilities have been graduating from high school (National Organization on Disability, 2001). There is also greater enrollment in postsecondary institutions among students in specific disability categories (Blackorby & Wagner, 1996). It is not known exactly how many students with disabilities, including those with psychiatric disabilities, are making the transition from high school to college. Current studies have not been designed to collect that precise information; however, research and data collection through the National Longitudinal Transition Study-2 are expected to yield better results by 2007 (The Institute for Higher Education Policy, 2004).

In the absence of a singular study reporting transition figures to postsecondary education, there are numbers recorded from other research projects examining different kinds of data. One such study is the National Postsecondary Student Aid Study (National Center for Education Statistics [NCES], 1999). This study collects data regarding the ways that students pay for postsecondary education and includes a reporting category for disabilities. For the 1999–2000 school year, 9% of all undergraduates (50,000 total) reported some kind of disability. Of that number, 17% indicated that they had a psychiatric disability. Within that category, 21% of the students were female and 11% were male. The Baccalaureate and Beyond Longitudinal Study (NCES, 1999) conducted further tracking of students with disabilities beyond college graduation; individuals with psychiatric disabilities had the highest rate of graduate school enrollment of all reported disabilities in this study.

These figures, however, only reflect the numbers of students with known or diagnosed psychiatric conditions upon entering college. They do not account for the incidences of psychiatric conditions occurring once an individual becomes actively enrolled. Statistics indicate that mental illness, especially schizophrenia and major depressive disorders, occur most frequently in people 15–30 years old (Kaplan & Sadock, 1998), a time period when many find themselves in postsecondary programs. For some students in the 17–22 year age range (especially those living on residential campuses), the pressures of college living—including being on one's own for the first time, experiencing overcrowded campus conditions, experiencing anonymity, facing the expectation of a fast-paced life, and facing societal-defined success—can be overwhelming and can precipitate the first psychiatric event in the person's life (DiGalbo, 2004).

Assessments of counseling center directors and studies of the presenting issues of students using these services on campus show the changing nature of problems confronting counseling staff. Up to the 1980s, students brought concerns related to study skills or career choice to college counseling centers (Archer & Cooper, 1998). During the 1980s, surveys began to point to an increase in more serious problems affecting students' psychological health (Heppner et al., 1994; Robbins, May, & Corazzini, 1985). Although students still brought more traditional concerns related to college life, symptoms of depression and anxiety began to be significant concerns (Archer & Cooper, 1998). These issues and symptoms persisted into the 1990s (Pledge, Lapan, Heppner, Kivlighan, & Roehlke, 1998), giving a different picture of the college community than had existed previously. Students with more intense mental health needs were appearing on campus, necessitating college administrators to accept the realities of changes in the student population over time. College administrators, staff, faculty, and students with psychiatric disabilities can work and live together with continued attention toward improved campus communications, maintenance of appropriate student support services, and the introduction of programs and interventions proven to be successful for these students.

Jake is a 29-year-old student who is currently a junior in college. He is majoring in information systems and plans to graduate next year. His strengths are in technology, reading, and motivation. Throughout high school, Jake had frequent mood swings. Occasionally, he participated in counseling, trying various medications at his doctor's direction. At age 17, he was hospitalized for several months. His doctor suggested that he had problems with depression and psychosis but provided little explanation. Jake frequently stopped taking his medication due to the side effects.

Jake's depression seemed to get better when he went to college, although he still experienced some episodes of depression. While at college, Jake would stay up for several nights in a row working on projects, with his mind racing as he multitasked. He enjoyed these late nights, as he was able to get much accomplished. These periods were also accompanied by impulsive spending, excessive socializing, and a feeling of euphoria.

Jake's recurring depression caused him to seek assistance at the university counseling center. He wanted a mood stabilizer to help with the depression. Through consultation with a psychiatrist and a thorough evaluation that considered Jake's manic experiences as well as his bouts with depression, Jake was finally appropriately diagnosed with bipolar disorder. He now realizes the importance of taking his medication to maintain stable moods.

TRANSITION TO POSTSECONDARY EDUCATION FOR STUDENTS WITH PSYCHIATRIC DISABILITIES

Transition programs are especially important to students with psychiatric disabilities. Because certain psychiatric conditions can occur later in an individual's life, some students entering college may have bypassed high school transition programs and, therefore, may not have benefited from the information offered. Regardless of when conditions emerge, the nature of these problems can influence academic mastery, social relations, and/or social connectedness (Jolivette, Stichter, Nelson, Scott, & Liaupsin, 2000). Among students with disabilities at the high school level, students with psychiatric disabilities have the highest dropout rate (U.S. General Accounting Office, 2003). For the students entering college (or other postsecondary programs), there is an indication that completion rates are low (Malmgren, Edgar, & Neel, 1998). Perhaps not so coincidently, employment rates are low as well (Jolivette et al., 2000). To provide safety nets, increase enrollment, and boost retention, both secondary and postsecondary institutions can initiate specialized academic support programs designed for students with psychiatric disabilities. These programs comprise a concept called *supported education* (Unger, 1998).

Since the 1990s, school systems and colleges have shown the value of supported education programs for individuals with psychiatric disabilities through a variety of demonstration projects (Bullis, Moran, Benz, Todis, & Johnson, 2002; Mowbray, Collins, & Bybee, 1999; Stringari, 2003). It must be remembered that services for those with psychiatric disabilities, as with all disabilities, are not a one-size-fits-all proposition. Students' needs may range from mild—benefiting from community or college counseling centers—to intense—needing housing, welfare, transportation, and interpersonal supports (Bullis et al., 2002; Megivern et al., 2003). Programs are somewhat different, reflecting the needs, ages, and educational situations of their students (secondary versus postsecondary); however, successful projects tend to focus on 1) the availability of an individual with whom to build a one-to-one relationship (e.g., case manager, peer support mentor); 2) vocational assessment and planning; 3) information or assistance with using campus resources (e.g., the library, the career center, financial aid opportunities) and meeting responsibilities (e.g., registration); and 4) development of personal skills to include skills in time management, studying, stress management, and interpersonal interactions (Bullis et al., 2002; Mowbray et al., 1999; Stringari, 2003).

The outcomes of the supported education approach have shown increases in overall productive activity for the students enrolled, as the students have been constructively occupied in school, work, or both for the time they are engaged with the supports (Bullis et al., 2002; Mowbray et al., 1999; Stringari, 2003). In addition, emphasis on resource information and human support has demonstrated a positive result in terms of fostering and building social networks (Mowbray et al., 1999).

Many postsecondary schools are already developing individualized academic programs for students with learning disabilities and attention-deficit/hyperactivity disorder (Kravets & Wax, 1999). With the critical need for students to develop self-reliance, self-advocacy, and self-knowledge, some colleges are beginning to adopt elements of a supported education program for all students with disabilities on campus (Getzel, McManus, & Briel, 2004). Specifics may include individualized career and academic study skills programs. In addition, schools may offer summer orientation programs prior to college entry, giving information about the school, resources, and support programs (see Figure 11.1 for a sample schedule from such a program).

Supported education models seem to be a natural outgrowth of the transition movement. Although colleges need to be diligent in monitoring the progress of their students with psychiatric disabilities, supported education appears to provide a win-win situation for students and campuses alike.

Jake and his counselor worked on time management techniques to prepare Jake for his classes and to reduce the anxiety of not effectively managing his time. Because Jake liked technology, they chose to explore a personal digital assistant (PDA). They entered all of the deadlines for his classes in his PDA and set up auditory reminders to notify him of upcoming events. They also put in reminders for when Jake should take his medication, as he would occasionally forget to do so. In addition, they worked on goal setting and breaking large projects into more manageable pieces so Jake would not become overwhelmed.

CHALLENGES AND EFFECTIVE STRATEGIES

Coordination of Community Services

For students experiencing mental illness in the high school years, services for the transition from secondary education to college are frequently disjointed. Moving from high school to college creates the perfect opportunity for rehabilitation counselors to discuss and map career goals, course selection, and skill development as students with psychiatric disabilities move toward adulthood. Likewise, connection to a mental health agency can provide continuity of care through uninterrupted coverage of medications or counseling services, both of which are vital to smooth functioning and adjustment in a new environment. Yet, Agran, Cain, and Cavin (2002) suggest that rehabilitation counselors are not often invited to attend individualized education program reviews in high schools. Furthermore, if a mental health agency encourages a student to

Time	Event	Staff
9:15 A.M.–9:30 A.M.	Welcome and overview of day Review campus resource notebook	Supported education staff
9:30 A.M.–10:30 A.M.	Introduction to self-advocacy	Disability support services (DSS) coordinator
10:00 A.M.–11:45 A.M.	Placement tests	Supported education staff
10:00 A.M.–11:45 A.M.	Parent session: What parents should expect from college and their children with disabilities	DSS coordinator Supported education staff Peer mentors (current college students with disabilities)
11:45 A.M.–12:15 P.M.	Pizza lunch	Peer mentors
12:15 P.M.–1:00 P.M.	Differences between high school and college	DSS coordinator
1:00 P.M.–1:30 P.M.	Student panel and question-and-answer session on college and the student with a disability: What should the student expect?	Peer mentors
1:30 P.M.–3:15 P.M.	Tour of relevant campus services (e.g., counseling center, library, DSS office, writing center, academic support services office)	Peer mentors
3:15 P.M.–3:30 P.M.	Question-and-answer session about the tour	Supported education staff Peer mentors
3:30 P.M.–4:00 P.M.	Time management	Supported education staff
4:00 P.M.–4:15 P.M.	Wrap-up	Supported education staff

Figure 11.1. Sample summer orientation for entering college students with disabilities. (From Virginia Commonwealth University, Rehabilitation Research and Training Center, Professional Development Academy. (n.d.). *What is STAR Plus?* Retrieved February 23, 2005, from http://www.student.vcu.edu/pda/starDescript.html; adapted by permission.)

consider college (Megivern et al., 2003), no provisions are made for coverage of day-to-day issues once the student turns 18 and is in college (Vander Stoep et al., 2000). Students themselves cite this obvious lack of connection as a frustration. Contact with a case manager or therapist to help navigate services and resources—as well as to deal with issues related to studies, social isolation, and educational goals—are seen as preventive if not essential to college completion (Megivern et al., 2003; Weiner & Weiner, 1997).

As the need for support comes to the forefront as a major issue in contributing to academic success for students with psychiatric disabilities, a new direction in the development of mentoring networks is beginning to appear. *Mentoring* describes a relationship between an older adult and younger individual. The older adult provides guidance, advice, and friendship (Bartlett, 2004). From this intense, time-committed relationship, the younger individual can gain knowledge, direction, and emotional well-being. A variation of this relationship, in the form of peer supporters or peer mentors, is being used on college campuses (Bartlett, 2004; Carter, 1994), in mental health agencies (West, Fetzer, Graham, & Keller, 2002), and in grant-run transition programs (Whelley, Radtke, Burgstahler, & Christ, 2003).

Peer supporters or peer mentors differ from traditional mentors in that they are part of a relationship that occurs between two people of the same age and status (Whelley et al., 2003). This relationship can make a difference in bridging the gap for students with disabilities in general, as well as for those with psychiatric issues, as they move on to college or employment (West et al., 2002; Whelley et al., 2003).

The value of this mentoring approach to transition is apparent, and its benefits are many. Peer mentors in the college setting are individuals with disabilities. Not only are they close in age to the incoming students with psychiatric disabilities, but they also have dealt with experiences related to disability. This allows the relationship to be one of equals, based on friendship and empathy, not domination (West et al., 2002). Students with psychiatric disabilities have the potential to form a trusting relationship, which the literature (Bartlett, 2004; Megivern et al., 2003; West et al., 2002) suggests can lead to academic success through the following:

- Lessening of psychiatric symptoms through social connection

- Learning the value of campus resources and how to use them through a student's eyes

- Learning tips regarding study skills and habits, scheduling, and course selection

- Gaining perspective on how to solve common campus problems

- Sustaining motivation and hope by seeing a fellow student with a disability succeed

The peer mentor approach to working with transition issues allows for many positive and powerful possibilities for students while also helping vocational rehabilitation managers, mental health counselors, and academic support services personnel who may have limited time and funds to work with the encompassing issues of students with psychiatric disabilities (Whelley et al., 2003). This approach holds much promise for students with the most complex emotional and academic needs.

Jake's counselor recommended several campus and community resources. For stress management, Jake was given information on utilizing the gymnasium on campus, which provided a place to exercise.
Not only did Jake lessen his stress level, he also found an added benefit of being able to concentrate better after exercising. The cost of the
gym was included in tuition, so this was at no extra expense to Jake.
Jake was also given information about another campus resource, workshops on study skills, which again was included in his tuition. Finally,
Jake received information from his counselor on a community support
group for adults with bipolar disorder.

Self-Advocacy and Disclosure

Fundamental to the success of every student with a disability is the development
of self-advocacy and self-determination skills. *Self-determination*, as defined by
Field, Martin, Miller, Ward, and Wehmeyer (1998), means seeing oneself as
being capable, understanding one's strengths and weaknesses, and being able
to direct one's own path in life. Included in the concept of self-determination
is the idea that an individual must understand what he or she needs to achieve
goals and move forward.

At the heart of self-advocacy is the understanding of the individual's
disability as well as an understanding of the essential times to disclose such
a fact. It is necessary for a student to understand that receiving accommodations
relies on disclosure of the disability to the campus disability support services
(DSS) office (U.S. Department of Education, Office of Civil Rights, 1998).
In a postsecondary setting, many elements come together to create success
for a student with a disability; however, the use of accommodations can make
a significant difference. Accommodations are adjustments or aids that address
the actual functional limitations of an individual with a disability and, in many
cases, are critical to the student's academic success. There are a number of
reasons why students with psychiatric disabilities choose not to disclose
their situations:

1. *A new experience:* As stated previously, a psychiatric disability may not
   appear until a student is in college. The individual may not know about
   the advantages and disadvantages of disclosing or the process involved.

2. *Stigma:* Mental illness still carries negative connotations. Disclosing such
   a condition poses considerable risks. Perceptions of being irresponsible,
   childlike, and dangerous create attitudes of fear and disrespect within the
   public (Hall, Brockington, Levings, & Murphy, 1993; Taylor & Dear,
   1980). A very real consequence to disclosure of psychiatric symptoms is
   loss of badly needed friends and social contact (Megivern et al., 2003).

3. *Lack of awareness:* Students experiencing psychiatric conditions prior to
   entering college may not know that DSS offices exist or that such offices
   can serve their particular needs (Megivern et al., 2003).

4. *Independence:* Young students entering college with the knowledge of their
   psychiatric disabilities may wish to be free of the labels and so-called

help they previously received from family, schools, and agencies. In their yearning to be like others, students may disregard knowledge or advice that could contribute to success (West et al., 2002).

To strengthen these students' chances of academic success, comfort level with their disabilities, and ability to make decisions related to disclosure, work is being done privately and publicly to develop self-determination curricula that can be introduced in high school or earlier (Fagen, 2001; Field & Hoffman, 2001; Libby, 2000; Paraschiv, 2000). These curricula may vary in components but generally strive to prepare the student in increased understanding of self and disability, assertiveness skills, and problem-solving abilities (Paraschiv, 2000).

One curriculum being developed at Virginia Commonwealth University's Rehabilitation Research and Training Center (VCU-RRTC) blends self-determination with mentoring. With this particular project, college students with disabilities will assist in teaching the curriculum to secondary level students. In the primary stages of developing the curriculum, focus groups done with college students with disabilities, including those with psychiatric disabilities, expressed a strong support for this approach (VCU-RRTC, 2004). The students indicated not only that they wished they had had the information from a self-determination model prior to entering college but also that they had had the opportunity to interact with a student with a disability who served as a guide and role model. As with supported education and peer support on a college campus, self-determination curricula combined with mentoring in high school seeks to provide the deepest level of supports geared toward aiding a student's success. For more information on self-determination, see Chapter 3.

> Jake and his counselor determined that Jake needed to work on strategies for success while attending college. They began by discussing in detail Jake's psychological evaluation. They also discussed the importance of accommodations and how to obtain them in postsecondary education settings. Jake decided that it was in his best interest to self-disclose to the college. Jake then took his documentation to the DSS office and received a letter of accommodation that stated he was entitled to extended time for taking tests, testing in a limited-distraction room, and notetaking services. Jake was nervous about approaching his professors with this letter because of the stigma attached to his disability. The counselor and Jake role-played several effective ways to disclose to his professors. One problem Jake had was giving too many details concerning his disability. The counselor and Jake worked on giving only the pertinent information as it related to his academics. Although he was still somewhat apprehensive, Jake felt more comfortable and approached several of his professors.

Faculty Awareness and Students with Psychiatric Disabilities

In the years immediately following the passage of the ADA, students with disabilities had an increasing presence on college campuses. Neither they nor their educational issues were well understood. The ADA required postsecondary educational institutions to accommodate or make adjustments for the functional needs of students with disabilities. Initially, making these adjustments bred resistance on the college campuses. Meeting the needs of students with disabilities, particularly making individual course arrangements, was seen as an intrusion and violation of academic freedom. With time and exposure to students with disabilities, faculty perceptions have softened (The Institute of Higher Education Policy, 2004).

Students with disabilities view faculty attitudes as crucial to their success on the college campus (Lehmann, Davies, & Laurin, 2000). Students with psychiatric disabilities may struggle with self-doubt, low self-esteem, and fear, so the willingness of instructors to understand their learning needs and to be available and supportive encourages the students to pursue their coursework (Weiner & Weiner, 1997). Table 11.1 offers other potential learning needs and characteristics of students with psychiatric disabilities. Not all students with mental health issues will possess every learning concern presented, but it is helpful to understand the variety of concerns that these students may have.

Many problems that students bring before instructional faculty can have simple and practical answers. For example, a student with a psychiatric disability may be easily overwhelmed by anticipating a semester's worth of activities. In one office visit, the instructor may be able to help the student set up a time line or calendar to lay out, keep track of, and plan due dates of various projects. If further assistance is required, the instructor might indicate that he or she is available for consultation during office hours as questions regarding assignments arise (Center for Psychiatric Rehabilitation, 1997).

Table 11.1. Areas in which students with psychiatric disabilities may have functional limitations

Experiencing medication side effects: drowsiness, fatigue, dry mouth and thirst, blurred vision, hand tremors, slowed response time, and difficulty initiating interpersonal contact

Screening out environmental stimuli: inability to block out sounds, sights, or odors that interfere with focusing on tasks and/or a limited ability to tolerate noise and crowds

Sustaining concentration: restlessness, shortened attention span, distraction, and difficulty understanding or remembering verbal directions

Maintaining stamina: difficulty sustaining enough energy for a whole day of classes on campus

Handling time pressures and multitasking: difficulty managing assignments, prioritizing tasks, and meeting deadlines; inability to multitask

Interacting with others: difficulty getting along, fitting in, contributing to group work, and reading social cues

Fear of authority figures: difficulty approaching instructors or teaching assistants

Responding to negative feedback: difficulty understanding and correctly interpreting criticism or poor grades; inability to separate person from task (i.e., personalization or defensiveness due to low self-esteem)

Responding to change: difficulty coping with unexpected changes in coursework, (e.g., changes in assignments, due dates, or instructors); limited ability to tolerate interruptions

Experiencing severe text anxiety: an emotional and physical inability to take an exam

From Center for Psychiatric Rehabilitation, Boston University. (1997). *How does mental illness affect the way I function at school?* Retrieved July 22, 2004, from http://www.bu.edu/cpr/jobschool/functed.htm, adapted by permission; and from Souma, A., Rickerson, N., & Burgstahler, S. (2002). *Academic accommodations for students with psychiatric disabilities.* Retrieved February 22, 2005, from http://www.washington.edu/doit/Brochures/Academics/psych.html, adapted by permission.

Beyond this approach, assessing the situation on a case-by-case basis is often the best way to determine effective strategies and accommodations (Center for Psychiatric Rehabilitation, 1997). Faculty members may wish to have a discussion with a student regarding specific needs. Faculty members are also well advised to contact the college DSS office when they have questions or concerns. Furthermore, conveying an accepting attitude is critical. Faculty members can ensure this through a syllabus statement that encourages students to disclose. They can maintain expectations for success by asking students how they can support their learning. Finally, faculty members should be aware of campuswide training that will keep them abreast of related issues (Backels & Wheeler, 2001).

RESEARCH CONSIDERATIONS: THE FUTURE AND TRANSITION

Although the ADA has been effective in opening the doors to postsecondary education for individuals with psychiatric disabilities, it has also highlighted the needs and elements required for these students to succeed in higher education and life in general. Navigation through higher education has continued to illustrate the need for smooth transitions. Students with psychiatric disabilities, as all students with disabilities, need strong content training, a sense of themselves, knowledge of colleges' expectations, and a sense of employment possibilities (Brinckerhoff, McGuire, & Shaw, 2002).

Common sense solutions addressing these students' instructional and emotional needs have emerged through consultation with individuals with psychiatric disabilities, schools (K–12 and beyond), mental health care providers and agencies, rehabilitation services, and researchers (Hagner et al., 1999; Unger, 1998). Although educators and social service providers can see the personal value and effects of these transitional strategies, there is little objective data to back up their implementation. Researchers need to begin to work with schools and supported education programs to devise well-designed or replicated studies verifying the effectiveness of various interventions (Davis & Clark, 2000; Megivern et al., 2003; Mooney, Epstein, Reid, & Nelson, 2003).

Davis and Clark (2000, pp. 273–274) noted several areas in which improved data collection could enhance the quality of schooling and life for students with psychiatric disabilities:

- Documentation of the typical progression of experiences and service use across transition domains for young people with and without emotional or behavioral difficulties. . . .

- Characteristics of the individuals being served

- Progress on the goals of these young people

- Types and amounts of services and supports used across the different transition domains. . . .

- Follow-up of individuals to assess their progress in the domains of employment, educational opportunities, living situation, and community-life adjustment after transition services end

In addition, data should be collected on dropout rates of students with psychiatric disabilities from both high school and college. Understanding what led to those experiences as well as what students have done since that time is important in designing and implementing future strategies (Thurlow, Sinclair, & Johnson, 2002).

Statistical reporting can lead to better education and life experiences for these students; it also lends power when talking to state and federal legislators. Statistics allow them to see the issues in a more straightforward manner. Once they understand the overall and community implications of these concerns, they have the rationale to allocate funding that has a direct impact on transition planning and services.

CONCLUSION

This chapter has focused on the issues of students with psychiatric disabilities in a postsecondary educational setting. With changes in the laws since the early 1990s, students with disabilities who were never thought able to attend college are matriculating to technical, 2-year, and 4-year institutions in record numbers. Included among these students are students with psychiatric disabilities. Although it is difficult to track exact numbers of students with psychiatric disabilities entering college, information from federal reports and university counseling centers indicate that these students are entering the campus at increasing rates.

To get the most out of their college experiences, students with psychiatric disabilities, as all students, need to be well prepared to enter campus life. Like students with other disabilities, students with psychiatric disabilities have additional issues that some students may not face. Therefore, it is especially important that students with psychiatric disabilities be aware of themselves, be aware of the impact of their conditions on daily functioning, understand access to as well as use and benefits of accommodations, and be informed of a variety of community and school support services that can provide the reinforcements often critical to college success. Ideally, students should be made aware of themselves and community supports and services throughout their elementary and secondary school experiences. Special emphasis should be placed on the high school years to make a smooth transition from a secondary to a postsecondary setting.

Certainly, changing attitudes toward and opportunities for individuals with psychiatric disabilities make a discussion on entering postsecondary education an actuality. These changes trigger the beginning of significant shifts and possibilities in the lives of people often dismissed as being incapable of productive work and contributions. As schools, students, and communities begin to work more closely together in understanding and meeting the needs of people with psychiatric disabilities, these individuals can expect to complete curricula leading to careers, independence, and respect. More important, new potential, energy, and creativity await both the academic world and society at large as it welcomes a new and vital force through its doorways.

REFERENCES

Agran, M., Cain, H.M., & Cavin, M.D. (2002). Enhancing the involvement of rehabilitation counselors in the transition process. *Career Development for Exceptional Individuals, 25*(2), 141–155.

Americans with Disabilities Act (ADA) of 1990, PL 101-336, 42 U.S.C. §§12101 *et seq.*

Archer, J., Jr., & Cooper, S. (1998). *Counseling and mental health services on campus.* San Francisco: Jossey-Bass.

Backels, K., & Wheeler, I. (2001). Faculty perceptions of mental health issues among college students. *Journal of College Student Development, 42*(2), 173–186.

Bartlett, T. (2004, May 14). Back from the brink: More colleges try to help students who struggle with their courses. *Chronicle of Higher Education, 50*(36), A39.

Blackorby, J., & Wagner, M. (1996). Longitudinal postschool outcomes of youth with disabilities: Findings from the National Longitudinal Study. *Exceptional Children, 62*(5), 399–413.

Brinckerhoff, L.C., McGuire, J.M., & Shaw, S.F. (2002). *Postsecondary education and transition for students with learning disabilities* (2nd ed.). Austin, TX: PRO-ED.

Bullis, M., Moran, T., Benz, M.R., Todis, B., & Johnson, M.D. (2002). Description and evaluation of the Aries Project: Achieving rehabilitation, individualized education, and employment success for adolescents with emotional disturbance. *Career Development for Exceptional Individuals, 25*(1), 41–58.

Carter, T. (1994). Mentor programs belong in college too. *Journal of Career Planning and Employment, 54*(2), 51–53.

Center for Psychiatric Rehabilitation, Boston University. (1997). *How does mental illness affect the way I function at school?* Retrieved July 22, 2004, from http://www.bu.edu/cpr/jobschool/functed.htm

Davis, M., & Clark, H.B. (2000). Transition: Current issues and recommendations for the future. In H.B. Clark & M. Davis (Eds.), *Transition to adulthood: A resource for assisting young people with emotional or behavioral difficulties* (pp. 267–276). Baltimore: Paul H. Brookes Publishing Co.

DiGalbo, L. (2004, June). *Meeting the challenges of persons with psychiatric disabilities in postsecondary settings: How do you meet the unique needs of students with disabilities?* Session presented at the meeting of the University of Connecticut, Postsecondary Training Institute, West Dover, VT.

Fagen, S.A. (2001). *Improving services for secondary students with emotional and behavioral disorders: Project Anchor.* Washington, DC: Academy for Educational Development. (ERIC Document Reproduction Service No. ED456588)

Field, S., & Hoffman, A. (2001). *Promoting self-determination in transition planning: Implementing the "Steps to Self-Determination" curriculum, October 1, 1998–September 30, 2001. Final report.* Detroit, MI: Wayne State University, College of Education. (ERIC Document Reproduction Service No. ED478265)

Field, S., Martin, J., Miller, R., Ward, M., & Wehmeyer, M. (1998). Self-determination for persons with disabilities: A position statement of the division on career development and transition. *Career Development for Exceptional Individuals, 21*(2), 113–128.

Getzel, E.E., McManus, S., & Briel, L.W. (2004). An effective model for college students with learning disabilities and attention deficit hyperactivity disorders. *Research to Practice, 3*(1). Retrieved January 20, 2005, from http://www.ncset.org/publications/researchtopractice/NCSETResearchBrief_3.1.pdf

Hagner, D., Cheney, D., & Malloy, J., (1999). Career-related outcomes of a model transition demonstration for young adults with emotional disturbance. *Rehabilitation Counseling Bulletin, 42*(3), 228–242.

Hall, P., Brockington, I.F., Levings, J., & Murphy, C. (1993). A comparison of responses to the mentally ill in two communities. *British Journal of Psychiatry, 162*, 99–108.

Heppner, P.P., Kivlighan, D.M.,Jr., Good, G.E., Roehlke, H.J., Hills, H.I., & Ashby,J.S. (1994). Presenting problems of university counseling center clients: A snapshot and multivariate classification scheme. *Journal of Counseling Psychology, 41*, 315–324.

The Institute for Higher Education Policy. (2004, June). *Higher education opportunities for students with disabilities: A primer for policymakers.* Retrieved June 30, 2004, from http://www.ihep.com/Pubs/PDF/DisabilitiesReport2004.pdf

Jolivette, K., Stichter, J.P., Nelson, C.M., Scott, T.M., & Liaupsin, C.J. (2000). *Improving post-school outcomes for students with emotional and behavioral disorders* (Report No. ERIC/OSEP Digest E597). Arlington, VA: ERIC Clearinghouse on Disabilities and Gifted Education. (ERIC Document Reproduction Service No. ED447616)

Kaplan, H.I., & Sadock, B.J. (1998). *Synopsis of psychiatry: Behavioral sciences/clinical psychiatry* (8th ed.). Baltimore: Lippincott Williams & Wilkins.

Kravets, M., & Wax, I.F. (1999). *The K & W guide to colleges for students with learning disabilities or attention deficit disorders* (5th ed.). New York: Random House.

Lehmann, J.P., Davies, T.G., & Laurin, K.M. (2000, May/June). Listening to student voices about postsecondary education. *Teaching Exceptional Children,* 60–65.

Libby, A. (2000). *Teaching self-determination and Arizona standards for K–12 students with disabilities lesson plan portfolio.* (Report No. U.S.; Arizona, 2000-00-00). (ERIC Document Reproduction Service No. ED449624)

Malmgren, K., Edgar, E., & Neel, R.S. (1998). Postschool outcomes of youths with behavioral disorders. *Behavioral Disorders, 23*, 257–263.

Megivern, D., Pellerito, S., & Mowbray, C. (2003). Barriers to higher education for individuals with psychiatric disabilities. *Psychiatric Rehabilitation Journal, 26*(3), 217–231.

Mooney, P., Epstein, M.H., Reid, R., & Nelson, R. (2003). Status of and trends in academic intervention research for students with emotional disturbance. *Remedial and Special Education, 24*(5), 273–287.

Mowbray, C.T., Collins, M., & Bybee, D. (1999). Supported education for individuals with psychiatric disabilities: Long-term outcomes from an experimental study (Statistical data included) [Electronic Version]. *Social Work Research, 23*(2), 89–102.

National Center for Education Statistics. (1999). *Students with disabilities in postsecondary education: A profile of participation, preparation, and outcomes* (NCES Publication No. 1999187). Washington, DC: U.S. Government Printing Office.

National Organization on Disability. (2001, July). *Education and disability statistics: A historical perspective.* Retrieved July 22, 2004, from http://www.nod.org/index.cfm?fuseaction=Feature.showFeature&FeatureID=109

Paraschiv, I. (2000). *Development of a high school curriculum that promotes self-determination and independence skills.* (Report No. U.S.; North Carolina, 2000-06-01). Washington, DC: Paper presented at annual meeting of the American Association on Mental Retardation. (ERIC Document Reproduction Service No. ED445455)

Pledge, D., Lapan, R.T., Heppner, P.O., Kivlighan, D., & Roehlke, H.J. (1998). Stability and severity of presenting problems at a university counseling center: A 6-year analysis [Electronic Version]. *Professional Psychology: Research and Practice, 29*(4), 386–389.

Robbins, S.B., May, T.M., & Corazzini, J.G. (1985). Perceptions of client needs and counseling center staff roles and functions. *Journal of Counseling Psychology, 32*, 641–644.

Souma, A., Rickerson, N., & Burgstahler, S. (2002). *Academic accommodations for students with psychiatric disabilities.* Retrieved February 22, 2005, from http://www.washington.edu/doit/Brochures/Academics/psych.html

Stringari, T. (2003, March). Community partnerships increase services and outcome for students with psychological disabilities. *Ijournal: insight into student services.* Retrieved July 7, 2004, from http://www.ijournal.us/issue_04/ij_issue04_TimStringari_01.htm

Taylor, S.M., & Dear, M.J. (1980). Scaling community attitudes toward the mentally ill. *Schizophrenia Bulletin, 7,* 225–240.

Thurlow, M.L., Sinclair, M.F., & Johnson, D.R. (2002). *Students with disabilities who drop out of school–implication for policy and practice.* Retrieved January 27, 2005, from http://ncset.org/publications/viewdesc.asp?id=425

Unger, K.V. (1998). *Supported education: Providing services to students with psychiatric disabilities.* Baltimore: Paul H. Brookes Publishing Co.

U.S. Department of Education, Office of Civil Rights. (1998). *Auxiliary aids and services for postsecondary students with disabilities.* Retrieved July 19, 2004, from http://www.ed.gov/print/about/offices/list/ocr/docs/auxaids.html

U.S. General Accounting Office. (2003). *Special education: Federal actions can assist states in improving postsecondary outcomes for youth.* Retrieved July 1, 2004, from www.gao.gov/cgi-bin/getrpt?GAO-03-773

Vander Stoep, A., Davis, M., & Collins, D. (2000). Transition: A time of developmental and institutional clashes. In H.B. Clark & M. Davis (Eds.), *Transition to adulthood: A resource for assisting young people with emotional or behavioral difficulties* (pp. 3–28). Baltimore: Paul H. Brookes Publishing Co.

Virginia Commonwealth University, Rehabilitation Research and Training Center, Professional Development Academy. (n.d.). *What is STAR Plus?* Retrieved February 23, 2005, from http://www.students.vcu.edu/pda/starDescript.html

Virginia Commonwealth University, Rehabilitation Research and Training Center. (2004). *Summary of focus group trends concerning self-determination skills of college students with disabilities.* Richmond: Author.

Weiner, E., & Weiner, J. (1997). University students with psychiatric illness: Factors involved in the decision to withdraw from their studies. *Psychiatric Rehabilitation Journal, 20*(4), 88–91.

West, T.E., Fetzer, P.M., Graham, C.M., & Keller, J. (2002). Driving the system through young adult involvement and leadership. In H.B. Clark & M. Davis (Eds.), *Transition to adulthood: A resource for assisting young people with emotional and or behavioral difficulties* (pp. 195–208). Baltimore: Paul H. Brookes Publishing Co.

Whelley, T.A., Radtke, R., Burgstahler, S., & Christ, T.W. (2003). Mentors, advisers, role models, and peer supporters: Career development relationships and individuals with disabilities. *American Rehabilitation, 27*(1), 42–49.

CHAPTER 12

Students with Learning Disabilities or Attention-Deficit/Hyperactivity Disorder

Michael F. Hock

Increasingly, students with learning disabilities and attention-deficit/ hyper-activity disorder (ADHD) are choosing to attend college (Brinckerhoff, Shaw, & McGuire, 1992; Dunn, 1995; Houck, Asselin, Troutman, & Arrington, 1992; MacDonald, 1987; Vogel & Adelman, 1992). As noted in other chapters, approximately 9% of all first-time, full-time college students have some type of disability (Henderson, 1999). Of this number, 3.5% report having a learning disability. This number has grown steadily since 1988 and has increased from 1.2% of all full-time college students to 3.5% in 1998. In addition, 3%–5% of the U.S. school-age population has been identified as having ADHD (Heilgenstein, Guenther, Levy, Savino, & Fulwiler, 1999; Salend & Rohena, 2003). One implication of this finding is that increasing numbers of school-age children with ADHD will eventually attend college (Reid & Katsiyannis, 1995).

Unfortunately, many students with learning disabilities and ADHD will experience difficulty in college due to an enormous gap between the academic skills they possess and the academic demands of the college environment (Bigaj, Shaw, Cullen, McGuire, & Yost, 1995; Dunn, 1995; Mellard & Hazel, 1992; Reid, Maag, & Vasa, 1994; White, 1992). College students are expected to read and comprehend a variety of challenging textbooks and other materials, be proficient in a broad array of study strategies and problem-solving skills, write research papers, have substantial knowledge of many topics in diverse content areas, make personal choices affecting time management and organization, and function autonomously (Brinckerhoff et al., 1992; Gajar, 1992; Hishinuma & Fremstad, 1997). Students with learning disabilities and ADHD tend to have difficulties in these areas, and the consequences of this gap between the expectations and abilities are not encouraging. These students are more likely to fail their college courses, and they graduate at lower rates than other students (Bursuck, Rose, Cowen, & Yahaya, 1989; Heiligenstein et al., 1999). Thus, although the door to college is open for increasing numbers of students with disabilities, many of these students leave college without the benefits associated with a degree and the skills necessary for future success.

In order to close the gap for the significant number of students needing help with reading, writing, and math skills and to enhance their postsecondary experiences, services are needed to markedly improve how these students perform (Patton & Polloway, 1992; Salend & Rohena, 2003). Several authors have suggested that programs for college students with learning disabilities and ADHD need to include the following components:

- Instruction in comprehension and creative study strategies (Brinckerhoff et al., 1992; Vogel, Hruby, & Adelman, 1993; White, 1992)

- Instruction in coping strategies, such as using computers for word processing (Polloway, Schewel, & Patton, 1992)—word processing programs are helpful for poor spellers and writers who must make extensive revisions to drafts (in particular, cut and paste features support revision and reorganization of drafted text)

- Access to computer labs (Keim, McWhirter, & Bernstein, 1996)—as noted in the previous entry, many students with disabilities need these tools to accommodate for their disabilities

- Instruction in working as a member of a team (White, 1992)

- Instruction in listening critically to others (White, 1992)

- Instruction in self-advocacy and self-sufficiency skills (Brinckerhoff et al., 1992; Dunn, 1995; Gerber, Ginsberg, & Reiff, 1992)

- Effective academic tutoring services (American Psychiatric Association [APA], 2001; Polloway et al., 1992; Salend & Rohena, 2003; Vogel et al., 1993)

- Medication treatment, as applicable for some students with ADHD (APA, 2001)

Of the previously listed services, tutoring is the service most often provided to college students with learning disabilities and ADHD (Bigaj et al., 1995; Figler, 1987; Keim et al., 1996; Mohr, 1991; Vogel et al., 1993; Zaritsky, 1989). Although traditional and typical tutorial services can be helpful, the usual outcome is, at best, immediate and short-term success, and at worst, learner dependency on tutors (Brinckerhoff et al., 1992; Hock, Deshler, & Schumaker, 1999). In addition, services that focus on helping students identify and discuss personal hopes, expectations, and fears for the future (i.e., goals)—and, in turn, develop individualized action plans that lead to the attainment of the identified goals—can be very helpful in ensuring that students with disabilities have a successful college experience (e.g., Brinckerhoff et al., 1992; Reid & Katsiyannis, 1995; Vogel et al., 1993).

This chapter focuses on two evidence-based interventions that are foundational to success in college for students with learning disabilities and ADHD. The first intervention is an intensive skill- and strategy-based tutoring program called Strategic Tutoring (Hock, Deshler, & Schumaker, 2000). The other intervention, called Possible Selves (Hock, Schumaker, & Deshler, 2003), is designed to discover students' hopes and goals for the future and to develop action plans that lead to attainment of identified personal hopes and goals.

STRATEGIC TUTORING

Because tutoring is a service often provided to students with learning disabilities or ADHD, there is a need to utilize a tutoring model whereby tutors can teach skills and strategies while helping college students with their coursework. Such a combined tutoring model is necessary because students must be kept afloat in their courses while learning to function independently. Students must demonstrate their ability to respond to the demands of postsecondary courses very early in their college careers, so it is important that tutoring services be provided early and in an intensive fashion by skilled tutors. Thus, the tutoring model must do the following (Bigaj et al., 1995; Brinckerhoff et al., 1992; Hock, Deshler, & Schumaker, 1993):

- Address the immediate academic needs of the students regarding assignment completion and growth of real-world knowledge in general.

- Ensure that students acquire specific content knowledge that supports understanding of the course curriculum.

- Ensure that students acquire critical strategies for learning and problem solving.

- Establish mentorships between tutors and students that support student commitment to learning and attaining personal goals.

The Strategic Tutoring Model

Traditional tutoring may provide a useful service for some students. Students who are usually successful without tutorial support may, on occasion, "get stuck." That is, although they generally can complete their assignments independently and are already successful learners, they may need help with a specific problem or assignment. Traditional tutors can help such students by re-explaining content and showing students what to do without teaching a skill or strategy related to the assignment. This form of tutoring predominates most tutoring programs (Hock et al., 1999).

Given the nature of college and university expectations and the academic characteristics of students with learning disabilities and ADHD, however, an intensive, nontraditional approach to the tutoring process is needed. Specifically, this new approach to tutoring incorporates a strategic teaching process in which the tutor takes the central role as both planner and mediator of the learning. That is, within this model, the tutor not only teaches the content and helps with assignment completion but also presents the strategies required to make the content learned meaningful and useful. Under this new role, tutors have a multifaceted agenda:

- They must carefully organize and transform the content into a form that is "learner friendly" and easy to understand.

- They must consider which strategies students need to learn the content.

- They must teach students how to use those strategies.

- They must establish mentoring relationships with the students they are tutoring so that those students can become expert learners.

Thus, effective tutoring becomes a delicate balance among content goals, teaching strategies required for achieving those goals, facilitating students' learning experiences through strategy instruction, and engaging students in learning apprenticeships (Collins, Brown, & Newman, 1989; Hock, 1998; Jones, Palincsar, Ogle, & Carr, 1987; Rogoff, 1990).

This approach to tutoring is called the Strategic Tutoring Model (see Figure 12.1). It is an instructional tutoring model in which tutors teach students skills, strategies, and/or content knowledge. This model was based on more than 25 years of research conducted at the University of Kansas Center for Research on Learning (KU-CRL), which has focused on teaching strategies and content to academically at-risk adolescents and adults, including those with learning disabilities and ADHD.

The Strategic Tutoring Model requires that during tutoring interactions, the tutor must follow a well-defined four-phase instructional sequence when a student needs assistance with an assignment or academic task (see Figure 12.2). In Phase 1, the tutor must assess the student's current approach to the task at hand by asking questions to determine the nature of the assignment and the strategies the student uses when completing similar tasks. Once the tutor has clarified the assignment and helped the student identify strategies that he or she currently uses, the tutor discusses the rationale for learning a more effective strategy. Then, the tutor asks the student to commit time and effort to learn a more effective strategy.

In Phase 2, the tutor and student co-construct a learning strategy that addresses the student's academic needs. The strategy is co-constructed by weaving the student's current strategy together with a more efficient and effective strategy provided by the tutor. The tutor then carefully explains each step of the new strategy and checks to make sure that the student understands each step. During this phase, the tutor and student can also build a completely new strategy. In building a new strategy, the tutor and student begin working on the assignment, and after the tutor has a clearer understanding of the

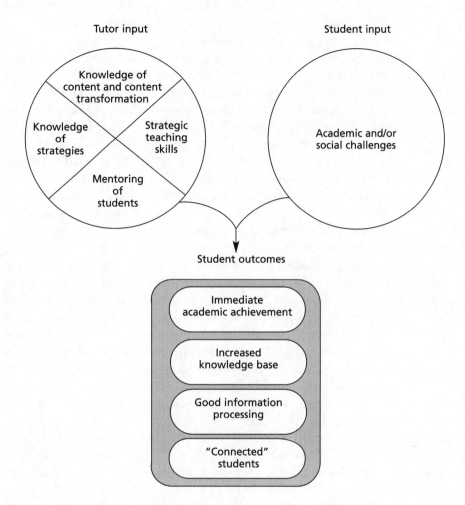

Figure 12.1. The Strategic Tutoring Model.

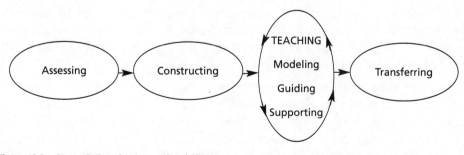

Figure 12.2. Strategic Tutoring Instructional Phases.

strategy necessary to complete the task, the tutor and student reflect on the process they have been following and identify the strategy they have been using. This becomes the strategy that is taught to the student.

In Phase 3, the tutor models the strategy for the student by thinking and problem solving aloud on a task that is similar to or actually part of the student's current assignment. For example, the tutor might model how to use a paraphrasing strategy while reading the student's psychology textbook. The tutor also checks the student's understanding of how to use the strategy by guiding the student through application of the strategy to the student's current assignment and provides positive and corrective feedback, gradually helping the student to become independent in strategy application.

Finally, in Phase 4, the tutor discusses and plans with the student ways that the student can independently transfer the newly acquired strategy to future and similar academic tasks. The goal of Phase 4 is to support the student as he or she learns to independently apply the strategy to a variety of assignments and in settings other than the tutoring center.

Strategic tutors focus on four goals as they interact with students. First, they ensure that students receive the necessary assistance to realize immediate academic achievement with pressing class demands. They recognize that if students do not complete their work and prepare for exams appropriately, they will not be able to maintain school enrollment. Second, they focus on increasing students' existing content knowledge bases. This is important because learning new content is enhanced when students have command of important prior knowledge. Third, to encourage students to move from a position of high dependence on tutorial assistance to one of independence as learners, tutors must focus on helping students become "good information processors" (Pressley, Borkowski, & Schneider, 1987). Some indicators of students being good information processors include the following: 1) they know a large number of useful learning strategies; 2) they understand when, where, and why these strategies are important; 3) they can select and monitor strategies wisely and engage in reflection and planning while learning; 4) they believe in carefully deployed effort; 5) they are intrinsically motivated; and 6) they know a great deal about many topics and have rapid access to that knowledge. The fourth goal is that tutors ensure that students are mentored, feel connected to the college or university, and are motivated to put forth effort. In short, strategically tutored students must be actively involved with learning and consistently infuse good information processing concepts with learning strategies in order to gain expanded knowledge bases.

Selection and Training of Strategic Tutors Strategic tutors may be selected from a variety of individuals who have different backgrounds. For example, tutors may be peers, graduate students, volunteers from the local community, teachers, or professional staff hired to provide a philosophical commitment to teach students skills and strategies while helping them complete assignments. These individuals have knowledge of the content to be tutored and have skills in and knowledge of strategic tutoring methodology and techniques.

Once tutors are selected, they must receive training and support in conducting strategic tutoring sessions. The content of such training should include an overview of the strategic tutoring model, examinations of expert models of strategic tutoring sessions, and, most important, individual coaching in role-play and real-life tutoring sessions (Hock, 1998). Training of this nature will require 10–12 hours of instruction led by someone who has expertise in tutoring and instruction.

Strategic tutoring services should be accessible to students through the college or university's disability support services office. Strategic tutoring services should also be differentiated from tutoring services that provide content help only. That is, strategic tutoring services are needed for students who struggle while learning, not students who do not understand how to complete a particular assignment or two.

Efficacy of Strategic Tutoring   Several research studies have been conducted to validate the efficacy of strategic tutoring with at-risk college students, including students with learning disabilities and ADHD (e.g., Hock, 1998). In one study, 28 first-year university students who were academically at risk, including two students with learning disabilities, were assigned to strategic tutors and received weekly subject-area tutoring in English composition 101. The mean ACT composite score for this group was 17.73. The reading comprehension percentile mean score was 36 as measured by the Stanford Diagnostic Reading Test, Third Edition (Karlsen, Madden, & Gardner, 1984). A comparison group of 28 higher achieving students was chosen as a contrast condition. The comparison students had scores on all measures that were significantly higher than students receiving strategic tutoring. For example, the comparison group mean ACT score was 23.39. Table 12.1 summarizes the achievement data for both groups.

Table 12.1. Achievement data of student participants discussed in Hock (1998)

Achievement scores	Experimental (n = 28)	Comparison (n = 28)	Degree of significance (p)
Mean ACT/SAT composite[1]	17.73	23.39	.0000*
Mean high school core grade point average	2.82	3.29	.0106*
Mean writing score[2]	9.22	10.32	.0317*
Mean algebra score[3]	9	15	.0001*
Reading comprehension percentile[4]	36th	N/A	N/A

[1]SAT scores were converted to ACT composite score equivalents
[2]Informal writing assessment
[3]The Kansas Algebra Informal Screening Test (The University of Kansas Mathematics Department, 1990)
[4]Stanford Diagnostic Reading Test (Karlsen, Madden, & Gardner, 1984) Blue Level Comprehension Subtest percentile scores
*p = .05

Students in the experimental group met with their strategic tutors for approximately 3 hours per week for $3^1/_2$ months to receive English Composition 101 support. During these tutoring sessions, students and tutors worked on preparing for or completing actual theme-writing assignments. Tutors embedded theme-writing strategy instruction while they provided support for current assignments. Students in the comparison group worked individually on their English composition 101 course assignments but had access to other university tutors. Overall results of the study indicated that students who were academically underprepared for university coursework (including students with disabilities) and received strategic tutoring were able to perform at a level equal to their better prepared peers on measures of strategy knowledge, grades earned on English composition themes, and overall course grades in tutored subjects. Thus, the power of intensive, ongoing tutorial support provide by skilled tutors seems to be a powerful intervention for underprepared college students.

Case Studies

Two of the students who participated in a study had learning disabilities (see Hock, 1998). The determination of learning disabilities for this particular university required that students present documentation of their learning disability. The documentation had to be recent (within the last 3 years) and had to specifically state the nature of the learning disability. Both participants presented documentation from their high school diagnostic and evaluation teams. Both diagnostic and evaluation teams used discrepancy formula procedures to determine the presence of a learning disability.

Information concerning one of the students indicated that she had become a successful student at the university while working with strategic tutors. For example, by the second semester of her freshman year, she had improved her cumulative grade point average (GPA) from 1.60 to 2.20. During her first semester, she received an *F* in one of her classes but had passed all other classes with *C*s, including English Composition 101 and intermediate mathematics/algebra. She earned a second semester GPA of 2.80 (with a *B* in college algebra). Reports from her tutors indicated that she put forth effort in tutoring sessions, attended group review sessions, and seemed motivated to learn. Unfortunately, a family crisis and added family responsibility led the student to leave the university. She withdrew from school in good academic standing after three semesters.

The other student with learning disabilities in this study had transferred to the university from a junior college (see Hock, 1998). Additional information indicated that he had learned to be a more effective student. For example, while his first-semester GPA was very low (1.03), he earned a second-semester GPA of 4.0 in college courses for algebra, biology 102, introduction to child psychology, and career and life planning. After two semesters, the student's cumulative GPA was 2.51. He attended the university for another semester and earned a semester GPA of 2.32. Comments from his tutors indicated that he worked very hard, improved his skills, and put in extra time to get ahead.

In another study of strategic tutoring that replicated the previous study, three of the students who participated were students with learning disabilities or ADHD. All of the students were male (see Hock, 1998). The first student earned a *C* in English Composition 101 and a cumulative GPA of 2.50. The student also earned 12 credit hours for the semester. These scores and grades are slightly below the mean scores earned by his peers without learning disabilities in the experimental and comparison groups. However, his semester GPA was equal to the scores earned by his peers without learning disabilities.

Additional information concerning this student indicated that he made a successful transition from high school to the university. For example, he reported that he had met or exceeded his academic expectations for the first semester. His tutors reported that he committed significant time and effort to academics, and they believed that he was learning how to be a more effective student. The tutors reported that significant instructional tutoring would still be necessary for the student to maintain the current level of success and eventually attain independent learner status.

The second student with a learning disability in the replication study earned a *C* in English Composition and a cumulative GPA of 2.62. The student also earned 13 credit hours for the semester. These scores and grades compared favorably to the mean scores earned by his peers without learning disabilities in the experimental and comparison groups.

This student had been particularly challenged by writing tasks in high school and found the demands of the university English Composition 101 class to be difficult. He struggled greatly with his early theme-writing assignments and became frustrated with the class and his instructor. He continued to work with a tutor and eventually committed to learning a more effective process for writing themes. As a result, his theme grades gradually improved from *F*s to *C*s to *B*s. The student's attitudes toward the class, instructor, and the writing of themes changed dramatically. His grades in other classes were high, reflecting his strengths in mathematics and science. Through three semesters, his cumulative GPA was 2.87. During one semester, he earned a GPA of 3.50. The transition from high school to the university was a challenge, but he was eventually very successful.

The third student, who had ADHD, earned a score of 20% on a theme-writing strategy pretest and self-reported that he had not taken his prescribed medication for ADHD prior to completing the pretest. He earned one of the highest scores of all students in the study on the posttest (70%) and reported that he had taken his medication prior to the posttest. In addition, he earned a *C* in English Composition 101 and a cumulative GPA of 2.91 after two semesters. The student earned 11 credit hours for the semester. These scores and grades are approximately the same as the mean scores earned by his peers without ADHD in the experimental and comparison groups with the exception of semester GPA. His semester GPA was higher than that of other experimental or comparison students. The number of credit hours he earned was lower than for the other students on average. The student with ADHD continued to improve dramatically in theme-writing skills and grades earned on themes. For example, he earned 149 and 148 points out 150 points possible on his last two themes during the second semester of his freshman year.

All students with disabilities who participated in the strategic tutoring intervention experienced some measure of academic success. More important, they did not experience such a disastrous first semester that they were dismissed from the university or dropped out. They seemed to benefit from strategic tutoring equally as well as their peers without learning disabilities or ADHD and made progress toward graduation.

GOAL BEHAVIOR AND POSSIBLE SELVES

Successful college students, including those with learning disabilities and ADHD, seem to be goal oriented, planful, and driven. Unfortunately, not all students are so focused on academic or future goals. Without this motivation to learn, the willingness to exert effort is greatly reduced. The good news is that goal-directed behavior can be nurtured in college students, including students with learning disabilities or ADHD. Thus, educators and counselors need to be concerned with facilitating motivation by using strategies to enhance learner effort and commitment to learning.

Learners of all ages are more motivated when they can see the usefulness of what they are learning and that what they are learning will lead to something of significance for themselves and others. In short, when learning is effectively tied to future purpose and outcomes, motivation to set goals and invest the necessary effort to meet goals is enhanced (e.g., Pintrich & Schunk, 1996). Without this commitment, significant numbers of learners may be left behind due to their lack of commitment and focus on meaningful and personal goals. Because of the need to develop intrinsic motivation, research since the early 1990s has focused on the development of programs to help students become committed to putting forth the effort needed to be academically successful.

Students who see learning as a way to acquire skills and knowledge that will increase competence in goal areas that *they* value are more likely to put forth the effort needed to attain those goals (Bandura, 1982; Blumenfeld, 1992; Borkowski et al., 1992; Dweck & Leggett, 1988). These students are often labeled intrinsically motivated and are said to be mastery oriented (Ames & Archer, 1988). That is, they are driven to put forth the effort necessary in academic situations because the reward they seek is directly related to what they personally value. In effect, the process and goal attainment related to learning is the reward (Deci, Hodges, Pierson, & Tomassone, 1992; Lepper, 1988; Maehr, 1989; Wehmeyer, Palmer, Agran, Mithaug, & Martin, 2000). Conversely, learning for the sake of achievement is driven more by extrinsic factors (Dweck, 1986; Lepper, 1988). Students who are motivated to achieve to get a certain grade, for example, may be considered extrinsically motivated.

Unfortunately, if these students believe that high levels of achievement and performance are beyond their reach, they may disengage from learning. Thus, it is useful to help students think in terms of mastery goals that are related to what they personally value and that help them attain the future selves to which they aspire.

Developing Possible Selves to Nurture Student Motivation

Hazel Markus, a professor of psychology at Stanford University, drew attention to the term *possible selves*. Markus said, "Possible selves are ideas about what one might become in the future" (Markus & Nurius, 1986, p. 954). Markus and her colleagues reported that ideas about one's self in the future can be very motivating. That is, individuals with clear ideas and goals about what they want to do, be, and be like seem more willing to put forth the effort needed to attain these hoped-for ideals. For example, a student who has identified becoming a computer network support technician as a possible self is more likely to work hard to graduate from college and get the necessary training for that career than a student who has never thought about a career. In addition, Markus and Nurius (1986) reported that some individuals will work just as hard to avoid the possible selves that they fear. For example, students who have thought about the possible self of living on welfare with no money to support a family may be more likely to work hard in school than students who have not seriously considered such outcomes. In either case, possible selves can increase one's motivation to work hard to attain specific goals because possible selves are an essential link between self-concept and individual motivation (Cross & Markus, 1994; Leondari, Syngollitou, & Kiosseoglou, 1998; Markus & Nurius, 1986; Oyserman & Markus, 1990a, 1990b).

The Possible Selves Program

The possible selves concept seemed promising in terms of helping students become more motivated to learn. However, although several individuals had reported interventions based on the Markus possible selves concept, no one had developed a program that can be used by educators at all levels of schooling to enhance the academic motivation of students, especially those students having difficulty in school. As a result, the Possible Selves Program (Hock et al., 2003) was developed to increase student motivation by having students examine their future and think about goals that are important to them. Specifically, students participating in the program think about and describe their hoped-for possible selves (selves they would like very much to create; a wish or a dream regarding themselves), expected possible selves (selves they are fairly sure they can create), and feared possible selves (selves they wish to avoid). Once students describe their possible selves, they create a Possible Selves Tree (Borkowski et al., 1992; Day, Borkowski, Dietmeyer, Howsepian, & Saenz, 1994; Estrada, 1990), which has branches and other elements representing the students' possible selves. The tree is used as a metaphor to help students examine the key roles they will assume in life; their hopes, expectations, and fears for the future; and the overall condition of their tree. In effect, students examine their personal tree and are challenged to evaluate and take action to nurture their tree so it can become strong, well-balanced, and beautiful. Finally, students set goals related to the actions they need to take to nurture their trees, make plans for reaching the goals, and then work toward those goals.

Researchers have suggested that once students have examined their possible selves (i.e., hoped for, expected, and feared), they are more inclined to believe that they can do well in school and in life (Day et al., 1994; Estrada, 1990; Hock, Deshler, & Schumaker, 2002). They begin to view learning as a pathway to their hopes and expectations and as a way to prevent feared possible selves from materializing. Thus, learning becomes more relevant, and students increase their willingness to put forth effort and commit to learning.

Program Components   There are six components in the Possible Selves Program. The first component, *Discovering*, helps students answer the question, "What are my strengths and interests?" During this phase, a counselor engages students in activities designed to help them identify areas in which they have interest and skills and feel good about themselves. The goal is to find an area in which each student has had positive experiences that he or she is willing to share (e.g., soccer, computer games). By finding an area about which the student feels positive, the "pump is primed," and the student may become more willing to share information related to areas about which he or she may not feel so positive (e.g., learning).

Thinking is the second component of the program, and it is designed to help the student answer the question, "Who am I?" Students complete a structured but open-ended interview with a counselor, either individually or as part of a group. During the interview, students are asked to identify words or phrases that describe them in targeted areas (i.e., as a learner, person, and worker and in a strength area). They are also asked to define their hopes, expectations, and fears for the future in each area. In this way, an outline of the current self and possibilities for the future is developed within each area. Sample interview questions for the learner area include the following:

- What statements or words best describe you as a learner?
- What do you hope to achieve as a learner?
- What do you expect to achieve as a learner?
- What do you fear as a learner?

The targeted areas and number of questions within the interview can be modified to fit the age and interests of the students (see Figure 12.3 for a sample questionnaire to use during the Possible Selves Interview).

As a student responds to questions and describes himself or herself, the student can also record answers to the interview questions. Additional questions

Possible Selves Questionnaire

What words or phrases best describe you in the following areas? Respond verbally or write down brief responses to the questions. Remember, there are no right or wrong answers to the questions, so respond honestly and to the best of your ability.

Section 1: Individual Strength

1. What's one thing that you are really good at doing?

2. What are some of the things you hope to achieve in this area?

3. What are some of the things you expect to achieve in this area?

4. What are some of your fears in this area?

Section 2: Learner

1. What words or phrases best describe you as a learner?

2. What are some of the things you hope to achieve as a learner?

3. What are some of the things you expect to achieve as a learner?

4. What are some of your fears as a learner?

Section 3: Person

1. What words or phrases best describe you as a person?

2. What are some of the things you hope to achieve as a person?

3. What are some of the things you expect to achieve as a person?

4. What are some of your fears as a person?

Section 4: Worker

1. What words or phrases best describe you as a worker?

2. What are some of the things you hope to achieve as a worker?

3. What are some of the things you expect to achieve as a worker?

4. What are some of your fears as a worker?

Figure 12.3. Sample questionnaire to use as part of the Possible Selves Interview.

are asked about the student's hopes, expectations, and fears for the future in at least three domains (learner, person, and worker—or an individually selected strength area), and these responses are also recorded. For example, one university student responded to the question "What do you hope to achieve as a learner?" by stating, "I hope to not flunk out of college, get at least a 2.5 G.P.A., learn the skills I need to open my own tech support business, and I really hope to earn my degree in computer science" (Hock, Schumaker, & Deshler, 2003, pp. 6–7). When the same student was asked, "What do you hope to achieve as a person?" he responded by stating, "I hope to be more responsible, to take care of my obligations, and take care of details as expected." Clearly, these goal statements provide direction for this particular student and allow college support service counselors to put the support and services they provide in the context of the student's hope and goals for the future. In short, support and services are seen by students as helping them reach *their* goals.

Once the interview has been completed, the third component of the Possible Selves Program is introduced: *Sketching*. This component helps students answer "What am I like, and what are my possible selves?" It is during this stage that students draw a Possible Selves Tree. The counselor begins by stating something such as, "You've listed a lot of important information about yourself. Now, you're going to pull that information together by creating a Possible Selves Tree. The tree will have limbs that represent you as a learner, person, and worker (or as a person with strengths in a certain area). It will have branches that represent your hoped-for and expected possible selves in those areas. You will represent your feared possible selves with dangerous conditions for your tree, such as lightning, termites, and poison in the soil. You'll use the exact words recorded in the interview to add branches and roots to the tree and the dangers around it. You can add to or modify the statements you made. Later, I'll ask you to evaluate your tree and tell me if it really represents the ideas you shared." Next, the tree is drawn and evaluated, and preliminary goals are discussed concerning how to keep the tree strong, make it fuller, protect it from fears, and provide it with nourishment. In short, the student is asked to briefly think about the tree and ways to nurture it.

The fourth component of the program, *Reflecting*, helps students answer the question, "What can I be?" It provides an opportunity for a student to evaluate the condition of his or her tree and set goals for the future. During this activity, for example, the student might realize that nurturing in the learner and person areas is needed if balance and fullness are to be achieved. This reflection activity can include a discussion of how learning can support the total tree. Because career hopes may be lost without improved academic performance, the student may be more inclined to commit time and energy to learning if the direct relationship is clarified. For example, if a student expresses the hope of earning a degree in computer science, he or she might set goals to attend class regularly and earn a 2.50 in all classes.

The fifth component, *Growing*, helps students answer the question "How do I get there?" It is utilized to get students to start thinking about specific ways to nurture and "grow" their tree and attain identified goals. If, for example, a student identified the hope for a career as the owner of a retail business during the Reflecting component, the student and counselor can take the short and long-term goals that are necessary to attain this possible self and develop a plan to reach these goals. It is hoped that the student will discover (with the counselor's guidance) the following that will support attainment of the student's hopes and expectations for the future: learning how to problem solve, earning a college diploma, learning business math skills, and learning different reading strategies in order to comprehend important material. In addition, the student may discover that these same goals help the student avoid the feared selves that have been identified (e.g., a person who has no job, money, or friends). During the Growing activities, a well-developed Action Plan is constructed by the student and counselor. The Action Plan lists a specific hope, a short-term goal underpinning the hope, the specific tasks that must be completed to reach the goal, and a time line for completing all of the tasks. The Action Plan provides a "pathway" to support the attainment of long-term goals and hopes for the future.

The sixth and final component is *Performing*. It helps students answer the question, "How am I doing?" During this phase, students regularly revisit the Possible Selves Tree, the goals established to nurture the tree, and the action plans. Task completion is reviewed; goals and action plans are modified; goal attainment is celebrated; new goals are added; and hopes, expectations, and fears are continually examined. In addition, whenever the value of learning is questioned, the tree can be used to demonstrate how specific learning experiences and student effort contribute to the strength of the student's tree (i.e., his or her future).

Research Supporting the Possible Selves Program   A few studies have been conducted on the effects of the Possible Selves Program with university-level students. Two studies were conducted with freshmen university students, including students with learning disabilities or ADHD who were not well prepared for the academic demands of college. In the first study (Hock et al., 2002), 60 students were randomly assigned to one of three conditions. For the control condition, 20 students received tutorial support from trained tutors and academic advising from counselors. Tutorial support consisted of unlimited access to subject-area and academic-skills tutors as needed. Academic advising was delivered by counselors in the university's office of student support services and consisted of bimonthly meetings during which students' academic progress was monitored and discussed. Counselors encouraged students to put forth effort and achieve success in their classes. The 20 students in the career-counseling condition received the same tutoring and counseling services as students in the control condition, with the addition of 6–8 hours of career-counseling activities over the course of a semester provided by staff associated with the university's counseling center. Specifically, these students were administered the Strong-Campbell Interest Inventory (Strong, Hansen, & Campbell, 1985), and the results of the inventory were discussed with a counselor in one-to-one sessions. Students then explored possible careers using resources available at the counseling center. The 20 students in the Possible Selves condition received the same tutoring and counseling services as the control group, and they participated in the Possible Selves Program that consisted of the Thinking, Sketching, and Reflecting components (i.e., the students did not receive the Discovering, Growing, and Performing components because they had not been conceptualized as part of the original intervention). The Possible Selves Program took 6–8 hours to complete and was presented to students in one-to-one interactions with a counselor.

The results of this study showed that at the end of the first semester of the freshman year, students in the Possible Selves Program group scored significantly higher than students in the control group and the comparison group on measures of goal identification. That is, they identified more goals as possible for them in life. It is interesting to note that the number of goals identified by students in the other conditions actually declined over the course of the first semester, while those of the Possible Selves group increased slightly or were maintained. Thus, freshman students not involved in the Possible Selves Program reported fewer academic goals than they did on pretests administered at the beginning of their first semester at the university. Also, at the end of 6 years, the Possible Selves students had earned higher GPAs than the students in the other groups: The mean GPA for the Possible Selves group was 2.65. The mean GPA for the control group was 2.25, and the mean GPA for the career-counseling group was 2.41. Moreover, 75% of the Possible Selves group had graduated from the university, compared with 45% of the control group and 60% of the career-counseling group. The overall graduation rate for all students entering this university was 54%. Thus, students who participated in the Possible Selves Program graduated at a rate that was 21% higher than the general student population, 30% higher than students in the control group, and 15% higher than students in the other counseling group.

The original Possible Selves Program that was implemented in the previously noted study was revised to include additional steps (Hock, Deshler, & Schumaker, 2002). The two new steps included developing elaborate goal-directed action plans (Growing) and periodic monitoring and feedback on the completion of tasks and action plan goals (Performing). In this study, 32 freshmen students (matched for ACT scores, gender, and high school GPA) were randomly assigned to a control or an experimental group. Upper-class students were recruited and taught how to guide others through the Possible Selves Program. Two of these peer mentors were assigned to each group of four to six students who had been assigned to the experimental group. Each group met for 1 hour per week for 12 weeks during the fall semester. The peer mentors taught the Possible Selves lessons during that time. The control students met individually with counselors during the same time period and for the same number of hours.

Students in the Possible Selves Program significantly outperformed the control group on measures of role identification and goal setting in the areas of academics and personal life. That is, the Possible Selves group identified significantly more roles for themselves as learners and people than did the students in the control group. In addition, they identified more goals for themselves as learners and people, and the goals they identified were more specific than the goals identified by the control group. These differences were statistically significant. Finally, retention of students at the university was greater for the Possible Selves group than for the control group. Although students in both conditions still had 1 year left in a 6-year time period in which they might graduate at the time of this printing, 75% of the students in the Possible Selves group were on track to graduate or had graduated, and 56% of the students in the control condition were on track to graduate or had graduated. Thus, the retention results for the Possible Selves Program as taught by peer mentors with small groups of students are similar to the retention results of the original possible selves study in which academic counselors worked individually with students. It is interesting to note that the peer-mentored students in the second study identified significantly more roles and goals than did the counselor-led Possible Selves students in the original study. The performance of students with learning disabilities or ADHD did not significantly differ form the other students in the Possible Selves studies.

CONCLUSION

The Strategic Tutoring and Possible Selves Programs show promise as interventions designed to enhance academic proficiency and motivation and to improve student performance across different instructional levels on key outcome measures of college success. Specifically, students who participated in the Strategic Tutoring and Possible Selves Programs earned higher GPAs in required courses, earned more credit toward graduation, and identified more life roles and goals than did their peers. Their academic performance was significantly higher than similar students who did not receive strategic tutoring. In addition, students who participated in the Possible Selves Program identified personal goals that were significantly more specific in nature than the goals of other students. These goals were instrumental in helping university-level students to earn higher GPAs over extended periods of time and to graduate at a higher rate than other students with similar profiles. Thus, the Strategic Tutoring and Possible Selves Programs seem to be effective interventions that increase the type, number, and specificity of goals students identify and the academic achievement that they attain. In turn, academic achievement and possible selves goals may be important in enhancing future academic motivation and performance by making school experiences and learning activities relevant to students' hoped-for future possible selves. Once students become more academically proficient and begin to see the relevance of academic skills, knowledge, and effort as the means to attain what they have identified as important hopes for the future, commitment to learning may follow.

It is hoped that students, including those with learning disabilities or ADHD, will be able to improve their academic performance; hold on to their dreams of success in their chosen fields; and expand the vision of what is possible for them in the future to include goals for becoming college graduates, good people, learners, family members, and productive workers. As a result, the outcomes that students achieve may be markedly enhanced in ways that make a difference in the quality of their lives.

REFERENCES

American Psychiatric Association. (March, 2001). *Attention deficit/hyperactivity disorder: Fact sheet.* Arlington, VA: Author.

Ames, C., & Archer, J. (1988). Achievement goals in the classroom: Students' learning strategies and motivational processes. *Journal of Educational Psychology, 80,* 260–270.

Bandura, A. (1982). Self-efficacy mechanisms in human agency. *American Psychologist, 37,* 122–147.

Bigaj, S.J., Shaw, S.F., Cullen, J.P., McGuire, J.M., & Yost, D.S. (1995). Services for students with learning disabilities at two- and four-year institutions: Are they different? *Community College Review, 23,* 17–33.

Blumenfeld, P.C. (1992). Classroom learning and motivation: Clarifying and expanding goal theory. *Journal of Educational Psychology, 84*(3), 272–281.

Borkowski, J.G., Day, J.D., Saenz, D., Dietmeyer, D., Estrada, T.M., & Groteluschen, A. (1992). Expanding the boundaries of cognitive interventions. In B.L. Wong (Ed.), *Contemporary intervention research in LD: An interventional perspective.* New York: Springer-Verlag.

Brinckerhoff, L.C., Shaw, S.F., & McGuire, J.M. (1992). Promoting access, accommodation, and independence for college students with learning disabilities. *Journal of Learning Disabilities, 25*(7), 417–429.

Bursuck, W., Rose, E., Cowen, S., & Yahaya, M.A. (1989). Nationwide survey of postsecondary education services for students with learning disabilities. *Exceptional Children, 56,* 236–245.

Collins, A., Brown, J.S., & Newman, S.E. (1989). Cognitive apprenticeship: Teaching the craft of reading, writing, and mathematics. In L.B. Resnick (Ed.), *Knowing, learning, and instruction: Essays in honor of Robert Glaser* (pp. 453–494). Mahwah, NJ: Lawrence Erlbaum Associates.

Cross, S.E., & Markus, H.R. (1994). Self-schemas, possible selves, and competent performance. *Journal of Educational Psychology, 86*(3), 423–438.

Day, J.D., Borkowski, J.G., Dietmeyer, D.L., Howsepian, B.A., & Saenz, D.S. (1994). Possible selves and academic achievement. In L.T. Wineger & J. Valsinen (Eds.), *Children's development within social contexts: Metatheoretical, theoretical and methodological issues* (Vol. 2, pp. 1–21). Mahwah, NJ: Lawrence Erlbaum Associates.

Deci, E.L., Hodges, M., Pierson, L., & Tomassone, J. (1992). Autonomy and competence as motivational factors in students with learning disabilities and emotional handicaps. *Journal of Learning Disabilities, 25*(7), 457–471.

Dunn, C. (1995). A comparison of three groups of academically at-risk college students. *Journal of College Student Development, 36,* 270–279.

Dweck, C.S. (1986). Motivational processes affecting learning. *American Psychologist, 41*(10), 1040–1048.

Dweck, C.S., & Leggett, E.L. (1988). A social-cognitive approach to motivation and personality. *Psychological Review, 95,* 256–273.

Estrada, M.T. (1990). *Improving academic performance through enhancing possible selves.* Unpublished master's thesis, University of Notre Dame, South Bend, IN.

Figler, S.K. (1987). Academic advising for athletes. *Journal of Sport and Social Issues, 11,* 74–81.

Gajar, A. (1992). Adults with learning disabilities: Current and future research priorities. *Journal of Learning Disabilities, 25*(8), 507–519.

Gerber, P.J., Ginsberg, R., & Reiff, H.B. (1992). Identifying alterable patterns in employment success for highly successful adults with learning disabilities. *Journal of Learning Disabilities*, 25(8), 475–481.

Heiligenstein, E., Guenther, G., Levy, A., Savino, F., & Fulwiler, J. (1999). Psychological and academic functioning in college students with attention deficit hyperactivity disorder. *Journal of American College Health*, 47(4), 181–191.

Henderson, C. (1999). *College freshmen with disabilities: Statistical year 1998*. Washington, DC: HEATH Resource Center and American Council on Education.

Hishinuma, E.S., & Fremstad, J.S. (1997). NCAA college freshman academic requirements: Academic standards or unfair roadblocks for students with learning disabilities. *Journal of Learning Disabilities*, 30(6), 589–598.

Hock, M.F. (1998). *The effectiveness of an instructional tutoring model and tutor training on the academic performance of underprepared college student-athletes*. Unpublished doctoral dissertation, The University of Kansas, Lawrence.

Hock, M.F., Deshler, D.D., & Schumaker, J.B. (1993). Learning strategy instruction for at-risk and learning disabled adults: The development of strategic learners through apprenticeship. *Preventing School Failure*, 38, 43–49.

Hock, M.F., Deshler, D.D., & Schumaker, J.B. (1999). Tutoring programs for academically underprepared college students: A review of the literature. *Journal of College Reading and Learning*, 29(2), 101–122.

Hock, M.F., Deshler, D.D., & Schumaker, J.B. (2000). *Strategic tutoring*. Lawrence, KS: Edge Enterprises.

Hock, M.F., Deshler, D.D., & Schumaker, J.B. (2002). *Nurturing possible selves in students through peer interactions: Surfacing personal goals*. Manuscript in preparation.

Hock, M.F., Schumaker, J.B., & Deshler, D.D. (2002). *The role of possible selves in improving the academic focus and performance of university students*. Manuscript in preparation.

Hock, M.F., Schumaker, J.B., & Deshler, D.D. (2003). *Possible selves: Nurturing student motivation*. Lawrence, KS: Edge Enterprises.

Houck, C.K., Asselin, S.B., Troutman, G.C., & Arrington, J.M. (1992). Students with learning disabilities in the university environment: A study of faculty and student perceptions. *Journal of Learning Disabilities*, 25(10), 678–684.

Jones, B.F., Palincsar, A.S., Ogle, D.S., & Carr, E.G. (1987). *Strategic teaching and learning: Cognitive instruction in the content areas*. Alexandria, VA: Association for Supervision and Curriculum Development.

Karlsen, B., Madden, R., & Gardner, E.F. (1984). *Stanford Diagnostic Reading Test, Third Edition*. San Antonio, TX: Harcourt Assessment.

Keim, J., McWhirter, J.J., & Bernstein, B.L. (1996). Academic success and university accommodation for learning disabilities: Is there a relationship? *Journal of College Student Development*, 37, 502–509.

Leondari, A., Syngollitou, E., & Kiosseoglou, G. (1998). Academic achievement, motivation and future selves. *Educational Studies*, 24(2), 153–163.

Lepper, M.R. (1988). Motivational considerations in the study of instruction. *Cognition and Instruction*, 5(4), 289–309.

MacDonald, R.B. (1987, April). *Evaluation of an alternative solution for the assessment and retention of high-risk college students*. Paper presented at the Annual Meeting of the American Educational Research Association, Washington, DC.

Maehr, M.L. (1989). Thoughts about motivation. In R. Ames & C. Ames (Eds.), *Research on motivation in education: Vol. 3. Goals and cognitions* (pp. 299–315). San Diego: Academic Press.

Markus, H., & Nurius, P. (1986). Possible selves. *American Psychologist*, 41, 954–969.

Mellard, D.F., & Hazel, J.S. (1992). Social competencies as pathway to successful life transitions. *Learning Disability Quarterly*, 15, 251–265.

Mohr, E. (1991). *A study of peer tutor training programs: A League report* (Report No. JC10305). Overland Park, KS: League for Innovation in the Community College. (ERIC Document Reproduction Service No. ED 322 777)

Oyserman, D., & Markus, H.R. (1990a). Possible selves and delinquency. *Journal of Personality and Social Psychology, 59*(1), 112–125.

Oyserman, D., & Markus, H.R. (1990b). Possible selves in balance: Implications for delinquency. *Journal of Social Issues, 46*(2), 141–157.

Patton, J.R., & Polloway, E.A. (1992). Learning disabilities: The challenges of adulthood. *Journal of Learning Disabilities, 25*(7), 410–415, 447.

Pintrich, P.R., & Schunk, D. (1996). *Motivation in education: Theory, research, and application.* Upper Saddle River, NJ: Merrill/Prentice Hall.

Polloway, E.A., Schewel, R., & Patton, J.R. (1992). Learning disabilities in adulthood: Personal perspectives. *Journal of Learning Disabilities, 25*(8), 520–522.

Pressley, M., Borkowski, J.G., & Schneider, W. (1987). Cognitive strategies: Good strategy users coordinate metacognition and knowledge. In R. Vasta & G. Whitehurst (Eds.), *Annals of child development* (Vol. 5, pp. 89–129). Greenwich, CT: JAI Press.

Reid, R., & Katsiyannis, A. (1995). Attention-deficit/hyperactivity disorder and Section 504. *Remedial and Special Education, 16*(1), 44–52.

Reid, R., Maag, J.W., & Vasa, S.F. (1994). Attention deficit hyperactivity disorder as a disability category: A critique. *Exceptional Children, 60*, 198–214.

Rogoff, B. (1990). *Apprenticeship in thinking: Cognitive development in social context.* New York: Oxford University Press.

Salend, S.J., & Rohena, E. (2003). Students with attention deficit disorder: An overview. *Intervention in School and Clinic, 38*(5), 259–266.

Strong, E.R., Hansen, J.C., & Campbell, D.P. (1985). *Strong-Campbell Interest Inventory.* Palo Alto, CA: Stanford University Press.

The University of Kansas Mathematics Department. (1990). *The Kansas Algebra Informal Screening Test.* Lawrence: Author.

Vogel, S.A., & Adelman, P.B. (1992). The success of college students with learning disabilities: Factors related to educational attainment. *Journal of Learning Disabilities, 25*(7), 430–441.

Vogel, S.A., Hruby, P.J., & Adelman, P.B. (1993). Educational and psychology factors in successful and unsuccessful college students with learning disabilities. *Learning Disabilities Research and Practice, 8*(1), 35–43.

Wehmeyer, M.L., Palmer, S.B., Agran, M., Mithaug, D.E., & Martin, J.E. (2000). Promoting causal agency: The self-determined learning model of instruction. *Exceptional Children, 66*(4), 439–453.

White, W. (1992). The postschool adjustment of persons with learning disabilities: Current status and future projections. *Journal of Learning Disabilities, 25*(7), 448–456.

Zaritsky, J.S. (1989). *Peer tutoring: Issues and concerns* (Report No. JC900123). Long Island City, NY: LaGuardia Community College. (ERIC Document Reproduction Service No. ED 315 134)

CHAPTER 13

Dual Enrollment as a Postsecondary Education Option for Students with Intellectual Disabilities

Debra Hart, Karen Zimbrich, and David R. Parker

There is a growing national trend for developing innovative postsecondary education options for youth with intellectual disabilities. This trend is motivated by the following factors: extremely poor postschool outcomes experienced by youth with disabilities, the negative impact of high-stakes testing on youth with intellectual disabilities (further restricting already limited postschool options), a growing cadre of youth who have been included in general education classes and have studied the K–12 curriculum, and the expectations of youth and their families that inclusion will continue into postsecondary education. Educators who have developed postsecondary programs and services typically have done so in isolation, often on a case-by-case basis (at the behest of parents) and without the benefit of lessons learned from evidence-based practices. Thus, there is a need to identify programs and services that support youth with intellectual disabilities and to begin to build a database of knowledge for families, youth, practitioners, policy analysts, and researchers.

This chapter presents an overview of current postsecondary education options for youth with intellectual disabilities and a discussion of initial research on the effectiveness of these options for improving outcomes for youth with disabilities. First, an overview of the motivating factors related to student outcomes that prompted this movement is discussed. Next, the results are summarized regarding a national survey conducted to identify which postsecondary education options are available for youth with intellectual disabilities. Third, a model that supports students with intellectual disabilities who are dually enrolled in high school and college is highlighted. Finally, recommendations for future research are provided.

DEFINITION OF INTELLECTUAL DISABILITY

The term *intellectual disability* refers to a learning or cognitive disability that significantly affects a student's access to the general curriculum without a strong system of educational supports and services. In addition to cognitive limitations, this disability often is characterized by significant limitations in adaptive behavior as expressed in conceptual, social, and practical adaptive skills (American Association on Mental Retardation, 2002). Although students with mental illnesses and emotional disturbances may have such adaptive behavior issues, this is a particular issue for those with intellectual disabilities related to mental retardation, autism, cerebral palsy, or multiple developmental disabilities.

OVERVIEW OF OUTCOMES FOR YOUTH WITH DISABILITIES

Due to the very poor postschool outcomes for many youth with disabilities, considerable attention has been paid to developing evidenced-based practices to improve these outcomes. The resulting data clearly highlight the need for change:

- "Only 35 percent of people with disabilities reported being employed full or part time, compared with 78 percent of those who do not have disabilities" (National Organization on Disability [N.O.D.], 2004).

- "Three times as many individuals with disabilities live in poverty, with annual household incomes of less than $15,000" (N.O.D., 2004).

- Since the mid-1990s, youth with mental retardation exiting high school are the only disability category not to experience a significant increase in earning above minimum wage (Wagner, Cameto, & Newman, 2003).

- Only 15% of students in special education programs go on to any type of postsecondary education (Lichtenstein, 1998).

- Only 8% of youth with intellectual disabilities participate in postsecondary education (Blackorby & Wagner, 1996; Neubert, Moon, Grigal, & Redd, 2001).

- "People with disabilities are less likely to socialize, eat out, or attend religious services than their counterparts without disabilities" (N.O.D., 2004).

- Life satisfaction for individuals with disabilities lags behind that of people without disabilities—34% of people with disabilities say that they are very satisfied, compared with 61% of people without disabilities (N.O.D., 2004).

N.O.D. President Alan A. Reich said, "Looking back four years, or ten years, to our earlier N.O.D./Harris surveys, we see Americans with disabilities heading in the right direction. But people with disabilities remain pervasively disadvantaged" (N.O.D., 2004). In addition, according to N.O.D. (2004), Harris Poll Chairman Humphrey Taylor found, "The severity of disability makes a significant difference in all of the gap areas, and people with severe disabilities have much greater disadvantages." Furthermore, Robert Hall stated, "Depending on the severity and type of disability that one has, some doors open but certain other doors close" (N.O.D., 2004). This trend is clearly evident when examining participation of youth with intellectual disabilities in postsecondary education options. Since the mid-1980s, considerable federal and state resources have been allocated to improving outcomes for students with disabilities, including those with intellectual disabilities, as they make the transition out of high school. Inclusive postsecondary education outcomes have been limited, despite these resources and mandates (Butterworth & Gilmore, 2000). Compared with their peers without disabilities, youth with intellectual disabilities have significantly lower participation rates in postsecondary education, have lower than average earnings, are disproportionately represented in low-skilled jobs, have limited access to employee benefits, and experience higher rates of poverty (Stodden & Dowrick, 2000). If they participate in any kind of postsecondary education experience, youth with intellectual disabilities are likely to attend segregated transition programs located on a number of college campuses across the country (Hart, Mele-McCarthy, Pasternack, Zimbrich, & Parker, 2004; Neubert et al., 2001).

Although data show an increase in the number of students with disabilities attending colleges, especially colleges with open enrollment (e.g., community colleges), these are students with sensory, mobility, and/or learning (rather than intellectual) disabilities (U.S. Department of Labor, Bureau of Labor Statistics, 1999). Postsecondary education is one of the most effective ways for individuals to increase their employability (Henderson, 1999; Horn & Berktold, 1999; Kaye, 1998; U.S. Department of Labor, Bureau of Labor Statistics, 1999). Typically, youth with intellectual disabilities are not recruited and do not enroll in postsecondary education (Blackorby & Wagner, 1996; U.S. Department of Labor, Bureau of Statistics, 1999; Hart, Zafft, & Zimbrich, 2001). However, even limited postsecondary education experience or participation in *any* type of postsecondary education (e.g., auditing one college course, completing a certificate program) correlates positively to chances of securing competitive employment for youth with intellectual disabilities (Zafft, Hart, & Zimbrich, 2004; Gilmore, Bose, & Hart, 2001; Stodden & Dowrick, 2000).

Typically, youth with intellectual disabilities either drop out of school or remain in special education programs beyond their 18th birthday while their peers without disabilities graduate and go on to college, technical school, and/or full-time employment. This discrepancy has prompted a growing interest in the development of relevant programs and services at the college level for youth with intellectual disabilities. As noted, some youth who have been included in K–12 general education and their families expect continued inclusive options after age 18. School systems and local colleges are beginning to respond to this need by developing dual enrollment programs for people ages 18–21 who have intellectual disabilities (Hart et al., 2004).

NATIONAL SURVEY ON POSTSECONDARY PROGRAMS FOR YOUTH WITH INTELLECTUAL DISABILITIES

A national survey identified 25 postsecondary education programs that use a dual enrollment strategy (Hart et al., 2004). *Dual enrollment* refers to students who are enrolling in postsecondary education and secondary education simultaneously. This is usually done by secondary students to use local education funds to pay for postsecondary education. Programs fell into one of three categories of postsecondary education models: substantially separate, mixed, and totally inclusive. The majority of the programs offered a mixed option, wherein youth with intellectual disabilities were supported, on a limited basis, in taking regular college courses. Some others offered segregated services with no opportunity or supports to enable these students to take general education courses. Only a few colleges offered totally inclusive postsecondary education options with adequate supports provided so youth with intellectual disabilities could participate in general education college courses of their own choosing. More inclusive postsecondary education models, composed of evidenced-based practices, are needed (Whelley, 2003). These would include options that support youth to develop a career path related to a primary area of interest. Overall, there is a dearth of information on postsecondary education programs and services for youth with intellectual disabilities and minimal data on the effectiveness of the options that do exist, particularly in relationship to improving postsecondary outcomes (Hart et al., 2004; Neubert et al., 2001). Figure 13.1 illustrates the breakdown of programs according to the following program types:

- *Substantially separate program:* Frequently, these programs are referred to as life skills or transition programs. This description provides information about programs that are based on a college campus, but it should be noted that they are also found in community-based settings. Students who attend these programs typically do not have sustained interaction with others in the general student body and they do not have the option of taking standard college courses with peers who do not have disabilities. The curriculum is focused primarily on skills, with functional rotation through a limited number of employment slots (e.g., maintenance, food preparation, filing), either on or off campus, providing some semblance of work experience for participants.

- *Mixed program:* These are programs that are housed on college campuses. The difference between mixed and substantially separate programs is that

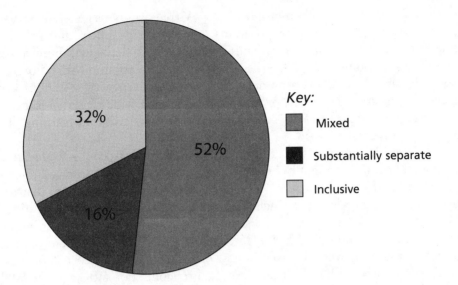

Figure 13.1. Types of service delivery model.

students with disabilities have some interaction with students who do not have disabilities (e.g., in the cafeteria, at sporting events). Most important, students have the option of taking typical classes and being supported in inclusive college courses, even though most of the curriculum is focused on functional skills, with rotation through a limited number of work experience slots.

- *Inclusive, individual support model:* Students receive individualized services and supports (e.g., an educational coach, assistive technology), which ensure access and success in college courses, certificate programs, internships, and/or degree programs. All services are student centered, based on student choices and preferences, and inclusive of those available to the general student body. Some programs also offer internships and employment-related supports.

More than half of the programs surveyed ($n = 25$) were mixed ($n = 13$), about one third were inclusive ($n = 8$), and about one fifth were substantially separate ($n = 4$). Most frequently, services provided in mixed programs were offered in separate settings or segregated classrooms, but in some instances students were supported to take standard college academic courses and to participate in campuswide recreational and social activities. Overall, mixed program curricula tended to focus on functional life skills.

Mixed and substantially separate programs have been around longer than inclusive programs. Some mixed and separate programs have been in existence since the late 1980s, in comparison with inclusive programs, most of which have been in operation only since the late 1990s.

Substantially separate programs tended to be larger than either mixed or inclusive programs, with 60% having more than 21 students and some as many as 70 students, across multiple classes. Mixed programs generally served 11–15 students, and inclusive programs 6–10 students. All of the inclusive programs surveyed (100%) have had fewer than 15 students with intellectual disabilities attending college at any one time. The most common disability type served by any service delivery model were students with cognitive disabilities or mental retardation; however, programs also served a wide range of students with other developmental disabilities such as autism, significant learning disability, and mental illness.

Figure 13.2 illustrates funding sources for these postsecondary education models. The most frequently cited resource (95%) was school district/Individuals with Disabilities Education Act (IDEA) funds for transportation. Instructional assistants or education coaches and vocational assessment were identified as provided by 65% of the school districts. There was a fairly even distribution in the way funds were used by the 25 colleges. Overall, 75% of the programs indicated that they were involved in cost or resource sharing: 78.6% of these costs were shared with their local vocational rehabilitation (VR) agency, 50% with their college's disability support services office, and 42.9% with their department of mental retardation/developmental disabilities (DMR/DD).

Figure 13.3 shows barriers to program implementation. Overall, 61.1% of the 25 postsecondary programs identified attitude as the most significant barrier to overcome. Examples of attitudinal difficulties include a belief that students with learning and intellectual disabilities do not belong in college and/or a belief that the curriculum will be "watered down" for these individuals.

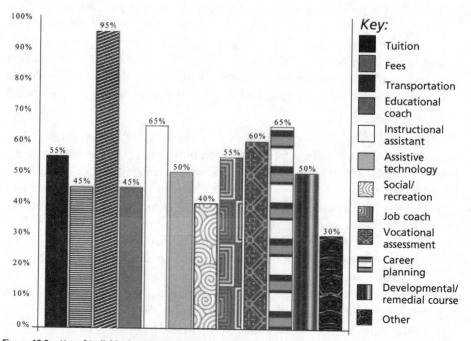

Figure 13.2. Use of Individuals with Disabilities Education Act (IDEA) funds.

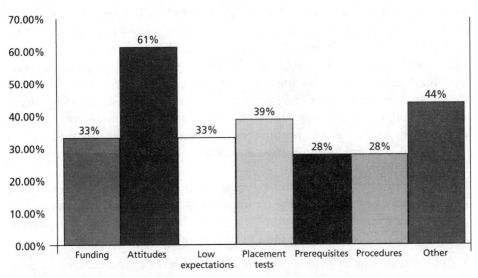

Figure 13.3. Barriers to program implementation.

Barriers listed under "Other" (the second biggest category) included transportation, entrance standards, and a lack of transition planning. The individual education program (IEP) meeting was the most frequently cited (68.18%) vehicle for determining whether a college program is appropriate for a particular student.

Discussion of Survey Results

This survey provided an initial data set on postsecondary education programs as a relatively new model of transition services for individuals ages 18–21 with learning and intellectual disabilities. Given the newness of this development, it was not surprising that only 25 programs were identified that qualified for this study. The number of programs was too small to provide a sufficient sample size to allow for detailed statistical analysis of differences in programmatic outcomes. Additional research is needed to determine the effectiveness of postsecondary education experiences in improving postschool outcomes for youth with intellectual disabilities. The next section discusses one inclusive postsecondary education model, developed in the late 1990s through a model demonstration project, which was funded by the U.S. Department of Education's Office of Special Education Programs (OSEP).

COLLEGE CAREER CONNECTION MODEL

In response to the dearth of inclusive postsecondary education models for youth with intellectual disabilities and to address the needs of these individuals and their families, the Institute for Community Inclusion, a University Center for Excellence on Developmental Disabilities at the University of Massachusetts–Boston, worked with staff from three school districts in Massachusetts to develop the College Career Connection (C³) Model. This dual enrollment model was the product of a demonstration project funded from 1998 to 2001 by OSEP. Project staff at the Institute worked with faculty from three diverse, urban high schools and their local colleges to provide inclusive participation in typical college activities for high school students ages 18–21 who had intellectual disabilities and who had expressed interest in postsecondary education. Overall, the model was built around students' strengths and preferences; it also incorporated a collaborative interagency team, the Student Support Team (SST), to create innovative strategies that support student access to inclusive college settings.

The nature of the C³ Model is graphically represented in Figure 13.4. The model took into account the unique aspects of individual students, including their aspirations for the future, family wishes, and cultural background. It was based on the following guiding principles:

- Individual student vision determined the direction and controlled decision making.

- All options explored with students were inclusive and occurred in settings that reflected a natural proportion of students with and without disabilities.

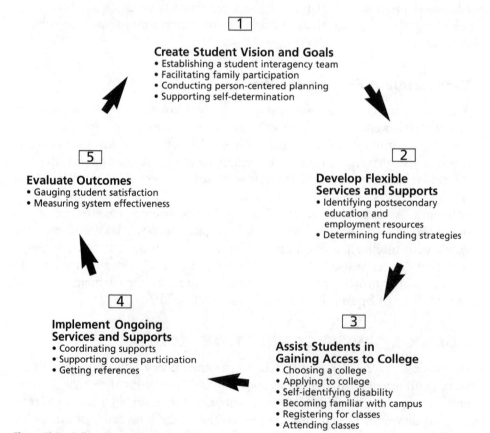

1

Create Student Vision and Goals
- Establishing a student interagency team
- Facilitating family participation
- Conducting person-centered planning
- Supporting self-determination

5

Evaluate Outcomes
- Gauging student satisfaction
- Measuring system effectiveness

2

Develop Flexible Services and Supports
- Identifying postsecondary education and employment resources
- Determining funding strategies

4

Implement Ongoing Services and Supports
- Coordinating supports
- Supporting course participation
- Getting references

3

Assist Students in Gaining Access to College
- Choosing a college
- Applying to college
- Self-identifying disability
- Becoming familiar with campus
- Registering for classes
- Attending classes

Figure 13.4. College Career Connection design.

- There were no special programs or specially designated classes (i.e., segregated classes or course sequences just for students with disabilities).

- The development of supports emphasized individual needs and preferences rather than a one-size-fits-all approach.

- Collaboration among systems (e.g., high school, college, adult services) was necessary for the process to be effective.

Implementation of College Career Connection

The following sections describe how the C^3 Model was implemented. Some of these activities occurred simultaneously and, depending on circumstances in each of the three school districts, the order may have differed slightly from the following sequence.

Create Student Vision and Goals   An initial activity of the C^3 Model was to identify students with significant disabilities as project participants. Criteria included finding youth ages 18–21 who had an intellectual disability and who 1) had expressed interest in postsecondary education, 2) were interested in learning more about the project, and 3) had family members who were interested in student participation in the project. Approximately eight students with significant disabilities per school district ($N = 25$) were identified to take part in the project. Then, through a facilitated, person-centered planning process, each student (with the help of friends, relatives, and others who knew the student well) developed a list of likes and dislikes, strengths and weaknesses, preferences, and areas of potential future interest.

To support individual student goals, each participating high school developed an interagency SST composed of a wide range of individuals including students, family members, school-to-career personnel, teachers, guidance counselors, college personnel, Workforce Investment Act (WIA) personnel, service coordinators from DMR/DD, counselors from VR, independent living staff, and service providers. Additional SST membership varied according to the needs of particular students and the local community. The role of the SST was twofold: 1) to identify individual services and supports for participants and 2) to develop solutions to systemic barriers. The SSTs met monthly to brainstorm the array of services that could best support individual students to reach their goals and cost-sharing arrangements that could be used to provide services. For example, the school district might pay for transportation and an educational coach at college, the VR agency might provide a tuition waiver or cover the cost of initial job coaching, DMR/DD might pay for some type of assistive technology, and the student and family might pay for books.

Facilitating family participation was another important aspect of the model's first step. For that purpose, orientation sessions provided an opportunity for family members and students, as well as key SST members, to learn about the project, to ask questions, and to express any concerns or hesitations about participation. During each session, project staff reviewed the need to better prepare youth for adult life and described how the project would provide access to postsecondary educational options and other individualized adult outcomes. Project staff provided follow-up contact with students and families throughout the remainder of the project.

Develop Flexible Services and Supports   To assist students in achieving their identified vision for postsecondary education, each SST developed a sample menu of individualized services and supports from which students and their family members could choose (e.g., educational coach, transportation training, career connections to employment, mentoring, technology, social networks). For example, one student learned to travel independently through the city's travel-training program so she could attend a social activity on the college campus. Other students learned to use public transportation through a program sponsored by their high schools. Also, through the collaborative efforts of SST members, several districts were able to develop cost-sharing arrangements between institutions and agencies to fund individualized services and supports and thus maximize limited transition dollars.

Assist Students in Gaining Access to College   Each action plan ultimately involved assisting the student to gain access to college, which may have included a continuing education course, on-line courses, a sampling of unrelated classes, or an entire course of study. Overall, the planning process helped establish each student's vision and also laid the foundation for the remainder of the project activities for students and all three SSTs. Once a student's career goals and support needs were identified, funding mechanisms were determined and responsible personnel were outlined in the student's action plan. Then the process of gaining access to college began. In the C^3 Model, several areas were considered to assist a student interested in going to college. These areas included choosing a college, applying to college, self-identifying disability, becoming familiar with the campus, registering for courses, and attending classes. In general, this process began 6–12 months prior to actual admission to college and continued, to a greater or lesser extent (depending on the individual student), throughout each semester that the student attended classes.

Implement Ongoing Services and Supports   Once various services and supports were identified, SST members shared responsibilities to ensure that students gained access to the needed services and supports in an efficient and timely way. For example, one DMR counselor orchestrated activities during the 3-week semester break so that students could maintain their schedules rather than spend downtime back at high school. Ongoing supports generally included an orientation session at the college and additional visits to the campus to ensure that students learned their way around; could locate student support service facilities; and were able to identify safety net/support system elements, such as where to meet when plans unexpectedly changed or how to use a cellular telephone to get help.

Evaluate Outcomes Ongoing evaluation strategies were instituted to ensure effectiveness of the process, adequacy and timeliness of services and supports, and overall satisfaction with the outcomes of the person-centered approach. Evaluation methods included focus groups, satisfaction surveys, and ongoing tracking of student outcomes. Every student had an opportunity to discuss his or her individual interests and needs with the entire SST during each semester to assess progress and address any concerns. In addition to the local teams, a project advisory committee was used to guide and evaluate project activities and to assist project staff in addressing emerging barriers in a systematic fashion.

Significance of College Career Connection

The development of the C^3 Model was significant for the following reasons:

- It offered a chance to pursue academic or vocational curriculum in inclusive settings.

- It addressed a significant need for more inclusive postsecondary education options for individuals with intellectual disabilities and the need for further research on the efficacy of these options.

- It provided opportunities to develop employment skills and make career connections.

- It helped individuals with intellectual disabilities to expand social networks and become involved with people without disabilities.

- It promoted the development of people with intellectual disabilities as lifelong learners.

What was most innovative about the C^3 Model was that it expanded the traditional concept of "transition" from a one-dimensional employment model to a model that includes inclusive postsecondary education as an option for students with disabilities. Dual enrollment is not a new concept, but the application of dual enrollment for students with learning and intellectual disabilities is exciting because these individuals historically have not been afforded the option of a postsecondary education. Access to postsecondary education may expand opportunities for students who have learning and intellectual disabilities to become involved in the larger society, as an innovative outcome of emerging social and public policy (e.g., the New Freedom Initiative, 2001). Moreover, as mentioned previously, college experiences may increase competitive employment opportunities for these students.

Exploratory Follow-Up Survey
to Determine the Effectiveness of the C^3 Model

To explore the outcomes of the programs involved in the survey, a follow-up survey (Zafft et al., 2004) was conducted in which outcomes for 20 students who were involved in C³ programs were compared with outcomes of 20 students who were not involved in C³ programs ($N = 40$). This study was funded in part by a subcontract with the National Center for the Study of Postsecondary Educational Supports: Rehabilitation Research and Training Center at the University of Hawaii. A brief discussion of the findings follows, with suggestions for further study.

All students participated in substantially separate education programs at the participating high schools, with the vast majority of students enrolled in life-skills programs rather than in the general education curriculum. The survey was developed by project staff and administered to all participants. One finding was that participation in postsecondary education correlated positively with two employment variables: competitive employment and independent employment. Students who participated in postsecondary education worked fewer total hours per week in paid employment (on a "part-time school and part-time work" schedule) than did their peers who did not participate in postsecondary education. Students who participated in postsecondary education used more accommodations when in college than in high school, and they made use of the additional types of accommodations that were available in college. Furthermore, students who participated in postsecondary education were more likely to receive a high school diploma. In addition, 16 of the 20 (80%) students who participated in postsecondary education chose to continue at college after completing their first class.

Some of the information reviewed in this summary reinforces research-based practices that are being supported in school systems already:

- Encourage students to develop robust visions of their future.

- Help students to keep their options open through participation in typical college-preparatory activities (e.g., college information night, college visits, college orientation).

- Ensure that students include a goal for pursuing postsecondary education in their IEPs, which Blackorby and Wagner (1996) noted as a practice that increases the likelihood (all else being equal) that students will enroll in college.

- Create greater access to the general curriculum through the use of a broad range of accommodations, including assistive technology and universal design strategies, while in high school.

- Connect students to postsecondary education before they leave high school, through models that form a bridge to the adult community of lifelong learners and workers (e.g., dual enrollment).

- Integrate evidence-based practices that support students with intellectual disabilities in gaining access to and succeeding in postsecondary education into personnel preparation programs.

As with much research, however, the results described here raise more questions. The next section suggests future research and actions to pursue.

SUGGESTIONS FOR FUTURE DIRECTIONS

First, as postsecondary education programs develop, they must be identified and surveyed. Similar efforts in Canada, Australia, and Europe may be surveyed and added to the discussion, both by way of comparison with national trends in the United States and as resources for additional evidence-based practices from which to learn. This information then needs to be compiled and made available to educators and the general public through linkage with national clearinghouses (e.g., the HEATH Resource Center), higher education associations (e.g., the Association of Higher Education and Disability [AHEAD]), and relevant national centers (e.g., National Center for the Study of Postsecondary Education Supports: Rehabilitation and Training at the University of Hawaii, National Center on Secondary Education and Transition, National Center for Workforce Development).

Second, research on the effectiveness of current approaches must be undertaken to determine the relative success of each in assisting individuals with a wide range of learning and intellectual disabilities (e.g., emotional or psychiatric disabilities, mental retardation, significant learning disabilities), youth at risk of academic failure, and second language learners in accomplishing any (or all) of the following:

- Graduating from high school

- Completing a certificate program

- Graduating from a 2-year college

- Matriculating into a 4-year college

- Identifying and developing a preferred career path

- Securing meaningful, inclusive, competitive employment of their own choosing

- Having friends

- Becoming self-determined

- Participating actively in a fulfilling life in the community at large

Third, identification and research on the effectiveness of strategies, such as state and local resource mapping that uphold restructuring and reallocation of existing resources, must occur to develop a systemic infrastructure that supports all youth in making the transition to postsecondary education and employment. For example, examine cross-agency resource alignment for creating and improving collaboration between and among individuals, their families, one-stop career centers, and adult service organizations.

Fourth, it would be useful to research the total student experience in postsecondary education to identify the nature of intellectual *and* social growth of individuals with disabilities, including those with intellectual disabilities. In particular, it would be interesting to identify how a college experience raises expectations of teachers, parents, and perspective employers for people with intellectual disabilities.

Finally, policies and practices must be identified to eliminate barriers for youth with learning and intellectual disabilities in gaining access to postsecondary education (e.g., expand use of assistive technology and other accommodations in high school, change requirements for receiving a diploma in order to be eligible for financial aid, drop prerequisite course requirements, raise expectations).

CONCLUSION

The transition out of high school is complex. It requires thoughtful, flexible, and tested models that support students with intellectual disabilities in achieving a productive life based on options of their choosing. It is particularly troubling to see young people working in menial jobs for extremely low pay and without benefits. Therefore, a moral imperative rests with the disability research community to closely examine ways to support better postschool outcomes for these individuals. Given that inclusive postsecondary education options for people with learning and intellectual disabilities are still new and relatively rare, the overview presented in this chapter provides an example of a successful service model for practitioners and advocates. Dual enrollment for students with learning and intellectual disabilities promises to be a creative educational option to improve graduation rates and the attainment of meaningful, inclusive, competitive employment.

REFERENCES

American Association on Mental Retardation. (2002). *Definition of Mental Retardation.* Retrieved on June 30, 2004, from http://www.aamr.org/Policies/faq_mental_retardation.shtml

Blackorby, J., & Wagner, M. (1996). Longitudinal post-school outcomes of youth with disabilities: Findings from the National Longitudinal Transition Study. *Exceptional Children, 62,* 399–413.

Butterworth, J., & Gilmore, D. (2000). Work status trends for people with mental retardation FY 1985–FY 1998. *Research to Practice, 6*(4), 1–4.

Gilmore, D., Bose, J., & Hart, D. (2001). Postsecondary education as a critical step toward meaningful employment: Vocational rehabilitation's role. *Research to Practice, 7*(4), 1–4.

Hart, D., Mele-McCarthy, J., Pasternack, R., Zimbrich, K., & Parker, D. (2004). Community college: A pathway to success for youth with learning, cognitive, and intellectual disabilities in secondary education. *Education and Training in Developmental Disabilities, 39*(1), 54–66.

Hart, D., Zafft, C., & Zimbrich, K. (2001). Creating access to college for all students. *Journal for Vocational Special Needs Education, 23*(2), 19–31.

Henderson, C. (1999). *College freshmen with disabilities: Statistical year 1998.* Washington, DC: HEATH Resource Center and American Council on Education.

Horn, L., & Berktold, J. (1999). *Students with disabilities in postsecondary education: A profile of preparation, participation, and outcomes.* Washington, DC: U.S. Department of Education, National Center for Education Statistics.

Kaye, H.S. (1998). Is the status of people with disabilities improving? *Disabilities Statistics Abstract, 21,* 1–4.

Lichtenstein, S. (1998). Characteristics of youth and young adults. In F. Rusch & J. Chadsey (Eds.), *Beyond high school: Transition from school to work* (pp. 1–31). Belmont, CA: Wadsworth Group.

National Organization on Disability. (2004, June 25). *Landmark Disability Survey Finds Pervasive Disadvantages.* (2004). Retrieved February 3, 2005, from http://www.nod.org/index.cfm?fuseaction=page.viewPage&pageID=1430&nodeID=1&FeatureID=1422&redirected=1&CFID=1702969&CFTOKEN=1372791

Neubert, D.A., Moon, M.S., Grigal, M., & Redd, V. (2001). Post-secondary educational practices for individuals with mental retardation and other significant disabilities: A review of the literature. *Journal of Vocational Rehabilitation, 16,* 155–168.

Stodden, R.A., & Dowrick, P.W. (2000). The present and future of postsecondary education for adults with disabilities. *Impact, 13,* 4–5.

U.S. Department of Health and Human Services. (2001). *New Freedom Initiative.* Retrieved September 29, 2003, from http://www.hhs.gov/newfreedom/init.html

U.S. Department of Labor, Bureau of Labor Statistics. (1999). *Report on the American workforce* (USDL: 99-252). Washington, DC: Author.

Wagner, M., Cameto, R., & Newman, L. (2003). *Youth with disabilities: A changing population: A report of findings from the National Longitudinal Transition Study (NLTS) and the National Longitudinal Transition Study-2* (NLTS2). Menlo Park, CA: SRI International.

Whelley, T. (2003). Students with Intellectual Disabilities and Postsecondary Education: Discussion of Developments in Practice and Policy. *Proceedings of the 2003 Capacity Building Institute.* Manoa: National Center for the Study of Postsecondary Education Supports, University of Hawaii–Manoa.

Zafft, C., Hart, D., & Zimbrich, K. (2004). *College career connection: A study of youth with learning, cognitive, and intellectual disabilities and the impact of postsecondary education.* Arlington, VA: Council for Exceptional Children, Division of Developmental Disabilities.

Creating Opportunities for Employment

CHAPTER 14

Internships and
Field Experiences

Lori W. Briel and Elizabeth Evans Getzel

articipation in internships and field experiences puts students in higher education on the fast track for career success. Students who engage in several career-related work experiences while in college, including internships, are able to secure employment more quickly after graduation, are more likely to be employed within their field of study, and are generally more satisfied in their work positions than graduates with no career related experience (Kysor & Pierce, 2000). With technological changes in the economy and corporate trends supporting downsizing and restructuring, many businesses use cooperative education, internships, and part-time jobs to provide an economical way to screen, train, and develop potential full-time employees (Brooks & Greene, 1998; Carter & Franta, 1994).

The Vault Annual Survey showed that 86% of college students complete one or more internships by graduation and that a growing 69% of college students complete two or more internships by graduation (Internship Survey, 2000). Employers, faculty, and students recognize the increasing value of internships as a mechanism to display skills and abilities and to apply academic knowledge in a practical way (Reardon, Lenz, & Folsom, 1998). Internships allow students to transfer their academic skills to the employment setting.

Employers have identified job-related work experience as very important when recruiting college graduates for entry-level employment (Reardon et al., 1998) and note that it positively influences the ability to obtain an interview through résumé screenings (Perry & Goldberg, 1998). Clearly internships and field experiences play a vital role in the career growth of students completing a college degree. These experiences are even more critical for college students with disabilities.

Significant numbers of college students with disabilities have had limited career development activities in high school, have had little or no meaningful work experience, and therefore have difficulty considering the influence of their disability when deciding on a career (Hitchings et al., 2001). Students more commonly have an understanding of the academic impact of their disabilities, with less awareness of how their disabilities could affect them on the job (Hitchings & Retish, 2000). By providing ample opportunities to acquire work experience prior to graduation, while still in the protected environment of internships, students can confirm their career preferences, develop employment histories, and identify the services and supports that will maximize their opportunities for employment success (Getzel, Briel, & Kregel, 2000). Furthermore, internship and cooperative education programs can help students to address some of the barriers they will face when seeking employment; simultaneously, the attitudes of employers about the potential of individuals with disabilities can be influenced and even changed for the better (Burgstahler, 1995).

COMPREHENSIVE CAREER PLANNING

To compete in the global economy, internships and work experience need to be a part of students' higher education experience. Among the individuals who face the greatest challenges to direct and manage their chosen career in this competitive marketplace are young adults with disabilities. These individuals lack needed information about available careers, how to identify what modifications are necessary to perform a job, and how to request needed modifications from an employer (Getzel et al., 2000; Hitchings et al., 2001). If these pressing needs of students with disabilities remain unaddressed in college, they will continue to face barriers when attempting to pursue their chosen careers.

Since the mid-1990s, Virginia Commonwealth University (VCU) has designed the Career Connections program to enhance employment opportunities for individuals with disabilities prior to graduation. Students with disabilities are able to obtain services and supports to acquire internships in their field and maximize the use of university and community services. Students self-identify their need for assistance and direct the implementation of the services provided. The intent of the program is to ensure that students with disabilities exit the university with marketable skills and are linked to services in the community once they enter the workplace.

The program addresses specific issues that students face. Students are often unclear about how their disabilities affect their performance on a job. They are unable to articulate how their accommodations transfer to the workplace. These students lack needed work experience to build a résumé of success prior to graduating from VCU. The program has shown to be particularly effective for students who have significant difficulties with transferring from an academic to a work environment. Some students with disabilities cannot fully benefit from traditional career planning services. They need comprehensive career planning in order to successfully complete their academic programs. For instance, some students do not have the grade point average to qualify for an internship through the university, making it difficult for them to gain the work site experience they need. Other students served through the program need assistance to practice appropriate behavior in a work environment. In addition, some students who enter the program have been recently diagnosed as having a disability and need assistance with advocating for supports and learning about their rights and responsibilities in the workplace.

The years of experience gained by working with students has led to the development and refinement of a process that enables students to gain the experience and employment-related knowledge they need. The VCU Career Connections program works closely with all entities on campus, in particular the university's career center, to enable students to obtain the full range of services, supports, resources, and networks available both on campus and in the community. For example, the program seeks VCU alumni who are interested in meeting with current students to discuss employment in their field and to share postgraduation experiences. The common experience of attending VCU and pursuing a similar degree helps to build bridges into the employment community and creates an opportunity for either current or future employers to understand the skills and talents of students with disabilities. Based on the needs of students and the collaborative relationships established, the program has created a process that incorporates the following elements:

- Assist students in establishing a postschool career objective.

- Identify learner accommodations in the academic setting that can be subsequently transferred to the employment setting.

- Assist students in identifying university and community resources that will assist them during college and after graduation.

- Assist students in identifying one or more work experiences prior to graduation (especially if an internship or practicum is not required), including mentorships, cooperative education placement, and internships.

- Assist students in their transition from the academic setting to the work site, clinical setting, or internship site.

- Provide follow-along services to ensure transfer of learner accommodations and access to services and supports, including assistive technology, personal assistant services, or transportation services through rehabilitation agencies or other community organizations.

Equally important to the success of students involved in a comprehensive career planning program is the need for colleges and universities to become familiar with the issues that students with disabilities face when seeking and completing internships. Information and training are needed to assist faculty, field liaisons, and site supervisors to develop proactive strategies that support students in this process, along with a clear understanding of their roles and responsibilities and those of the students. New and innovative strategies, especially in the area of technology, increase the opportunities for individuals with disabilities to apply their knowledge in internship and clinical settings. Keeping faculty, staff, and field liaisons abreast of these changes is an important aspect of this program.

The material selected for this chapter provides information, strategies, and ideas to assist students with disabilities participating in field placements or internship programs. The content draws from the practices developed at a 4-year university with an academic and medical campus. The program continues to grow and change as universities and colleges (both 2- and 4-year) adapt the process on their campus.

THREE CRITICAL CONSIDERATIONS

Internships and cooperative work opportunities can facilitate career preparation and development for students with disabilities (Briel & Getzel, 2001; Mazurek & Shoemaker, 1997). Issues faced by students with disabilities are threefold. First, students lack information about the Americans with Disabilities (ADA) Act of 1990 (PL 101-336) and the rights afforded to individuals with disabilities in an employment setting. For example, half to two thirds of college graduates with learning disabilities surveyed rated their knowledge and understanding of the ADA as poor, and only half reported receiving ADA information and instruction during their college career (Witte, 2001). Second, students may have limited experience with or understanding of the demands of a work site and therefore lack awareness of which accommodation solutions or compensatory strategies may be available to address performance issues (Briel & Getzel, 2001). Third, field liaisons, site supervisors, and advisors may be unclear about the guidelines for disclosing, requesting, and providing accommodations at the work site. Scott, Wells, and Hanebrink (1997) concluded that although the university has primary responsibility and is ultimately liable for providing reasonable accommodations and ensuring auxiliary aids for students with disabilities who are participating in its programs (whether on or off campus), the internship provider generally assumes the duty for providing accommodations on its site. It is important for colleges and universities to address the unique preparation needs for students with disabilities and to implement strategies and critical program elements that will enhance the skills of program staff and students.

Disclosure in the Internship or Work Environment

Students with disabilities have varying knowledge of the protections afforded them under the ADA. VCU Career Connections staff initially assess a student's understanding and application of this significant legislation. Some students need basic information about the definition of disability, reasonable accommodation, and the concept *otherwise qualified*. Students need to know how an employer can address disability in an interview, which questions are legal for employers to ask, and how to respond to illegal questions in an appropriate manner. Most students need clarification on the process of disclosure and the options involved. They need information and strategies on how to compensate for the impact of their disability on performance. Table 14.1 highlights resources to tap for foundational information about the ADA.

The most important consideration students must make is whether, when, and how to disclose their disability to an employer or field liaison. Generally, students must contact site supervisors, complete applications, and interview for positions. This may be a student's first experience with deciding whether to disclose his or her disability in a community setting. Students often feel tremendous pressure to hide their disability and try to self-accommodate. Too often, disclosure occurs after a student receives a failing grade (Ashland Regional Technology Center, 1997).

The VCU Career Connections staff provide specific instruction on methods to disclose a disability. Critical to making this decision is a student's understanding of his or her own strengths and limitations, the essential functions of the position, potential accommodation solutions, and the supervisor's prior experience. The specific need for disclosure will dictate the choices for when to disclose a disability. Table 14.2 delineates potential positives and negatives for timing the student's disclosure. (Chapter 15 offers additional information on making this decision; e.g., see Table 15.4.)

Each student should review his or her options, weigh the possible outcomes of each choice, and determine what he or she feels most comfortable doing. Students should plan disclosure in a way that gives the potential employer enough time to be informed and coordinate accommodations, without giving the individual too much time to second-guess his or her decision. For example, a student who uses a wheelchair should call 1–2 days before the interview to inquire about an accessible location for the interview. This gives the business ample time to coordinate an appropriate location.

Equally important to review are guidelines for disclosure, regardless of when the disclosure takes place. Students need to be aware of potential employer discomfort or unfamiliarity with disability and be prepared to educate the employer in a comfortable, casual manner. Students should avoid technical, medical diagnoses and instead use functional language. It is important for

Table 14.1.   Resources regarding the Americans with Disabilities Act (ADA) of 1990 (PL 101-336)

The ADA: Your Employment Rights as an Individual with a Disability (U.S. Equal Employment Opportunity Commission)
http://www.eeoc.gov/facts/ada18.html

The ADA: Questions and Answers (U.S. Equal Employment Opportunity Commission)
http://www.eeoc.gov/facts/adaqa1.html

Americans with Disabilities Act Portal (Job Accommodation Network)
http://www.jan.wvu.edu/portals/individuals.htm

Frequently Asked Questions About Employees with Psychiatric Disabilities (Center for Psychiatric Rehabilitation, Boston University)
http://www.bu.edu/cpr/catalog/articles/1997/macdonald-wilson1997.pdf

Small Employers and Reasonable Accommodation (U.S. Equal Employment Opportunity Commission)
http://www.eeoc.gov/facts/accommodation.html

Table 14.2.   Pros and cons of disclosing at certain points in the employment or internship process

When	Potential gains	Potential setbacks
In a cover letter	Advance time to prepare positive written disclosure and to tailor your abilities to the duties of the job description	Potential employer's preconceptions may hinder opportunity for an interview Unable to read potential employer's body language and mood
In a résumé or on a job application	Establish an upfront relationship and communication	Potential employer may have stereotypes about disabilities and may not offer you an interview
When a potential employer calls for an interview	Establishes open communication and gives potential employer time to review Americans with Disabilities Act (ADA) of 1990 (PL 101-336) compliance information	May not get serious consideration during the job interview
Before the interview	Shows respect to potential employer Gives potential employer advance notice to secure any accommodations that may be needed during the interview and time to research proper etiquette or refresh his or her knowledge of the ADA	Potential employer has advance time to yield to his or her stereotypes about disabilities
During the interview	Opportunity to read potential employer's body language; to time the disclosure; and to disclose in a brief, positive manner	Potential employer may feel uneasy and ill prepared to respond with appropriate and legal questions
After the job offer	May have legal recourse if disclosing your disability negatively affected the hiring decision Time to get accommodations in place before the job starts Positive relationship has already been established	Potential employer may feel that you have been dishonest in the application process, which may erode trust
After the job begins	Gives opportunity to establish credibility before disclosure Gives freedom to talk with co-workers about disability-related issues	May take time to secure requested accommodations Employer may believe you have not been honest, which may negatively affect your relationship with him or her
When performance difficulties arise	Difficulties may not arise (i.e., you may never need to disclose)	Employer may have difficulty changing perceptions of your work performance, feel betrayed, or wonder why you waited so long
Never	Disability information is kept private	Not protected from discrimination under the ADA

Source: Aase and Smith (1989).

students to model how the employer should view their disability. Having opportunities to role play and practice their disclosure is recommended. VCU Career Connections staff videotape this practice session and let students critique their disclosure. Table 14.3 illustrates more extensive guidelines and gives specific examples of disclosing techniques. It is important for students to review all of the guidelines with a career advisor, faculty liaison, or disability counselor and devise the most effective plan.

Transferring Academic Skills to Employment Settings

College students with disabilities are often not prepared to arrange job accommodations or environmental modifications (Brodwin, Parker, & DeLaGarza, 1996). Due to limited exposure to work sites, role models, and employment settings, students may not be aware of how their disability affects their work performance; therefore, they may not be aware of which accommodations to request. Internships provide an excellent opportunity to assess the current and future support needs for individuals with disabilities (Getzel et al., 2000). VCU Career Connections staff work with students with disabilities to determine how accommodations in the classroom setting can transfer to the workplace. For example, portable devices such as adaptive keyboards or magnifiers generally transfer easily to a work setting.

Determining effective compensatory strategies becomes even more important. Students must explore assistive technology or alternative methods to complete a task within the time frames of the job. Using speech-to-text software may increase word processing speed or audiotaping client sessions may replace notetaking. It is important that students with disabilities have access to necessary supports as they make the transition to an internship setting to acquire professional skills. University faculty, disability support services, career advisors, rehabilitation counselors, and site supervisors must work with students and assist them with the identification of immediate and future support needs.

The Role of the University

In compliance with Section 504 of the Rehabilitation Act of 1973 (PL 93-112), colleges and universities have a responsibility to ensure equal access and accommodation for students with disabilities during the recruitment period, the admission process, and the term of enrollment (29 U.S.C. § 794). Section 504 imposes a responsibility to reasonably accommodate an otherwise qualified student with a disability unless such an accommodation would fundamentally alter the program or constitute an undue burden. The ADA also prohibits discrimination against qualified people with disabilities and has extended coverage to include places of employment, state and local government services and buildings, public accommodations, transportation, and telecommunications (42 U.S.C. § 12101).

Table 14.3. General guidelines and examples on how to disclose disability

Guideline	Example
Be optimistic; focus on your job qualifications.	*Cover letter:* "As an individual with a lifelong physical and speech disability, I learned early on to focus on my intellectual abilities and to develop strengths within my limits. For example, I received my first computer when I was 5 years old and learned to operate it independently. Today, I am proficient in many software applications and operating systems and in system troubleshooting."
Stress current involvement in a positive activity that shows your ability to manage your disability.	*Résumé:* "Member of the American Blind Skiing Foundation"
Give the employer information on what he or she needs to do or provide regarding communication, directions, or supervision.	*Telephone call prior to the interview:* "I am calling to confirm my interview scheduled at your company in 2 days. Could you please tell me where to find your office's accessible entrance?"
Educate the employer by articulating or demonstrating how you can perform the essential functions of the job. Have resource information available for the employer.	*During the interview:* "Have you ever heard of a screen reader? I have a learning disability and have difficulty reading in the traditional way. However, when I hear written words, the information makes so much sense. My screen reader has enabled me to succeed at college, and I know it will be useful on this job."
Face employer concerns by talking about your compensatory strategies or accommodation solutions.	*During the interview:* "You may be wondering how I can type letters with my physical disability. I have a great software program that allows the computer to type as I speak words. It can be loaded onto most computers. I would be happy to show it to you sometime."
Explain the benefits of your disability regarding your personal growth or perseverance.	*During the interview:* "After experiencing a brain injury, I learned the value of connecting with professionals. I can be resourceful and creative to get a job done."
Use general, functional terms to briefly explain the impact of your disability on the job; avoid technical, medical diagnoses.	*After the job offer:* "During the interview, you explained that work was generally assigned at a staff meeting. I find that I work best when instructions are both written and verbal. I have a disorder that makes processing verbal information a challenge. Could you accommodate me in this way?"
In a private setting, remind your employer about your right to confidentiality.	*After the job is accepted:* "Thank you in advance for keeping this information confidential."
Frame the disclosure around how you work best.	*A few weeks on the job:* "I have noticed that I am having a difficult time completing my work assignments. I have a medical condition that requires frequent breaks in order to do my work. Would you allow me to work later to enable me to take more breaks? I always get the job done when I manage my schedule in this way."

It has been traditionally understood that under Section 504 of the ADA, field work coordinators, faculty, and/or instructors do not have the right to disclose a student's disability to any field work site without the written permission of the student (Title I at 42 U.S.C. §§1211(d)(3) & (4); 29 C.F.R. §§

1630.14–1630.16). Although the Family Educational Rights and Privacy Act (FERPA) of 1974 (PL 93-380) provides faculty with access to educational information in institutional files regarding students with whom they are working, disability-related records provided by a physician, psychiatrist, psychologist, or other recognized professional are not subject to free access under this act (Association on Higher Education and Disability [AHEAD], 1996). However, differing views exist. There may be times when a student with a hidden disability elects not to disclose to the site supervisor but an informed field liaison has legitimate safety concerns for the student and/or the population with whom he or she may be working. It is suggested that university officials could modify their FERPA policy by specifically identifying field placement site supervisors as school officials (J. Kincaid, Esq., personal communication, April 1, 2004). This would enable field liaisons to identify the student as having a disability and to share accommodation requests with site supervisors without the required consent of the student. This type of disclosure to school officials would be set forth in the institution's annual notification of rights to students and would be discussed with the student ahead of time.

Career advisors have expressed interest in clarifying responsibility for the provision of accommodations in internship settings. The University of Minnesota's General Counsel made preliminary efforts to delineate the separate, distinct roles and responsibilities of university representatives and prospective employers (LRP Publications, 1999). According to these administrative guidelines, the university is responsible for providing accommodations for off-campus work-study jobs or for-credit internships. The employer is responsible for providing accommodations for noncredit, nonpaid internships. The exchange of money means that the employment relationship between the student and the internship site takes precedence over the student's relationship with the university. However, if the internship is both paid and for-credit, the student, the DSS coordinator, and a representative from the internship site agree up front who will pay for accommodations. Provision may also be made through vocational rehabilitation services or other community resources. The university is responsible for providing guidance to the internship site regarding the provision of academic adjustments or accommodations. In addition, the university must monitor what happens in the internship environment to ensure that no discrimination occurs against students and that students are provided with all necessary accommodations.

ESSENTIAL COMPONENTS TO STRENGTHEN INTERNSHIP PROGRAMS

Engaging in Individualized Planning

The driving force of the VCU Career Connections Program is developing an individualized career plan. At the initial meeting, a student and the program staff delineate the student's long-term career goal and course of academic study.

Through discussion, additional information is obtained about the student's learning style, past academic and employment successes, effective accommodations or compensatory strategies, previous connections with university or community services, and personal interests and activities. Information is also gathered on how the student decided on the career goal and which steps are involved in achieving the goal. Overall, the plan focuses on the employment preparation needs of students and the necessary supports and services to help prepare students for the career goals that they have established. Necessary academic and community supports are incorporated into the plan, which is designed to ensure that students exit school with marketable skills and are linked to community services once they enter the workplace (Getzel et al., 2000). Program staff members work with the student to develop the plan, but the student directs the decisions concerning specific activities that the plan will address. The student and the program staff continually update the career plan to determine which future steps are needed to reach the student's goals.

Identifying Effective Learner Accommodations

As part of the comprehensive career planning process, the VCU Career Connections program works closely with students and the campus DSS office to assist students in identifying effective accommodations in the classroom. For students with learning disabilities, traumatic brain injuries, or neurological disorders resulting in memory deficits, accommodations may include audiotaping lectures, obtaining notetaking services, or modifying the format of tests. The use of compensatory strategies, methods, and techniques to address cognitive challenges are also identified and explored with the student to determine what might be effective for him or her. Examples of these strategies include using mnemonics or graphic software to enhance student learning or color coding the paper of various forms to distinguish among them.

Information is also gathered on the student's general learning style, past work history, use of accommodations, or successful compensatory strategies. The VCU Career Connections program utilizes learner accommodation information throughout the program to ensure that the most effective strategies are identified and used by students. This is accomplished by 1) encouraging students to consider the identification of these strategies while developing their individualized career plans; 2) initiating the development of learner accommodations that have proven effective in both educational and employment settings; and 3) transferring the use of effective compensatory strategies and assistive technologies through a sequential process of pregraduation work experience, job placement, and postplacement assistance (Getzel & Kregel, 1996).

Using Multiple Approaches for Instruction

As part of the services offered, VCU Career Connections staff members provide on-site consultation for field supervisors to identify potential instructional strategies that may be useful for students with disabilities at the work site. Traditional placements often begin with a period of observation. For students with hidden, sensory, or multiple disabilities, it is recommended that this period be as interactive as possible. For students with attention-deficit/hyperactivity disorder (ADHD) or memory challenges, learning occurs more readily when students are involved as participants. Site instructors can assign short tasks, ask questions, or take notes at a meeting to encourage active learning. Effective instructional strategies depend on the learning style of the student, the targeted skill, the work setting, and the availability of the site supervisor. Most students benefit from an initial demonstration of the task, followed by an opportunity to perform part or all of the task. Immediate, specific feedback on performance is generally best if this type of supervision is possible. Attention to the social nuances of the work environment and clear behavioral expectations may be required. Specific instruction may need to be provided on general work skills or interpersonal relationships. For example, an individual with ADHD may need information on establishing personal boundaries and professional co-worker relationships. Students with psychological disabilities may need a specific plan for stress management. The instructional strategies described in Table 14.4 have proven effective for students participating in the VCU Career Connections Program. These strategies are designed to provide increased structure for the student and to actively engage him or her in the learning process. Opportunities are also built in for the supervisor to give the student specific, immediate feedback.

Providing Access to Technology

Students with disabilities need to have access to technology that promotes positive career outcomes, learn how to use technology to meet work demands, and be able to transfer this technology to the work site (Burgstahler, 2003). Ever-changing and improving technology presents some challenges for students to be able to obtain and explore the latest version of technology that

Table 14.4. Tips for using multiple approaches to instruction

Make the initial observation time interactive (e.g., assign a short task within the demonstration).

Engage the student in a task and give direct feedback on his or her contribution.

Modify or restructure a routine to provide repeated practice of a targeted skill.

Model a task; have the student immediately repeat the same task.

Assist the student with breaking complex tasks into smaller components; use checklists or templates.

Extend the learning time for initial skill acquisition; allow for more repetition.

Role-play leadership activities or social interactions.

Ensure that the student has a method to review information (e.g., notes, tape recorder).

Discuss and identify stress management strategies; encourage use of these at the job site.

Provide clear boundaries for co-worker relationships.

Videotape and review intern performance; provide constructive feedback.

might best meet their specific needs. Some adaptive software and hardware is usually available for use through the campus DSS office. However, many other devices are personalized for the student and need to be purchased individually for use on the job. This is an important reason for students to be aware of community resources, such as the local department of rehabilitative services (DRS) office. For students at VCU, the Virginia Assistive Technology System (VATS)—a state-operated, federally funded grant program—increases awareness of and accessibility to assistive technology for individuals with severe disabilities through a variety of activities that offer information and technical assistance on devices, services, and funding resources. For example, the VATS could provide information about the Virginia Assistive Technology Loan Fund Authority, which makes low-interest loans available to individuals with disabilities to purchase a wide variety of special equipment.

The VCU Career Connections staff have found that the use of technology on the job is becoming a more common solution for task completion. Speech-to-text software enables students with limited physical abilities or significant learning disabilities to create reports, summarize information, and communicate via e-mail. One-handed keyboards may increase the word processing speed for individuals who have partial use of their hands. As with learning any new strategy, students first need to observe a demonstration of the piece of equipment and receive an explanation of how it may be useful to them personally. Second, instruction must be provided on using and customizing the technology to meet work-related needs (McManus, Getzel, & Briel, 2004). For example, using a personal digital assistant equipped with audio reminders of individually loaded task deadlines serves as an effective tool to establish a time management plan.

Building Collaborative Relationships

University policy should encourage the development of collaborative relationships among field departments, the DSS office, career services, and community agencies to adequately serve students with disabilities. Each entity has common goals for students with disabilities, and sharing knowledge and expertise can be mutually beneficial. It is well documented that employers (including individuals serving as site supervisors) have reservations and lack information about hiring and supervising people with disabilities (Hernandez, Keys, & Balcazar, 2000; Peck & Kirkbride, 2001). Students, career services staff, and field liaisons must be prepared to address this potential barrier and to provide employers with information and support that alleviates any fears.

Career Connections developed a resource team, composed of local disability professionals who are committed to serving the career development needs of college students with disabilities. This team includes representatives from the local Department for the Deaf and Hard of Hearing, the local Department for the Blind and Vision Impaired, VATS, and the local DRS office, as well as local psychologists. Faculty, field liaisons, and site supervisors have access to the expertise from each agency based on the questions or needs that arise with their students. The resource team does not meet as a group, but its members are available to provide their expertise to university personnel. For example, when questions arose about the most appropriate adaptive equipment for a student with a visual impairment to use on an internship site, the VCU Career Connections staff facilitated a consultation with a representative from the Department for the Blind and Vision Impaired to determine, with the student, what technology would be most effective.

Students completing internships are at a critical juncture in their career development. University and community services must partner together in order to maximize services to students. Acquiring a new set of skills takes instruction, practice, and feedback for all students. For those with disabilities, it is even more important to connect a student with community adult service agencies for conducting assessments, identifying accommodation strategies, and coordinating access to and use of technology.

Establishing connections with community resources can be an important—and often essential—component of successful placements for some students with disabilities. Knowing how to obtain assistive technology at the work site or support to address behavioral issues related to a disability may be critical information for students to fulfill their requirements. Students may not know what type of technology would be useful to them or may need assistance with securing funding for adaptive software. For example, a student who was deaf was working with colleagues who were unfamiliar with sign language. Program staff contacted the local Department for the Deaf and Hard of Hearing, and a teletypewriter (TTY) was loaned to the internship site. In addition, sensitivity training sessions were conducted for co-workers. The nonprofit employer had not anticipated the need for a TTY, much less the expense of installing the accompanying telephone line. Coordination with the DRS proved successful in addressing this concern.

Providing Training and Technical Assistance for Faculty and Site Supervisors

University and college personnel need to take the lead in ensuring that their faculty and staff are well informed about the ADA and its implications for field work. Face-to-face training sessions need to be coordinated so that faculty liaisons and site supervisors understand the differing responsibilities of the university and the student. Information and training may be appropriate regarding the definition of disability and how a disability, especially a hidden one, may affect work behavior. For example, VCU conducted a 1-day, statewide workshop for occupational and physical therapy preceptors to focus on successful practices and strategies for students with hidden disabilities in clinical settings. Myths about disability were discussed, along with practical application of strategies on the site. Because increasing numbers of people with psychological disabilities are attending college (Sharpe, Bruininks, Blacklock, Benson, &

Johnson, 2004), personnel must be given functional information and decide on strategies to implement to address any performance issues. Supervisors need to be provided with guidelines for providing feedback to someone with a psychiatric disability (e.g., focusing on job behavior, not medication management) (Khubchandani, 2003).

It is important to choose an internship site that maximizes a student's strengths and can accommodate his or her learning style. Students must identify the most critical factor or factors in determining their ideal placements. For example, one student with a mental health disability functioned optimally in the morning hours and prioritized his site selection according to ones that offered this time slot. Although this factor limited the student's options, taking this particular factor into account was important for his growth, ability to learn, and ability to be successful. Another student with a traumatic brain injury selected a smaller setting that had a basic daily routine. This regular routine established a structure, which provided a solid foundation to develop professional skills.

The first 2–4 weeks of an internship provide an excellent opportunity to assess the need for future supports at the site, particularly for students who are uncertain if any modifications will be needed (Getzel et al., 2000). The site supervisor can be instrumental in identifying key areas in which the intern may benefit from supports. The university faculty and intern should receive initial feedback about the intern's attendance, organizational skills, initiative, co-worker interactions, time management skills, and performance skills. During this initial period of the internship, relevant instructional strategies can be recommended, accommodations can be requested, or community supports can be arranged to ensure that the student is receiving effective training and performing at the level expected at the internship site. For example, one student with a traumatic brain injury was arriving late to his placement or reporting to the site on unscheduled days at a local hospital. Support was provided to explore alternative ways to follow a schedule, including use of a daily calendar, a two-alarm watch that displays days of the week, and a monthly wall calendar at home. A second example concerned a student with a learning disability who was having difficulty completing written reports in a timely manner. The VCU Career Connections staff assisted this student with exploring effective compensatory strategies for organizing material, synthesizing details, and using proper grammar. Some strategies included the use of graphic organizers, the use of writing software programs, and the development of a framework for several reporting styles.

The use of a team approach is recommended for employers, faculty, or students who are uncertain about how to address support needs. Often, assistive technology equipment can be loaned on a short-term basis or technology can be purchased to move with the student from job to job as his or her career progresses. The benefits of partnering with agencies are numerous.

Creating Business Networks for Future Employment

Students need to establish a record of successful work experiences in their field. Therefore, the VCU Career Connections program enables students to have numerous opportunities to acquire work experience prior to graduation. The program offers several activities that assist students in learning more about career opportunities and helping them demonstrate their abilities to potential employers through résumés and references. Some of the activities are short term to help the student obtain a general idea about a job and the qualifications necessary to work in a specific field. These short-term experiences primarily include informational interviews and job shadowing. Informational interviews enable a student to discuss particular jobs with employers in a nonthreatening environment, obtain a general idea about an occupation, and gather real-life information (e.g., the daily rewards and stressors in the field). Job shadowing is also a short-term activity in which a student is able to spend as much as a day or as little as a few hours following someone through his or her work routine. The student can observe activities in the actual work setting and experience firsthand what it might be like to work in that profession.

As noted previously, the Career Connections Program emphasizes connecting with VCU alumni. Sharing a common experience, such as attending the same college or university, provides a solid base to establish a relationship and discuss familiar campuswide events, courses, and instructors. It also provides the employer with an opportunity to emphasize the personal qualities and skills that promote development in a particular field and gives relevance to specific courses in the student's academic program. VCU's Alumni Externship program operates for a week between the fall and spring semesters and during the week of spring break. Alumni invite a student to job shadow at the work site for one week. The experiences coordinate with many different majors, so students can match a placement to their interest area and apply for the externship. This opportunity has proven to be an excellent avenue for students to meet professionals in the field, build a network of business contacts, experience a work site, and get a feel for a job's demands and environment.

More extensive work experience opportunities are offered through internships or cooperative education. Cooperative education opportunities often complement a student's course of study, build a record of work experience that can be used to enhance future employment-seeking activities, and identify needed services and supports. Internships are often one or two semesters long and are directly tied to the individual's academic course of study. These experiences are often culminating activities that can be used to assess an individual's need for subsequent support services. A unique aspect of VCU's program is that staff are available to go into a work site during each of these experiences to assess the student's need for accommodations, identify student and employer preferences, and assist the student in designing and implementing effective interventions.

Evaluating Services and Supports Provided

It is important to obtain feedback and input about the services and supports provided to student participants as well as to faculty members, field liaisons, and on-site supervisors. Prior to completing their internship experience, students are asked to respond to a survey through a structured telephone interview. The questions focus on the extent to which students benefited from assistance provided through the program. The feedback assists in reviewing the strengths of the services provided and enables staff to evaluate which changes are needed to better serve students.

The training and technical assistance programs or sessions offered as part of the program offer a primary source of feedback from faculty, field liaisons, and on-site supervisors. Feedback is obtained about the information and strategies provided through the training. When program staff members work on site with a student, meetings are scheduled during times convenient to the on-site staff members. This has proven to be an invaluable method for obtaining immediate feedback about the strategies or supports students are using, and it helps to reduce the likelihood of problems occurring late in the field experience or internship. These meetings also serve as a model for on-site staff and students to discuss the students' strengths and difficulties.

GETTING INITIAL WORK EXPERIENCE

Tom contacted the VCU Career Connections Program a semester before his anticipated graduation. He was majoring in business and finance, had a strong interest in securities and stocks/bonds, and wanted to learn about potential jobs in his field. Tom had cerebral palsy that significantly affected his speech and mobility. He used a scooter for traveling long distances and a walker for shorter distances. Traditional communication was difficult. At times, repetition was necessary. Tom took advantage of notetaking services and extended time for tests and assignments, both of which were afforded him through the DSS office. He told the Career Connections staff that he had a DRS counselor in high school but was not currently receiving services from that agency.

To assist Tom in exploring and understanding possible career options, the staff gave Tom informational web sites to review and was referred for participation in the National Disability Mentoring Day sponsored by DRS. The site selected for his mentorship was SunTrust Bank, which is the leader in Virginia's Business Leadership Network. Tom was able to meet key representatives from the bank and learn what each department required and expected from their employees. Through this experience, Tom was given contacts to other businesses. Informational interviews were arranged, and Tom learned about additional certification options for working in the finance field. Tom obtained information to review regarding certification programs.

Tom graduated with a grade point average of 2.2. A month after graduation, the VCU Career Connections staff invited him to participate in the Workforce Recruitment Program for College Students with Disabilities, a coordinated effort among the Career Connections program, the university career center, and the DSS office. This program is sponsored by the U.S. Department of Labor's Office of Disability and Employment Policy and the U.S. Department of Defense, which interviews students with disabilities across the country. Tom decided to participate. The staff worked with Tom to ensure that his résumé highlighted his skills, and he elected to disclose his disability in a positive way through his cover letter. He worked with the staff to review interview skills, including typical questions and possible responses.

Tom expressed concern about his typing speed. The program staff arranged a visit to his home to see how Tom's computer equipment was set up and to observe Tom's typing skills. It appeared that Tom underestimated his typing ability to a degree, but his speed still presented a potential roadblock to meeting employer expectations and time lines for efficient communication and report writing. Tom only had use of his right hand for typing. He used large gross motor movements and then, with concentrated effort, used the side of his thumb to strike the individual keys. He was able to recognize errors and self-correct. To address this issue throughout college, Tom relied heavily on extended time to complete assignments and for test taking.

Staff talked with Tom about his experience with adaptive equipment and software. Tom recalled having a keyguard in high school but not using it very much. Specifically, staff addressed his experience with one-handed or other modified keyboards and word prediction software. Tom recalled that he received an assistive technology evaluation in high school and, as a result, had used word prediction software (which he did not find helpful at that time). Because of the enormous growth in technology since he last used such technology, the Career Connections staff recommended that Tom contact his DRS office and request that his file be reopened for the purpose of evaluating his current assistive technology needs. Tom met with a counselor and was able to use different technologies in the counselor's office. The result of the evaluation was a recommendation for a smaller keyboard and the use of word prediction software.

A few months later, Tom received a summer job offer for a budget analyst through the Workforce Recruitment Program. The personnel manager asked Tom to send her a list of any accommodation requests. The Career Connections staff recommended that Tom request a specific job description that would delineate his work responsibilities. The DRS counselor was able to tell the employer the specific keyboard and software information that needed to be purchased. Tom purchased this technology for his home use as well.

By linking to the VCU Career Connection Program, Tom was able to take advantage of the business partnerships established on both the state and national levels. By networking with the Business Leadership Network, the Workforce Recruitment Program, and DRS, Tom was prepared to gain work experience through a full-time summer position in his field and to explore the use of adaptive software and hardware to determine their effectiveness in enhancing his skills. After fulfilling his commitment to his summer job, Tom would be in a better position to identify his career interests and job support needs.

CONCLUSION

Internship and work experience opportunities are instrumental in shaping the career path for individuals with disabilities. Opportunities for students to explore areas of interest, experiment with effective accommodations, and make valuable connections with employers must be integrated into the college career planning process. For many students with disabilities, the first work experience paves the way for future career growth and advancement. It is critical for students with disabilities to have access to individualized supports that will promote their learning and prepare them for a professional career (Getzel & Kregel, 1996).

Work experience programs for students with disabilities provide opportunities for students to apply the knowledge and skills that they have acquired to a work environment. The VCU Career Connections staff found that for a majority of the students participating in the program, their first real professional working experience occurred during their internship. The staff was able to work with students to resolve such issues related to assistive technology, disclosure of a disability, and work accommodations. In some cases, students who had successfully completed their academic studies were in jeopardy of not graduating because they were experiencing difficulties completing their internship program. In large part, this was due to the lack of exposure to work environments. The internship enabled these students to develop and implement strategies to determine which methods were most effective to successfully complete their requirements. As a result, the students were more prepared to begin a career in their chosen field, having the knowledge and experience gained through their work experience. Internship programs provide a critical link between the academic setting and the work environment to enable all students, particularly students with disabilities, to apply their knowledge and determine the work environments that best match their skills and abilities.

REFERENCES

Aase, S., & Smith, C. (1989). *Career development course sequence.* Minneapolis: University of Minnesota, Career Connections and Disability Services.

Americans with Disabilities Act (ADA) of 1990, PL 101-336, 42 U.S.C. §§ 12101 *et seq.*

Ashland Regional Technology Center (KY), Case No. 07-96-1285, 10 NDLR 303 (OCR Region VII 1997).

Association on Higher Education and Disability (AHEAD). (1996). *Confidentiality and disability in higher education.* Columbus, OH: Author.

Briel, L.W., & Getzel, E.E. (2001). Internships in higher education: Promoting success for students with disabilities. *Disability Studies Quarterly, 21*(1), 38–48.

Brodwin, M., Parker, R.M., & DeLaGarza, D. (1996). Disability and accommodation. In E.M. Szymanski & R.M. Parker (Eds.), *Work and disability: Issues and strategies in career development and job placement* (pp. 165–208). Austin, TX: PRO-ED.

Brooks, J.E., & Greene, J.C. (1998). Benchmarking internship practices: Employers report on objectives and outcomes of experiential programs. *Journal of Career Planning & Employment*, *59*(1), 37–56.

Burgstahler, S. (1995). Cooperative education and students with disabilities. *Journal of Studies in Technical Careers*, *15*(2), 81–87.

Burgstahler, S. (2003). The role of technology in preparing youth with disabilities for postsecondary education and employment. *Journal of Special Education Technology*, *18*(4), 7–21.

Carter, J.K., & Franta, P. (1994). Placement services in today's economy. Job development programs. Service learning: A new priority for career centers. *Journal of Career Development*, *21*(2), 111–115, 127–134.

Family Educational Rights and Privacy Act (FERPA) of 1974, PL 93-380.

Getzel, E.E., Briel, L.W., & Kregel, J. (2000). Comprehensive career planning: The VCU career connections program. *Work*, *14*, 41–49.

Getzel, E.E., & Kregel, J. (1996). Transitioning from the academic to the employment setting: The employment connection program. *Journal of Vocational Rehabilitation*, *6*, 273–287.

Hernandez, B., Keys, C., & Balcazar, F. (2000). Employer attitudes towards worker with disabilities and their ADA employment rights: A literature review. *Journal of Rehabilitation*, *66*(4), 4–17.

Hitchings, W., & Retish, P. (2000). Career development needs of college students with learning disabilities. In D.A. Luzzo (Ed.), *Career counseling of college students* (pp. 217–231). Washington, DC: American Psychological Association.

Hitchings, W.E., Luzzo, D.A., Ristow, R., Horvath, M., Retish, P., & Tanners, A. (2001). The career development needs of college students with learning disabilities: In their own words. *Learning Disabilities Research and Practice*, *16*(1), 8–17.

Internship Survey. (2000). *Results of Vault 2000 internship survey*. Retrieved March 4, 2004, from http://www.vault.com/surveys/internship/survey2000.jsp

Khubchandani, A. (2003). *The ADA and internships: Your responsibilities as internship and postdoctoral agency directors*. Retrieved August 4, 2004, from http://mirror.apa.org/pi/cdip/internship directors.html

Kysor, D.V., & Pierce, M.A. (2000). Does intern/co-op experience translate into career progress and satisfaction? *Journal of Career Planning & Employment*, *60*(2), 25–31.

LRP Publications. (1999). Attorneys create accessibility guidelines to assure internship opportunities. *Disability Compliance For Higher Education*, *4*(10), 16.

Mazurek, N., & Shoemaker, A. (1997). *Career development needs of college students with disabilities: Implications for secondary and postsecondary service providers* [Research report]. (ERIC Document Reproduction Service No. ED 412 708)

McManus, S., Getzel, E.E., & Briel, L.W. (2004). Providing intensive educational supports at Virginia Commonwealth University. *Impact: Feature issue on achieving secondary education and transition results for students with disabilities*, *16*(3), 24–25.

Peck, B., & Kirkbride, L. (2001). Why businesses don't employ people with disabilities. *Journal of Vocational Rehabilitation*, *16*, 71–75.

Perry, A., & Goldberg, C. (1998). Who gets hired: Interviewing skills are a prehire variable. *Journal of Career Planning and Development*, *58*, 47–50.

Reardon, R., Lenz, J., & Folsom, B. (1998). Employer ratings of student participation in non-classroom-based activities: Findings from a campus survey. *Journal of Career Planning & Employment*, *58*(4), 36–39.

Rehabilitation Act of 1973, PL 93-112, 29 U.S.C. § 794.

Scott, S.S., Wells, S., & Hanebrink, S. (1997). *Educating college students with disabilities: What academic and fieldwork educators need to know*. Bethesda, MD: American Occupational Therapy Association.

Sharpe, M., Bruininks, B., Blacklock, B., Benson, B., & Johnson, D. (2004, August). The emergence of psychiatric disabilities in postsecondary education. *National Center on Secondary Education and Transition Issue Brief*, *3*(1), 1–6.

Witte, R. (2001). College graduates with disabilities and the Americans with Disabilities Act (ADA): Do they know their employment rights? *Learning Disabilities: A Multidisciplinary Journal, 11*(1), 27–30.

CHAPTER 15

Career Planning and Placement

Lori W. Briel and Paul Wehman

T he pursuit of a career is a major defining element of identity for people in U.S. society. Career choice has the potential to open doorways to a host of enriching experiences, such as financial security, home owner-ship, active participation in community life, access to health care and retirement benefits, and development of friendships and social networks. Most students who earn a college degree expect to benefit from their years of academic effort both professionally and financially. The anticipated course of action involves securing an entry-level position in their field of study and then combining time and experience, resulting in increasing levels of challenge, responsibility, and performance. Simple as it sounds, graduates with disabilities often face great obstacles in achieving these goals.

Historically, a majority of people with disabilities have been unemployed or underemployed. Through the support of vocational rehabilitation counsel-ors and community service providers, people with disabilities have made tre-mendous inroads into the employment sector; however, the impact of federal legislation such as the Americans with Disabilities Act (ADA) of 1990 (PL 101-336) is continually being debated. Although employers express positive global attitudes toward workers with disabilities, their willingness to hire applicants with disabilities still exceeds their actual hiring (Hernandez, Keys, & Balcazar, 2000). Employers still present barriers to hiring people with disabili-ties, including attitudinal bias, social discomfort or unfamiliarity with people with disabilities, a belief that people with disabilities cannot effectively perform the nature of the work in their company, and fear of high accommodation costs (Dixon, Kruse, & Van Horn, 2003; Hogan, 2003; Peck & Kirkbride, 2001). In addition, employers have limited awareness in identifying and secur-ing workplace supports for individuals with disabilities (Unger & Kregel, 2003).

Through effective federal transition initiatives, a growing number of individuals with disabilities are electing to pursue a college education and, upon graduation, take on the challenge of obtaining a professional position that allows for career advancement. Comprehensive career preparations at this stage bring to the forefront the various roles and responsibilities of students, career counselors, and employers as each entity seeks to understand the ADA and its implications. Individuals with disabilities seeking employment must have a plan to disarm employer fears that may include details of who will disclose, to whom, when, where, why, and what will be disclosed (Allen & Carlson, 2003; Bolles & Brown, 2001). Concurrently, university career counseling center staff are requesting more knowledge about disabilities, including how to talk with people about their disabilities, how to advise students regarding disclosure, what accommodations employers expect to make, and how accommodations actually work on the job site (Aune & Kroeger, 1997).

Colleges and universities need to address the career preparation needs of students with disabilities. One half to two thirds of college graduates with learning disabilities surveyed rated their knowledge and understanding of the ADA as poor, and only half reported receiving ADA information and instruction during their college career (Witte, 2001). Many students with disabilities lack the work-site experience from internships or work co-op opportunities that help to identify effective accommodations and necessary supports, practice disclosure skills, and refine career goals (Briel & Getzel, 2001; see also Chapter 14). Graduates with disabilities can be successful and progressive in their career development. Additional supports that help students prepare for careers and acquire job-seeking skills need to be embedded into the educational structure of postsecondary institutions.

OVERCOMING OBSTACLES TO CAREER SUCCESS

Barriers to Employment

College students with disabilities seeking to fulfill their professional goals face career-related challenges above and beyond those of traditional students. In addition to needing regular job preparation and networking skills, students with disabilities need a solid understanding of the impact of their disability on daily life, communication, and job performance. Students also need the skills to proactively address employer fears through the provision of educational information and accommodation solutions. Table 15.1 highlights specific career development issues that students, instructors, and career counselors have to address.

Students with disabilities must acquire a certain level of acceptance of their disability. Supportive family members or teachers often model an affirming view of disability, with a focus on strengths and an understanding of limitations. Conversely, some students transform negative feedback from instructors or authority figures into motivation for success. Newly diagnosed students, such as those with learning or psychological disorders, may still be grappling with their own stereotypes of the disability. Learning about the

Table 15.1.   Career development needs of students with disabilities

Being comfortable with their disability

Building self-esteem and confidence

Learning about their disability and its impact on learning or the work environment

Becoming familiar with compensatory strategies and assistive technology

Learning about protections afforded and responsibilities under the Americans with Disabilities Act (ADA) of 1990 (PL 101-336)

Acquiring self-disclosure skills and the ability to request accommodations

Obtaining workplace supports through community resources

Learning how to manage insensitive employer comments and attitudes

Gaining traditional employment experiences

academic impact of a disability is often at the forefront of a university setting; however, through career development activities and the employment search process, additional challenges may come to light. The development of self-advocacy skills begins by recognizing and understanding the disability and its impact in all areas of life.

Too often students with disabilities lack the necessary work-site experiences to fully understand the impact of disability on career choice or to determine what strategies, technology, or supports might be needed on the job (Getzel, Briel, & Kregel, 2000). With extra effort being required to complete academic requirements, time may be minimal to coordinate workplace experiences such as part-time jobs or job shadowing. Traditional summer work opportunities may be replaced by the fulfillment of academic requirements. Students may repeat a course to obtain a better grade, or those taking a reduced courseload may make up classes during this time. Ironically, many students with disabilities learn best through experiential learning yet are excluded from established internship programs due to grade point average requirements. In discussing their college and high school experiences, some college students shared that effective compensatory strategies are often learned via trial and error (personal communication with Virginia student focus groups, February 2004). Without the experience to raise awareness of a need, students erroneously believe that they are prepared for the next environment (e.g., the workplace).

In addition to work-related skills, employers are seeking candidates with qualities that are generally referred to as *soft skills*. Using effective written and verbal communication, interpersonal, and teamwork skills; demonstrating motivation, initiative, and a strong work ethic; and displaying honesty and integrity enhance an employee's desirability (Gerber & Price, 2003; National Association of Colleges and Employers, 2004). As a number of graduates with disabilities soon discover, the nature and scope of disability extends beyond the classroom. A student with an auditory processing disorder may need compensatory strategies to carry on daily conversations with co-workers or supervisors. Students with attention-deficit/hyperactivity disorder may need specific instruction on listening, conversing, and meeting work deadlines.

Otherwise, employers may interpret difficulty with work performance as a motivational deficit.

Compounding the preparation for employment is the fact that many of the traditional classroom accommodations may not transfer to a work setting. For example, it is not reasonable for employees to regularly request extended time for assignments or to ask that all directions be put in writing. As students begin the pursuit for employment, it is important for them to develop skills so they can assume responsibility for their disability, compensate on the job, and manage the impact of the disability to increase productivity and efficiency. These skills include understanding the impact of their disability on work performance, identifying workplace solutions or accommodations, and articulating this information to the hiring supervisor in an effective manner.

Since the late 1990s, there have been tremendous advances in the area of technology to enable individuals with disabilities to read, write, communicate, and work with greater ease and efficiency (Langton & Ramseur, 2001; National Organization on Disability, 2002; Senator, 2000). Assistive technology, as defined by the Technology-Related Assistance for Individuals with Disabilities Act of 1988 (PL 100-407) is "any technology used to increase, maintain, or improve the functional capabilities of individuals with disabilities." Yet, even when income, education, and age are considered, people with disabilities are less likely than those without disabilities to use the Internet (U.S. Department of Commerce, 2002). As a result, it is imperative for college students with disabilities who are in need of technology to connect with community agencies or resources to arrange for participation in an assistive technology assessment or to sample technology and identify funding solutions. Further exploration of software with word prediction capabilities or the use of personal digital assistants to support organizational skills may also be indicated (Getzel, McManus, & Briel, 2004). College students with disabilities need access to technology that promotes positive career outcomes; a medium to learn how to use the technology in the most effective way; and a seamless transition as they move from academia to career environments (Burgstahler, 2003).

Students with disabilities need a greater awareness and understanding of the ADA as it relates to employment. In a survey about career preparation needs, college students with disabilities were not satisfied with their understanding of the roles and responsibilities required by the ADA at the work site (Rumrill & Hennessey, 2004). Transition initiatives from high school to college have been instrumental in educating postsecondary students with disabilities about the procedures on campus to obtain classroom accommodations afforded under the ADA and Section 504 of the Rehabilitation Act of 1973 (PL 93-112) (U.S. Department of Education, Office for Civil Rights, 2002). However, few established mechanisms exist for college students with disabilities to obtain information about the ADA and to learn about the roles and responsibilities of employers and employees with disabilities. The process to request accommodations differs significantly in workplace and college settings. Although both entities require the student or employee to initiate disclosure, smaller companies may have neither a central person nor a human resources department to house an employee's medical documentation nor an identified advocate to assure that the employee's request for accommodation is fulfilled. It is imperative that students learn about the protections afforded them under the ADA.

It is also important for students to make an informed choice about whether and how to disclose disability to an employer. Determining if, when, and how to disclose disability to an employer is a culminating factor in the employment equation for individuals with disabilities. The competitive nature of the job search for students with disabilities and the decision to disclose disability is complicated by negative attitudes of employers (Allen & Carlson, 2003). Studies reveal that adults with learning disabilities are underutilizing the provisions of the ADA in the workplace and that many individuals rarely self-disclose (Price, Gerber, & Mulligan, 2003). Less than 30% of college graduates with learning disabilities disclosed to employers, although greater numbers stated that their learning disability affected their work in some way (Kakela & Witte, 2000; Madaus, Foley, McGuire, & Ruban, 2002). Training, counseling, and resources need to be available to students in order to make an informed choice in this matter and to acquire the necessary skills to disclose effectively.

THE ROLE OF CAREER CENTER: NETWORKING AND JOB PREPARATION

Most college career centers offer all students an assortment of services to provide career guidance, develop job-seeking skills, and prepare students to eventually secure a placement at the completion of their academic requirements. Common approaches include 1) courses, workshops, and seminars that offer structured group experiences in self-assessment, career planning, résumé development, job-access skills, decision making, and related topics; 2) group counseling activities; 3) individual counseling; 4) placement programs that include on-campus interviews, career fairs and networking opportunities, and internship opportunities; and 5) on-line résumé services and databases (Enstrom, 2003; Herr, Cramer, & Niles, 2004).

Results from a Job Outlook survey indicated the top 10 places employers find new hires (National Association of Colleges and Employers, 2004):

1. Internship programs
2. Company co-op programs
3. On-campus interviews
4. Employee referrals
5. Career/job fairs

6.   Faculty contacts

7.   Internet or company web site job postings

8.   Printed job postings to career center

9.   Student clubs/organizations

10. Internet job postings through campus web site

It is obvious that colleges and universities are prime vehicles for employers to meet their recruiting needs. Thus, it is essential that students with disabilities take advantage of the multiple opportunities provided by the career center.

There are three significant issues when addressing the career preparation needs of college students with disabilities. First, fewer college students with disabilities take advantage of campus work-based learning programs than their peers without disabilities (Burgstahler, 2001). Second, career centers deal with many employers who express fears and concerns about hiring individuals with disabilities. Third, in light of the increase in the number of students with hidden disabilities (Henderson, 2001; Sharpe, Bruininks, Blacklock, Benson, & Johnson, 2004), career center personnel may feel ill prepared to address student issues such as determining disclosure decisions and identifying and requesting accommodations at the work site. Equally perplexing may be the service needs of employers regarding matters such as using tax incentives or providing guidance to determine the essential functions of a position. Agency collaboration and business/industry outreach are key areas for best practice in the career development of college students with disabilities (Michaels & Barr, 2002).

Student Utility

Student participation can only be encouraged, not required. In addition to making a career center physically accessible, proactive strategies can be implemented that welcome student diversity. It is suggested that promotional materials include information for students with disabilities, such as who to contact for accommodations. The use of inclusive language on a web site could affect whether a student with a hidden disability decides to disclose to the career counselor. Instructional material about the ADA may be appropriate for a career center web site. All students need to be familiar with this significant legislation, as they may eventually have a co-worker with a disability, become an employer, or acquire a disability. In addition, it is recommended that all instruction, materials, and content incorporate universal design principles— that is, an instructional approach that benefits all learning styles without adaptation or retrofitting (Scott, McGuire, & Embry, 2002; see also Chapter 6). Career-planning workshops that include disability-related information— such as learning rights under the ADA, planning for disclosure of disability, learning about adaptive technology for reading and/or writing, and teaching the soft skills—are also recommended (Ryan & Harvey, 1999). Table 15.2

Table 15.2. Inclusive instructional strategies for career-related workshops

Include a statement in the workshop advertisement inviting students to discuss disability-related accommodations with career center staff before the workshop.

Conduct workshops in accessible locations.

Have printed materials and outlines available, prior to the workshop, for distribution in electronic format, large-print format, and regular and plain text formats.

Provide effective prompting during activities.

Use multiple modes of delivery: short lectures, discussions, hands-on activities, role plays, Internet-based interactions, and closed-captioned videos.

Provide graphic or pictorial versions of key concepts whenever possible.

Engage students in active learning.

provides additional instructional strategies to address the needs of diverse learners.

Employer Education

Progress is being made in efforts to educate employers and equip them with the knowledge and skills necessary to supervise an individual with a disability. However, surveys continue to report negative attitudes of employers with little to no experience with hiring an individual with a disability and employer fears regarding the cost of accommodation and ability of people with disabilities to meet workplace standards (Dixon et al., 2003; Hogan, 2003; Peck & Kirkbride, 2001). Significant positive experiences of employers need to be highlighted. For example, a vast majority of employers who have hired workers with disabilities reported that accommodations costs were often less than or same as expected, and rated working with people with disabilities as favorable (Unger & Kregel, 2003).

Career centers can begin to acknowledge the concerns and needs of employers by providing resource information on their web sites, including applicable educational materials in their libraries, and inviting questions about disability-related training on their intake forms. Table 15.3 lists specific examples of employer resources, products, and publications. Identifying a contact person in the career center to address disability-related questions may be a good starting point. This representative would not be a disability expert but could recommend resources for employers, such as ADA Technical Assistance Centers, or could network with the local department of rehabilitative services (DRS) office (a federal- and state-supported agency) or other community professionals to meet employers' needs.

Career Center Personnel

It is neither realistic nor expected that career counselors become experts in disability matters. Nevertheless, it is important for counselors to become familiar with the general disability-related issues that face students and employers.

Table 15.3.   Disability-related resources for employers

Americans with Disabilities Act (ADA) Tax Incentives Packet
This packet contains information on a small business tax credit and tax deductions available for
businesses of any size to improve accessibility for customers or employees with disabilities. It
includes the Internal Revenue Service (IRS) form and instructions for claiming the disabled
access credit.
http://www.usdoj.gov/crt/ada/taxpack.htm

The Center for Workforce Preparation (CWP) and Virginia Commonwealth University (VCU)
CWP and VCU address barriers to the employment of individuals with disabilities. Products and
publications are available at the web site provided.
http://www.uschamber.com/cwp/strategies/disabilities/default.htm

Disability and Business Technical Assistance Centers
These are 10 regional centers that provide informational guidance, materials, and technical
assistance to individuals and entities covered by the Americans with Disabilities Act (ADA) of
1990 (PL 101-336).
http://www.adata.org/dbtac.html
Toll-free: 800-949-4232

Hogan, G. (2003). *The inclusive corporation: A disability handbook for business professionals.*
Athens: Ohio University Press/Swallow Press.

Job Accommodation Network (JAN)
JAN is an information and referral service about job accommodations for people with disabilities.
http://janweb.icdi.wvu.edu
Toll-free: 800-526-7234

Thompson, A., Bethea, L., Rizer, H., & Hutto, M. (1997). *College students with disabilities and
assistive technology: A desk reference guide.* Mississippi State: Mississippi State University Project
PAACS (Postsecondary Accommodations for Academic and Career Success).

Virginia Commonwealth University Rehabilitation Research and Training Center on Workplace
Supports (VCU-RRTC)
VCU-RRTC offers a comprehensive web site to promote employment for people with disabilities.
http://www.worksupport.com

Traditionally, there has been little collaboration between the college
disability support service (DSS) offices and college career centers (Aune &
Kroeger, 1997; Rabby & Croft, 1991). In addition, very little, if any, input has
been sought by campus career services from employers concerning sufficient
employment preparation of college graduates with disabilities (Getzel et al.,
2000; Getzel & Kregel, 1996) and the self-advocacy needs of students with
disabilities (Bolles & Brown, 2001). Career Opportunities for Students with
Disabilities (COSD) is a federal initiative, funded through a grant provided
by the U.S. Department of Labor's Office of Disability Employment Policy
and formed to address this lack of collaboration. Composed of large and small
universities, well-known national employers, and U.S. government agencies,
this unique consortium focuses on the employment and career development
of college graduates with disabilities.

Career center directors must decide how to meet the professional development needs of center personnel. One powerful resource for partnership and
training is connection with the local DRS office. Both DRS offices and career
centers have a common goal of successful employment and career advancement
for college graduates with disabilities. DRS offices can collaborate with career

centers to provide sensitivity training to employers and career center staff members, discuss the roles and responsibilities of employers under the ADA, and explain the benefits of hiring individuals with disabilities. In addition, DRS offices can assist employers and graduates with disabilities in the job application process.

Career center personnel need to be equipped with information, resources, partnerships, and contacts to effectively meet the educational needs of students with disabilities and employers. It is important that counselors model inclusive behavior and normalize disability. Recommending key employment success strategies is essential: 1) identify a mentor at the work site to help the employee with a disability acquire the hard and soft skills needed to succeed on the job, 2) learn the tricks of the trade or shortcuts to increase efficiency, 3) determine work place politics and personalities, and 4) learn who to speak with if an employee makes a mistake on the job (Hagner, 2002; Whelley, Radtke, Burgstahler, & Christ, 2003). Desired support skills for career center personnel include providing employers with resource information about conducting interviews and students with questions to consider regarding the need to disclose disability to an employer. Table 15.4 lists categorial questions that students can answer independently or with a career counselor to assess whether disclosure may be necessary or beneficial. "Yes" answers may indicate solid preparation for and benefit of disclosure. "No" answers may indicate a need for more preparation or limited benefit of disclosure.

Career center personnel can also independently acquire knowledge about disability-related career development needs. This can be accomplished by reading current publications or professional journals, reviewing Internet resources, participating in distance education teleconferences or web casts, or enrolling in a continuing education course. Given the vast number of career possibilities for some graduates with disabilities, it is recommended that career counselors, faculty, and students with disabilities become familiar with established disability-friendly business networks at the local and national levels.

TAPPING INTO DISABILITY-FRIENDLY BUSINESS PARTNERSHIPS

People with disabilities form the single largest and most diverse minority in the United States, with one in five Americans reporting a disability (Fujiura, 2001; Hogan, 2003). Increasingly, disabilities are being viewed in the same context as cultural diversity (Smith & Sowers, 2002). Many large companies are recognizing the need to address changing labor demographics, customer demand, and diversity in the workplace to compete successfully in the 21st century (Fabian, 1994; Society for Human Resource Management Online, 2004). Big businesses are reporting that the recruitment, retention, and advancement of diverse candidates form part of their organization's overall

Table 15.4. Chart for gathering facts about whether disclosure may be necessary or beneficial

From the company	About the position	About the employer	About myself
Do I have background information about the company?	Have I requested a detailed job description for the position?	Does the supervisor use a flexible and personal management style?	Am I familiar with the protections provided by the Americans with Disabilities Act (ADA) of 1990 (PL 101-336)?
Do the company, its senior management, and its owner welcome and value diversity?	Do I know the essential functions and expectations of the job?	Does the employer have experience in managing differences or diversity?	Am I comfortable with my disability?
Has the company participated in any disability-related recruitment programs?	Can I talk with an employee who is currently in this position or in a similar one?	Does the employer focus on essential, rather than marginal, functions?	Am I aware of my strengths and functional limitations?
Is there a company policy on hiring individuals with disabilities?	Will my compensatory strategies (e.g., the use of adaptive software or assistive technology) change the traditional way of getting the job done?	What experiences has the employer had with hiring individuals with disabilities?	Will I need potential medical assistance?
Is preemployment testing required? What is the medium for testing?	Will I need accommodations for the application or interview process or at the work site?	Can I provide the employer with resource information about the ADA and my specific accommodation needs?	Have I explored technology or strategies to compensate for my limitations?
Does the company have an internship program?			Have I previously used accommodations at a work site?
			Have I practiced disclosure strategies with a family member, close friend, or career professional?

business strategy, according to a *New York Times* press release on February 13, 2003. However, small businesses (5–24 employees), which make up 70% of the nation's employers, are generally not as formal in their approach.

National and community initiatives are being put forth to attract, train, and accommodate a diverse labor force. Through collaboration and sharing of resources, more employers are being prepared to recruit, interview, hire, and accommodate an employee with a disability. (Table 15.5 provides summary and contact information for these initiatives.) One such collaboration involves business-to-business mentoring. The U.S. Business Leadership Network (USBLN) is a national program led by employers that engages the leadership and participation of companies throughout the United States to hire qualified job candidates with disabilities (Van Lieshout, 2001). This national organization supports development and expansion of state Business Leadership Networks (BLNs) across the country, serving as their collective voice. Supported by the U.S. Department of Labor's Office of Disability Employment Policy (ODEP), this nonprofit organization recognizes and promotes best practices in hiring, retaining, and marketing to people with disabilities.

Additional business affiliations can be accessed through local DRS offices. Frequently, regional business development managers at DRS facilitate the development of work force networks or alliances of work force development professionals to enhance partnerships with the business community. These networks provide the business community with easy, cost-effective access to diverse applicant pools through a variety of incentives and resources. Most

Table 15.5. Federally supported initiatives to employ people with disabilities

Employer Assistance and Recruiting Network (EARN)
EARN is a third-party referral service, sponsored by ODEP and the Social Security Administration, to connect employers to qualified candidates with disabilities.
http://www.earnworks.com
Toll-free: 866-327-6669

Job Accommodation Network (JAN)
JAN is a free consulting service providing individualized work site accommodation solutions, technical assistance regarding disability-related legislation, and education about self-employment options.
http://www.jan.wvu.edu

Social Security Pass Plan
This is a financial plan to set aside earned income to fund established career goals.
http://www.passplan.org

State department of rehabilitative services offices
These federal- and state-supported agencies promote the employment of individuals with disabilities.
Each state's department has its own web site; see http://www.vadrs.org for an example.

U.S. Business Leadership Network
This organization is supported by the U.S. Department of Labor's Office of Disability Employment Policy (ODEP).
http://www.usbln.com

U.S. Department of Labor
The U.S. Department of Labor offers a cross-governmental portal on disability-related information and resources.
http://www.disabilityinfo.gov

networks hold monthly meetings for members and offer an opportunity for an employer to present information about the company, hiring needs, and recruitment process. All of these employers have access to free disability awareness training for their employees through the DRS. The steering committee for the networks consists of a select group of community organization representatives and work force development professionals who work with diverse populations.

Work Force Development Initiatives

The Center for Workforce Preparation (CWP) is a grant-based nonprofit affiliate of the U.S. Chamber of Commerce that focuses on workforce development and quality education issues. The CWP assists member companies to recruit diverse and underutilized labor sources. In collaboration with Virginia Commonwealth University, the CWP is engaged in a 5-year project focusing on barriers related to the employment of individuals with disabilities. (See the web sites provided in Table 15.3 to obtain relevant publications and products.)

ODEP offers employers a variety of resources and initiatives to help businesses find and hire people with disabilities. The Job Accommodation Network is a free consulting service designed to increase the employability of people with disabilities by providing information about workplace accommodations, providing technical assistance regarding the ADA and other disability-related legislation, and educating individuals about self-employment options.

Another partnership established through the ODEP and the Social Security Administration's Office of Employment Support Programs is the Employer Assistance and Recruiting Network (EARN). This third-party referral service connects employers who have job vacancies to employment service providers who have direct access to job-ready individuals with disabilities. EARN also provides technical assistance to assist employers in locating appropriate organizations and information as they seek to hire qualified candidates with disabilities. Also provided is a national toll-free telephone and electronic information referral service designed to assist employers in locating and recruiting qualified workers with disabilities.

As big businesses recognize the value in recruiting a diverse work force, efforts are being put forth to develop internship and work experience programs that target college students with disabilities. For example, IBM has a diversity recruitment program entitled Project View that offers people who are Latino, African American, Asian, or Native American or who have disabilities the opportunity to explore IBM's national career options. This program includes an all-expense-paid, $1^1/_2$ day visit for students to explore career options with the company. (Table 15.6 delineates additional work experience opportunities available to students with disabilities.) These programs give students opportunities to have mentors in their field, assess workplace supports, and identify effective accommodations.

Table 15.6. Business partnerships targeting college students with disabilities

Entry Point!
Sponsored by the American Association for Advancement of Science, this program links students with disabilities majoring in science or technology with internships.
http://www.entrypoint.org

Lift
This "nonprofit corporation qualifies, trains, hires, and places information technology profession-als who have physical disabilities through contracts with major corporations, which eventually hire" the individuals directly.
http://www.lift-inc.org

Microsoft
Microsoft works with the Career Opportunities for Students with Disabilities (COSD) consortium to hire employees with disabilities.
http://www.cosdonline.org

The Washington Center for Internships and Academic Seminars Scholarship Program for College Students with Disabilities
This scholarship program develops leadership skills in public service.
http://www.twc.edu

Workforce Recruitment Program
This program is sponsored by U.S. Department of Labor's Office of Disability and Employment Policy (ODEP) and the U.S. Department of Defense. It provides opportunities for summer work and full-time employment.
http://www.dol.gov/odep/programs/workforc.htm

CONCLUSION

College graduates with disabilities can be successful in their pursuit of employment and career advancement in their chosen field. This growing population faces greater challenges than traditional students, including lack of work experiences that build career success and relevant information about the ADA. College career centers are becoming more aware of the career development needs of graduates with disabilities and play a key role in preparing students for employment. Equally important is the education that career centers can provide to a wide array of employers seeking college graduates. Connecting with established business partnerships, collaborating with community agencies, and making use of federal initiatives can lay significant groundwork for the success of graduates with disabilities. It is time for colleges and universities to proactively address the career development needs of all students and to embed services within the regular university service system.

REFERENCES

Allen, S., & Carlson, G. (2003). To conceal or disclose a disabling condition? A dilemma of employment transition. *Journal of Vocational Rehabilitation, 19*(1), 19–30.

Americans with Disabilities Act (ADA) of 1990, PL 101-336, 42 U.S.C. §§ 12101 *et seq.*

Aune, B., & Kroeger, S.A. (1997). Career development of college students with disabilities: An interactional approach to defining the issues. *Journal of College Student Development, 38*(4), 344–356.

Bolles, R.N., & Brown, D.S. (2001). *Job-hunting for the so-called handicapped or people who have disabilities.* Berkeley, CA: Ten Speed Press.

Briel, L.W., & Getzel, E.E. (2001). Internships in higher education: Promoting success for students with disabilities. *Disability Studies Quarterly, 21*(1), 38–48.

Burgstahler, S. (2001). *Access to the future: Preparing college students with disabilities for careers.* Retrieved December 7, 2003, from http://www.washington.edu/doit/Brochures/Careers/future.html

Burgstahler, S. (2003). The role of technology in preparing youth with disabilities for postsecondary education and employment. *Journal of Special Education Technology, 18*(4), 7–21.

Dixon, K.A., Kruse, D., & Van Horn, C.E. (2003). *Restricted access: A survey of employers about people with disabilities and lowering barriers to work.* Retrieved February 5, 2004, from http://www.heldrich.rutgers.edu/Resources/Publication/89/WorkTrendsXIVRestrictedAccess FinalReport.pdf

Enstrom, C. (2003, Fall). What your career center can (and can't) do for you. *Graduating Engineers and Computer Careers,* 32–34.

Fabian, E.S., Leucking, R.G., & Tilson, G.P., Jr. (1994). *A working relationship: The job development specialist's guide to successful partnerships with business.* Baltimore: Paul H. Brookes Publishing Co.

Fujiura, G. (2001, August/September). Emerging trends in disability. *Population Today.* Retrieved March 4, 2004, from http://www.prb.org/Content/NavigationMenu/PT_articles/Jul-Sep01/Emerging_Trends_in_Disability.htm

Gerber, P.J., & Price, L. (2003). Persons with learning disabilities in the workplace: What we know so far in the Americans with Disabilities Act era. *Learning Disabilities Research & Practice, 18*(2), 132–136.

Getzel, E.E., Briel, L.W., & Kregel, J. (2000). Comprehensive career planning: The VCU career connections program. *Work, 14,* 41–49.

Getzel, E.E., & Kregel, J. (1996). Transitioning from the academic to the employment setting: The employment connection program. *Journal of Vocational Rehabilitation, 6,* 273–287.

Getzel, E.E., McManus, S., & Briel, L.W. (2004, February). An effective model for college students with learning disabilities and attention deficit hyperactivity disorders. *NCSET Research to Practice Brief, 3*(1).

Hagner, D. (2002). *Career advancement strategies and tools: A guide to assist individuals with disabilities to advance beyond entry-level employment.* Cicero, NY: Professional Development Associates.

Henderson, C. (2001). *College freshmen with disabilities: A biennial statistical profile.* Retrieved January 8, 2004, from http://www.heath.gwu.edu/pdfs/collegefreshmen.pdf

Hernandez, B., Keys, C., & Balcazar, F. (2000). Employer attitudes towards workers with disabilities and their ADA employment rights: A literature review. *Journal of Rehabilitation, 66*(4), 4–17.

Herr, E.L., Cramer, S.H., & Niles, S. (2004). *Career guidance and counseling through the lifespan: Systematic approaches* (6th ed.). Boston: Allyn & Bacon.

Hogan, G. (2003). *The inclusive corporation: A disability handbook for business professionals.* Athens: Ohio University Press/Swallow Press.

Kakela, M., & Witte, R. (2000). Self-disclosure of college graduates with learning disabilities. *Learning Disabilities: A Multidisciplinary Journal, 10*(1), 25–31.

Langton, A.J., & Ramseur, H. (2001). Enhancing employment outcomes through job accommodation and assistive technology resources and services. *Journal of Vocational Rehabilitation, 16*(1), 27–37.

Madaus, J., Foley, T., McGuire, J., & Ruban, L. (2002). Employment self-disclosure of postsecondary graduates with learning disabilities: Rates and rationales. *Journal of Learning Disabilities, 35*(4), 364–69.

Michaels, C., & Barr, V. (2002). Best practices in career development programs for postsecondary students with learning disabilities: A ten-year follow-up. *Career Planning and Adult Development Journal, 18*(1), 61–79.

National Association of Colleges and Employers. (2004). Exploring the job market. *Job Choices: Diversity Edition,* 9–24.

National Association of Counselors and Employers. (2004, January 14). *Employers identify the skills, qualities of the "ideal candidate"* [Press release]. Retrieved February 7, 2004, from http://www.naceweb.org/press/display.asp?year=2004&prid=184

National Organization on Disability. (2002, May 15). *What is the technology gap?* Retrieved March 1, 2004, from http://www.nod.org/content.cfm?id=979

The New York Times Company. (2003, February 13). *Diversity policies have positive impact on company business performance, according to New York Times Job Market National Study; diversity initiatives moving more women and minorities into management* [Press release]. Retrieved February 7, 2004, from http://www.corporate-ir.net/ireye/ir_site.zhtml?ticker=NYT&script= 411&layout=-6&item_id=382320

Peck, B., & Kirkbride, L. (2001). Why businesses don't employ people with disabilities. *Journal of Vocational Rehabilitation, 16*, 71–75.

Price, L., Gerber, P.J., & Mulligan, R. (2003). The Americans with Disabilities Act and adults with learning disabilities as employees: The realities of the workplace. *Remedial and Special Education, 24*(6), 350–358.

Rabby, R., & Croft, D. (1991). Working with disabled students: Some guidelines. *Journal of Career Planning and Employment, 51*, 307–312.

Rehabilitation Act of 1973, PL 93-112, 29 U.S.C. § 794.

Rumrill, P.D., & Hennessey, M. (2004, July). *Surveying the employment concerns of college and university students with disability: A participatory action research approach.* Presentation at the 5th International Conference on Higher Education and Disability, Innsbruck, Austria.

Ryan, D., & Harvey, S. (1999). Meeting the career development needs of students with disabilities. How practitioners can enhance counseling efforts. *Journal of Career Planning & Employment, 59*(2), 36.

Scott, S., McGuire, J.M., & Embry, P. (2002). *Universal design for instruction fact sheet.* Storrs: University of Connecticut, Center on Postsecondary Education and Disability.

Senator, S. (2000). Technology and employment: In today's workplace, assistive devices can enable people with disabilities to do the job. *Exceptional Parent, 30*(11), 40–45.

Sharpe, M., Bruininks, B., Blacklock, B., Benson, B., & Johnson, D. (2004, August). The emergence of psychiatric disabilities in postsecondary education. *National Center on Secondary Education and Transition Issue Brief, 3*(1), 1–6.

Smith, M., & Sowers, J. (2002, Fall). Disability as diversity. *The Vine*, 1–3.

Society for Human Resource Management. (2004, October 12). *What is the "business case" for diversity?* Retrieved October 12, 2004, from http://www.shrm.org/diversity/businesscase.asp

Technology-Related Assistance for Individuals with Disabilities Act of 1988, PL 100-407, 29 U.S.C. §§ 2201 *et seq.*

Thompson, A., Bethea, L., Rizer, H., & Hutto, M. (1997). *College students with disabilities and assistive technology: A desk reference guide.* Mississippi State: Project PAACS (Postsecondary Accommodations for Academic and Career Success).

Unger, D., & Kregel, J. (2003). Employers' knowledge and utilization of accommodations. *Work, 21*(1), 5–15.

U.S. Department of Commerce. (2002, February). *A nation online: How Americans are expanding their use of the Internet.* Retrieved March 3, 2004, from http://www.ntia.doc.gov/ntiahome/ dn/nationonline_020502.htm

U.S. Department of Education, Office for Civil Rights. (2002, July). *Students with disabilities preparing for postsecondary education: Know your rights and responsibilities* [On-line pamphlet]. Retrieved January 7, 2004, from http://www.ed.gov/about/offices/list/ocr/transition.html

Van Lieshout, R. (2001). Increasing the employment of people with disabilities through the business leadership network. *Journal of Vocational Rehabilitation, 16*, 77–81.

Whelley, T.A., Radtke, R., Burgstahler, S., & Christ, T.W. (2003). Mentors, advisers, role models, & peer supporters: Career development relationships and individuals with disabilities. *American Rehabilitation, 27*(1), 42–49.

Witte, R. (2001). College graduates with disabilities and the Americans with Disabilities Act (ADA): Do they know their employment rights? *Learning Disabilities: A Multidisciplinary Journal, 11*(1), 27–30.

Index

Page references followed by *t* and *f* indicate tables or figures, respectively.